NARENDRA MODI

Yes He Can...

I0437114

D. P. SINGH

FOR MOTHER

As indeed all the mothers of the world

CONTENTS

Author's Note

PART I • STATE OF THE NATION

PART II • TWO HOPES

PART III • HERE COMES MODI

AUTHOR'S NOTE

Presently the world comprises of two great and sparring tribes. One sees the world getting progressively better, what with, thanks to great strides made in the field of science and technology, its vast majority coming out of its past of ignorance, stasis, misery and slavery, and marching ceaselessly towards a bright future. The other discerns unmistakable signs of doom, with depleting social trust, impossible-to-stop moral decay, looming religious wars, growing economic Darwinism, worsening resource crunch, environmental degradation, extinction of species, and ultimate annihilation. India too shares this split, but, additionally, it is cleft right down its middle by another great divide—of near-sightedness and farsightedness; conditions that go generally (but not always) with one's material circumstances as well as the awareness level.

Ironically, in addition to those too busy in making their two ends meet to be aware of anything other than the next day's meal, people most likely to be afflicted by nearsightedness are the ones who enjoy good life and regular sources of income. They have a mobile phone to play with, motor bike or car to zoom around and chase skirts, *'addha'* to enliven the evenings, and time and the mental level to obsess with things like fashion, cricket and Bollywood. They are either unaware of or refuse to draw lessons from their history, and are blissfully oblivious of the trends and goings-on in the world lying beyond their self-absorbed noses. Any talk of the perils their ancient culture and the faith-systems (which took collective endeavors of hundreds of generations of their ancestors to shape) face is anathema to them. Discussions about the kind of future they, their next generation, or the nation as a whole are going to suffer a decade or two down hold no traction with them. In short, disregarding or contemptuous of their past and unmindful of the future, they are mighty smug with their present, howsoever unenviable or contemptible their lives and the attitudes might appear others to be.

While nearsightedness is not exactly an affliction (but just the thing a good doctor or spiritual healer might prescribe for leading an uncomplicated and happy life), farsightedness is nothing less than a full-blown syndrome. Forever whining, carping, criticizing, castigating, berating and bemoaning every aspect of national-societal life, the lot of the farsighted is pathetic indeed. And this, when they have far less reasons to cavil, enjoy as they do generally a far better station in life than their nearsighted compatriots.

And even as the nearsighted are of firm view that the Arushi Murder, Sachin's 'mahashatak' and what Katrina confided in Sallu's ears are more portentous issues than things like the impending energy crisis, India's encirclement by China, or near-complete collapse of public education system in the country, the farsighted have problem with just about everything happening in the Universe. From local (nullah being built under JNURM collapsing even before its completion, or synthetic milk and chemically treated vegetables playing havoc with the organs and brains of infants and the adults alike), to national (assets of politicians, bureaucrats and the army generals rising in direct proportion to accidents, murders and suicides across the nation), to international (China buying up all the tradable energy and mineral resources of the world, or Salafism gaining ground among the entire Ummah), to stratospheric (depleting ozone layer or growing militarization of space by China): litany of laments carried by this sorry breed of do-good-nothings is dismal and tiresome indeed.

With much shamefacedness, your author admits to being a part of this incorrigibly morose breed, having million problems with just about everything his finicky and feverish mind can lay its hands upon. Otherwise, there is no reason in the world for him to be disturbed by the thought that no DM in any district of his state earns less than Rs 10 crores a year, even as no less than 10 thousands might be dying annually in his district of complications arising out of destitution and hunger. Or, for that matter, why should he be filled with anger and angst about the battering of baby Falak who was no relation to him, or dwindling of mangroves of Sunderbans which he has no intention of ever visiting? And, much like many of his friends, why doesn't he look forward to make his evenings enjoyable with the aid of Jack Daniel or Johnny Walker he is unable to understand and despairs much.

However, the divide discussed above is purely psychological in nature. India is divided at other – and much real, deeper and damaging – levels that require no great acumen or serendipity to sense or make out. Thus, in addition to harboring divisions of color, religion, sect, language and class that continue to serrate the socio-economic landscape of the world, India has got one more divide which is unique to it and far more insidious than them all. More than three millennia old and known as *'jaati'* (caste), this divide is so powerful as to overcome all other 'regular' divisions germane to the human specie. One may get to grow fair and handsome, convert to another religious faith, alter his mother tongue by trying to even dream in English, change his surname from Mahar to Mishra or the ideology from that of Marx to Rockefeller, yet his caste will continue to cling to him (or rather he to his caste) more closely than perhaps his own self-image. Otherwise nothing explains Nehru's attachment with the appellation of Panditji, despite his Harrow, Marx and Mill; Reddies of Andhra clinging madly to Rajshekhar Reddy and his son, despite them being outrageously corrupt, in addition to having converted to Christianity; or our very own Rahul Baba letting his caste-pride (either mistakenly or fraudulently, for it hardly behoves son to a Catholic mother and son to a son of a Parsee gentleman to term himself that) sneak out in the (in) famous *'I am a Brahmin...'* assertion.

But telling Indians about these divisions is like telling a warthog that he had those hateful warts too many. We are here onto a yet more pervasive and pernicious divide that our System has created and which has come to override all the divisions enumerated above. Abrahamic faiths cleaved the human society along 'we the faithful' vs. 'they the kefir line. Marx hypothesized the society divided into eternally warring camps of labor and capitalist. British imperialism created the division of predatory colonizers and the exploited colonized. Combining the worst aspects of caste, kefirhood, class and colonialism and transcending them all, *'Perpetrator/Victim'* is the new great schism that our polity and the *'System'* has succeeded in creating, dividing entire land into two distinct and great classes drifting apart from each other all the time like the continental landmasses. If allowed to deepen and broaden unchecked as it does now, the schism is likely to bring the whole project in democracy, liberalism, secularism, and nation and society building crashing down, swaddling the land in unending gore and blood.

Indeed, greatest charge against the Indian State is that it has segregated its citizens into two distinct and increasingly disconnected classes of perpetrators and victims. All other charges, viz., mind-numbing corruption, failure to arrange a dignified life for an overwhelming majority of the populace, or inability to secure nation's future inhere in that single charge. Thus, in the democratic-socialist state that India is supposed to be, anyone failing to attain a 'position' (i.e., getting to be a government officer, police inspector, elected 'representative', certified mafia, high class *dalal* or prostitute, and the like) in life loses his/her citizenship rights too. He does no more enjoy the luxury to live on an honest day's labor with his dignity intact. Forgetting any claims to rights or the dignity altogether, he has to take in, along with his two pieces of stale bread, a daily minimum quota of abuses and insults at the hands of the trustees as well as the minions of the state.

Moral of the narrative is that either one has to attain, any which way, a position in life whereof he can inflict million tyrannies and indignities upon his less fortunate fellow beings, or be prepared to suffer them. Such a relentless milieu has been fashioned that one has either to turn into a perpetrator, or be resigned to languish as a victim. No middle ground has been left by the system for one to aspire to lead an honest, dignified and noble life; thing deemed an inalienable right of every citizen in modern and humane nations.

Overriding and subsuming every other concern, task before all those harboring even an iota of love for the land and concern for its people is to recover that lost middle space and keep widening it ceaselessly. Simultaneous with that, private heavens created by the perpetrators for their seven generations (as also the public gulag that the rest of the nation has been turned into) have to be squeezed out of existence.

But how shall that middle space be recovered and who shall do it for the blighted land and its suffering majority? They say that hopeless is the lot of the people who await a Saviour to rescue them from the consequences of actions that may or may not belong to them. And that is entirely true. System – and not person – is what they should look forward to. And it is them only who have either to hammer the old system into shape, or create one anew.

The supposition however is true only for the autocracies where the overriding requirement is to usher in some variant of democracy. If you had already created the kind of democracy you thought accorded best with your 'genius' and the needs, your task gets limited to electing the right kind of persons to preside over its affairs. If however, for some reason, right kind of persons were not available for electing, it becomes absolutely critical to choose at least one right kind of person – call him Savior, 'man-Friday', or just a national

'Chotu' – to sit at the helm of the affairs. If the man was indeed right, carrying right attitude and vision, he would naturally select right kinds of persons to work to materialize his vision and the people's aspirations...

Democracy is expected to (and does) save societies and nations from the ravages of autocracy. It is said to possess a unique self-correcting mechanism, in addition to being a great healer. It can cure thousand societal ills, as it has shown time and again across many a nation. It could rather be termed a kind of socio-political wonder-drug capable of alleviating even the most intractable of societal ills and political wrongs. By all evident logic, South Africa should have sunk into a frenzy of vendetta after the end of the apartheid regime. Democracy however helped heal the wounds that had been suppurating for decades wonderfully.

In case of India too, even though it might appear sometimes to be exacerbating these, democracy has worked slowly but ceaselessly to repair the great chasm of caste and plaster over that of the communalism. It has prevented excesses and brought peoples together, making them perceive their respective destinies in a common nationhood, rather than separately or in antagonism to each other. It is a sure bet that India would have fragmented long ago under a dictatorship or more flawed democracy than it already is. Fissiparous and centrifugal tendencies had been running so deep that even after more than six decades of work it remains too fragile to survive a potential dictatorship.

And in addition to the capability of curing many of the socio-political ills, democracy has in it to heal itself too of the infections it happens to contract all the time as a fallout of less than democratic mindsets associating with its processes. Democratic praxis across nations like S. Korea, Indonesia, Turkey and Bangladesh furnish enough proof.

However, it has shown itself to be singularly inept in treating itself and the societies of one specific malady—and that is flesh-eating bacteria of corruption attacking directly at the moral fiber, social cohesion and political stability of nations.

It is not that corrupt democracies do not reform; example of South Korea is instructive. But the normal processes of democracy – running parties, fighting elections, luring voters, mustering majorities by sealing deals and entering into quid pro quos, combined with huge insecurity of career that keeps roiling the minds of the politicians – are usually designed in a way as to exacerbate, rather than mitigate the phenomenon of corruption.

Even as the best doctor can't treat himself of his Alzheimer's, democracy can't treat itself of the maladies that come to be rooted in its DNA. Corruption is most intractable and wasting of these. And even as million nurses or OT staff put together can't undertake even a single heart or brain surgery; procedures that only a brilliant and experienced doctor can; so too, not a billion voters or thousands of law-makers born of its infected womb, but only an exceptional leader of men can cure the democracy of this most intractable of its ills.

Naturally, that leader must not only be free of the afflictions that brought the democracy to that pass, he must bring much more to the table. For starters, he must be blessed with or be capable of, what could be termed, fine excess. The excess should run deep enough to make him anathema to the sections exploiting the flaws of the system to subserve their particular and selfish ends. He must be capable of raising their heckles every time his name was mentioned. That is because the person eager to make him acceptable to those he is supposed to whack into good behavior could only be expected to maintain the status quo ante. *'I must follow the people for I am their leader'* mentality is that of the poodles and those seeking power for personal ends, and not true leaders of men.

Further, besides being aware and sensitive towards the woes of democracy and the people, and capable and willing enough to address them, such a person should have a deep grasp of the reasons underlying those woes. For if the man wasn't even aware of the causes, or turned out to be dismissive of these as things that were 'in the nature of things' (ordained or natural lot of the 'teeming millions'), how could he be expected to even proceed with the job? It would be like handing over to a Pandit, conversant only with the Vedas and Puranas, or a Maulvi steeped in his Koran and Hadith, the charge of Manhattan Project. Whose fault would be that? Certainly not of that Pandit or the Maulvi, but those placing their faith (either out of ignorance or baser motives) in these sorry specimens of humanity.

Now, if a person is spotted, who, by long observation and common consent, comes to be deemed the only one fit for the job, it becomes supremely incumbent upon the people to enable that person to carry out the job for them. However, it is never advisable for the people to discard democracy or its scepter (the elections) even for a moment to let that person acquire even quasi-dictatorial powers, howsoever creditworthy his character or the record might be. 'If you are really that good as you had us believe, deliver results within the four bounds of democracy' — that should be the sentiment.

Care should also be taken to see that the person comes from within the system. It is of cardinal importance for him to be fully conversant with the strengths and the intricacies, as well as, the limitations and the weaknesses of the system in order to mould it to give out its best without wrecking it (willfully or accidentally) altogether. Experience of Pakistan with its dictators, who managed to wreak havoc with its polity in the name of saving it from its said excesses is hugely instructive in this regard. Manifold more diverse than Pakistan, India is singularly incapable of surviving any tinkering with its democracy.

Clearly, best bargain for a people is a savior emerging from within the system, however rotten it might be. He should be a person adept at pushing and testing the system and the people to bring out the best out of them, but fully aware of the perils of straining at the extremities. Like the mythical Raja Janak, he should be of and from the system, yet, like the proverbial lotus blossoming in the muck, quite distinct and detached from it. That is the only hopeful scenario for India (or, for that matter, other nations lying in similar quandary as India).

And, it goes without saying, that such a person should be acceptable to all the patriotic and justice-loving people desirous of leading a life informed by the virtues of enlightenment and rectitude, and making progress in accordance with the tenets of modernism and humanism.

Task before us is to find out whether our holy land and its hoary civilization, whose two millennia long caste reprehensibility was compounded first by six centuries of slavery, then overlaid by two centuries of imperialism, and, finally, aggravated beyond imagination by six decades long orgy of corruption and sins practiced in the fair names of democracy and people, has got so lucky as to have found a leader we could all place our collective faith in and give all out support (without, of course, compromising upon the essentials of democracy, liberalism and secularism) to enable him to extricate us from the mess we are stuck in and save our future for us.

Besides mulling over our wretched present and its probable causes, as also the dire future awaiting us all if the 'root cause' lying behind those causes was not dealt with soon, present book is an attempt to weigh the leadership options available to us on the parameters of merit, achievements and potential.

*

Part-I

STATE OF THE NATION

1

STATE OF THE NATION • Bird's Eyeview

We can't do better than begin with Mr. Vinod Mehta, Editor-in-Chief of perhaps most well regarded of the newsmagazines of India, *The Outlook*, who, despite being staunchest advocate of the ruling Congress Establishment, has been reduced to writing this dirge in his editorial piece of 9 September 2012:

> Thought things couldn't get badder? You have never been wronger.

> Just how much punishment can a nation take? Does some ingrained civilisational memory enable us to endure the almost limitless lashes? Are we a nation of practised masochists? At what point does people's rage spill out onto the streets? As a hardened journalist, I suppose I can absorb more shocks than the aam admi. So, as I picked up the dailies on Wednesday, I was prepared for new bad news and also prepared for old bad news having become badder, pardon the expression. I had the bar set pretty low. However, I quickly discovered it was not quite low enough.

> Disgust, disappointment, despair, dejection have become routine emotions for those unfortunate citizens whose day begins with the morning newspapers. Still, Wednesday, September 5, was exceptional, the mother of all black Wednesdays. The Coalgate scam had widened and deepened and now seemed to implicate almost the entire political establishment. Mukesh Ambani's RIL secured illicit favours from ONGC running into hundreds of crores. Mamata Banerjee misused funds earmarked for upgrading educational infrastructure to celebrate a Teacher's Day gala. Karnataka chief minister Jagadish Shettar, battling a drought, was forced to cut short a junket of state MLAs to South America due to public outrage. The CAG pulled up the National Highways Authority for a shady Rs 847 crore loss. Uddhav

Thackeray wanted permits for Biharis coming to Mumbai for employment. Narendra Modi's former minister, Amit Shah, was chargesheeted in a fake encounter case. Sri Lankan pilgrims visiting Chennai were attacked by militant Tamil groups, apparently, with Jayalalitha's approval.'

As you will have observed, I have excluded from the laundry list the usual quota of murder, molestation, rape, dacoity and other sundry unsalutary stories. The Delhi Police, well aware of their stinking reputation, took out large advertisements on September 5, pleading with Delhiwallahs: "Your city is not all about the bad news that you read every day. It's also about the good news that you don't read, like the numerous bombs we defused and accidents we prevented." And all this battering they choose to inflict on us in a single day!

Is there a way out? Even a short-term solution? Doubtless, the present dispensation has to be booted out, the sooner the better. But I cannot say with any conviction that those who will take their place will not feather their nest with equal zeal. When I started writing this piece, I was determined not to quote W.B. Yeats and his warning of what happens when the Centre does not hold: anarchy is let loose. We are heading in that direction, if we haven't already arrived there.

A GOOGLE Earth View of India. Even as the greater part of the world marches on to a future of freedom, prosperity and happiness, the state of affairs prevailing in our country, wherein hundreds of millions remain perennially a step away from the abyss; best and the noblest of the land stand dispirited and cowering, made to feel like chattels and helots by the state and its minions; and the worst are literally full of passionate intensity, enjoying unbridled power and wallowing in their ill gotten millions, can't simply be a matter of oversight or accident. And, most certainly, Gods or the Providence can't be so arbitrary, heartless, or cross with an entire people as to ordain utter destitution and degradation their collective and eternal destiny. So, what gives?

Before proceeding to dig into the anatomy and the causes of the state of affairs prevailing, we would do well to first have a Google-Earth view of this ancient land of *'gods and seers':*

Grave charges stood against the Presidential candidate but majority of the Parliament and the assemblies suffered no qualms in voting her in. Prime Minister of the nation reins but not rules, real power behind him being the Lady widely suspected to be the mastermind behind the scandal that has entered into international lexicon as a byword for high level corruption. He occupies his post only because, firstly, the Lady was not able to for some unspecified Constitutional snag, and, secondly, she was not confident about crowning her under-developed son.

All political parties, even those with regional or sub-regional reach and aspirations have hundreds, even thousands and tens of thousand crore rupees held in *benami* investments or stashed away in foreign accounts—to run vast party machinery, splurge on elections and to purchase elected members, more than willing always to sell themselves off to the highest bidder. Almost all of it happens to be black-money…illegal donations, bribes and cuts on deals.

Every single minister and the member of the elected bodies (Parliament, legislative assemblies and municipal, *panchayat*, or co-operative bodies)…indeed every *'leader'* or *'people's representative'* rolls about in ill-gotten wealth ranging from few crores to thousands of crores. Close to half of them have graver charges – theft, loot, fraud, rioting, kidnapping, murder, rape and running mafias – pending against them in either suitably obliging, or nearly dysfunctional courts.

Every single civil servant is either into bribes and deals to the best of his position and acumen, or pining for and striving to jump headlong into the pork barrel. Exception to the above rule is either a mental case already, or is likely to become one in due course. The net 'worth' of the smart and wise set of 'public servants' may range from a few millions for a lowly clerk and a few crores for the likes of engineers and sundry class-II officers, to hundreds, even thousands of crores for Class I (IAS, IPS, IFS, IRS, and the like) officers.

Grave corruption charges stand against top military commanders too. It is an open secret already that corruption runs deep and insidious in the Indian security establishment, nibbling away at its vitals. Slowly but inexorably, the Indian defense forces are turning into late nineteenth and early twentieth century versions of Russian and Turkish armies of Crimean, Russo-Japanese and the Great War infamy; gigantic apparatus eaten hollow by sleaze, apathy and self-indulgence of its higher brasses and other trustees. It might appear to be an enormous and fearsome African elephant to an outsider, but the fatal malignancy has turned it into a harmless wooly mammoth liable to be worsted grievously in the dog-eat-dog world developing out there.

The judicial system, specially at the lower level, fares little better. Indian judiciary could in fact be an apt study to investigate as to why the Islamic and other forms of kangaroo courts begin to look appealing to people and how the nations become failed enterprises.

And all that when millions of children and infants succumb annually to un-assisted births and sex-selective abortions, three millions to diarrhea, and another million or so to malaria, encephalitis, dengue and what not. Tens of millions of Indian *'citizens'* stand to fall to AIDS and hundreds of millions to direct and indirect consequences of environmental pollution and all-but-inevitable outbreaks of pandemics such as bird flue, swine flue, SARS, plague, and the like. Millions die from 'poverty-related' diseases: consumption, nutritional deficiency disorders and downright starvation. Millions die prematurely from organ failures, due primarily to contaminated food and water, and other lakhs from road accidents, electrocution, stampede and, what they term, 'freak' accidents, but not so freak coming to think of it, being rather regular features of this land steeped in apathy, ignorance and corruption. Millions are maimed or murdered wantonly in petty disputes over paltry property, measly sums of money, honor-killing, love-triangles, family disputes and such like—everything traceable to the state of degrading poverty, deficient education, and dehumanizing political and social milieu obtaining in India which has served to bring the 'social capital' and respect for human values to near-depletion levels.

Hundreds of thousands of promising lives are snuffed out prematurely by their own hands, thus taking the easy way out by taking their leave of *'Mera Bharat Mahan'* and *'Shining India'* with, perhaps, silent cries of *'Jai Ho'* upon their lips. Hundreds of millions continue to languish in distress and angst, fed up of the inequity and hopelessness of it all and always a step away from full-blown insanity. Children, even toddlers, are kidnapped either to be sold into slavery and prostitution, or blinded or maimed for beggary. They could end up being slaughtered for the transplantable organs or for spicing up *'dhaba'* dishes even!

Parents abusing children and the children making a short work of their parents, brothers murdering siblings, uncles raping nieces, husbands committing inhumanities against the wives, daughter-in-laws being burnt and parent-in-laws thrown out of their homes — such mind-numbing madness seems to have taken over this land and its denizens mere contemplation of which makes one go epileptic with rage, anguish and despair. Under the situation, a person failing to bury his normal human responses into a sink of unconcern and apathy, and turning into an insensitive brute exposes himself to grave danger of heart failure or insanity.

As for explaining the thing is concerned...the rot has gone so deep and wide that neither the usual suspects (communalism and the caste system), nor economic distress offer sufficient rationalization. It is not to deny that economy lies at the root of most of the things in our material world and, as China has shown so instructively, economic policies of the state have power to transform lives of hundreds of millions within their own lifetime. Indeed, it was China's example and the fear (exacerbated by balance of payment crisis of 1991) that had forced the Indian Establishment to undertake some economic reforms. Something however continues to stop the nation not only from reaping the full rewards of those reforms, but also stymie the redistributive measures (paltry and largely symbolic even as they are) meant to give the excluded sections something to chew upon. Further, no economic policy – crass-capitalist or full-blown socialist – stipulates that files be allowed to gather dust, projects delayed, time wasted and people forced to run from pillar to post to avail even the minimum of their citizenship rights and the dues. Clearly, something else is at work that lies at the root of it all.

And since the modern societies are coiled hopelessly in the grip of politics (*'If I seem to take part in politics, it is only because politics encircle us today like the coil of a snake from which one cannot get out, no matter how much one tries'*: Gandhi) this something could fairly be attributed to the polity, as also the kind of state or the 'system' wrought by that polity. As far as our country is concerned, it has become more than apparent by now that the state and the 'system' obtaining here have got a certain degree of malevolence about them, for they have been uncannily consistent in transforming the society's best – most resourceful and the enterprising – into its worst. Thus, as a direct consequence of the kind of electoral politics the country has come to be burdened with, potential heroes and deliverers of the society are being turned into social parasites and predators. It doesn't take them long to metamorphose into *'Rakshasa'* warriors of the yore who were famed to ride forth daily to devastate habitats, capture humans for cannibalism, defile the *'yajnas'* of the *'rishis'* and carry off their womenfolk. Contemporary *Rakshasas* too (bureaucrats, engineers, businessmen, industrialists, contractors and mafia-lords, and politicians and *dalals* of every hue and description), once fresh from their morning *'pooja'*, rush out riding their Boleros and Pajeros, Endeavors and Fortuners (or just stately Ambassadors) on almost a similar mission, in effect. Night and day, 365 days a year and whole of their lives, in the name of public service, providing leadership, and guiding the nation to prosperity and security, they, every mother's son of them along with his entire clan, remain engaged in but one thing: breaking and bending every law in the rulebook, flouting every norm of decent conduct, setting bad precedent, befouling the environment, looting public money, perpetrating fraud upon the people, screwing the motherland, and undermining the future of the society and the nation.

'But that is sheer madness', one is apt to cry out. 'Considering that the nation is the source, as well as the ultimate repository of all of one's karmas, it is nothing short of madness to wreck in this manner the nation where one took birth, plays his life out and is likely to die, his bones interred in its soil, even as those of hundreds of generations of his ancestors had been and of the coming generation would be. What genetic defect, environmental disorder or viral infection could be lying behind this syndrome?'

To find the answer, we would have to investigate the significant change in the overall environment of India, which, like some magic wand of an evil sorcerer, seems to have mutated the most genial, contented and temperate race of people into social monsters and insensitive brutes.

At least for the first few decades after the watershed event of Independence, physical environment of India remained as salubrious or deleterious as it had always been. Only significant change impacting the lives of the Indians seems to have been the polity they were bestowed with at that most crucial juncture of their history. Through rajas, sultans, badshahs and viceroys of every hue and description, they had managed to keep their traditional way of life and the thinking largely insulated from the outside influences. Democratic polity is an altogether different beast, however. Assumption, that democracy is 'for the people' and 'by the people' may not be wholly correct, but that the fact that it affects the people immensely in myriad of ways and even in spite of them is indisputable. As the saying goes, *'you might not be interested in politics but politics is always interested in you'*.

Thus next only to religion, and even more than that in the materialistic times of ours, it is the polity of a nation that creates the moral universe for its denizens to have their characters forged and play out their life's karmas in. Mere six decade praxis of the democratic polity that the Indians were led to live in, willy-nilly, has created a weltanschauung wherein infants are served as delicious dish in restaurants, four year old girls are blinded and maimed for beggary and prostitution, six year old boys are cut open to extract tradable organs, road-accident victims are left dying on the metro roads, pregnant women are forced to deliver and die at the gates of government hospitals bang in state capitals, and nobody appears to be minding, feeling outraged, or crying foul more earnestly or loudly than what the terms of political correctness demand.

Simply put, the kind of secular-democratic polity the people of India have been burdened with has devastated their moral cosmos, robbing them of their innate innocence and goodness. And as return gift, they have got from it everything vile except a little, dubious and utterly transitory kind of prosperity available only to a miniscule section of the populace. That seems to be the only thing the Indian State seems to have set itself out to work and claims credit for. And in a kind of Faustian bargain, in lieu of measly things like malls, mobile, motorbikes and the like, people have been wheedled of their character, goodness, contentment and the future. Looking closely, one can't escape being struck with a sinking feeling that, thanks to million acts of omission and commission committed by the Indian State (wrought by the kind of democratic polity the nation is burdened with), this ancient land of wisdom, compassion and innocence is plunging relentlessly into a state of, what could best be described as, *'jahiliya'*—that is, a milieu completely devoid of culture, morals, compassion, wisdom and social trust.

Even if one refrained from being a killjoy, choosing not to spoil the celebratory mood the Indian State and its protagonists have lathered up for their own consumption, he stands little chance against the *'Bold and the Beautiful'* brigade soaked in cricket, Bollywood, 'Page 3' and mall culture. With so many sports cars, wrist-watches, wines and cosmetic brands showering down daily upon the 'happening' place that India has lately become, it seems almost churlish to talk of more and more land coming to be stalked by water famines or Naxalism. How should it matter that, every single day, hundreds of lives are snuffed out just by open man-holes or electrocution—for the state-officials won't attend to mundane faults, being too busy devising mega-plans (because they yield mega-commissions) meant to catapult India right into the twenty-second century? That a family's breadwinner or the sole light of its eyes died in such a wanton and inconsequential manner seems particularly inconsequential when one is burdened with such weighty matters as having to decide between Hawaii and Hong Kong for his winter junket. Shouldn't it be held to be beyond all norms of etiquettes to talk about water, food and energy crisis looming over the land, threatening to drown it into interminable strife and anarchy, when one is dressed to kill, literally—ready to go to a pool-side party thrown by some defense contractor or hawala dealer, with all manners of imported foods, wines and girls laid out to enjoy?

What expectations could one have from a state whose almost entire elite (political leaders, bureaucrats, businessmen, media-barons and military commanders; pillars on which a fair, robust, and progressive state stands and who could themselves be termed, 'The State') is irredeemably compromised—not only not honest concerning its duty and the calling, i.e. serving the organizations and the institutions, and through it the nation and its citizenry honestly and diligently, but eating frenziedly into its vitals? One is left with absolutely no hope from the 'democratic' dispensation obtaining when the Chief Minister of its largest province, carrying more people than either Japan, Russia, Pakistan or Indonesia, could be so blasé, blatant and shameless as to claim that the state had become a Uttam Pradesh (ideal state) under his rule, even though there was no electricity or water supply for hours even in the largest of its towns, hardcore murderers and rapists moved straight from Jail to Cabinet meetings (and thence to Jail again to throw extravagant birthday parties replete with exotic wines, food and nautch-girls et al), and policemen-on-duty robbed citizens as a matter of routine even on the busy streets of the provincial capital?

And to make matters worse, the succeeding chief minister, corrupt and insensitive to the very heels of her imported sandals, made bold to claim to have become icon of development and good-governance, even though utter destitution, hunger, atrocities on the weak and the defenseless, and other inhumanities like parricide, fratricide and incestuous rape – natural outcomes them all of the kind of polity and the governance people are being subjected to in the name of democracy and public good – had been stalking the land, day in and out. Things promise to get only worse, for the dispensation responsible for bringing the things to the current pass shows little sign of reforming. People that feel no shame celebrating the disgraceful present; could they care less for the future?

And, pray, why should they? They have got sort of Sudarshan Chakra with which they promise to cut the head of every demon – unemployment, illiteracy, crime, inequality, casteism, population and communalism, as also every one of the vital insecurities (food, energy, defense and environment) – that dared cast its evil eyes upon the land and its people. This Sudarshan Chakra, rechristened *Eight Percent Growth Rate'*, is duly consecrated by high priests of international finance (IMF, World Bank and the like), new-age angels and gods of finance ministry mandarins (FII, hedge funds and the like), and heavenly bookkeepers of virtues and sins (credit rating agencies such as Standard & Poor and Moodies). You have just to point out the ogre troubling the people and your obliging PM would send the Chakra forth to slice its head off (in some indeterminate future, that is). The only quid pro quo is that in lieu of a few knick-knacks of dubious worth, the 'aam admi' should keep showing superhuman fortitude, along with complete faith in the credentials of the very state that has robbed him of everything vital, wholesome and transcendent.

Is clocking 6, 8, or even 10% rate of economic growth all about being a State? Is that it's only, or even the principal, raison d'être? Had that been so, then the best state would be where proven economists and managers, capable of ensuring highest economic growth, were placed at the helm of the affairs. A meritocracy running the affairs of the state with a single point agenda of ensuring highest possible rate of growth, and a plutocracy overlooking its performance – that would be the be-all-and-end-all of the state...its legitimacy, constitution, methods, scope and goals. Conceivably, criteria for judging the merit of a state and the political system would be applicable to all nations of the world. In that case, a meritocracy culled from all over the Planet could be placed to oversee the affairs of the entire world. That should mark the end of national boundaries and the 'End of History'. That conceivably is what the institutions like GATT, IMF, and the World Bank had been engaged in bringing about all these years. Yet, such has been the cussedness of people and the nations that misjudging their motives completely, they have kept reviling them no end!

By a logical corollary, the most rich and financially savvy person (one, whose portfolio of shares, plots, flats and the like give highest yield) must be considered the best of the human lot, while the things like character, ethics and etiquettes, or thousand manners of hobbies and accomplishments that take one's attention and efforts away from money-making, must be discounted for measuring true worth of men.

No rational man would however hold financial savvy the sole, or even significant, mark of goodness. Likewise, the states predicating their rational merely on economic indicators (creation of wealth, or even its judicious redistribution; grounds on which too the Indian State would be found to be severely wanting) place their foundation on a dubious and dangerous quicksand.

State is not merely an efficient or prudent financial executive or production manager. Market forces have proved themselves to be better and more sensible guides and agents in the matter than most of the states. State's role could best be described as that of a patriarch of a big clan. Patriarch's duty doesn't at all lie in slogging in the field to meet out his clan's immediate material needs. These could better be taken care of by the more dynamic and enterprising younger lot. His duty lay in ensuring that elements hostile to the clan had been kept at bay and sibling rivalries and dissensions within the clan were pre-empted or amicably settled before they got too big to contain. However, most onerous of his duties, which he could afford to ignore only at the risk of imperiling long-term security and the future of his clan, lay in seeing to it that the upcoming generations were marinated well in the mores, ethics and traditions of his clan and the tribe; that they entered their adulthood as persons of education and character, carrying sense of honor and full aware of their duties. That indeed is the preeminent – sacred, rather – of the patriarch's duties. Every other thing he could blithely leave to their own devices; they can't but turn out right.

That could be said to be the preeminent – perhaps the only – duty of the state as well

On every yardstick the Indian State could be seen to be carrying a disastrous report-card, as any short excursion outside its seat of power would make out. Simply dismal has been its performance in protecting or bettering its citizens' present. Even in the *'Lutyen's Delhi'* could be found veritable armies of retainers and flunkeys eking out a bare existence…devoid of any marker that they were citizens of a modern state. And barely five kilometers excursion to the outskirts of Delhi unravels the claims of the trustees of the Indian State in their entirety. Hunger, misery, disease, grime, illiteracy, ignorance and sheer moroseness and futurelessness are writ large upon every other face. And to think that one had more than three million square kilometers of hinterland to cover!

What is portentous still (as we shall discuss elsewhere in the book), the Indian State has disastrously failed in carrying out the most critical duty of a state, viz., securing the future survival of its citizens. As things stand (and it is no metaphor or a figure of speech), the Indian nation is standing at the mouth of a volcano. Insidious activities inside the volcano are at work all the time and ominous rumbles can be heard by perceptible observers. Scientific forecast: The volcano will begin spewing out lava within a decade and explode in another decade or two. And, to make the matters singularly ominous, all the nations of the world combined can't afford to shelter even one-tenth of the escaping billion-plus souls without themselves going down under.

Havoc wrought by the Indian State and its trustees upon the physical, moral and spiritual well being of the its citizens is great indeed. It has taken away their character and ruined their personality, rendering them a sickly specimen of human specie. More damaging still, it has humiliated and brutalized them to the extent that they are no more able to feel outraged by their wretched condition. Made incapable of realizing the need to reform, they can't be expected to exert themselves to even devise the ways, let alone making the requisite efforts. As chickens start landing to roost in a determined manner and vital insecurities begin to bite in right earnest, the failures would begin assuming increasingly grotesque forms. Security of livelihood and the lives would diminish progressively and the resulting strife, once set in, would get increasingly deeper, bloodier and chronic. Complete erosion of faith in the capacity and even the intentions of the state to deliver the good would make the average citizen averse to even exert himself (let alone making the required level of sacrifices) in the common cause. Humongous and strong to a casual eye, the state would become progressively mothballed and dysfunctional, and, much like an elephant, enormous and menacing-looking otherwise but eaten hollow by age or some fatal malignancy, prone to sudden collapse or implosion. By all accounts the Indian State is doomed in its present form. Apprehension is that if it were not soon replaced with another farsighted, committed and fair dispensation, entire society and the nation might implode amid unquenchable dissensions and anarchy.

Who is to be blamed for bringing the affairs to this pass? Is it the people who deservedly suffer the kind of state (holding company, so to say, of the Central and provincial governments) they supposedly fashion and continue to endure? Is not the state merely the alter ego or kind of 'super soul' of its citizens; projection, so to say, on a giant screen of all the combined egos and selves, characters and personalities, virtues and aspirations, and beliefs and convictions of its constituent millions, as also their prejudices, superstitions and other baser instincts? 'A people's moral fiber is the yarn the flag of their state is spun of. A state failing only means that the *'General Will'* of the people is failing; that they deserve to fail and suffer communally for being flawed individually. Therefore, rather than pry closely into the character of the state (its constitution, form and methods) to investigate the underlying cause of the societal rot or the national failures, one should rather dissect the character of the people and hold them to task,' along such lines run the logic of trustees, beneficiaries and the protagonists of the state.

That is specious logic, to say the least. Is the state such a harmless beast as its partisans make it out to be? By a crass mutilation of logic, the blame for the failures is sought to be put upon those whose lives and the livelihood the state has got firmly in its grip. It has paramount power to levy taxes and impose restrictions; powers which it never fails to use to the maximum possible extent. In return for being taxed to the bones, forfeiting vital freedoms, and subjected to million daily harassments by this 'coldest of all cold monsters', they are fobbed of with an election every five years. And to close the vicious cycle, that placebo of election too is duly hijacked by its devious patrons by presenting the people with the option of choosing Satan over the Devil.

Admittedly, there is no pressing need on their (i.e., The directors and principal shareholders in the venture of democratic states) part to pedal the sham of elections, democracy or universal franchise. However, historical experience has taught it that it always pays to keep a whipping boy (though it may turn out to be pretty inconvenient sometimes) to put blame upon for the consequences of their own misdemeanors, as also to let people take out their collective rage upon.

As far as the masses in India were concerned, utter lack of sense of history on their part could be held to be the biggest reason behind the continued success of the directors of the Indian State. The situation seems hopeless, for the masses, most of whom are either illiterate or only ill-literate, either do not have access to history, or are given only sanitized versions of it. In any case, they are unusually deficient in the ability to draw appropriate lessons from it. In the ancient and mediaeval India, 'varnasankara' (co-mingling of castes and resulting bastardization of the pure ones) had been the favorite whipping boy of the Brahminical Establishment, responsible for all the ills their world suffered. After the Independence, 'too much democracy' and universal franchise, along with political and job reservations became its favorite voodoo dolls, even though it continued to enjoy all the powers and freedoms to exploit and oppress the masses that it had since ages. Democracy and elections (fashioned by none else but it) came in extremely handy to deflect blame for its own shenanigans and to let the hoi polloi its steam off. It conceived and implemented schemes in a manner meant to serve its particular interests best. It enacted purportedly modern and secular laws, but appointed judges to interpret and custodians to execute these in a way designed to subserve and bolster the ancient laws of Manu.

And yet, 'People get the kind of dispensation they deserve'!

Admitted that people are uniquely bad and stewing deservedly in their own juices. What of the state then? How does it come into the picture? What is the need for it or the rationale of its existence? Why should people keep carrying it upon their backs—pay taxes, suffer unfreedoms and put up with thousand daily contumelies at the hands of its patrons and minions? If people get only as much as they are good or bad at, and the state is helpless in extending any assistance or guidance, why should they continue to feed the rotten Leviathan, along with its million progenies fouling the air around? Shouldn't it be replaced with something more beautiful and beneficent, which, instead of implying that people were cussed rascals getting their just desserts, exerts itself to utilize the faith and the power placed in it by them to enrich and ennoble their lives in every sense of the term?

Incontestably, the balance of logic lies in the favor of people and against the partisans of the state. Yet it gives no satisfaction, for the blame game settles nothing and the basic issues remain unresolved.

The failure, or rather the full implication of the failure, is not fully apparent yet. Even as a beautifully embroidered and perfumed shroud can conceal the hideous sight and odour of a rotting corpse for a long time, the high rate of economic growth reflected in media, mobile, mall and motor boom serves to cover the hideousness lying underneath the Indian economic scenery. It is only a matter of time before the bloated corpse burst out, throwing up fetid fluids and putrid smell for everyone to revolt and bolt. Worse, misery never comes singly. Revealed shall not only be the carcass of the contemporary Indian reality, but the entire set of hobgoblins would come tumbling down from the shelf of Indian history—jeering and leering, and spoiling to take revenge and settle scores.

The moment for final vendetta and blood-letting would arrive when any of the three vital insecurities, namely, food, energy and defense came to hit hard and deep. A slight nip or cut in the armour of a single insecurity remains manageable. Many states have been doing that all the time and have become rather adept in the art. However, in the face of the unresolved (and apparently unresolvable) Hindu-Muslim question, and the turn the entire neighborhood (indeed the world at large) has been taking lately, a single insecurity going somewhat out of control would inevitably trigger the other two. Before long, aiding and abetting each other, all the insecurities would join forces to tear the fabric of the society apart, bringing the entire system steeped in denial, myopia, self-regard, apathy and chicanery crashing down. Stating, that the consequences for a nation of more than one thousand million shall be grave would be an understatement of all times. Four-fifth of the adults functionally illiterate, three-fourth of the children perpetually underfed, and more than half of the population landless, jobless and futureless...only a few days' joblessness away from outright starvation at any given time—if that wasn't grave enough already, pray, what else could be? The new crisis would precipitate anarchy and catastrophe of a magnitude the history is yet to witness, Gulag, Auschwitz or Srebrenica notwithstanding. India stands doomed under the present dispensation. The rest of the world too can't escape being caught up in the tragedy and suffering enormous upheaval.

2

STATE OF THE NATION • 'Root Cause'

As things stand, India has come to suffer worst of the both worlds. While the new age enlightenment and the amenities offered by modern industrial civilization continue to elude majority of its peoples, old age innocence, delights, traditions, certitudes and the peace of mind have been lost to them for ever, and, as a result, they have come to acquire a very lopsided persona. Schizophrenic and hypocritical at the best of times, it has become a strange mix of exuberance and moroseness, generousness and misanthropy, and serenity and irritability. While the old world contentment has given way to the new-age greed, tools to satisfy that greed (health, education, skills, jobs and the overall 'eco-system') within the bounds of laws and ethical-societal norms continue to be denied to a great section. Result is that close to a billion people – entire populations of the US, W. Europe, Japan, Canada, Australia and Russia put together – are left awfully hungry, dispirited, ignorant and brutalized…with an abysmal past, little contentment with the present and even less confidence in the future. In addition to the puny and emaciated frames, ignorant brains, blank and idiotic expressions (wizened to some; difference of perception only) upon the faces, uncouth manners, slovenly appearances and gibberish talks crowding virtually every square yard of the land, what we are being witness to is virtually a tsunami of philistinism, crime and sin sweeping across the land whose depth, enormity and brutality beggars belief.

One really hates to recount the trillion times told trite tales – of unspeakable misery and indescribable pain, of wanton crimes and mindless corruption, daughters being sold into prostitution and sons disappearing only God knows where to, daughter-in-laws burnt for a mobike, brothers killed for paltry plot of land and parents maimed for booze-money. Had these things been 'in the nature of things' (i.e., inescapable lot of the human race, with people suffering universally from similar moral, ethical and social malignancies), then the prevailing situation wouldn't have been cause of undue alarm or angst. These had indeed been so in the ancient and mediaeval times when the world was sort of united in its ignorance, miseries and inhumanities. The situation however has undergone phenomenal change in the last couple of centuries, especially the past few decades. Many nations have broken free from their state of ancient miseries and degradations, and are taking great strides to secure a future of prosperity, hope, dignity and morality for their citizens. Conversely – and there can be no two opinions about it – the Indians continue to sink deeper all the time into a kind of black-hole, getting progressively greedy, insensitive, impatient, intolerant, cruel and inhumane...devilish, almost. Were they so bad always?

God No! In fact, Indians had always stood out as paragons of virtue, enjoying overabundance of all the fine attributes associated with the human specie. Despite three thousand years of caste hideousness, six hundred years of Islamic atrociousness and two centuries of British diabolicalness (repugnancies enough to rob any people of their basic decency and tolerance), the Indians continued to be celebrated for their temperance of character, as also compassion and forbearance even towards their sworn tormentors and exploiters.

Thus Huien-thsang, the Chinese pilgrim to India (7th century A.D.):

Though the Indians are of light temperament, they are distinguished by the straightforwardness and honesty of their character. With regard to riches, they never take anything unjustly; with regard to justice, they make even excessive concessions....

Idrisi, an eleventh century Muslim historian:

The Indians are naturally inclined to justice, and never depart from it in their actions. Their good faith, honesty, and fidelity to their engagements are well known, and they are so famous for these qualities that people flock to their country from every side.

Abul Fazl, minister to Akbar (16th century):

The Hindus are religious, affable, cheerful, lovers of justice, given to retirement, able in business, admirers of truth, grateful and of unbounded fidelity; and their soldiers know not what it is to fly from the field of battle.

Warren Hastings, British empire-builder (18th century):

They (Hindus) are gentle and benevolent, more susceptible of gratitude for kindness shown them, and less prompted to vengeance for wrongs inflicted than any people on the face of the earth; faithful, affectionate, submissive to legal authority.

Bishop Heber, no lover of Hinduism (early 19th century):

The Hindus are brave, courteous, intelligent, most eager for knowledge and improvements, sober, industrious, dutiful to their parents, affectionate to their children, uniformly gentle and patient, and more easily affected by kindness and attention to their wants and feelings than any people I ever met with.

Mountstuart Elphinstone, Governor of Bombay (19th century):

No set of people among the Hindus are so depraved as the dregs of our own great towns. The villagers are everywhere amiable, affectionate to their families, kind to their neighbors.... The Hindus are mild and gentle people, more merciful to prisoners than any other Asiatics. Their freedom from gross debauchery is the point in which they appear to most advantaged and their superiority in purity of manners is not flattering to our self-esteem.

Sir Thomas Munro, British general, statesman and Governor of Madras (early 19th century):

...Hindus are not inferior to the nations of Europe, and if civilization is to become an article of trade between England and India, I am convinced that England will gain by the import of cargo.

And, suddenly, every Indian and his auntie seem to have been caught in a frenzy of getting to be the World No.1 in everything that is reprehensible and inhumane. Culture of individualism and materialism brought by the Western-Industrial Civilization is blamed by many for the pandemic of greed and insensitivity sweeping across nations. The assessment is not wholly incorrect. No corner of the world or the human conscious remains unaffected by the balefulness spawned by industrialism and capitalism. However, the peoples around the world seem to have gathered their wits around them and are growing better all the time. They have been shedding their mediaeval sensibilities and the ways fast...and gifting these away (so it seems) to the Indians who appear to be lapping these up like hungry beggars.

It is obvious that the Indians have lost their moorings and the mojo faster than they got anchoring in modernism, wherein democratic and liberal values like gender equality and respect for individual's beliefs and the way of life are taken as granted, and commitment to education, hard work, and building up of an equitable and fair society gets sort of ingrained. Thus, education and knowledge are valued for their own sake and not as things to land degrees, while work is something to be respected and taken pride in, and not frowned upon as an undesirable burden or a thing beneath one's dignity.

Nothing ever happens without a cause. Behind every rise of a gale, fall of a sparrow or rumblings of an earthquake lays a cause rooted in the inexorableness of Nature. If however the thing concerns a people or a nation, the *'root cause'* must be traced to its particular socio-political circumstances. What *'root cause'* lies behind the unique and exceptional ills of India?

Two primordial ills, one unique to the land and the other exceptionally virulent and damaging, are assigned the root cause tags for India's many woes. Bigotry and discrimination on the basis of color, language, religion or class have always existed across ages and societies, taking toll of hundreds of millions of lives over the centuries, but what had been unique about India was its caste-system. Everything said about the Hindus was true till you ignored his caste related beliefs and the practices. As soon as the caste factor kicked in, Hindu turned into a pathetic caricature of every virtue attributed to him in the para quoted above.

Since the days of Baba Marx, economic factor too has come to be deemed as one of the (if not the only) prime movers of human history. To be truthful, the factor can't be ignored or dismissed just so, for, if it was not the lure of apple that led to his fall from the Heaven, then it was relentless search for food that brought man down from the trees and made him learn to walk straight on his twos and develop hunting tools, thus setting the wheels of civilization in motion.

Caste System: There could be little doubt that the caste-system (or its biological mother, the Varna system) was a great curse to the ancient land and its people. It made the brahmins lying cheats, Kshatriyas vainglorious oppressors, banias greedy rascals and everyone else...well, *'hewer of wood and drawer of water'*. Additionally, the evil institution restricted free movement of people and forestalled cross-pollination of ideas and dissemination of skills and inventions, stymieing thereby the vibrancy of trade and economy. As direct fallout, Indian states of the yore too were deprived of resources required to arrange advanced weapons, raise big standing armies and cavalry, and undertake defence against marauding-murdering hordes that descended upon the land all the time. Most damagingly, it kept at least four-fifth of the populace (and therefore commensurate proportion of able-bodied and martially-inclined men) completely out of combat and resistance. In an utterly violent age it was nothing less than suicidal. Faced with a people involved in pillage and warfare to a man, and whose faith served to unite them to a common and higher purpose (instead of dividing them into disparate atoms filled with feelings of repulsion towards each other, as it did with the natives), defeat and slavery became a foregone outcome.

Lying, cheating, vainglory, oppression, greed, defeat and slavery...there could be little doubt that the root cause behind almost all of the negativities the Hindus carried and slavery and degradations they suffered is the unique – and uniquely reprehensible – caste system.

And though it has distorted our polity to a certain extent, in that the people tend to ignore or explain away the shenanigans of the politicians from their own caste group, preferring to vote them over more suitable candidates from other castes, blame for all the miseries and degradation the nation continues to suffer even in the new millennium can't be laid at the door of the caste system alone. And, most of the time, people too can't be blamed for voting their caste-people, for theirs usually is a choice between a tweedledum and tweedledee. Fact is that despite what we usually see at the election-time and despite the caste-based reservations (or because of them), the actual everyday rigors and the fallouts of the caste system could be said to have abated to a considerable extent. But, then, the misery and the degeneration of the society, and its growing urge to embrace defeat and slavery once again too should have abated to that extent. Yet exactly the reverse seems to be happening. Where else should then we look for the *'root cause'*?

Communalism: Hindu-Muslim communal situation too has been assigned (by the Hindu Right as well as the secularist-left) the *'root cause'* label. But, except for being, perhaps, once a decade feature of a hundred or so localities of a dozen or so towns (among India's thousands), only one grave and long-term damage could be attributed to the Muslim presence in India: Failure or reluctance of the Indian State to enforce vigorous population control measures, due primarily to the fear of violent backlash from the Muslims who continue to remain implacably hostile to the idea. However, this too can't be attributed entirely to the Muslims, being principally a failure of the

Indian State. Further, it is by no means certain that they (that is trustees of the Indian State) would have proceeded with these measures even in the absence of Muslims or their resistance. And it is a fair bet that (as usual) the state machinery would have succeeded in making a complete hash of the thing, leading to violent reaction from the Hindus even. So this hypothetical charge too remains a non-starter.

Of course, the nation's polity has been distorted by communalism (as it has been by caste). But, unlike the caste system, communalism (rather the continued presence of Islam) had had its beneficial aspects too. Thus – and not withstanding Gandhi – while the caste-system has brought no conceivable gain to the Hindus, India or the humanity in general, the presence and the fear of Islam has at least one redeeming feature to it, in that, post-Independence, it has prevented the Savarna Hindus from running totally amok over the rights and the lives of the non-Savarna Hindu majority, and, thereby, making complete mincemeat of the society. Bare fact is that the overall rot runs so deep that by no means can it be traced back or attributed to the (alleged) cussedness of the Muslims. Further, whatever the blame assigned to the Muslim communalism, the Hindus too, being the inevitable other party, must share the culpability.

Thus the two ills might have taken heavy toll upon the societal wellbeing and economic progress in the past, or may be doing that to quite an extent even in the present, their impact upon the national-economic affairs has diminished of late. After all, a subtle caste system has always existed in countries like China and Japan but that hasn't stopped them from getting to be objects of emulation and envy among the nations. Likewise, it hasn't prevented the US, termed a melting pot of nationalities, or Malaysia, where religious and ethnic minorities constitute some 40% of the population, from arranging rich and harmonious life for their citizens.

Economic policies: Economic policies, especially the Fabian-socialist of Nehru and knavish-extortionist of Indira Gandhi have been held by not a few to be the root cause behind most of the ills of the nation. Fact is that *'economy the root cause'* theory can be pedaled persuasively regarding almost all of the woes of a person, as also that of the world as a whole. For, whereas a rich person gets to enjoy good nutrition, education and health as a matter of course, the extremely rich sheds his caste, religion and ethnicity too for all practical purposes. And these are the sum total of the woes of the world, both individual and collective. Any beggar worth his Blackberry could tell you that the root cause of most of the ills bedeviling him or the nation at large (as also the panacea for them) remains economy. Economic assets and jobs to arrange food on children's plate, and money for their treatment and the school fee so that they turned out to be healthy, educated and skillful, able to put up yet more hard work in more skillful and paying jobs than their parents had and raise yet more healthy and educated generation in their turn so as to enable it to turn out yet more…well, that exactly is the way the advanced, rich, harmonious and happy nations came to be what they are. In order to put the people and the nation on such a treadmill, the economy must grow at a rate equal to the expanding families and exploding wants, and then some…to bring up, in a decade or so, hundreds of millions to the happy perch where tens of millions stand now.

But the economy is not growing—at least at the rate required to arrange enough education and jobs to keep those millions busy enough to keep the Devil from making their empty brains its lair. That is, life is not growing rich, promising and charming enough for them to refrain from risking their freedom and enjoyment by killing their parents, siblings or girlfriends for incredibly petty issues or paltry sums of money. Obviously, the level of their upbringing is not such as could make them value the rights, beliefs and freedom of others, or even their own.

Economic policies have been blamed…and are to be blamed, without a shadow of doubt. They have played a crucial role in making nations great and their citizens healthy, educated, liberal, progressive and rich. US, Europe, Japan, Taiwan, and the like on the one side, and the erstwhile Communist nations on the other are great exemplars. And nothing can bring out the effect of economic policies on a people's fortune and the well-being more evocatively than the Chinese of the pre and post Deng era. Lessons from the debacle of Soviet Bloc, combined with the fear engendered by revolutionary rise of China forced India to commence opening up its economy and reap commensurate fruits. But, sadly, the fruits fell quite unevenly across the social spectrum and the growth story is threatening to come unstuck. Question is: Why, even after two decades of reforms (period, in which China exploded, setting off to another Long March to super-prosperity for its citizens and superpowerdom for itself), India continues to look…well, quite like itself, that is, a great heap of emaciated, diseased, illiterate, uncouth, fractious, deprived and depraved louts?

More than its avatars and seers like Ram, Buddha and Guru Nanak or the yogis levitating naked in the freezing heights of

Himalayas, more than its rope-tricks and snake-charmers, more than its tigers and elephants and pageantries and princes, and even more than Gandhi, Taj Mahal or the IT, what India is coming to be known is a land mired irredeemably in corruption. It has come to be a land whose high and mighty – industrialists, businessmen, politicians, bureaucrats, media barons and the like – conjure up more the images of Huns, Mongols, vandals, thugs and conquistadors of the yore who knew nothing better than to loot and destroy the hapless lands they happened to set foot upon, rather than of righteous, sincere and caring trustees of an unfortunate nation with an implicit mandate to improve the lives of its denizens and secure its future. Premium accounts in Swiss and Panama banks and mansions in England, Dubai and Monaco, contrasted with nearly a billion mired in destitution, diseases, starvation, squalor and ignorance—what might Ram, Buddha, Gandhi or the IT avail to make the world think well of such a nation?

There is no prize for guessing that the discussion is leading to another – and hopefully final – *'root cause'*. And that root cause is *'Rangdari'* phenomenon which has come to be the principle defining feature of the nation, marinating the entire society, politics and the economy in its toxic juices. Besides putting the well-being and the future of 1200 million and their coming generations to grave peril, it has served to cleave this benighted nation sharply into two distinct categories of perpetrators and victims, leaving but little space in between for a simple, self-respecting and law-abiding citizen to survive with dignity. One can't really avoid discussing so consequential a thing in some detail.

The Rangdari Land. As a direct consequence of the depredations of 'people's leaders' and 'public servants' – direct avatars of the thugs and pindaris of the uniformly dark 18th century – the land that should have become a veritable Ram Rajya, has been turned into, what could best be called, 'Rangdari Land'. Rangdari phenomenon is direct new age successor to what had been the principal hierarchical feature of this blessed land for more than three millennia, namely, the varna/caste system. It would be no exaggeration to say that it has come to be the central feature of the Indian political, social and economic system, and is being practiced, in one form or another, from one corner of the land to the other.

All said and done, the much-maligned caste system had one overriding objective behind it: To enjoy wealth and services flowing from the sweat of other's brow. Though not exactly slavery as prevailed in the ancient and the mediaeval world, it was much worse than that in many aspects. Reason being that in the caste system slavery was compounded by adamantine chains of religious injunctions as laid out in the scriptures, and, therefore, what to say of the possibility of escape or manumission, it rendered contemplation even of such things as liberty or free-will impossible. Now the present thug-syndicate, going by the name of political and administrative establishment, has also created for itself a similar position of privilege with a singular objective: Earning unearned wealth by robbing all others of the fruits of their labor and enterprise. This syndicate draws its authority and sustenance from the new age scripture of Constitution. Little surprise in that, for the gumboots gifted to the native heathens by the departing British (GoI Act of 1935, which provided template for the Constitution of 1950) were bound to turn out to be ill-fitting and bloodying.

Now having acquired modern features and connotations, and fortified beyond assault by the Constitution and its laws, this varna-caste gangsterism of the old has become much more deadly and efficient, and could be summed up in a single – and supremely appropriate – expression of *'Rangdari'*. Rangdari indeed is an extremely apt term to define the character the Indian polity has come to acquire under the present Reich. It is in happy consonance with Indian social, religious, political and economic traditions of three thousand years. And whereas, throughout its history, the land suffered horrendously at the hands of the old rangdars drawing authority from the religious scriptures, the present day rangdars or neo-Savarnas are natural products of the secular scripture of the modern age, viz., 'Constitution of India'. Rangdari is much more than such simple things as bribes, extortion or commissions – pejorative terms applicable to lowly creatures like police constables, lower grade clerks or small-time goondas; 'small fishes' that do not enjoy the 'eco-system' of complicity and protection involving, or able to muster the all-out support of, the entire 'system' (that is, higher ups in police, politics, bureaucracy and the judiciary). A Rangdar is the 'system' itself against which there is no appeal or recourse. Those naïve or daring enough to even contemplate that are sure to turn out to be either dead or mad. The entire epistemology of the phenomenon could be expressed in a single sentence: *I have no legal or moral claim, but since, thanks to the complicity of the state, I have got a little power in my hands, I will help myself at the expense of the people or the state, or both'*. That in a nutshell is Rangdari.

It is no coincidence that the term Rangdari evolved and came into vogue in Bihar, the bastion of caste and exploitation, but, much like some insidious weed, the phenomenon has come to prosper and proliferate in every single climatic zone of the country. It has managed to create a new hierarchy of caste, far potent and pernicious than the actual thing had ever been. Replacing the old dichotomy of savarnas and shudras, a new paradigm of neo-savarnas and neo-shudras has come into operation. Politicians, government servants, moneybags and middlemen have come to be the part of the neo-savarna category of rulers, oppressors and exploiters; all others, constituting nine-tenth of the populace, are ghettoized as neo-shudras. Though kinsmen and compatriots to the majority set, the swagger, insensitivity and brutality of the rangdars makes them appear as if they were part of some occupation army.

It is a verity that the uniquely divisive and sinister caste system the Indian society had managed to afflict itself with had turned this paradise of a land, bursting at seams with all the bounties required in the ancient times to make a nation the crown of nations, into a land of wants, inhumanities, discord, unfreedoms and downright slavery. It also is an irrefutable given of our times that the new caste system of rangdari won't let this nation and its denizens achieve the true level of their potential and happiness. Stewing in its destitution and ignorance as a consequence, the overwhelming majority shall continue to be a slave in the hands of the rangdar minority.

Ironically, the gross anti-people infamy is being indulged in by the blasted gang in the name and service of the people itself. Practically everyone plying the nefarious commerce calls himself either a 'public' servant or 'public' representative, even though he is servant only to his lust and villainy, and represents the interest of none else but himself and his clan. Everyone seems to be filled with maniac energy of a wild tribe on hunt astride his favorite SUV, even as the hapless prey (law-abiding Indian, working his shirt off to make his two ends meet) runs for its dear life like a frightened boar being sticked from all sides. It would have been a scene to enjoy on the Discovery or Animal Planet, hadn't the implications for the society and the nation been that grave and irreparable.

Just about everyone – from lowly peon, patwari and ward-member to gram pradhan and panchayat adhyaksha; clerk and office-head to constable and inspector; engineer and doctor to PCS, IPS and IAS officer; MLA and MP to cabinet minister and party president; military top brass to ministers, chief-minister, and even the Prime Minister and the President of the nation (that is, virtually everyone enjoying constitutional sanction and authority of some sort) - is busy exacting his quota of rangdari...gnawing away frenetically at the roots of the society and the nation as if there would be no tomorrow.

Other societies and nations have their best set (most intelligent, dynamic and enterprising of the lot) giving out its best: nurturing and bettering the society, ensuring justice and fair play, and helping the less fortunate of their compatriots come up and contribute their mite to national-societal cause. In India we have these sections – historical privilegentsia as well as the new soldiers of fortune – engaged 24x7 in the demolition job — decimating the society and the nation with a viciousness and vigor the Nazis couldn't do to the Jewish nation. With the very fence engaged in polishing off the crop, there could be no reward guessing the fate of the husbandman.

Now the greatest defense of rangdari is that, viewed in a larger context, there is not much overall harm done since most of the country's wealth remains within the country; either invested back (so-called FDI is ninety percent rangdari money and the p-notes ninety-nine), or spent on purchasing goods, spurring the land's economy. Further, what they earn is a small part of the governmental budgets or people's money. This salt-in-the-flour amount should be accepted as a kosher thing and not be blamed for the overall rot afflicting society or the nation. State officials used to be paid huge salaries during the British period. Comparison would reveal that even taking the bribes and cuts into account, their total take-home doesn't match that in majority of the cases.

That is dissemblance at best. Diabolicalness of the logic can only be compared with Manuwadins justifying caste system and untouchability in terms of Karma-theory, Mullahs holding the non-conforming and the non-believers *wajib-ul-katl* in the name of Koranic injunctions, or the Pope anointing confirmed mass-murderers and tricksters as Christian saints.

If one sat down in real earnest to count the ultimate implications of the devastation the rangdars have been subjecting our nation and the society to, he would have found out that these had easily outweighed the damage done to them by the Manu Smiriti, Puranas, Koran, Bible and Das Capital put together. Only some broad items are outlined here:

It is daylight robbery, besides being completely immoral. Availing of a thing you are not entitled to, or doing things you are under oath or obligation not to, can't be justified by any amount of sophistry. And while the immorality of the thing is obvious, the crassness and callousness of the phenomenon, wherein millions starve even as a few make merry at their expense or in spite of them, should be apparent too.

It is high treason: For nothing imperils the national security more than a society gone immoral and corrupt, and its citizens rendered starved, ignorant, sick and cynical. In that sense, calculated conduct of the rangdars is more insidious and deleterious, imperiling the moral, morale and the future of the society, than isolated acts of terrorism indulged in by misguided elements.

Argument or notion that rangdari money remains within the country and is invested back or spent to spur economy and development is misleading in entirety. Investment in palatial homes, prime plots, luxury cars, jewelry and fine wines, which most of the ill-gotten money is normally invested in (if not sent abroad) can't compensate for the schools and hospitals and power houses and the like that would otherwise have been built to improve and save lives. And the argument that rangdari money is invested back in the country to give spur to the economy is countered by the fact that the selfsame rangdari system impedes investment in really productive sector of industry.

Simply put, 10-500 crore a year that a District Magistrate normally earns in an year (depends upon his posting; Kaushambi, Kabirnagar, Kanpur, Ghaziabad or NOIDA, as far as the state of UP was concerned) to purchase properties in Delhi, Dubai or Dartmouth, could easily save twenty thousand to one lakh children from utter malnutrition or build dozens of middle-class schools in the rural areas. And given that there are at least 500 'officers' and 50,000 other employees of various departments that had their 'bal-bacchey' (families) to take care of, besides thousand of politicians and office bearers of 'democratic' bodies, the rangdari turnover in a single district could easily top a DM's income fifty times over!

Further, thanks to this blighted rangdari, ten crores spent on a public works project don't yield a crore worth of benefit even. That is no revelation or wild accusation, as the quality of any MNREGA or JNURM work would testify.

The only proper and effective way to quantify the consequences of rangdari would be to see it in terms of lives devastated directly and indirectly by the actions of a public official. Thus, if a newly born child of a poor household (destined to turn out to be ill-nourished and near-illiterate) requires Rs. 20,000 a year to be raised as a well-cared for child, 20 crore a year earned by a typical UP district magistrate could be deemed to be robbing 10,000 such children of that opportunity. Even if one chose not to multiply it with, say, a factor of

100 (that is, total estimated yearly rangdari turnover in a district), direct and indirect consequences of the venality and insensitivity of so high an official, and the punishment he should be given from the overall short and long-term societal and nationalist viewpoint could well be imagined. Needless to state, rangdar ministers and chief ministers damage the people and the nation many times more than even that and deserve according punishment.

Though amassing apparently for hundreds of generations, this myopic and self-indulgent breed of new rangdars may not get to enjoy its ill-gotten wealth its own entire lifetime even. Unwilling to forsake its hubris, countless times the rangdar set of the old (which constitutes the majority of the new rangdar set) was worsted, enslaved, raped, humiliated, converted and killed mercilessly. History is set to repeat itself all over—for the last time this time around, by all reckoning. For, the enemy has turned wiser, global and infinitely deadlier, demonstrating, for those caring to observe and infer, its intentions to follow 'take no prisoners' policy. Badly mauled and truncated though, they had been lucky to escape the millennium long onslaughts of the supremacists and imperialists of the yore. There is no chance now of surviving the latter's infinitely thoroughgoing and deadly 21st century avatars.

Does anyone harbor any doubt that corruption corrupts the society in every which way? Contrary to what Nehru and Indira Gandhi implied, and the people with their hands in the till try to convince themselves and the others, it devastates lives and hinders progress of the nation. Otherwise, why should it be that the highest percentage (greater in absolute numbers than entire populations of every country other than China) of illiterates, ill-nourished, landless, assetless and shelterless mass of people should stand in the name of India? Why, now this very day (20 July, 2012), when these lines are being penned, there is a news item that UNICEF has estimated yearly deaths of children in India due to diarrhea and pneumonia at 10 lakh and India remains at the top among 75 nations studied…above every single sub-Saharan nation even. Are we Indians that uniquely sinful, accursed or godforsaken? Name any affliction known to the human kind – blindness, handicap, rickets, TB, diabetes, heart-disease, leprosy, diarrhea, malaria, and the like – and we are right at the top. It is as if the global *'Hall of Shame'* has been reserved forever by India in its name. From transport bottlenecks to man hours lost in queues, from cohorts of ill-literates coming out of the apology of schools to people dying of spurious drugs, from crashing MIGs to derailing trains, from dengue to encephalitis, from daughters being raped to sons being killed, from young girls lured away to be sold into flesh-trade to young boys kidnapped to be sacrificed to organs-trade, from wannabe migrants to Europe suffocating to death in containers to people reliving their bums on the roadside—virtually every ill that is absent in Japan, Malaysia and Singapore, and is fast disappearing from China, Brazil and even Indonesia can be laid at the doorstep of this blighted rangdari.

We all are bothered by rising level of crime in the society, especially the more brutal kinds of recent vintage: Children, even infants, being mutilated, raped and sodomized; sons, even daughters, killing parents for booze or mobile money; juveniles friends kidnapping and murdering friends for ransom; and girls turning up raped, killed and stuffed up in bags daily on the roadside or in railway compartments. That is all very well—feeling so outraged, depressed and concerned about the new depths the society seems to be plumbing every other day. What is not well is that either we fail to discern, or make it convenient to ignore the umbilical link these seemingly novel crimes have with the rising level of rangdari in our society. Naked truth is that, in every respect, corruption is the mother – giving birth to, hatching, feeding, teaching it the preying skills and protecting it from the consequences – of all the crimes. That way, the seemingly benign corruption is manifold insidious and deleterious than even the most outrageous of the crimes.

Indeed, corruption is way too toxic than a crime, for it extends inspirational *'value-add'* to it by making it go unpunished. A crime will have little inspirational value if it entailed quick and exemplary punishment, thereby depriving the perpetrator of its gains and leaving him far worse off then he had been before committing it. But non-punishment of crimes (due primarily to corruption and apathy prevalent in our police force and the judiciary; and they can't be an island of honesty and work-ethics amid a sea of corruption and sloth), and insensitivity and brutalization that the pervasive phenomenon of rangdari has subjected the entire society and the 'system' to, has a magic effect upon those susceptible to a life of criminal adventurism.

It is a no-brainer that corruption breeds sense of injustice all around and every criminal act has its root in injustice, real or perceived. Even as having to pay bribery is positively galling, seeing the corrupt not only going unpunished but flourishing splendidly is no pleasant feeling either. It renders one feeling small and cheated. Sentiment, that one is not treated fairly by a powerful set of people or the society as a whole bruises the ego leading to build up of anger. In evolved persons this anger turns into resolve to fight the injustice through physical or intellectual means. In the weak it leads ultimately, after feeble and futile attempts upon resistance, to a sense of resignation, self-pity and escapism. However in the persons that are neither evolved nor weak or escapist, a poison ivy of indignation takes root. If allowed to go untreated or not cut off early, it flourishes unabated, leading gradually to his own demise as a normal human being and accumulation of hatred towards the society. A life of crime and depravity gets to be the logical next step.

Every time a bribe or undue favor is asked in lieu of a legitimate work, or a right is denied on account of a man's birth-status (caste, class, color or creed), a poison ivy is planted. And they have been planting millions of such poison ivies daily and then wonder what the society is coming to!

It is common knowledge that a witness to domestic violence is more likely than not to turn out to be violent in his own married life. Similarly, childhood victims of crime or rape are not, as logic or conventional wisdom might suggest, likely to turn out to be saints or crusaders against crime; rather the other way round. Now, as things stand in India, every single person – right from his/her childhood to adulthood, from the birth-certificate age to death-certificate, whether seeking pre-nursery admission or a driving license – is likely to suffer or witness at least a hundred cases of invidious distinction, official apathy or pure bribe-extortion. It means that barring the exceptional cases of those innately evolved or undergone some kind of cathartic experience, every single denizen of the land is likely to acquire a corrupt, callous and corroded, if not downright brutalized and depraved, mindset.

That, seeing, reading and listening to the tales of crime and sin, one more gory, bizarre and hair-raising than the other which our newspapers and the TV channels are crammed with, we do not die daily of shock and anguish is in itself indicative of brutalization wrought upon us by the corrupt milieu we have grown up in. Though the trend is by no means unique to India, it can't be denied that things have been rendered inordinately fetid here.

Whatever the level of corruption, and damage it is doing to the morals, health, education and the general well-being of the people and the future of society and the nation, not many people appear to be sufficiently angry or indignant about it. Even *'lakh-crores'* that raised the heckles of people in the wake of 2G scam has become sort of de rigueur. Politics of Karnataka and Andhra (or any other state for that matter), where out and out robbers seem to have hijacked entire states and yet are treated as heroes and gods by the people, is evidence of the depth to which the rot has set in. Things seem to have attained their peak. It may not be long before the inexorable 'Laws of Karma' struck, making millennium-long slavery, along with million murders, rapes and conversions that came in its wake appear a teddy-bear picnic.

In spite of the scriptures-sanctioned rangdari that our caste-feudal society had been soaked in, the British had managed to inject a new morality, accountability and rectitude in our rotten public standards and mores. British rulers and the bureaucracy established new standards (as also deterrents and punishment against lapses) in the matters of work-ethics, punctuality and probity. That helped many Indians come out of their feudal and slavish mindsets, and reform and modernize their public conduct.

But alas! Our own leaders (and most respected, iconic and powerful ones at that; only these kind of leaders are capable of establishing new standards) let us down badly, making things go back to square one. Yes, we are talking Nehru, Indira and Rajiv here. It is not that they were personally venal (they had no need to; entire nation was sprawled at their feet), but their fear of losing power and, therefore, the need to worst the opposition at all costs induced them to make the election process expensive beyond the capacity of the opposition. That made them (as also the opposition, wherever it happened to acquire power) do things that became part of the folklore of corruption. Each did at least one thing that got etched in the collective public consciousness, seeping down in due course to the very foundation of its moral pillars.

Fittingly, our very own 'Father of the Nation' had begun the game by courting the likes of Birla whose name remains byword for filth-money and all manners of shady doings. Nehru's fondness for such proven rotten eggs as TT Krishnamachari, Pratap Singh Kairon and Dharam Teja served to loosen the inhibitions of the Congress leaders and the bureaucracy. Indira (Nagarwala) and Rajiv (Bofors) kept up the tradition. Presently, the Sonia-Rahul-Manmohan triad's 2G, CWG and coal-block scam have lowered the morals to the extent that, apparently, no new depth remains to fathom.

Natural outcome is that we are back to the age of Saiyid Brothers, Mohammad Shah Rangeela, Mir Jafar and Amichand—of unparalleled moral degradation, all round stasis and unbridled conspiracies, scandals and open loot, consequenting into two century long colonization and destitution of the land. There should be little wonder then that India languishes right at the bottom of every list that connotes health, education, character, evolution and overall happiness, and very top of the ones connoting hunger, wants, ignorance, sickness, moral decrepitude and bleak future. That being the case, and the things promising only to go down further, one should not be shocked or outraged by the assessment that this nation is doomed. The rangdari system of the old first kept the majority of the land low for two millenniums and then the entire nation under slavery for close to six centuries. Rangdari of the mediaeval type (feudalism) got it colonized for two centuries. As the history moves now with the speed of thought, the rangdari system of the modern variety will destroy the nation altogether much before it had the opportunity to celebrate a century of its Independence.

Even with his moral fiber destroyed, an individual can manage to survive, though he would do so less as a human and more as a beast. He can't implode by himself and the social safety net and the laws of the land are there to protect him from the Darwinian forces lying out. Nations don't enjoy that luxury; international safety net as it is there is extremely weak and the Darwinian forces just too strong. But much more than that, nations are particularly prone to implosion from the onslaught of forces and tensions that keep working inside all the time and against which there is no safety net except the one woven from its own moral fiber. No one can say that India hasn't either lost its moral fiber already, or is in the final stage of doing so.

From looming energy and water famines, to depleting green cover, to dying cities, to collapse of morals and the morale of just about every individual as well as the institution...litany is a long laundry list of lamentations. Yet the greatest long term damage that the new rangdari has done is to render the nation and the society completely oblivious and inured to the dangers lurking within and the outside our borders. Most resourceful, dynamic and intelligent are either too pleased and satisfied with themselves, or too bitter, envious and cynical, even as the common run of men is left with no time or capacity to even think of his own future, letting alone that of the society and the nation. Since the reader has shown his concern by persevering this far by the trite tale, the author feels, much like the Ancient Mariner, encouraged to discuss two of the biggest and most imminent (but by no means the only) dangers staring in the face of the nation and its billion plus.

✳

3

TWO AGENTS OF DOOM • Hunger Wars

Talking of vital insecurities facing beasts and the humans alike, food insecurity comes right on the top, just alongside the security of life. All other considerations pale into insignificance. Neither could this tract have been conceived, nor would anyone care to read it on a hungry stomach. Let alone book writing or reading, for a good ninety percent people, food, if push came to real shove, is likely to take precedence over even such exalted things as personal or national honor and freedom, fraternal or conjugal love, or even God and religion. Indeed, there could be no comparison. Food stands in a league of its own, having in it to transcend even such deeply held taboos as beef, pork, non-kosher or non-helal food, or even cannibalism.

The thing is no less true about nations. Of course, tiny states such as Brunei or Burundi can't be expected to deal with all manners of insecurities on their own; one or the other kind shall always remain the bane of their small size. Yet, in the nature of their smallness is written their security, as they can very well adjust to any emergent situation without inconveniencing others too much. However, large states such as US, China, Japan, Russia, Brazil, Indonesia, Nigeria, Bangladesh, Pakistan and, of course, India stand in a different league. Their legitimacy, stability and integrity hinges upon their capability of providing their citizens with all manners of securities largely on their own. Needless to reiterate, food security is paramount among these.

They aver that India is in the process of developing into a superpower and may indeed become one within a decade or two. Not everyone is sanguine about the assertion. What, however, everyone is sure about is the fact that India is going to become the most populous country of the world by the end of the next decade. One hundred and fifty crores by 2030; Whew! What else does a nation require to become a superpower? Step aside you Chinese, Pakis and the Yankees! We are going to be number one in this game of numbers! And we have worked hard to achieve this position — persisted with trampling upon the rights of our own people, starved them and kept them illiterate, denied healthcare to them, continued to tolerate and vote thoroughly myopic and self-serving dispensations, and corrupted ourselves to our bones. No other people in the world have made such Herculean efforts to reach the top.

That is all very well, but a population means food, first and foremost. Population is not merely ballast to build super highway to superpowerdom. One hundred and fifty crore souls is not three hundred crore legs merely—marching to the borders to the tunes of martial band, carrying one hundred fifty crore flags with 'Mera Bharat Mahan' blazoned in scarlet one side and 'India Shining' in saffron the other, and trampling

The enemy under three hundred crore boots. It is also one hundred and fifty crore mouths baying and as many tummies growling for food every six hours, failing to get which they are certain to set the entire nation, along with its superpower ISO certificate, to fire.

What the food requirement of this arriviste superpower is likely to be in 2030? Back of the envelop calculations reveal that to keep up with its enhanced population and the newly acquired superpower status (calories, proteins and vitamins requirement of every denizen brought at par with the developed nations), India would need to enhance the production of food grains by a factor of more than two (550 million ton requirement/240 million ton current production), of pulses by three (45/14), oil seeds by ten (200/20), meat by ten (11 kg/1 kg per head), milk by seven, sugar by three, fruits by ten and vegetables by five.

Somebody perhaps unlearnt his lessons in arithmetic, or, in his rush of jingoism, made it convenient to forget the connection of superpower status of a nation with the food needs of superpower citizens.

Or, may be, he mistook superpowerdom with super-slumpowerdom. But, even the needs of a super-slum power shall be impossible to meet two decades hence.

The production of food grains, pulses, oilseeds or sugarcane has hit a plateau, with little possibility of a significant rise in productivity, due primarily to inefficient agricultural setup, uneconomic land holdings, shrinking irrigational resources, rising cost of inputs, dwindling fertility of the soil, abysmal educational level of the peasantry, and corruption and apathy of the government agencies. Production is virtually stagnating for past several years and the booming population is bringing the per capita availability of food grains incessantly down. It has now reached the level prevailing in the fifties when India was considered to be a perennially starved country. Food grain availability peaked in 1964-65 at 480 grams per day per person; it was 430 gram in 2011. With the social setup turning increasingly more in-egalitarian by the day, the ever growing rich and the middle class has begun consuming much richer food now, thereby cornering disproportionate share of just about every food item – grains, pulses, meat, sugar, oil, fruits, vegetables, and the like. As a direct consequence, availability of food grains for the poorest sections has got even worse than what their grand parents had managed to have in the fifties, even as their intake of proteins and vitamins – building blocks of the body and its sustainers – has dwindled to nil for all practical purposes.

As for record surplus food grain stocks with the government, so much so that millions of tons of grain rots in the open for there remain no place to stock it…well. Set against the fact of more than three-fourth of the nation's children running underweight, receiving even less nutrition than even the godforsaken children of the sub-Saharan Africa, only a feckless and criminal dispensation can have the gall to present that as a matter of great satisfaction and pride the way the Indian State does. In any case, this is the last decade the Indians are likely to see grain stocks of any size.

Now, even if by some miracle, and despite stupendous odds like receding water table and growing infertility of soil (not to talk of climate change), India managed to achieve the world average productivity levels in every crop variety (rising by 30% in case of rice, 60% in case of wheat, and 250% in case of coarse grains), and managed too to halt shrinkage of the arable land, the production of food grains shall still reach 370 million ton—far below the 550mT required for a decently fed nation. And, that is leaving the things like pulses, oilseeds, meat, milk and fruits (items the Indians can never hope to match the world in) out.

Within a generation time, the land holdings, majority of which are uneconomical even now, are set to be fractionalized further by a factor of two to three. More than four-fifth of these shall become marginal—unable even to return the cost of labor invested in them.

Millions upon millions shall be forced to abandon husbandry, swelling the ranks of hungry and naked cohorts and swamping the (so-called) towns to complete collapse.

About one third of India's land is already degraded or is in varying stages of degradation. With further growth in population and enhanced industrial-economic activities, much land is set to be lost to building projects of hundred kinds—roads, schools, hospitals, power stations, factories, housing and the like. To make matter worse, resulting effluents-pollution and the human activities shall rob much additional proximate land of its productivity. It is estimated that around 20% less land shall be available for cultivation in the next twenty years. As for the world, according to the FAO, availability per capita of arable land shrank from 4250 m^2 in 1960 to 2250 m^2 in 2005 and is set to decrease to around 1800 m^2 by 2030. According to Oxfam's calculations, the amount of land bought around the world by private investors from 2000 to 2010 could produce enough food to feed 1 billion people. In India alone, some 50,000 villages have disappeared from 1995 to 2010, cannibalized by its relentlessly expanding towns.

Moreover, it is but natural that the market forces will induce the farmer to switch to commercial (non-foodgrain) crops to subserve the bourgeoning needs of the economically well off sections. That would further reduce the land available for cereals production, making these scarcer and costlier, and thus driving the economically weaker sections (overwhelming majority, in effect) further off the food cycle (carbohydrate-cycle rather, for they have already been driven out of the protein, vitamin and fats cycles, for all practical purposes). That would complete the internal colonization by the 'Shining India' of the excluded and disinherited India of 'teeming millions' by making them perennially starved, as the dalits of the land had always been. Didn't somebody surmise that history repeats itself, first as a tragedy, then as a farce? Well, in the topsy-turvy land the India is, farce is being played out first; tragedy is awaiting it a decade down.

Caught up already in an interminable struggle to make its two ends meet, a great majority shall neither have means enough to indulge in such luxuries as birth control, nor patience enough to let its children waste their years in the schools to receive a useless kind of education. Far better would it be to make them earn a few bucks by working in dhabas and homes, or through begging and stealing. For, under the developing situation, the mid-day meal, which arranges but a few morsels of dubious quality for a child, is unlikely to work either for it or the family. The phenomenon is pretty common even now, but the trend is likely to intensify as food items, consuming two-third of the family income of the poor even now, get increasingly scarce and costly. As the timer on the food-bomb ticks away inexorably, the 'great expectation' of the 'Shining India' that, with the passage of time, and without them bothering to make requisite mental and physical efforts and sacrifices, the swelling tide of its prosperity shall be enough by itself to lift other ninety percent boats stuck in the mud of vicious cycle of destitution, ill-health and ignorance is set to turn into great consternation. And that wouldn't be the sole thing to worry its head off. Innumerable and hard-to-detect landmines lie buried beneath the super highway they hope to ride along to 'Destination Superpowerdom'.

The Green revolution happened, for the technology and the methods – hybrid seeds, chemical fertilizers, and pesticides, tube-well irrigation, advanced sowing and plantation techniques etc – were readily available to copy and catch up with. Incidentally, it came as a great relief to the Establishment for helping to dilute the pressure on the front of land redistribution, clamor for which would have become too great had the looming specter of mass-starvations turned true. Presently, there is no revolutionary technology or farming techniques out there to be copied to bring about a second Green Revolution. Without taking intelligent and sensible options like fundamental restructuring of the land holding pattern across the country and making massive investments in irrigation and other modern techniques (obvious impossibilities under the kind of weltanschauung the nation reels under), it would be increasingly impossible to even maintain the agricultural output at its present level, not to talk of enhancing it further to meet out the leapfrogging needs of the surging population. Biotechnology and GM seeds, new white hopes of the previous decade, have turned out to be a chimera largely…at least in the case of food grains. In any case, it is predicated upon enormous research and capital investments that India, with its run down institutions mired in corruption, red-tape, apathy and ineptitude, and lack of foresight and will on the part of the self-indulgent political and administrative class, is singularly ill-equipped to undertake. Unpredictable medium and long term consequences of the adoption of GM technology will always remain a deterrent for a country of India's size. America can take even fifty percent crop loss in a wrong turn of event. All that it would have to do is to curtail its meat consumption and ban food grain exports; little matter to them that it would cause millions of deaths in other parts of the world. But even twenty percent crop-loss shall consequent into millions of starvation deaths and great turmoil in a country like India.

Whatever manner we choose to analyze the facts and data concerning population figures, land availability, food productivity, or the possibility of modernizing agriculture in the face of worsening land-holding pattern, one conclusion can not be escaped: That instead of entering the Superpower League, India is set to face a crisis of *'never before in the human history'* proportions. And, we haven't taken the likely climate change and other potential environmental calamities into our account. Even a slight turn in climate is certain to transform the nation's roadsides into open graveyards ala Bengal of the early forties and China of late fifties. Kalahandi and Kutch of nineties shall be replicated in every bloc, with not enough Punjabs there to meet out the shortfall.

Some eternal hopefuls aver that world is awash in food supply and thanks to great untapped plains and forests of South America, Africa, S-E Asia and Australia, there shall always be plenty to feed the worl population, whatever it got to be.

That is utter fallacy, to put it mildly. World is not awash in food even now, that is, if all the hungry mouths were to be fed properly. Moreover, all of the world regions are beginning to suffer from dwindling water supplies, with enough water not available to meet the irrigation demands of the grain bowls of the US even, even as Australia and Africa's droughts get increasingly debilitating. All the great aquifers of the world are depleting fast due to relentless tapping with bore wells. America being a hugely surplus country regarding food production, and given the mentality of the Americans and their way of life, many agricultural farms shall be the first to wind up in case things needed to be prioritized between meeting irrigation, industrial and urban needs. Americans are not the type who would, in the name of humanity or even God or Christ, consent to close down even few thousands of millions of their private swimming pools or golf courses to save starving millions of Congo or Koraput.

Some worthies hope that a technology is bound to emerge (as if technology was oath-bound to shield the humans from the consequences of their follies and recklessness) in due time to take care of the future food needs (whatever the population level) of the world.

That is entirely ignorant, fatalistic, anti-human and anti-national, head-in-the-sand kind of view. Are nations' or the mankind's destinies to be made a function of wishful assumptions of some irrationally sanguine souls? The hoped-for technology may take twenty years or fifty to evolve, or may not come about at all. There are many reasons militating against the optimistic assumption.

To begin with, a technology is developed in response to some emergent need and the developing nations are the neediest, India being the upper most in the rank. Is it doing enough in the field, or is there any sign of some white horse of technology emerging out of the *Saagar-Manthan* our great agricultural 'research' institutes, first class exemplars of bureaucratic stasis and corruption, are engaged in? Do we expect the Americans or Europeans (reeling forever under glut situations) to pour enormous capital and intellectual resources in agricultural research so that Indians, Pakistanis, Bangladeshis, Nigerians, Egyptians, Iranians, North Koreans, Somalis and the like (that is, people who nurse nothing but envy or animus towards the West) may not die of hunger, even as they went on growing their populations to flood their lands and diverted their resources towards developing N-weapons and Jihadi organizations to subvert them? Even if it (i.e. the West) managed to catch hold of a miracle technology to meet out the world food requirement for all time to come, it would (and should) do everything to suppress its further development and dissemination for its own good, as also that of the world as a whole. That is besides the fact that the extant food-surplus position of the West is going to be the biggest tool (bigger perhaps than the oil even) in its hands to leverage the world politics to meet its strategic aims.

Further, even if the world food supply grows significantly in the future, it is unlikely to benefit India much. China turned a food-deficit nation many years ago and, despite three decades of one-child policy, its population is yet to be stabilized. It is expected to rise by about two hundred million before stabilizing fully. Moreover, revolutionary rise in the prosperity level of its citizens has made its food consumption grow much faster than the rate of population growth. To compound that, and in consonance with the rising income levels, the food habits of the Chinese are also undergoing rapid transformation with increasing share in their food mix of meat and the poultry which need anywhere between eight to fifteen times more resources (land, water and fertilizers to grow feed) to produce than the cereals. It is a sure bet that in coming years China will contract up all food surpluses available in the world market, outbidding India and the similarly placed nations many times over. Given its unremitting hostility towards India, it may do that deliberately in a particularly stressed year so as to trigger riots and destabilization.

As is likely to be the case concerning every other conceivable commodity (copper, zinc, uranium, coal, oil, timber and the like), the two giants of Asia are set for a vicious dogfight in the international food market too. And much like every other arena, China is certain to worst India by a wide margin in this most critical of bazaar places too. Reason is not simply the rapidly bourgeoning economic might or diplomatic clout enjoyed by China, or the astuteness and patriotism of its ruling junta in direct contrast to the Indian ruling elite. Awful truth is that China has got too many dragons – nuclear proliferation, North Korea, Greenhouse Gases, propping up of retrograde regimes around the world, US and European debt, South-China Sea, and the like – stashed up in the vaults of its Forbidden City. The threat of unleashing even one of these shall be enough to deter the declining West from going against its vital interests.

And blackmail is not the only weapon in China's arsenal; far from it. It has got many 'favors' or 'concessions' too to offer to the world, particularly to the craven and terrified West. It is another matter that most of these concessions are of a bit negative kind: Not abetting the Islamists, not supplying military technology to Islamic nations, not building up naval presence in the Atlantic or military bases in the renegade African and Latin American nations, not arming the Space, not indulging in covert cyber war, not impeding rare-earths exports, not attacking Taiwan...list is endless, with China always on the top. One could, if he so wished, call these concessions instruments of great blackmail, for China it all is part of legitimate diplomacy. It goes without saying that offering these 'concessions' doesn't compromise China's sovereignty or its national interests even a bit.

India, on the other hand, has little to offer on the positive front and lesser still on the negative. It can't afford to sell nuclear or military technology to the Islamic nations, nor threaten making common cause with the nations like Saudi Arabia, Iran and Pakistan to abet Jihadi Islam; things the West most fears from China. Moment it (India) tries to blackmail the West, its goose is as good as cooked.

It may be found illuminating here to judge as to where at the beginning of the present century do the two population giants of the world stand in the matter of this most critical of securities.

China's agricultural production is one and a half times that of India. Its present population of 1.3 billion is set to maximize at around 1.4-1.5 billion and decline thereafter. India's population of 1.2 billion (official figures; actual figure may be much higher) is increasing with a growth rate of about 1.8% (2 crore mouths a year) and seems nowhere near stabilizing. More than three quarters of its population is light years away from consuming recommended quantum of just about everything: carbohydrates, fats, sugar, protein, minerals and vitamins. More than half fail to get enough cereals of whatever quality. More than a quarter remains perennially a step away from outright starvation. More than seventy-five percent of the children across vast swathes of the country are malnourished; Indian officialese for semi or full-blown starvation.

What the situation is likely to be in Y 2030? With nearly forty crore mouths added, India leaves China far behind in terms of population. Land under agricultural usage gets shrunken by more than ten percent, even as vast swathes of land turn water stressed or run completely dry. Cereal production declines more rapidly as more and more of the extant land is diverted to commercial crops for export—inland, to meet out the shifting dietary preferences of the 'Shining India', as also to export meat, poultry, flowers, wines, exotic vegetables, organic food, and the like to the West Asia and the West so that more and more mobiles, laptops, gold, cosmetics, apparels and accessories to fulfill the fads and fancies of the selfsame 'Shining India', fancy cars, luxury boats and commercial planes to enable it to reach its destinations quickly and comfortably, and advanced weaponry to keep its sense of security intact, could be imported unrestricted.

China on the other hand would have reached its population plateau. Even at present, with per capita consumption of cereals one and half times and that of meat more than two, it is feeding its population much better than India. Yet, even after the population had peaked, its demand for food is likely to keep growing apace in view of growing percentage of adults in the population mix and rapidly rising income levels across all sections of its populace. As such, China's need for imports is not likely to abate in a foreseeable future. However, not a single Chinese is likely to starve even in case all marketing surpluses evaporated from the international markets. All that would be needed to be done on its part is to reduce its consumption of meat and poultry that takes eight to ten times cereals to produce.

As regards India, even if its production and consumption of cereals were deemed as adequate as of now (which they patently are not; Chinese consume fifty percent more than the Indians and they are not the best fed people of the world by any means), its demand-supply gap is likely to increase by more than a quarter by 2030. Notwithstanding sanguine forecasts of the officialdom, India's population growth rate is not going to abate much. Contrarily, it could even rise as the percentage of the sections resistant or hostile to the concept of family-planning rises rapidly; situation exacerbated by the fact that more and more numbers are likely to fall into destitution and ill-health, and, therefore, beyond the ambit of family planning. Situation on the front of proteins, fats and vitamins (that is, pulses, legumes, vegetable oil, sugar, meat, milk, vegetables and fruits) is set to get manifold worse as internal colonization is certain to leave more and more people completely out in the dumps.

As things stand, and entirely unlike China, India's position would be desperate in the future, particularly in a drought year. India would practically starve, while China shall have to reduce its meat consumption merely. Growing social unrest is certain to deteriorate into widespread communal riots, leading to breakdown of the administrative apparatus and making further break up of the nation a distinct possibility. The powers inveterately hostile to India and its natives – evangelical-imperialist sections of the West, Jihadi-genocidal Islam and hubristic-supremacist China – won't lag behind in extracting their pound of flesh off the beleaguered elephant. Inevitable fallout of all of the above will be that to purchase food from the hard-bargaining West controlling the food market, and to purchase internal peace from the Chinese supported Naxalites and Islamic Ummah supported Jihadis, India will have to surrender major chunks of its national sovereignty to all three of its historical tormentors.

More portentously still, even with the West inclined to help India out (of course with humiliating conditions attached), there might just not be enough to meet out the shortfall. After all, population is still surging in most parts of the world, even as consumption patterns change with still greater pace to impact the world food security negatively. It is difficult to see how India's self-serving leaders and churlish economists shall be able to deal with the developing food riddle. Hundreds of millions have already been thrown out of the food-cycle by their own compatriots; how would they be able to compete in the international markets in which both bulls and the bears (so to say) remain implacably hostile to them is beyond comprehension.

China however is not India's only competitor, or even the most formidable or hostile one. China's future food imports are likely to turn out to be piffle in comparison to what the Muslim nations are set to do. Already close to one and a half billion and exploding like a supernova, their population is set to burgeon to 2.25-2.5 billion a quarter century hence. Only a few of the Muslim nations are contemplating (or can dare to) population control and nearly all of them (except Indonesia, Malaysia and Bangladesh) lie in arid zone, with little prospects of increment in their agricultural production. Even if a few of these were self-sufficient in food production as of now, their astonishingly high population growth rates will make them perennially and abysmally dependent upon food imports. Additionally, even if some of them began undertaking population control measures today, legislating two-child norm, their population shall continue to grow for at least half a century.

As if to compensate for that crippling disadvantage, most of these nations enjoy a decisive advantage over poor countries like India or those belonging to the sub-Saharan Africa. They are awash with oil and can afford to spend obscene amounts to meet out their food requirements. Even if some of these were not, their rich brethrens, especially Saudi Arabia and the UAE, could be depended upon to bail them out to the extent of preventing starvation deaths.

By no means can India hope to compete with these two mighty and influential competitors in China and Islam. As things stand, even now, when it has built up considerable stocks and the world food market is relatively elastic, it is unable (or unwilling) to feed hundreds of millions of its undernourished and the starving. Situation, when the world food surpluses will in all likelihood be contracted out many years in advance (at the prices of gold, literally, or on the basis of commercial or strategic quid pro quo), could well be imagined.

Inevitable fallout would be coming of a great weapon of blackmail in the hands of marketable surplus nations. Dispensing (or withholding) food favors is going to be a deadlier bargaining counter than oil or the military might. And this weapon shall firmly be in the hands of the Western Christendom. Tables shall be turned upon the growingly anti-West Muslim nations, but a particularly unfortunate nation (unfortunate in having short-sighted, self-serving and rapscallion elite running its affairs; and not resources or potential) shall be crushed in the pincer movement of escalating oil and food prices, as fierce rivalry takes hold of the two camps, forced to set off the escalating cost of essential imports by jacking up the prices of the essential exports.

By no means is the foregoing a too improbable logic or uncharitable premise. Oil has been used as a weapon many times in the past and with devastating effect. It is still being used without let or relent by the N-bomb building Iran and Jihad exporting Saudi Arabia.

Who knows it better than India which has made it into its second nature to genuflect before the oil-rich Islamic nations, even to the extent of undermining its medium and long-term national interests? There should be little doubt that, in a scarcity situation, food can be used as a weapon of coercion and blackmail manifold more devastatingly than oil has ever been. In fact, it is as good a weapon as one could ever get. Again, India should know. Sixties of PL-480 and *'ship-to-mouth'* humiliations is not a Jurassic Age that can never come back. They (the US and the West) won't be serving their national interests and hegemonic goals if they failed to skin the cow of food-blackmail to its very bones by manipulating and dictating foreign, home and economic policies of the food-deficit nations. Simple expedient of sparking mayhem and revolution by denying food exports would suffice to bring recalcitrant regimes to their heels. Witness what their cat's paws (IMF, World Bank, rating agencies etc.) do to the nations that stumble and fall into their snare. Things are set to get hundred-fold worse when the world as a whole gets permanently and seriously food-deficit.

And it would be a weapon that won't age or go obsolete. That is because the momentum of population growth is impossible to stanch even in the medium term. China hasn't stopped growing yet despite unparalleled efforts spanning more than three decades. Africa as a whole is set to double its population every quarter century or so till at least the end of the present century. A mango-republic like India, with its cucumber-like dispensations can't be imagined to be gathering guts enough to enforce population control measures. It is impossibility in case of Islamic nations, for either they look upon exploding Muslim numbers as weapons in aid of their cherished transcendental goal, or are mortally afraid of even talking about it for fear of inviting violent Islamist backlash. Evidently, their faith-induced myopia or fear makes them ignore the phrase, 'to get hoisted with one's own petard'. To wit, beginning Dakar and Damascus, thence to Delhi and ending at Dacca, food slavery of the most disgraceful kind is writ large upon a wide arc upon the world map. It is there in the mindset of Africans, ready to raise a brood of ten and arrange antibiotics and anti-malarial drugs to save them, but not ready, in the name of poverty and ignorance, to undergo even free vasectomy. It is there in the preposterous hopes and antediluvian goals born of misconceived ideals, goals and the polity of many an Islamic nation.

And it is there in the mindset of corrupt and feckless trustees and the partisans of the Indian State who are as oblivious of the future of the nation as they are disregarding of its past and unashamed of its present. Be forever a slave or face mayhem and anarchy—that is the inescapable fate the Indian State is setting up for the Indians. Overweening self-interest leading them by nose, the reigning dispensations are busy pushing the nation up the garden path to superpower chimera, next to which lies a precipice.

Conclusion is unexceptionable. Sanguine souls, hoping once again to find, kill and bury the poor Malthus by sheer weight of their unfounded optimism are staking the lives of hundreds of millions of Indians, and the freedom and the future of a venerable nation on the alter of naiveté, ignorance and indifference. Vast tracts of cultivable land (much more than under cultivation then) had been lying fallow in the times of Malthus; almost entire earth has been brought under farming now. Irrigation potential was lying virtually untapped then; no stream or aquifer has been left pristine or plentiful now. HYV seeds and chemical fertilizers were hardly known in Malthus times; fertility of soil is milked to exhaustion by their overuse now. And the new white hope of the world (GM technology) is turning out to be a big white lie, at best, and could turn out to be blackest of tragedies if allowed to have complete sway.

All these shortfalls could have been met, or put up with patiently, had the food scarcity situation been a passing phenomenon. After all, many a families undergo adversities, see them through with fortitude and dignity, and manage to emerge stronger and more cohesive than before. However, even an otherwise cohesive extended family will fail to cope up with the situation if it became known, that, instead of getting alleviated in a reasonable frame of time, the adversity was going to be worse with each passing day. Me and my immediate family, 'each to his own', big fish/small fish, dog-eat-dog and survival-of-the-fittest are the kind of sentiments likely to overcome every one of its members. Tough and the resourceful would get going, even as the weak, who the blame for the situation would conveniently be put on to, are likely to be made short work of.

It is no secret that India is far from being a loving family or a cohesive society. Rather, among all the big and middle sized nations, it is most likely to fall apart amid chaos and genocides under a calamitous situation. As things stand, it remains at the cutting edge, so to say, of a great religious conflict even under the best of times. Prospects for conflict and chaos are not only not going to be abated, but, as we shall see, aggravate with each passing day. Food crisis, as and when it happens to strike in true earnest, is only going to hasten the inevitable.

And sure as death it is going to strike this fabled land of milk and honey. Widespread starvation and 'malnutrition' deaths are a well-recorded fact of national life even in these times of relative plenty. Footprints of starvation deaths have already spread out from the perennially drought prone areas of Andhra, Orissa, and Vidarbha to the heartland of Green Revolution: Gangetic plains and even Punjab.

Thus, according to 'Hunger Index' prepared by International Food Policy Research Institute, while India ranked 66th out of 88 developing countries surveyed in the matter of per capita calorie consumption, relatively better off Indian states such as Haryana and Tamil Nadu fell in the 'alarming' category and even Punjab came under 'serious' category, ranking below countries such as Nicaragua and Honduras.

What has kept the illusion of business-as-usual on the food front from being completely exposed, and countless *'malnutrition'* deaths treated as ignorable blips of little national significance, is the stratagem on the part of the state of creating the illusion of *'buffer stock'*. The practice of keeping buffer stock of food grains (or of any other commodity, for that matter) by the state is in itself admittance of the fact that the demand-supply situation of that commodity stands in a precarious balance. It is a statement that the state expects a crisis situation to emerge anytime and carries means enough to see it through. Governments down the decades have followed the practice of keeping buffer stocks of food grains. That only means that the food situation never became good enough for it to contemplate keeping its hands off. Yet it did precious little to strike at the root cause of the malaise.

What is likely to shatter the happy illusion of 'self-reliance' that the partisans of the State have managed to peddle till now is complete wipe-out of the 'buffer stock' in a decade or so. Hundreds of thousands of yearly deaths, which at present are successfully brushed under the huge Persian carpet called 'malnutrition', would come to be acknowledged for what they really are – starvation deaths, naked and proper. That is the time the moment of reckoning for the callous and myopic Indian State and its rapscallion partisans would have come. Terror and hysteria are milder terms to express the sentiment that is likely to take over the sections of people that till the other day had been staunch partisans of the State. They would be the first to question the legitimacy and the raison d'être of the state they had been benefiting from for several decades.

That however would be the wake up call—no, not for the State, but for everybody else: big merchants as well as small-time traders, farmers big and small, and the public at large. That would be the signal to get into action and start hoarding. Grain would disappear from the markets faster than the morning dew does before the rising sun. And can the situation be controlled or averted? You bet!

It would do well to recall here that shortfall in cereals availability when the great Bengal Famine struck in the early forties was around 4-6% merely...not something really earth-shaking or unmanageable. But wild rumors and panic-hoarding made the situation go completely out of hand and, before anyone could grasp the enormity of the situation, three million corpses had been littering the roadsides of Bengal. What India is going to face within a decade is shortfall (over and above what is normal in the 'normal' times) of Bengal Famine proportions in a normal year and anything around 10-15% in a drought year. Consequences can't even begin to be imagined.

As soon as the perception takes hold that the government buffer stocks had been dwindling and food grain in the international market was either not available or had been advance-contracted by China and the rich Islamic nations, an unprecedented panic would take the entire land in its hold. Rumors would fly thick and fast. Mass hysteria, followed by a hoarding spree – millions of households rushing pell-mell to buy at least a few quintals; small farmers hoarding a few tons for their own consumption and the next year's seeds; medium and big farmers hoarding hundreds of quintals of their produce to sell at windfall profits; and, finally, traders small and big hoarding up from tens to thousands of tons – would wipe the market clean of food grains within no time. And that is when the food riots, that should have broken out long ago – in Orissa, in W. Bengal, Chattisgarh, Bihar, East UP, Bundelkhand or Vidarbha, where millions of 'citizens' of a purportedly free, democratic, and socialist superpower-in-the-making live only a little better than the Jews did in Nazi concentration camps – would break out in the right earnest.

And if food riots break out, can communal riots remain far behind? And how long, if these became interminable feature, deteriorating into genocides as they would inevitably be, could intervention by the outside agencies, always on look out for troubled waters to fish in and who have never made a secret of their intentions to break India apart, be averted?

Moreover, being elder brother to its estranged brothers, its own set of problems is not the only thing India has to reckon with. There is Bangladesh as usual, with Pakistan next in line, whose population, except for some aberrations like Nigeria and sub-Saharan nations, continues to grow at the fastest rate even among the Muslim world. Consider the report:

The Financial Express, Dhaka, May 6, 2012

The country's environmental experts and scientists believe that if the population growth, unplanned urbanization, and industrialization continue at the present pace, Bangladesh will lose all its arable land by the end of this century (within five decades, according to another report). For a resource-constrained country, frequently battered by natural calamities, over-population is the foremost barrier to economic development. And population growth does not only mean feeding extra mouths but also exerting additional pressure on various resources like arable land.

The graveness of the situation may easily be perceived if juxtaposed with the stark reality that cultivable land of the country is decreasing at the rate of 1.0 per cent per annum due to indiscriminate urbanization and industrialization. Added to this, climate change triggered by global warming has cast a negative impact on agriculture production in the country. Hence, if the volume of the country's agricultural land continues to shrink due to uncontrolled growth of population, unplanned industrialization and urbanization, a bleak future is really awaiting the people of this country. Bangladesh is losing 80,000 hectares of farm land every year, as the country's fast growing population looks for new land to build homes and entrepreneurs go deep into the countryside to set up factories. If the trend is not reversed now, the country would permanently lose its food security, making the poor population more vulnerable to volatile international commodity prices.

No prize for guessing where all the Bangladeshis – all of the 40-50 crores – will head to? In fact, in another post dated May 24, 2009, the same paper had said that much...

A report titled 'Climate Change as a Security risk' said that the probable loss of arable and residential lands through flooding in this part of the world would result in increase in internal and external environmental migration and strained relations between countries....

By 2050, India and Nigeria would cultivate 0.06 hectares of grainland for each person, less than one tenth the size of a soccer field. China, Pakistan, Bangladesh and Ethiopia would drop even lower, to 0.04-0.05 hectares. Faring worse would be Egypt and

Afghanistan with 0.02 hectares, as well as Yemen, the DR Congo, and Uganda, with just 0.01 hectares.

Within two decades, availability of land per capita in Pakistan is expected to sink below where the Bangladesh's stand now. And considering the fact that most of Pakistan lies in arid zone and the availability of irrigation water is set to dwindle rapidly as rivers emanating from the Himalayas dry out, it is likely to fare even worse than Bangladesh in the matter of food availability. The burden will of course fall on its 'brother-in-N-arms' on the eastern border.

Can the Indian State do anything to bring the situation under control? Let's see:

The state could, of course, force the big traders to bring their stock out into the open, but can it do that to millions of households or the farmers, big and small? If sheer desperation made it do the unthinkable, i.e. sending forces to search each and every household and the farmstead, a veritable *'intefada'* would break out all over the land over this life and death issue. It would be the end of the Indian Democracy story, for imposing interminable emergency and shooting thousands of rioters year after year would be the only possible way of preventing uncontrollable anarchy and mayhem. In retrospect, better it would have been for millions of Indians had the infamous Emergency been continued indefinitely and rather than been forced to starve, killed in communal riots, or shot to death by the law-enforcing agencies of their own state, they had been stopped from taking birth in the first place.

All of the above will have put paid to all the growth, investment, superpower, and shining or resurgent India stories that have lulled the nation into a dangerous somnambulance, making it sleepwalk to the edge of a pit-less abyss. It would put India, along with the likes of Somalia, Sudan, Congo, Zimbabwe, Afghanistan and Pakistan, in the league of 'failed' states and amongst most dangerous countries of the world. Designated a failing police nation with absolutely no future, Indians will have none to thank but themselves for continuing to elect utterly myopic and self-serving politicians who failed to take steps to secure the land from the old Chinese malaise and the lamentation: *'Too many people, too little land'.*

To continue, whole of the state's attention and resources shall be consumed in managing procurement and distribution of food, and containing internecine violence that is bound to acquire progressively sinister and divisive forms. Gone will be the talks of infrastructure development, bringing in foreign investment, clocking double-digit growth rate and turning Mumbai into Shanghai, Bangalore into Singapore, Calcutta into Kuala Lumpur, or Delhi into Beijing. Much like Sudan or Somalia, it will be food, food, food and food. Like Pakistan, where all public discourse and the state policies have come to be stuck around Al Qaeda, Taliban, LeT, or TTP, it will be Maoists, Naxalites, Islamists, Saffronists and their innumerable clones here in India. What company or industry would like to set up shop in a land torn asunder by as lowly and demeaning thing as food riots? And that, when the regions of East Asia, Eastern Europe and Latin America beckoned with social peace, investment friendly policies, galloping infrastructure, booming markets, and educated, pliant and able-bodied work-force.

What is more, food scarcity and the related violence, monstrous even as it is likely to be, would be only one aspect of the situation. Like some mythical creature, the single-headed ogre will likely metamorphose into a hydra-headed monster…infinitely bigger, uglier and deadlier than its original avatar. There would be unavoidable politics, corruption, discrimination and favoritism in distribution of food stocks left with the state. Charges and counter-charges would flow thick and fast. Beleaguered provinces, no matter what political dispensation obtaining, would try to put the Centre and other provinces in the dock for their own incompetence and corruption. North will accuse the South of not producing enough for its needs and the South the North of population proliferation, with the East crying itself hoarse and nobody listening.

However, most portentous of them all would be the charge of discrimination laid against the State and the Executive by the Indian Muslim organizations and assorted secularists. That will inflame the passions no end and counter-charges, of Muslims treading the path of the pre-Partition Muslim League, won't be long in coming. There would soon be free for all, raising political temperature of the country to the N-reactor level for, mind you, unlike the Shah Bano or Babri Masjid kerfuffle, it will be a life and death issue this time around. Moreover, awareness that the situation was likely to grow only bigger and deadlier by the day in view of unchecked population growth and the related fallouts, the passions are unlikely to abate, hardening the position of the warring factions irrevocably. Hindus would demand privilege, Muslims strict adherence to population ratio. One way or another, tens of millions of Indians are certain to disappear from the face of the earth every year.

Fix a quota for the Muslims in the famine relief, the secularist and the Muslim Organizations would clamor even as the mostly Hindu bureaucracy, with a sullen conviction that it was unchecked and deliberate proliferation by the Muslims that was responsible in the main for the situation, can't help discriminating against them. Hindutva Organizations would be solidly behind it, vociferous and illogical as always in their rant.

'It is only the unbridled, deliberate, and plainly anti-national and anti-humanity proliferation by Jihadi mindsets that is responsible for the crisis,' so would run their arguments. 'And, by the way, what are those fifty million Bangladeshis doing here? Throw them out at once as an immediate relief measure and make universal sterilization a compulsion for medium to long term relief', would be their immediate demand.

That would hardly be acceptable to the Muslims, in general, and the Islamic-supremacist mindsets among them, in particular. By then, the agenda of bagging India for Islam would have become far too advanced, entrenched and confident, and the legitimacy and potency of the India State and the political system undermined considerably. Acquiescing in compulsory family planning measures would be putting paid to the dream of taking over India as the necessary and most decisive step towards creating an International Islamic Caliphate and delivering the world to the Islamic God. That would be nothing short of blasphemous. It would be the time to think another unthinkable. If the issue came to be that of life and death (or the life after death) then nothing was left to fear or feel squeamish about. When the bad had indeed come to be worst, nothing could conceivably be lost and everything gained by raising the demand that was going to be raised in any case—if not at that point of time, than a decade or two later. In short, demand for another Partition would be the only logical (and legitimate, in the eyes of the Muslims) outcome.

'But you had got long ago what you demanded, worked for and got, but, in a supreme display of cussedness and perfidy, chose not to go to. You are still welcome to go there…indeed, it was about time you did, otherwise we would be compelled to do that for you. That was the denouement you had been fashioning for yourself all this while by indulging in willful reproduction. Go and live in your Dar-ul-Uloom that your Quid-e-Azam had demanded and wrenched for you. It was about time we also created our own ideal State where we could live without fear of getting outnumbered, overwhelmed and wiped out.'

So would run the argument of the Hindus gone mad by angst arising out of their own past mistakes and existential fears shaking them to the very core of their individual and the racial being.

Battle lines would thus be drawn clear, bloody and insurmountable, with interests, futures and lives of more numbers at stake than they had been anytime in the history of India or the mankind. Amid accusations and counter accusations, famine deaths, flight of capital, collapse of economy, wearing away of the legitimacy of the Indian State, and communal fires blazing all across the land, consuming villages and urban neighborhoods, it would be 1947 all over again, only complicated and compounded many times over.

That is not a theoretical or hypothetical scenario by any reckoning. Arab Spring, which continues to roil the Arab world till now, was due in part to the escalation in the prices of food commodities in the wake of crop losses around the world in 2008. And here is a report about the most mind-numbing and belief-beggaring genocide of the post-World War phase:

Earth Policy Institute :

The experience of Rwanda highlights the potentially serious ramifications of land scarcity. Between 1950 and 1990, Rwanda's population tripled from 2.1 million to 6.8 million. The per capita grainland availability fell to 0.03 hectares. James Gasana, Rwanda's Ex-Minister of Agriculture and Enviornment has noted that rapid population growth led to farm fragmentation, land degradation, deforestation, and famine. These stresses ignited the undercurrent of ethnic strife, erupting in civil war in the early 1990s and culminating in horrific genocide in 1994, when some 8,00,000 people were killed. Gasana points out that violence was concentrated in the communes where food supply was inadequate...

As for India, the fat would truly be in fire when the food crisis came to be compounded (as it inevitably would) by the energy crisis. Food riots degenerated into interminable communal riots and the Jihadi Ummah sensing a kill, call for curtailing or completely stopping the oil supply to India would go out to pressurize it for conceding another Pakistan. It would be most red of the red rags ever shown to a people in the entire human history. No Gandhi or Nehru would be there this time around to hold back the people. That would be the time for taking over of India by a Hindu Hitler, consequenting into N-confrontation with the Muslim nations and beginning of the much-delayed WW III.

Issue involved in Mahabharata was pure ego. Issue involved in Partition was hypothetical...Muslims might suffer discrimination and injustices at the hands of vengeful Hindus. Issue this time around would be more rooted, phenomenal, everlasting and universal: Who was to be blamed for the crisis, who was to die of starvation, and whether Islam shall be able to win this most crucial of battles in its quest for world dominance, or would it prove to be the point of inflexion whence the dreams and the hubris of Islamic suprematism had been laid to rest for all time to come, and rationalization and modernization of even the most antediluvian of the Islamic mindsets begun in real earnest.

4

TWO AGENTS OF DOOM • Demographic Destabilization

Independent of such things as food, water or energy crisis – and even if all of these came to be addressed by a magic wand, as it were, turning this nation of 1200 million deprived and tortured souls into a land of proverbial milk and honey – there remains one thing that has potential to, and is destined to, turn India into a Lebanon of eighties and Bosnia of nineties, only magnified thousand fold. What could that possibly be?

Hindu-Muslim relations remain quiescent, if not exactly cordial, for past one decade. Babri Masjid and post-Godhra outrages seem to have affected a kind of catharsis for Hindus they had been spoiling for since long. On the other side, Pakistan's experience with extremism and jihad seems to have cooled the ardor of some of the Islamist-minded of India, besides diverting the attention and energy of ISI from mission-break-up-India towards the home and Afghan fronts. Hindus have been in the habit of blaming Muslims for many of the ills besetting the nation. However, the world records shattering corruption that has emerged as the greatest evil shaming and undermining India, and for which only the Hindus have been responsible in the main (though impact and devastate it does both the communities alike), has forced them to deflect their barbs from their favorite voodoo doll. Though not refraining from taking potshots now and then, in the heart of their hearts they have come to realize too well that most of the ills besetting the nation are not the doings of the Muslims.

Thus, they have come to realize that to go on blaming the Indian Muslims for the ills they have no role in creating would be nothing but skirting the real issue, without facing which no real solution can ever be found. At the most, the Muslims as a community are as responsible for the national ills as any other community. As a matter of fact, their contribution towards the nation's economy as a whole may be disproportionately higher, for they are predominant supplier of semi-skilled labor-force that forms the backbone of the quasi-industrial economy that India is. Further, compared to the Hindu-dominated government and the Public Sector that batten on the real labor and weighs down the national productivity and the progress by its corrupt, slothful and obstructionist ways, they are immeasurably hard-working and productive.

It is not that the Hindus don't realize the contribution the overwhelming majority of the Muslim community makes towards the national economic and cultural life. They don't also feel squeamish in acknowledging the fact that, measured w/w, an average Muslim is more hard-working, dexterous and honest than an average Hindu. Or, that the Muslims are just like them—caught up in every day problem of making a decent existence possible, anxious about the future of their kids, contemptuous of corrupt politicians and chary of criminals within their community or the neighborhood. That, much like them, all but a minuscule section among the Muslims harbors the mentality and objectives that are entirely materialistic in nature. Spirituality or transcendental concerns are as far away from their minds as that of any Brahmin worth his sacred thread. And they are as contemptuous and exasperated of the Islamic fundamentalists as an average Hindu is of the outfits like Bajrang Dal, Abhinav Bharat or Ram Sene.

Were an independent international commission to be constituted to assess the roles of various communities of India, measured in terms of their contributions towards societal and economic wellbeing of the nation as well as the negativities besetting it, apportioning blame and credit wherever due, the verdict would be clear and near-unanimous: Majority of the Muslims would be declared friends of India and the true sons of the soil, while significant sections of the Hindus (but majority of the upper castes), holding patents in Indian-ness, Hinduism, patriotism and what not, would come to be termed clear villains, akin to parasites and pests.

Most of the Hindus understand that well. That is the reason they have weathered grave and regular provocations with understanding and forbearance, making them take the series of terrorist outrages intended to provoke them into violence against Muslims in stride. Even the Great Bombay Carnage failed to evoke any amount of rancor against the Indian Muslims, for the Hindus knew too well that their own weaknesses, combined with the congenital corruption and the pusillanimity of the ruling elites had brought the mayhem upon the land.

What is the rub then? If Muslims were so good indeed and the Hindus so understanding, why does the Hindu-Muslim issue continues to be looked upon as a simmering volcano; underground powder-keg fated to turn into conflagration of unimaginable proportions? Why the gnawing-growing anxiety in everyone's conscious and a vague certitude in his guts? Why this great wall of suspicion and fear that continues to stand forbidding and foreboding even in these times of apparent cooperation and peace? Why then, despite all round – and well acknowledged – contributions to economy, culture, language or the arts, the Muslims have begin evoking anew an inordinate amount of fear, mistrust and hostility in the hearts of the Hindus, and are, time and again, made to feel like unwelcome squatters in their own country?

Is that a gut reaction of an irrational, fearful and reactionary animal called Hindu, or do there exist some valid reasons for it? Had those wary of the Muslims constituted only a miniscule minority, their fears and animus could be brushed aside as figments of fevered imagination of constitutionally bigoted minds. But when the numbers of those expressing the sentiment openly run into hundreds of millions, and another hundreds of millions too continue to nurse similar sentiments in their hearts (though preferring to keep these to themselves out of self-interest, prudence or political-correctness)… well. So many millions can't just be tarred with the easy appellation or slur of communal rascals or frightened bastards.

So, other than the issues related with historical grievances, or the extant or looming crises of the quotidian nature (food, water, energy and the like), what could possibly be the cause likely to turn the land into…well, an interminable Bosnia, only magnified a hundred times.

Bluntly put, the root cause lies in the Abrahamic concept dividing the humanity into irreconcilable faithful/heathen-kefir camps and exhorting the faithful to engage in relentless crusade/jihad against the later, thereby creating mindsets soaked in sentiments of contempt, loathing and suprematism on the one hand, and suspicion and fear on the other. However, the crisis would precipitate in India when the new demographic equilibrium that had been obtained the post-Partition is disturbed sufficiently to come irretrievably unhinged from its pivot. That is, when Muslims become sufficiently confident again, the Hindus nervous in commensurate measure, and the situation so over-pregnant with old tensions and new possibilities that desire for a resolution, whatever the cost, begins to appear more attractive than putting up with the hugely uncertain, nervous and frustrating status quo.

Without going into the details of how, why and what of the thing, suffice to state that the ratio of Muslims in India's population is increasing relentlessly, while that of the Hindus is declining correspondingly, so much so that it in an arc fifteen hundred kilometers long, beginning Saharanpur in UP to Malda on the Bangladesh border (and thence into the heart of Assam and even further) and two hundred kilometers wide to the south, it has been approaching the levels what had obtained in the areas that had ultimately seceded as Pakistan. Overall, Muslim share of India's population has more than doubled, rising from 8% at the time of Independence to around 20% at the beginning of the second decade of the present century. It was around 25% before the Partition even with the Muslim majority areas, which constitute Bangladesh and Pakistan now, included. What is more, considerably lower (around 10%) percentage of Muslims residing in the heartland of India had managed to raise sufficient lather to force Partition for the benefit of their Muslim brethrens in the east and the west. With growth rate of the Hindus declining fast in line with the imperatives of modernity and exigency of survival, and majority of the Muslims choosing to stick with their reproductive practices, the ratio of Muslims in India's population mix is set to grow even faster in the coming decades.

Question is: Is there something fishy, deliberate or exceptionable in that?

After the urge to preserve one's life, that to propagate is second most germane thing to the living beings. The urge to propagate tends to be a run-away thing usually, but the checks put into place by Nature in the form of constraints upon the food supply, a system of food-chain and death by exposure to elements, keep it in a rough balance.

As with every other specie, Nature had been taking care of the excess human population too since the earliest times. However, faster development of man's brain gave him access to tools that helped him overcome Nature's considerable odds, enhancing his survival rate as compared to other species. As a consequence, his population stabilized at a considerably higher level than what it would have been had he not learnt to walk on his twos, build shelter and fire, and make heavy club, fish line and bow.

First the taming of the animals like cattle and goats, and then development of agriculture saw human population grow exponentially, but so did the wars, famines and pestilence. It precluded the population run-away, stabilizing it at a new, though considerably higher level.

Advent of Industrial Age, bringing in its wake things like chemical fertilizers, pesticides, modern irrigation methods, high-yielding variety seeds and life-saving drugs completely upset the new balance that had come to hold between man and the Nature. Population exploded, vegetation and life-forms got decimated, earth got scorched and water bodies and environment fouled.

Population explosion caused by synthetic products brought in its wake synthetic products to control it. It was eminently logical and necessary development, and there needn't have been any moral quibbling over it. When you have no qualm traveling by cars, trains or planes; wearing clothes, cosmetics and perfumes; using fertilizer-produced food and synthetically produced medicines; undergoing cosmetic surgery and organ transplants; and, above all, visiting fertility clinics and undergoing artificial insemination – everything in direct contravention to how Nature meant you to move around, look or live – why bring morals or religious sensibilities into picture in the matter of wearing condoms, popping-in birth-control pills, or undergoing sterilization alone?

World population, which had continued to grow throughout, albeit slowly, has exploded since the nineteenth century due to a variety of well-known reasons. It has grown from around 2 billion in 1920s, to 4 in mid-seventies, to 7 in the beginning of the present decade. Though the rate of growth has slowed down significantly of late, absolute numbers continue to increase more than ever due to considerably higher population base and more cohorts than ever coming into the child-bearing age. As a result, the world population is set to attain a figure of around 10 billion by the middle of the present century. While population of many a nation has stabilized lately and even begun declining, many others hope to see it stabilized (in line with the imperatives of modernity and sanity, or the state's persuasive or coercive intervention) within a decade or two. Yet there are a whole lot of nations that remain far from joining the trend and their populations may grow 30 to 100% in next quarter century.

While many of these nations (mainly the oil-rich Muslim nations north and west of Afghanistan) can afford to go on exploding (though the environment as a whole can't) for a few more decades, others patently can not. Yet many of the latter go on adding to their numbers despite clear prospect of falling ever deeper into the pit of scarcities, deprivation and general mayhem that they languish in even now. Why do they do so?

As far as the non-Islamic Third World nations (except a few

Catholic ones in the sub-Saharan Africa, where Catholic populations are locked in mortal confrontation with the Muslims) are concerned, secular modern trends, combined with population control measures have largely stemmed the baby-boom. A few of these are still unable to join the trend, due primarily to poverty and ignorance their populations continue to suffer from, denying them access to knowledge and means of birth control. In many cases there is resistance due to religio-cultural reasons, though there seems to be no extraneous-sinister motives to pullulating. Absent the negative reasons and they could be depended upon to be join the world trend gladly.

As for many of the Muslim nations or the populations, the issue as a whole appears to be a unique mindset that refuses to heed the imperatives either of modernity or of pragmatism. It is direct product of the interpretation they put upon their ideology—command purportedly it gives, assurance it extends and the promise it holds. Command is to people the whole world with the faithful till no kefir or kufr remained extant in the world. Assurance is ultimate victory for the faithful of the Islamic God and reward is eternal paradise for them.

As per the eternal and incontestable wisdom of such mindsets, the whole world (including the insensate objects) is Muslim. All those not believing in Islam are ignorant squatters, at best, and willful enemies of Islam, otherwise. To recapture the world for the Islamic God is the holy duty of every Muslim. Striving incessantly to enlighten whole world about the glory of Islam (either through preaching and persuasion, or through the force of sword) was a Jihadi duty with every Muslim which he could ignore only at the risk of imperiling his Hereafter. It was understandable however that not every Muslim could afford to (or feel inclined to) preach the holy word or wage direct holy war. But there was a way out for him: Jihad through proliferation route. If the Muslims became just too many, they would naturally crowd out the unfaithful, whom God in his infinite wisdom was misguiding towards their destruction by making them invent and adopt satanic measures of birth control, from the face of the Earth.

That perhaps is the reason as to why the educated Muslims that had begun taking to two-child norm earlier have been going in for 'plus-one' scheme now. Word has been spread, and seems to have struck root, that have as many children as you plan to or feel comfortable with, and then one more for the sake of Islam for fulfilling your part of the holy duty of Jihad. Thus, if every Muslim couple kept producing one more child then the rest (when the whole world had graduated to adopting two child norm), then, may be in a century or three, the entire world would get to be Muslim. And in the matters transcendental, even a millennium counts for nothing.

However, it was the non-Islamic nations where the need to adopt the plus-one scheme was supreme, even if they did wisely by adopting two-child norm in the already Muslim majority nations. That exactly is the reason that while in the nations like Bangladesh and Indonesia even the low-educated poor Muslims have begun taking to two child norm, in the non-Muslim majority US, Europe, Sri Lanka, China, Singapore, Australia and India, this 'plus-one' is never going to go away.

Otherwise, nothing explains the fact that in spite of near-total literacy and much better financial status, the population growth rate (PGR) of the Muslims of Kerala (constituting more than a quarter of its population) is as high as 2.3% per year, which is more than even the national PGR of 2.11 and is double the PGR of the Hindus (including the scheduled castes and other marginalized sections) there. Not only that, though full educated, their total fertility rate (TFR; children a woman would have over her lifetime) at around 3.6 is more than even the illiterate women of India (3.4), way more (2.2) than even the women that have received some kind of education, much more (1.9) than the women that have received education up to high school, and unconscionably more (1.6) than the ones that have received education up to intermediate.

Not only that, TFR of full-educated Kerala Muslim women was far higher than those belonging to such bastions of conservatism as Iran (1.87) even, and far higher than the Muslim nations enjoying similar women educational levels and freedom, such as Algeria and Tunisia (below 2.0).

Overall, the fertility rate of Muslims in India is 4.4 against 3.4 for India over all. Thus, the fertility rate of Muslim women is 1.1 children higher than the Hindu women.

Though the difference may appear small, but conclusions and implications are huge. Firstly, considering the fact that Muslims are concentrated in the urban areas, the level of their TFR must be way below the Hindus that are sprawled across the hinterland. Secondly, one point higher TFR simply means that when, ultimately, the over all fertility rate of India approached the desirable replacements levels, the Muslim population shall continue to increase inordinately. For, mind you, one more child per family means twenty crore more babies than others for a Muslim population of forty crores (by, say, 2035), who would in their turn produce ten crore more babies and so on. And here lies the immense long-time significance of the plus-one urgings of the Muslim thinkers and the preachers.

The miracle of difference of 'One' in the TFR can be seen in the fact that if the global TFR falls today to 1.6 (about Europe's level today), then the world population in 2050 will be 8 billion and falling. But if the global TFR remains at 2.6 (about what it is today) then the world population in 2050 will be 27 billion (four times more than today) and rising exponentially.

Thus, if the Hindu TFR comes down to 1.6 (which it is likely to) at some point of time, there shall be only a marginal increase in population then on, but if the Muslims continued to adhere to the one-plus policy (which they are likely to, going by the conduct of Kerala Muslims), the Muslim population of India shall increase four times by 2050 (that is equalizing that of the Hindus) and growing exponentially.

Indeed, the phenomenon can be discerned in all the non-Muslim majority nations, or even those nations where the Muslims hold a precarious majority. Thus, whereas, in Muslim nations like Indonesia, Morocco, Algeria, Tunisia, Turkmenistan, Turkey, Azerbaijan, Bahrain, Iran, Maldives and Albania, the TFR has come down to replacement or near replacement levels (children just enough to replace their parents; held to be around 2.1), the similarly placed Muslim populations (socially, educationally and financially) in all of the non-Muslim majority nations refuse to follow the trend, sticking to *'combat fertility'* mentality.

Thus in Israel, while the TFR for Jews is 2.7 and the Christians 2.2, for the Palestinians of Gaza strip it is 4.5. An average Nigerian Christian woman has 5 children, her Muslim counterpart has 7. Why, even in Malaysia, TFR for the Chinese, Indian and the native Malays (wholly Muslim) stand at 1.8, 2.0 and 2.8 respectively. And as stated earlier, fertility rates of Muslims of Europe is three times higher than the native Europeans. In fact, 'Combat' fertility rate was responsible for reducing the Christian population of Lebanon from 77% of the total in 1900 to 35% by 1975, and turning Kosovo and Bosnia into Muslim majority territories within a few decades.

Coming back to India, whereas the population of the sub-Continental Muslims has grown around six times since the Partition, that of the Hindus has increased only three times. And according to the 2001 census, the Muslim population of India has grown 200 percent in four decades while the rest of the country grew by 134%.

The million houries worth question however is: Must Muslims

and the others be guided by and feel obliged to follow their image of how the earth should look like? Should it swarm with hungry and ignorant multitudes polishing off all the vegetation and the forms of life from the Planet...everything obliterated to give way to or feed but single specie professing a single faith?

Many Muslims and Muslim nations may feel duty-bound to follow the interpretation put upon the Holy Book by their preachers, 'scholars' and the ulemas. But the existential question that the thinking Muslims and other people and the nations must ask themselves is: Are they too as duty bound to put up with the wisdom disseminated by people whose sole – and unconcealed – wish and the objective is to undermine, overwhelm and decimate other faiths, beliefs, cultures, nations and the species? What does hold more value for them: Imperatives of modernism, exigencies of the environment and the future of their generations, as also the faiths, culture and the way of life bequeathed by their ancestors and continued peace and harmony of their land, or willful undermining of all these in the name of misplaced beliefs or secularism?

The blame for the inordinate population growth among the Muslims can't certainly be put upon such mundane things alone as poverty, unemployment, lack of education or discrimination that the cussed Muslim 'intellectuals' and the Mullahs (egging on the Muslims to breed in the cause of Islam), or their gratuitously obtuse apologists try to make out. For, as social mores and lifestyles change and awareness grows, Hindus, Christians and the others, far more poor, un-employed or ill-educated than the Muslims living in Brussels, Amsterdam, New York, Serbia or Saudi Arabia, commence joining the family planning trends. Nothing other than the idea of eternal jihad and ultimate world domination ingrained in the subconscious of the adherents of Islam can explain the phenomenon, wherein little religious compunction is observed in practicing just about everything (cosmetics, surgery, anesthesia, fertility-treatments and even organ transplants) other than the means of birth-control. And the thing is germane not only to the few poor, illiterate or half-educated living in the boondocks of Yemen or Somalia, but to almost all of the rich and well-educated of New York and Copenhagen too. Patently, it goes well beyond the realm of culture or innocuous irrationality and belongs firmly to the domain of deliberate and planned.

One great reason for inordinate population growth of Muslims is early-age marriage of girls, and here too the religion comes into the picture. When you are against your girls acquiring higher education, moving around in public places and do jobs for the fear of them associating with the kefirs and getting kefir, secular or non-Islamic ideas in their heads, thereby losing their 'sacred hatred' towards the infidels, the only proper thing to do is to marry them off at the earliest age possible. Thus, if a normal non-Muslim girl marries at the age of twenty five and has a child or two by the age of, say, thirty, her Muslim counterpart is likely to have four or five by that age, having been married at the age of eighteen or so. And by the time both get to attain the age of fifty-five, our Muslim girl may be enjoying a company of twenty or so children and grandchildren, even as her Hindu or Christian counterpart had called it a day with maximum of six. Thus in a period of three to four decades, the Muslim population increases by around twenty against, perhaps, six of the non-Muslims.

Now that is what explains the phenomenon wherein, even though the Muslims constitute roughly 25% population of Brussels, top seven baby names were Muslim (that means more than seventy percent new births were Muslims) and, like Amsterdam of Holland, it is well ahead on road to turn into a Muslim majority city in less than two decades. Likewise, as a result of immigration and extremely high population growth rates (the Muslim birth rate in Europe is three times higher than that of the non-Muslims: *'Brookings'*), Muslims could outnumber non-Muslims in almost all of the towns of France, indeed all of the Western Europe by the mid-century. No prize for surmising that dhimmification and expulsion or genocide is the sure and logical fate of the natives of Belgium (indeed all of the Europe). Indeed, this neo-Jihad can very well be visualized to giving birth to neo-Nazism, aiming either to hound out and expel, or to exterminate Muslim populations, though the final outcome of the Armageddon would be far from certain.

And then they argue that the Muslims have problems of poverty and illiteracy because of the other's doing and the latter are duty bound to make sacrifices (by way of taxes for their support and uplift) to compensate for their inhuman conduct towards them! That exactly is the design and the dream of the Muslim clerics, ulemas and 'intellectuals', as also many of the lay Muslims—to fill the world with their own kind and then work to shame others for their poverty, illiteracy and unemployment, demanding compensation and sacrifices from others in the name of equity, justice and humanity.

Population experts of the world postulate that the population of the world would stabilize somewhere around 9 billion level by Y 2050. They do so on the basis of secular trends observed in non-Islamic nations where the factors like improved economic, educational and health levels; growing desire to live life to the full…in an uncluttered and decent manner; and mounting awareness of horrendous social, economic and environmental consequences if the population growth was allowed to have free run, have led to sharp declines in birth rates. That is naiveté at best and dissembling of the worst kind, mostly. They make it convenient to ignore (in the interest of political correctness) the fact that many of the secular, scientific, rational and economic beliefs and assumptions begin gasping for breath as they enter the Islamist mindscape, only to die at the altar of imperatives of Jihad.

There could be little doubt that if a technology to keep feeding as many mouths as kept opening up to the world came to be devised, the world population would never stabilize even if it reached a good 100 billion. For the Divine Command, as interpreted by the antediluvian mindsets, was not for up to the twentieth, twenty-first or the twenty-fifth century only, but for all time to come. However (and mercifully), though God may have his designs for rewarding his faithful and eliminating kufr and the kefirs, Mother Nature has its own way of doing things. For starters, it is completely faith-blind in the matter of rewarding its creation or exacting retribution for its misdeeds. One could keep taking from it only as a grateful son and not as a band of robbers. If, like beasts and insects, man wills its numbers to be limited by the single factor of availability of food, it would have its wish fulfilled…dying like beasts and insects of starvation, diseases and fights for food and territory.

So, running over and overwhelming the infidel lands by billion Kalashnikovs and purposeful procreation might be essential for the project of world dominance, but as sole instrument of it (as against gaining technological supremacy and pedaling soft power), as is being sought to be adopted by the Jihadi minds among the Muslims, it is sure to boomerang badly, turning into a never-ending nightmare –for everybody around no doubt, but for the Muslims primarily and most consequentially…

For, though, it entails the clearest and presentest danger for the non-Muslim nations, the success of this strategy depends solely upon taking undue advantage of the sense of liberalism of the others. Relentlessly trying and testing their goodwill and tolerance till it first turned neutral, and then into ill-liberalism, intolerance and…well, the unimaginable and the unspeakable…hoping all this time that the balance of population and the power turned the Muslim way before the push came to shove: Could that be termed a rational thinking or wise strategy? But, then, as we all know by experience, rationality and understanding in the matters of faith (that is, accepting that all others faiths and the faithful had equal claim to life, liberty and honor) has not been the forte of the religious extremists belonging to Abrahamic faiths.

Suffice to state in the end that demography and changes in demographic configuration have underlain all ethnic conflicts in the past and that is not likely to change in the foreseeable future. Every massacre or holocaust in history has been effected either to change the demographic equilibrium, or the attempts to restore it.

However, as far as India's population explosion and the dire fate awaiting it on the account is concerned, the Muslims can be blamed only partially. As India was fighting for and preparing for freedom in the early decades of the twentieth century, population had been exploding uncontrollably and famine was endemic. It had been recognized all around that leapfrogging population would eat away all the future productivity gains. Neither anyone could have predicted, nor was it wise to depend upon the revolutionary developments in seed technology that took place decades later and brought Green Revolution. Yet, what had been the stand and the nostrum of Gandhi, the prophet of Hindus? Main *'root cause'* behind the reluctance of succeeding dispensations ruling over the nation to even talk of birth control may be found here. Since, besides being informative and revealing, an average reader may find Gandhi's loathing and terror of sex for pleasure and birth-control interestingly outrageous, it is being presented in some detail...

Miss Sanger was an influential and dynamic American birth-control advocate. She traveled to India in November 1935, embarking on a nine-week tour of the country that totaled over 10,000 miles of travel. She interviewed Gandhi at his Wardha ashram regarding his views about sex and birth-control. She summed up Gandhi's loathing of sex to, "I am convinced his personal experience at the time of his father's death was so shocking and self-blamed that he can never accept sex as anything good, clean or wholesome." (It is another matter that Gandhi remained a 'sex-enthusiast' for decades after his father's death and came to nurse life-long obsession with it.) Conversation went like this:

> Miss Sanger: So it means that sexual union when children are desired is love, and when they are not desired it is lust?

> Gandhi: 'Exactly so'. And he described how he had often sought carnal pleasure with his wife when she was unwilling. 'Lust dies

and love reigns instead'.

Miss Sanger: 'Then throughout a whole lifetime you expect the sexual union to take place only three or four times?'

Gandhi: 'Yes, people should be taught that it is immoral to have more than three or four children, and after they have had these children they should sleep separately. If people were taught this, it would harden into custom. And if the social informers cannot impress this idea on people, why not law?'

That is, he would have a police constable stand, baton in hand, between the beds of every husband and wife that had had their law-ordained fill of three or four children. By the same logic, in China of today of one child norm, the couple would be allowed sex only on their golden night and then packed off to separate labor camps. That would be really great and....well, Gandhian!

When Miss Sanger suggested that there were perfectly natural means of preventing childbirth—lemon trees grew at Wardha, and so did cotton, and a swab of cotton dipped in lemon juice served as an easily available contraceptive—Gandhi objected strongly, saying that a cotton swab was an unnatural interference in the processes of nature and only continence was natural. Women must learn to *'resist'* their husbands and if necessary, they should abandon their husbands.

Apparently for Gandhi, while using a cotton swab dipped in lemon juice (perfectly natural and...well, 'organic' device) was unnatural interference in the processes of nature; suppressing natural sexual desire and suffering all manners of physical and psychological travails were not.

It failed to strike the old pate that to the men willing to fall into pit of sin by way of gratifying his sexual urges, use of condom or artificial contraceptive could possibly do no more harm, even as did a world of good to the world at large by limiting the population. And, pray, why should a man's lust be permitted to make his hapless victim suffer? For, it was women, utterly powerless to resist sexual aggression that remained greatest sufferer of excess-children syndrome, not infrequently paying with their life. And wasn't that dog-in-manger attitude on part of Gandhi—denigrating others for being lustful sinners when he had had his fill, having been a *'lustful husband'* (Gandhi's description of himself) to boot?

During the conversation, Gandhi told Miss Sanger that he was advising women coming in his contact to resist their husbands' amorous advances, even to the point of abandoning them if they failed to behave. Now, what was the inevitable implication of

Gandhi's prescription? It is a sure bet that even if all the moral force – of Buddha, Christ and Gandhi combined – had been brought to bear upon the man folk, they were not going to desist from demanding sex from their wives. Now, if the wives took heed of the advice of His Holy Wisdom, resisting the *'lustful'* demands of their husbands, they all were going to be out on the streets to live on their own – either kicked out by their men, or abandoning them of their free will, as their Savior suggested. What would have been the fate of such women...illiterate or only half-literate, lacking skills necessary to make a living and kicked out, with a child or four in tow: Either unspeakable drudgery, with children begging in streets, or falling prey to flesh-traders, bringing the 'lust' and 'sin' things back to square one.

Clear implication is: Gandhi would rather the Indian died of overpopulation, diseases, misery and starvation than employ means of birth control. Such being the wisdom of the nation's prophet, should there be any wonder that the land is veritably crawling with starving millions and has not only not got rid of the 'lust' and 'sin', but is busy establishing ever new records in things like rape, incest and paedophilia.

In any case, Muslims can only be held responsible for twenty two crore more souls added to the kitty of India over the past seven decades (3 crores at the time of the Independence vs. 25 crores now, of whom around five crores are Bangladeshi migrants). For the rest of sixty crores (thirty crores then, ninety crores now), the Hindus should thank nobody but themselves.

But what to do about the Muslim populations now who are bent upon defying the modern secular trends and do not feel squeamish in cocking a snooze upon the evident logic and imperative of long term survival? That may be bad for them and the world as a whole, but here we are more concerned with the section of Indian Muslims who seem to be seized by a mentality that has outnumbering the Hindus, and in double quick time too, as its primary goal. How are the fallouts of this mentality likely to pan out in the coming decades?

Things look quiescent on the surface today. However, and as we all know, nothing is permanent in the world and what goes up must come down. What could be taken as mathematical certainty is that wars devastating many a nations today shall not be there tomorrow. Peace shall there be; whether it was peace of a graveyard or a successful civilization is beside the point. Likewise, peace holding today in many other parts of the world shall not hold tomorrow. In

India's case, deliberate attempts upon demographic transformation of the land are bound to reach a point of criticality or inflexion, shattering its precariously held peace for all time to come.

Though no sure tab could be put upon that point of inflexion, it could come as early as in a decade when the Hindus, the negatively impacted community of shift in the demographic equilibrium, get the word that they had been reduced to a percentage below seventy, but it would surely within a quarter century when the percentage dips below sixty. That point of inflexion could come much earlier if a major incident or trend, having in it to disturb the sense of security and the well being of the nation or its majority community, happened. Unprecedented upsurge of Islamic fundamentalism across the world, spate of major terrorist strikes across the country, assassination of some important and well-regarded national leader of caliber and potential, disruption in oil supplies for whatever reason, war with Pakistan or accidental or deliberate nuclear attack emanating from there, rise of some Islamic party with clear overtones of separatism in its agenda and, of course, the bourgeoning food crisis—are some of the possibilities that are by no means far-fetched or beyond the realm of probable, and have it in them to advance the point of inflexion bang into the present.

That point of inflexion would be a point of no return, destabilizing, for all time to come, the equilibrium that has largely held till now and after which there could be no going back; literal snapping where even the desire to have things patched up, smoothened or reverted back to the working levels ebbs away. That point was reached for the Muslim League of Jinnah in 1937 when Nehru had contemptuously rejected any suggestion of power sharing with it, leading to irreversible change in its attitude, whereof opposing, denigrating and snubbing the Congress and exploiting the lack of spine or character of its leaders for its designated ends, whatever the cost to any party or the community, became its (and that of 97% of the Muslims') sole obsession.

It is not that only the minority community can feel insecure or suffer existential fears, claiming, as a psychological recompense to those fears, the right to be overwrought, belligerent, obstreperous, demanding and violent. Or that the majority community, ensconced in its knowledge of being in majority, is duty bound to remain forever quiescent, forever forgiving and forever elder-brotherly. The latter may be the case if the demographic equilibrium either holds firm or shifts to its advantage. However, seemingly deliberate attempts upon disadvantaging the majority community regarding that most vital of the factors in community relations can't but make the situation extremely fraught; much more so in case of India where the majority community has a litany of issues going back a millennium and the minority community has powerful mentors abroad, besides having an ideology that is implacably hostile towards the faith, beliefs and the practices of the native majority.

It has more often been the case that the fear of dwindling percentage haunts the majority community more than it does the minority. Reason is plain: Dwindling percentage of a minority doesn't alter the situation for it, nor does it change the inter-community relations to its disadvantage. It remains a minority as it had already been. If anything, the situation in most of the cases changes for the better, for feeling less threatened, the majority gets psychologically more amenable to showing greater tolerance – indulgence even – for it. Thus the Parsees, Jews, Buddhists, Syrian Christians, Ahmediyas, Dawoodi Bohras or the Bahaiis that have never felt threatened or discriminated against in India,

However, reversal of status from being a majority to minority can't but be a terrifying prospect for the majority community. That is more so if the chief calling card of that minority, even in the twenty-first century, remains its pathetic attachment to the values, mores and codes of sixth century Arabia, combined with overweening desire and violent attempts to enforce these upon all others. That is infinitely more so for the Hindus of India who have nothing but bloody and humiliating historical experience with Islam and its adherents.

Another factor is that the majority looks upon itself as (and usually is) the real inheritor of the land and its cultural legacies. The situation gets mitigated to a considerable extent if both the communities cherish the same religious beliefs (if the differences were linguistic, ethnic or racial), or, in the case of otherwise, different faiths have their foundations in the same land (Hinduism coexisting with Jainism, Buddhism and Sikhism). Absent any of these leavening factors, the attempts upon subversion of demographic equilibrium to the disadvantage of the majority are sure to develop into a factor of internecine discord.

Dwindling percentage evokes no sense of insecurity or fear among the Parsees, Sikhs, Jews or Jains in India, nor does it raise the fear-quotient of the Christians and the Jews in the Muslim nations any more than what they already reel under. Most often, these communities transform themselves into economic and intellectual elite, compensating themselves in terms of social status and economic well being for what they lose in numbers, thus making best out of what in many cases is a depressing situation. The majority community too doesn't look upon these communities or their economic power and status as a threat and a satisfactory, if not altogether great or ideal, equilibrium holds.

Or, for that matter, the dwindling percentage of the upper castes, vis-à-vis the other Hindu castes: it evokes no sense of insecurity in the former, even if they do not quite relish the latter's job-reservations or their new-found political swagger. Their chief concern remains jobs for their wards, and that unfavorable sentiments against them do not turn into open discrimination and attempts upon marginalization.

Conversely, the minorities sink to the bottom if discrimination against them is excessive and persistent. In such cases, a person among them getting rich or famous immediately invokes hostility and is cut down to size, even as the prejudiced majority looks upon nonchalantly, even smugly. It is the case with the Hindus, Christians, Buddhists, Parsees and the Muslim minority sects in practically every Muslim land. What prevents the situation from going totally out of hand there, preventing the applecart of the tolerance of the adherents of the 'Religion of Peace' from keeling over completely, is favorably growing Muslim population ratios vis-à-vis the non-Muslims. It keeps the prevalent state of affairs deeply satisfying and tolerable for the Muslims. Prospects of alteration of predominantly Muslim character of their society obviated, they can afford to be tolerant, even indulgent towards their minorities. It is another matter that that still is not the case, as the treatment of Christians in Nigeria, Egypt, Indonesia and Pakistan, of Shias in Arab countries and Pakistan, of Bahaiis and Parsees in Iran, Sikhs in Afghanistan, Ahmediyas in Pakistan, and of Hindus in Pakistan, Bangladesh and Malaysia amply makes out. No informed and truthful mind would doubt that had the situation there been what obtains in all the non-Muslims lands regarding the Muslims (that is, had the rate of population growth of the non-Muslims outpaced that of the Muslims in the Muslim lands), the non-Muslims would have been Gulaged and Auschwitzed long ago.

We could take the case of the State of Malaysia – an economic and technological tiger (thanks largely to the Malaysians of Chinese decent) and purportedly a modern and modernized nation, touted by self-deluding and truth-denying secularists as a shining example of pluralism, multiculturalism and peaceful co-existence that Islam purportedly stands for.

Delving only a little deeper into the Malaysian state of affairs, one can easily make out that unquestioning acceptance of the standard Islamist pattern – preferred faith and the faithful vs. barely tolerated kefirs, who must know their limits and the true place, and must bow to state sponsored Islamism in its various facets – is the price the non-Muslims have to pay to escape interminable harassment, incarcerations and impediments in business. Further, there could be little doubt that even the above qualified 'pluralism' and 'tolerance' is skin deep and a pure show off. It is the fear of economic collapse, ostracizing by the neighboring nations and the West, and, most of all, the terror of the big Dragon, ever mindful of the interests of the people of Chinese decent all over the world, that makes the Malaysian Muslims a far better specie than they actually have grown to be and prevents the trademark Islamic contempt and intolerance for its minorities bursting out in all its hideousness. Contrarily, treatment of the Hindus, who have no patron anywhere in the world, continues to follow the classical Islamist pattern.

However, the elemental factor preventing the apple cart of Muslim 'tolerance' from keeling over in Malaysia and precluding the rise of a leader in millenarian mould with the usual stirring call of 'Islam in danger' is the favorably growing Muslim population ratio vis-à-vis the non-Muslims. It keeps the prevalent state of affairs deeply satisfying for the Muslims of Malaysia. With prospects of alteration of predominantly Muslim character of their society obviated, they feel unafraid in harnessing the talent and enterprise of the Chinese and other non-Muslims for strengthening their patently Islamic state. It could be averred with certainty that had the situation been otherwise, that is, the rate of population growth of the non-Muslims outpaced that of the Muslims, Malaysia would have been turned into Lebanon of the seventies long ago. It must be mentioned here that Lebanon could regain its stability only when the Muslims became assured of their ultimate triumph by way of population revolution.

In any case, the case of Muslim population explosion vis-à-vis the Hindus stands on a different plane altogether. In the case of the Hindus, horrendous memories – of loot, destruction of temples and towns, rapes, massacres and forced conversions – come tumbling down from the cupboards of history. Muslim crime-lords making the lives of Hindus miserable, their daughters and sisters being abducted and converted with impunity, interminable extortion, riots and pogroms and terrorists attacks, with the pseudo-secular spineless Indian State and the anti-Hindu political parties and Human-rights organizations looking away as usual, if not exactly applauding it—that is the fate an informed and concerned Hindu visualizes for himself in case the Muslim population crossed a threshold mark. Thinking of the pre-Partition days, and what happened to and is still happening in Pakistan, Bangladesh and even Kerala and the Indian-ruled Kashmir, he can hardly be blamed for the grim visualization. After all, bearded hordes descending from all over the world and running riot upon the land and flogging, amputating and stoning-to-death anyone daring to violate their version of Sharia is a vision that scares the daylight out of the educated and forward-looking Muslims of Pakistan too. Taliban rule in Afghanistan and North Waziristan were solved examples, so to say. If the Hindus add rape, conversions and massacres to that scenario, could they be accused of being irrational, paranoid or scare-mongering?

That is the vision evoked in the mind of an average knowledgeable, thoughtful and concerned Hindu, having some knowledge of what India and the world have suffered from the day the murdering-marauding hordes arose from the deserts of Arabia. What is more, right from Nigeria to Egypt to Iraq to Iran to Pakistan to Bangladesh to Malaysia, persecution, humiliation and marginalization – dhimmification, in a word – of the minorities continues unabated. It is only that the drive has acquired less violent and more nuanced (but not the less insidious or relentless for that) forms. The vision sure is immensely disconcerting, having in it to set off a nuclear chain reaction across the world as it approached realization.

Does that image have an iota of logic or truth behind it, or is it a figment of imagination merely of a misanthropic and paranoid Brahminical mindset; one that has known throughout its history nothing better than to hate, despise, revile and subjugate anyone who is not of his religion, caste, sub-caste, clan and family, in that order? Let us investigate—

During the six decades post-Independence when the Hindus bred merrily, Muslims more than doubled their population ratio to about 20%. Now with the growth rate of Hindus declining all the time and the Muslims holding theirs steady, they could bring it par with the Hindus in another half century or so. If you add Pakistan and Bangladesh too to that, the population of Hindus in the Indian subcontinent could get to be about one-third of the Muslims (it was three times in the pre-Independence unified India)) by that time. That gives birth to an altogether new possibility—infinitely bloody and nightmarish than even the demand of another partition.

And the possibility is that, within a decade or two, instead of demanding another partition, the Muslims may demand doing away with the original Partition by restoring the sub-Continental borders to their original state:

> We admit to our fault in demanding vivisection of the holy land, paining thereby our dear Bapu and hundreds of millions of our Hindu brothers no end. Now we want to expiate for our collective sin by doing a grand 'punar-milan' (reconciliation). Hindus should have no objection to that for isn't it the thing they have been pining for all along and many among them would give away their right hand for?

Now that would be enough to fill the sub-Continental Muslim hearts with delirium and religious frenzy not seen among the faithful since the Saladin days, even as the Hindu hearts sank more ponderously than a dead dog. And to make matters worse and unstoppable, here is not even a Berlin wall to stop cross-border forays and intermingling. Who could possibly have guts to fire upon the surging hordes (backed by N-armed Pakistan Army) of tens of millions if, say, a Hafeez Saeed mobilized millions in Pakistan, some millenarian leader did likewise in Bangladesh, and a Imam Bukhari, Zakir Naik or Owisi, duly supported by the likes of Sonia, Mamta, Lalu, Kuldeep Nayyer, Romila Thapar, Khuswant Singh, Digvijay Singh, and the like mobilized millions of Indian Muslims, as well as, the utterly idiotic and suicidal dhimmi Hindus to cross-over to obliterate the *'artificial'*, *'inhuman'* and patently un-Islamic boundaries dividing the long-lost *'brothers'*.?

Hindus constituted 30% of population of East Pakistan at the time of Partition. Killings, forced conversion and forced-migration to India have pared that down to about 8%. And that was when there was a Hindu-majority state across the border to instill some restraint. With India gone and the Hindus reduced to minority, what would become of them could be anybody's guess. If the scenario, quite within the realm of probable (indeed certitude), still fails to shake the Indians out of their self-indulgent somnambulance, pray what else would? We would see, and in our lifetime too, a holocaust of a level that would make Hitler and Genghis Khan turn in their graves with wonderment and envy, reproaching themselves for being such soft-hearted nannies in their own lives.

Let there be no doubt about it. Not just India, but the entire world is bound to face a particularly dreadful certitude at some point of time. If it is not India first, it would be some place else, but India, as anyone can discern, is most ripe for the thing. Certitude is: A purposefully increasing, and unable or unwilling to assimilate 'One' is destined to be engaged, at some point of time, in an existential confrontation with the oblivious, stagnant and complacent 'Hundred'.

5

THEN THERE IS A THIRD

Even if all of the foregoing (that is, ills, ailments and worries bothering the nation) came to be solved ultimately, there is one vexation or danger that is not likely to go away, being entirely independent of (even though getting immense boost from) such things as poverty, illiteracy, population and the like. Ideologies of Wahabism, Salafism and Jihadism, and all that these entail – willful ghettoization of minds and the lives, increasing intolerance, communal polarization and violence, marginalisation of women, urge to impose one's worldview and the lifestyle upon the others, making unreasonable demands upon the society and the state, and deliberate flouting or bypassing of the laws of the land not deemed in consonance with the imperatives of the faith – are likely to strike ever-deeper roots, grow and keep roiling the land till one of the two unimaginables came to pass.

Reason is quite simple: Concept of suprematism in the Abrahamic faiths (but particularly the Islam) as them being the only, final and unquestionable source of Truth. Everything else is either untruth or a redundancy, and therefore liable either to be brought into conformity with their respective injunctions and commandments, or obliterated from the face of the Earth. If a significant section of the world continues to hold on to an ideology holding that close to a billion people – as slogging, loving, caring and full of human feelings, virtues and follies as anyone out there but worshipping a non-Abrahamic God (or gods) – were all children of Devil living in a state of untruth and sin, and therefore fit candidates to be either brought around to follow the sixth century Arabic way of life and thought, or obliterated altogether, than it gets to be as futile of hoping for peace to prevail upon the land as the possibility of war happening upon the Moon or the Mars.

Poverty, illiteracy or joblessness; things usually blamed by the moronic or dissimulating apologists of Islamism; have nothing to do with the rise in Islamic fundamentalism or Jihadism. Ideas for religious violence and wars, and subjugation, conversion and extermination of the non-Muslims emanate more from the full bellies and fat purses sitting in well-appointed army clubs, opulent mosques and palatial bungalows than from the hungry tummies engaged 24x7 in making the two ends meet. Ideas, strategies and the capital for forging or procuring cannons to undertake Jihadi assaults come from the well-off sections, even though cannon-fodder is provided by the unwashed masses. That is the reason as to why one of the richest countries of the world (Saudi Arabia) is busy grooming and supplying millions of mullahs and billions of dollars to spread Wahabism (which turns into Jihad, naked and pure, as soon as it touches the infidel lands, or *Dar-up-Harb*) across the world, and it is the rich Punjabi of Pakistan (rather then the poor Baluchis or Sindhis) who is extending ideological, moral and financial support to Jihad in the sub-Continent, even though ground troops are provided by poor Pashtuns and others.

Not unlike the Brahmin-Kshatriya compact that worked (in)famously in India for close to three millenniums and till the last century, the Islamic imperial-supremacist arrangement (the classical *Piri-Miri*) worked very well for the Muslim societies too. The feudal section held sway in its own field and enjoyed the luxuries of the world with the sanction and moral support of the Qazi-Mullah segment, and the later in turn enjoyed supremacy in its field with the support and protection of the former. The arrangement worked great till the end of the last century. But, much like all such unholy nexuses, it is coming under increasing strain in the new millennium. Reasons are manifold.

The Western Civilization, with its ideas, culture and million material charms has made the things go topsy-turvy for Islam and the Muslims. Compounding that is the characteristic perfidy of the rich privilegentsia, which, much like its counterparts throughout the world, wants to have the cake and eat it too. Simply put, it wants the laws and mores that it usually devises and professes to be in love with to be applied to the other lesser mortals, and not it. Presently, it dreams of establishment of Sharia-rule throughout the world by subjugating all the nations in the cause of Islam through a combination of proliferation, proselytizing and violence. And though hugely enjoying the warmth coming off the fires raging in the infidel lands lit by the jihadi advance-guards enjoying its moral-financial support, it doesn't want these fires or the harsh imperatives of Sharia scorching its well-appointed drawing rooms and the libertine lifestyles. Thus, neither does it want the bombs it had arranged for the purpose of cowing down and subjugating the infidels to destroy its neighborhood, nor does it desire to go back to the sixth century Arabia of lifelong gazing into the bums of camels. It doesn't want any of its comforts and freedoms, many of which run patently against the spirit and the letter of Islam curtailed. In short (as it had been in the mediaeval age) it wants its darling Islam to rule the world through the agency of Mullahs and Jihadis, and not them rule over it or apply every one of the injunctions and the imperatives of Sharia applied to it.

In their turn, the mullahs and jihadis won't mind doing their bidding, as they love nothing more than the idea of bringing the entire world under the flag of Islam. They would gladly spare (for the time being) their protagonists and the financers the rigor of Islamic laws but for a huge glitch. And it is that the world out there is just too strong and not at all prepared to be subjugated by them...at least as fast as they would want it to be. More gallingly still, after a few initial decades of indulgence and dithering, it (the non-Islamic world) is coming round to giving back more than it gets. Simply put, it is too powerful, too enlightened, and too much into enjoying its freedoms and the luxuries to even countenance the sight of the ignorant louts, let alone giving in to their worldview.

But the Mullah-Jihadi cohort, weaned on the belief of incomparable superiority of Islam and all-out support of the God for his faithful is one impatient lot. Accepting or reconciling to the possibility that the entire world may not ever come to fall to the charms or the intimidations of Islam, and, for that reason, choosing the easy expedience of holding back the steeds of Jihad, would be great blasphemy. It would be akin either to not believing the promises of the God or willful flouting of these. Entire world belonged to Islam and all the non-believers were either ignorant squatters, or headstrong enemies of Allah in direct employ of Satan. Now, ignoring that dire fact and refusing to be engaged in interminable Jihad to recover the world for the God...thing couldn't be contemplated even. Sad fact, however, was that many of the Muslims were refusing to actively engage in meaningful or ceaseless jihad. Not only they appeared to be reconciled to the vile status quo, but were happy socializing with the hated idolaters and enjoying many charms the Western Civilization, steeped in Satanism, offered. Why were they behaving that way? There must be some problem or lapse somewhere.

Oh yes! It is right here…in our neighborhood, among our own people…those who call themselves Muslims and profess to be one of us but are, in fact, hypocrites; Muslims all but in the name, sullying the good name of Islam. They are people who don't even observe the simple imperatives of Islam: Observing veil, putting on beards, wearing ankle-length pyjamas, observing five-time prayers, not listening to music, shunning Western education, mores and the art-forms, not nursing sacred hatred for all things un-Islamic. They even stoop to greeting the non-Muslims and engaging in social intercourse with them! Such Muslims were *takfir* (kefir in all but the name) and, therefore, *wajib-ul-kat* (apt for killing).

'You want us to convert the entire world to Islam but yourself ignore or flout the tenets of Islam. That is what makes Allah cross with the Muslims and prevents their victory over the world. That way you become, inadvertently or willfully, the more `clear and present` enemy of Islam. The word of Allah must first be implemented in all its sanctity in the Muslim lands and the societies. Before we embarked upon our mission to expand Islam in the world out, we will see to it that you had followed these to the last details', gets to be the sentiment.

And here is that the supreme contradiction and the hypocrisy of the Muslim elite mindset comes to the fore in all its vividness. 'We had given moral, intellectual and financial support to these rascals to apply Sharia all over the world, not us. And damn this state (though wrought and ruled by us); what is it doing to prevent these elements from prying into our lives and stalking our homes, and to protect our freedoms and the lives', the rascally set gets reduced to asking in exasperation and despair.

This is the theme in different stages of development – in Egypt, in Turkey, in Nigeria, Algeria and Syria…indeed, practically every one of the Muslim nations. However (and appropriately), it is being played out in all its glory and viciousness in the 'Land of the Pure' created by Allah for its chosen people.

More mundanely, the 'Land of the Pure' was created by the Muslims of India for their brethrens over there. Partition was affected and millions raped, converted, butchered and displaced. It was such a cathartic event. But did the mindsets of the Muslims opting to remain in India undergo any catharsis, or even a little change? You bet.

Though not exactly the root cause, reservations on the ground of religion were the spur and the instrument to enact Partition and all that it entailed for India, including the Indian Muslims. But, even as the rivers of blood were in full spate, and let alone burying or burning them, the two principal communities of the sub-Continent had been founding it impossible to even count their dead, the never-say-tired-or-ashamed set was back to its old ways—whining, complaining, trying to put the Hindus to shame and demanding reservations. And thanks to our ever obliging and supremely secular Nehru and his acolytes, it had been able to carry it off almost but for the intervention of Sardar Patel, who, intervening in the debate on Constitution on August 28, 1947, was reduced to calling the spade for what it was:

> I once more appeal to you to forget the past...You have got what you wanted. You have got a separate state and, remember, you are the people who were responsible for it, and not those who remain in Pakistan...What is it that you want now? In the majority Hindu provinces you, the minorities, you led the agitation...Now again you tell me and ask me to say for the purpose of securing the affection of the younger brother I must agree to the same thing again, to divide the country again in the divided part. For God's sake understand that we have also got some sense...

Question is, when even so cathartic experience as the Partition, which took a toll of millions (including the Muslims) and turned, for all practical purposes, a goodly percentage of India's inhabitants into persona non grata in their own land, failed to deter them from demanding all over again what had come to be the mother of all red rags to the majority, would the experience of Pakistan deter them from turning yet more adventuresome this time around? In answer to that question lies the future of Muslims, in particular, and India and the Hindus, in general.

Wahabism (and its armed wing, Jihadism) has entered India since long and is busy recruiting soldiers, establishing and strengthening the network, and fine-tuning India-specific strategy made at the headquarters overseas to the specific requirements of the land. The Hindus are worried, as indeed are their leaders...and for understandable and obvious reasons. However, the perceptive and the far-sighted of the Hindutva enthusiasts, and equally dense and myopic of the Islamist-Jihadi mindsets are, despite massive show of concern, smacking their lips in excitement and anticipation for the day when the Jihad would be dancing naked in the streets of Indian towns and even the villages. And, for that very reason, discerning and the farsighted of the Muslims leaders and the intellectuals are turning into a bundle of anxiety and forebodings. Everyone has his own reasons for differing levels of elation or anxiety.

Ordinary Hindus (and Muslims) and their leaders are, of course, worried about the fallouts—further rising of the wall of suspicion between the two communities and resulting communal tensions; daily blasts, riots, *bandhs*, street-battles and disruption of routine of life, making the problems of living go worse than they already are; progressive weakening of the economy and the country; permanently hovering clouds of war with Pakistan growing denser, imperiling of the future of everyone around...

And that exactly is the reason behind the excitement of the Islamist-Jihadi elements. In fact, that is what they have been working for all along; otherwise there would be no problem. They have little doubt, that, even now, when they constitute a distinct minority, if only the Muslims began behaving like true Muslims, the kefir-set, howsoever great its majority, stands no chance against them and no earthly force can stop this bastion of idolatry and sin from turning into a land of the pure and the virtuous. Hadn't a lad of thirteen taught kalima to the whole of the Sindh on the strength of barely a few hundred soldiers and Bakhtiar Khilji converted the great province of Bengal and its supposedly great ruling dynasty to Islam almost single handedly? Or, for that matter, the conquests of Mahmud of Ghazni and Malik Kafur... That is the power of true Islam. Now, if India could be captured and united with Pakistan and Bangladesh, the Hindus would have but one option to choose out of three, viz., converting to the true faith, getting slaughtered wholesale at the hands of victorious ghazis, and migrating to other non-Muslim countries (for the time being only, for, Inshallah, these lands too shall fall, by and by, to the sword of Islam).

Their strategy, conceived and managed from Saudi Arabia and Pakistan (though almost entire Ummah is aware of it and involved in the project), and run in conjunction with the Indian Muslim political and religious leadership and the 'intellectuals', is three fold: Proliferation, subversion and radicalization.

Proliferation route has been discussed in the previous chapter. It means, in simple terms, painting this land green by well-directed immigration (mainly from Bangladesh) and purposeful procreation.

Subversion is to make the country's economy go bonkers by frequent disruptions and diverting the focus and the resources of the nation away from development and progress. The cowardly Hindus are to be cowed down into a state of stupefaction and submission, and the resolve and the confidence of the Indian State in its self-worth and the capability is to be broken by making unrelenting assaults: Muslim political and religious leaders breathing down its neck, shaming it for not doing anything for the Muslims and forcing it to yield ground inch by inch; enacting a riot here and a terrorist strike there, and then launching a torrent of tirades for harassing 'innocent' Muslims when it dared to apprehend someone; and then, when the situation had got ripe, a final decisive assault made to make the weakened elephant collapse with a dull thud. But, all this while, full care had to be taken to make all of it look as if it was not the part of some grand strategy enacted and directed from Cairo, Jeddah and Islamabad, but scattered responses of aggrieved and anguished Muslims and their leadership in response to unprecedented oppression and genocide being enacted by the Hindus and their State.

However, the grand project can't take off unless the Muslims of the country had been radicalized suitably—that is, filled with sentiments of incomparable superiority of Islam, and revulsion to the very idea of living alongside the idolaters and the polytheists. Of course, underlying all of that is the threat of the wrath of Allah and interminable Hell if they failed to engage in continual Jihad by thousand means.

Excitement and anticipation of the perceptible Hindutva leaders and thinkers too is for similar reasons. They are exasperated nothing more than by the slow-spreading poison of Islamism against which they have not been able to formulate any effective strategy. Hindus being what they are – historically illiterate, utterly apathetic to the dangers lurking around them, extremely myopic...unable to see beyond their selfish noses, and hopelessly divided along caste, region and linguistic lines – these avowed defenders of Hindus find it extremely difficult even to connect (let alone sensitize, unite and rouse) meaningfully with the Hindu masses. Pretenders to secularism, manifold more savvy, articulate and devious then them, and the awful corruption prevailing in the land makes their task of enlightening the Hindus about the dangers of spreading Islamism and the need to take concrete action to defend against it yet more problematic.

Under such a hopeless situation, things like frequent show of strength by the Muslims, increasingly intemperate remarks and demands made by their religious and political leaders, growingly hostile attitude of an average Muslim affected by extremist sentiments, and, of course, frequent bomb-blasts, riots and the like, come as a godsend. And if the Jihad of Al Qaeda-Taliban variety got to be a reality, it would be as if, in the garb of guiding and helping His believers, the Islamic God itself had come to the aid of the Hindu God (or gods). If the Jihadism grows fast enough and begins to display its colors in the true earnest (as the Hindutva-brigade fervently hopes), the future they are mortally afraid of would be now when they still feel capable of meeting the onslaught of Islamism head on and besting it, and not a few decades later when they fear of growing too weak (in comparison to Islamist forces grown too strong) to tackle it. Armageddon as soon as possible – that is the dream of every perceptive votary of Hindutva.

And that explains the anxiety of the discerning Muslims. They are aware that, either which way, the Muslims like them are going to suffer inordinately. It is not that they do not want or are hostile to the idea of Islamic takeover of India and thence the world. But they can see well that take over of the Muslim societies by the Islamic laws (which don't go much beyond the Caliph-Qazi-Kotwal stage), and that of the Muslim minds by the Islamic thought (which rejects Western Education, along with its Darwinism with utmost contempt) could mean only one thing: Qazi-Kotwal establishment holding their lives in its antediluvian-murderous grip and the forces of Darwinism exacting their revenge by defeating and subjugating Islam and its adherents, whenever the crunch came. And if the utterly myopic Wahabi-Jihadi Islamists persisted in their blatant and violent attempts to spread their worldview in the non-Muslim lands too, the crunch would come so much earlier. That is the reason they want it done in a peaceable manner, presenting, to whoever cared to listen, the severely pruned and sanitized version of Islam as a religion of peace.

And if indeed Islam came to hold sway over India after unimaginable bloodshed, consequenting into, perhaps, 100 to 500 million casualties (without or with N-exchange) in the sub-Continent – that would hardly be a relief to the Muslims like them. Contrarily, as Afghanistan, Sudan, Somalia, Iraq and NEFP Islamist experiences have amply brought out, that would be the beginning of their troubles as Muslims living in *Dar-ul-Aman*, and shall be nothing in comparison to what they allegedly suffer as a minority in *Dar-ul-Harbs* around the world. Things they have come to love almost as much as Islam – democracy, freedom from veil and beards, music, cinema, TV, internet, mobile, literature, pizzas and burgers, jeans and T-shirts, liberal and performing arts, and million other things that the 'un-Islamic' cultures and sciences have spawned – would get to be out of bounds for them, replaced with things that any rational and freedom-loving modern person is likely to hate from his guts.

Even as implausible (though not impossible) the above scenario is, it is the third – and totally plausible, indeed inevitable – emerging reality that keeps them in a state of fretfulness. And this clear and present reality is that the Muslims, particularly the educated and moderate Muslims, as a whole are going to be caught in a pincer movement from which there appears to be no escape.

As things stand, what with the Americans going to pull-out of Afghanistan in a state of near-defeat, combined with the miraculous resurrection of Al-Qaeda in its many avatars and triumphant march of Salafist parties in the countries hitherto inaccessible to them, extremist-Jihadi elements are going to be immeasurably exuberant and bolder, convinced of their invincibility and sanguine about their future. And with hopelessly myopic, demoralized and feckless regimes obtaining in India, and millions problems outlined in the previous chapters that are set only to grow, there should be little doubt that they are going to have a field day in this land that has always been running choc-a-bloc with million mutinies.

Things however are never so easy or simple as they might appear. In any case, they are not going to be simpler than what they are for the Jihadi-Salafist cohorts in Pakistan where their progress is halting and patchy, and the success far from certain. And hugely impatient and violent as they always are, the Indian Jihadis too, much like their Pakistani counterparts, are likely to take to bombing the Hindu gatherings and other crowded places, and bullying and killing the moderate and sane voices among their own community. Result: Freedoms and the lifestyle of the moderate Muslims badly curtailed with the rise of Talibani elements in their neighborhoods; Hindus getting more and more suspicious, hostile and discriminating towards them; rise of avowedly anti-Muslim Hindu rightist leaders and political parties, advocating extreme solutions; and shrinking of economic space and job opportunities for the Muslims, in general, and educated ones among them, in particular.

Consider an entirely plausible (indeed inevitable) scenario... A devastating bomb blast occurs at the workplace of a private company like TCS or Infosys, or in the office or the plant of a strategic establishment such as ISRO, Defence, or the N-Establishment. Investigation bears out that it had been an insider job, and a network of Jihadi mindsets had taken root there, as also in many similar establishments. Now, it shouldn't bear telling that that would be the end of the road, more or less, for the Muslim aspirants seeking job there. And to think that a decade down, when the Jihadi chickens had come home to India to roost in the right earnest, the scenario is likely to play out in virtually every domain of the national economic life!

And to think that the hatred of Jihadis for India and everything it possesses, offers and connotes – ancient religion and the civilization, cultural vibrancy and tolerance, freedoms it offers, and the economy that helps keep the things quiescent and running – is immeasurably more than what it is for, say, Pakistan; just about everything here being destroyable or *wajib-ul-katl*!

Now, the growing suspicion, alienation, segregation and pauperization of the Muslims…that would warm the cockles of the hearts of the Islamists no end. That is because alienation, disaffection, sense of grievance and anger are the things they work to bring about, being rich grist for their radicalization mill. A vicious cycle would be created and the normal educated and upwardly mobile Muslim, desirous of leading a normal and happy life unencumbered by dogmas or labels and in a spirit of mutual respect, faith and coexistence, would be caught badly in a pincer movement. Thugs, philistines and louts would try to dictate his life in the Muslim neighborhoods, even as the Hindus would be increasingly chary of them living amid them or working alongside.

Further, the Hindus too won't remain unaffected by the increasing Talibanism. As always, the Hindu girls will be the primary target and the tool. We would see veritable explosion in the cases of abduction, molestation, luring away, and forced conversion and marriage of the Hindu girls as the favorite device to humiliate and cow down the Hindus and exacerbate communal tension. As things stand, the Hindus already have their own variety of thugs and louts to contend with. Now taking cue, these rascals would get a new lease of life and try to dictate and control the lives within their respective bailiwicks. Controlling the freedom and sexuality of women would get to be the favorite pastime of these ill-literate, do-good-nothing cohorts. Taliban would have done the job of talibanising India without even converting the Hindus to Islam.

That is the inexorable possibility, which, even as it warms the cockles of the hearts of the Hindutva and Islamism enthusiasts alike, fills the hearts of the progressive Hindus, desirous of seeing India a truly secular and noble place of peace, prosperity, justice, moderation and coexistence, as also of the moderate Muslims thinking along the similar lines, more or less, with consternation and forebodings.

They could seek to dismiss the above narrative as obnoxious rant of a prejudiced and paranoid mind, holding little verity or plausibility. That may be so. But what would they say to the outpourings of alarm and angst flowing from the pens of Muslim intellectuals enjoying impeccable credibility and published in such venerable and reputed newspapers as Dawn? Or, for that matter, to the wakeup call of Shahin Sultan, editor of the acclaimed online magazine, 'New Age Islam', and one of the few rational and courageous voices in the world of Indian Muslim journalism?

Supremely expressive of the above narrative and the conclusions is this article by Mr. Shahin Sultan:

> Islamic radicalism has been defined in a variety of ways: as a synonym for extremism, militancy, terrorism or the ideologies of Wahhabism, Salafism, Deobandism, Qutubism, or Maudoodism and so on. But I would define Islamic radicalism as a totalitarian Islamic-supremacy movement that believes it has a monopoly over Heaven, truth and justice. This movement is leading towards the alienation of Muslims from the mainstream world community – even from their own multicultural, multi-religious societies in non-Muslim majority countries.

> Militancy and terrorism are outgrowths of such attitudes and may not be specifically directed towards the goal of establishing an Islamic State. It may just be calling, in an ostensibly peaceful manner, for establishing so-called "Shariah-controlled zones" in the middle of secular societies.

> But radicalism is turning violent in many places because violence is implicit in the very idea of having a monopoly on truth. But violence, specially sustained episodes of violence depend on a variety of factors including infrastructural support, the attitude of the state etc. So to my mind a worldview that has not yet led to violence need not be considered any less radical. If nothing else, supremacist attitudes that may provoke others to violence have themselves to be considered as inherently violent.

> Looked at from this perspective, Islamic radicalism is going mainstream worldwide, and no less so, in the East. The Af-Pak region in South Asia is known to be the crucible of violence and terror perpetrated by Islamic radicals. But Southeast Asia too is not far behind. After all, the second most violent attack on civil society, after 9/11, took place in Bali, Indonesia, on a nightclub, in which 202 people, mostly Australians, were killed....

> A host of religious and sectarian militias in Pakistan, some even run by Islamist political parties, are a serious danger not only to Pakistan and neighbouring India, but also to the world at large. They are all allied at one level or another with the global Jihadis and Al-Qaeda.

> To me the most disturbing feature of what is happening in the East is the radicalization of Muslim societies. It's not the madrasa-

educated alone who are being radicalized. Muslims who have come out of normal, government or private institutions are being equally radicalized under social pressure. The investment of tens of billions of petrodollars in promoting a dry and desiccated version of Islam, devoid of its rationality, humanity and spiritualism, has created an atmosphere that is affecting many impressionable minds. When the Governor of Pakistani Punjab, Salman Taseer was killed by his own bodyguard last year, it was difficult to find a Mullah ready to lead his funeral prayers. When the killer was taken to court hundreds of lawyers threw rose petals at him, calling him their hero. The judge who sentenced him to death had to go into exile.

All that the martyred leader of Punjab had done was to appeal for Presidential clemency for a hapless Christian lady who could not have possibly insulted the Prophet (peace be upon him). No one asked how a Christian could be accused of blasphemy and tried under apostasy laws when she doesn't believe in Islam or the prophethood of Mohammad.

Following Salman Taseer's assassination, the only Christian in the federal cabinet of Pakistan, Shahbaz Bhatti was also murdered. He too had expressed sympathy for and pleaded the case of Aasia Bibi, the convicted Christian lady. Aasia Bibi's case brought to light the fact that it's not only Christians and Hindus who are persecuted for their beliefs but also Muslim minorities such as the Shiites, Ahmadis and Ismailis, who are routinely harassed, discriminated against and killed. The Human Rights Commission of Pakistan has just published a report that states, inter-alia, that at least 20 to 25 girls are abducted and converted to Islam against their will every single month in Pakistan.

Pakistan is a state created in 1947 on the radical idea that Muslims could not co-exist with other religious communities....

With this historical background one can understand the radicalization of Pakistani society. But what explains similar attitudes in Indian Muslim society? If one goes by India's Muslim Press, the reaction to Salman Taseer murder was just the same as in Pakistan. For a little perspective, I must state that in the Indian sub-continent, there are two major Islamic schools of thought, represented by Bareilwis and Deobandis. Deobandis are Wahhabis and all the Pakistani madrasas that taught armed Jihad were run on the Deobandi curriculum. Bareilwis constitute the overwhelming majority of the South Asian Muslims. They believe in seeking intercession from Sufi saints, as do Hindus, Sikhs and other communities in India. They go to these shrines together and this naturally creates a sense of sharing in a semi-religious atmosphere and helps national integration. Salafis,

Wahhabis and other radicals do not like Muslims to interact with other communities, much less on a religious kind of platform.

As has already happened in Pakistan, Deobandi, Wahhabi, Salafi imams are now being forced upon Indian Bareilwi mosques. This is sometimes leading to violence as well. Wahhabis have become so aggressive that they beat up people and stone their houses for daring to say prayers in a village mosque without having a beard. This happened in a Saharanpur district mosque during Ramadan three years ago. The clean-shaven Muslim's seven-year old daughter got hurt in the severe stone pelting and died.

Frightened with incidents like this and aware of what was happening in Pakistan, the heads of the 80 most important Sufi shrines of India got together a few months ago and organized a massive rally of Muslims in a town in Western Uttar Pradesh. Then for the first time in a public meeting in India they spoke about "growing Wahhabi extremism," actually using the phrase. Over a hundred thousand Muslims gathered in Moradabad and heard warnings of growing Wahhabi extremism from scores of clerics from India's largest shrines. This should have been major news in the Muslim press, but not one newspaper reported the event. Three newspapers did report the gathering and speeches but completely censored any mention of Wahhabi extremism.

Wahhabism having developed this kind of influence in a multi-religious society like India should ring alarm bells....

Clearly Radical Islam is on the rise and going mainstream as much in South and Southeast Asia East as in the Middle East or elsewhere. This is an alarming situation, and the biggest danger comes from the fact that the proverbial silent majority is too silent. Even where it is beginning to stir, moderate Islam is finding that it does not have adequate resources to counter this rising tide.

The recent effort of the Sufi shrines in India is a case in point. Even when they stirred themselves to action, they could not make an impact and are once again lying low. By and large governments seem unwilling to intervene, seeing it as an internal war within Islam. It indeed is a war within Islam; it is Muslims who are the main target of Salafi radicals; and it is they who will have to gather the courage to fight.

Throughout Islamic history, such violent radicals have disturbed the peace. They have been decimated many times and have risen again only to be defeated again. Islam's humane spiritualism and its stress on rationality have always proved superior to their ideological aridity.

But this time the radicals, the Wahhabis are in a far stronger position than before. They have got so far because a certain wealthy Arab state which claims to be the guardian of our holy places and which is protected by the only superpower in the world is behind this radicalism. Saudi Arabia considers Wahhabi Salafi radicalism its state ideology. You cannot even enter the country with a copy of the Holy Quran that is not published by them. For Saudi Arabia, spreading radicalism is an imperialist project. Along with their desiccated version of Islam, they also insist on exporting Arab culture, language, dress and architecture.

The Saudis have demolished nearly 300 monuments connected with Islamic history. Just a few remain. History conflicts with their ideology. It places Prophet Mohammad and his story in the matrix of time and gives it a context. If read in context many of the militant verses of the Holy Quran would appear to be relevant only for the time and situation they were revealed in; they cannot be applied universally. This will hamper what has to be a permanent war on infidels. Given a historical context only peaceable verses of the Quran, mostly revealed in Mecca, will remain relevant for all time. Wars will have to be stopped. Arab imperialism will not be able to make headway. The Army of suicide bombers recruited in Pakistan and elsewhere will have to be retrained for other jobs. In order to reach Heaven, Muslims will have to engage permanently in what the Prophet called Greater Jihad, struggling against our nafs, fighting one's own evil impulses.

Owing to its enormous oil wealth, Saudi Arabia's imperialist project has the support of nearly all governments in the world including those – like the United States – that have been its victims....On the side of mainstream Islam, (or what I hope is still mainstream Islam) there is no one. All governments, in Muslim-majority or non-Muslim majority countries deal with Saudi Arabia, either to buy their oil or/and sell them weapons.

Hundreds of plane-loads of semi-literate preachers fly from Jeddah to the far corners of the world almost every day converting Muslims to Salafism. Many Muslims, who still hate to be called Wahhabi, have nevertheless developed Salafi attitudes. You will find many Muslims in Pakistan and now also in India walking down the street in Arab dresses, for instance. Beards and hijabs have become common not only in the East but even in the West. Women, whose grandmothers never wore a veil, burqa or a hijab, are donning this symbol of slavery everywhere. Some moderate, liberal Muslims are themselves so affected by Salafi propaganda coming from all sorts of media that in their own minds they have started considering themselves hypocrites. Some are leaving Islam and calling themselves ex-Muslim. These responses are no help....

Confirmation of these sentiments and the fears from the 'Land of the Pure' comes across in this article from a well-respected journalist from there and published in 'New Age Islam':

Islamic Radicalism: Pakistan Entrapped in A Vicious Circle of Militancy and Cowardice of the State.

Mujahid Husain
19 April 2012

Al-Qaeda and Taliban militants have once again started attacking Pakistan, this time in a more organized manner. It was being said, after the successful military operations in tribal areas that Taliban and Al-Qaeda sympathizers have been chased away. But the reality is totally opposite. Indeed it is the Local and foreign militants who have driven away security forces and other peace-promoting organizations from there...

On the other hand it is not possible now to restrict the growing power of Taliban in Waziristan. Taliban has taken full advantage of the growing tension between Pakistan and U S over the NATO supply line. It is not beyond the realm of possibilities that Pakistan security forces, the state machinery and other institutions will have to face more intense attacks. Terrorists have become more organized with public support and have increased their effectiveness much more than before. Intellectuals and media are busy singing their praises. Imams in the Friday prayers' Khutba in mosques call them the 'architects of Islam'.

Al-Qaeda has brought its strategy of sectarian killings from Afghanistan into practice in Baluchistan and other northern parts of Pakistan in addition to the coastal town of Karachi which is already notorious for such massacres. Hazara tribesmen are being mercilessly butchered in Baluchistan and other northern parts of the country....

Today all the terrorist and militant organizations have joined hands. Controlling them has now gone out of country's capability....

Although these forces are ruling the roost for the last three decades they also know that they need to be more powerful to carry out their agendas after 2014 when American and NATO forces leave Afghanistan. They are aware that it will be easy for them to gain power in Pakistan if somehow they get united. Pakistani media is ready to greet the militant warriors in Islamabad as it is continuously paying respect and showing reverence on TV to such terror groups.

Neither does civil society of Pakistan look keen nor does it have the capability to stop religious militants taking power in Pakistan as all the liberal and secular individuals have already been brought to book or killed. To gauge the situation it is enough to mention that SAFMA offices in Lahore and Islamabad have faced serious threats. Pamphlets with the photographs of the journalists attached with SAFMA are being printed. These pamphlets describe them as enemies of Pakistan and Islam.

In short a powerful wave of militancy and terror can be seen everywhere in Pakistan which will not only destroy the structure of THE 'state', whatever little is left of it, but it will pave the way for sectarian violence on the basis of religion and sect. Its possibilities are getting obvious and palpable.

And some really innocent souls, who think that it is the Hindu attitude, discrimination and oppression that lie at the root of growing Muslim alienation and extremism, and Hindus are safe as long as they chose to remain meek, tolerant, noble and good, could do well to go through the following article published in *Dawn*, leading English language newspaper of Pakistan. It bears telling here that established by Mohammad Ali Jinnah, *Dawn* is truly a great newspaper and few of the extant sane and courageous Muslim voices could be heard in its articles and the blogs. In fact, I consider some of the columnists and bloggers of *Dawn* among the best in the world (better than even those writing in, say, *The New York Times* and *The Economist*, and eons ahead of the cheapskates that our leading newspapers like *'The Times of India'* or *'The Hindustan Times'* harbor) not only regarding the nobility of views and sentiments, but also the quality of language and style.

Perils of intolerance
I.A Rehman
Dawn, 16th August, 2012

LAST week's case of Sindhi Hindu families traveling to India should be a wake-up call for all those in positions of power in Pakistan. They will continue their present policies towards minorities at grave peril to themselves and the state....

But the real issue is not travel restrictions for minorities, it is the trend among them of giving up on Pakistan. The inconclusive debate on whether last week's travelers wanted to leave the country for good should not prevent anyone from accepting the fact that the rate of emigration by minority families has been rising for quite some time.

Reports that a good number of Hindu families from Ghotki, Mirpurkhas, Sukkur and Jacobabad have migrated to India cannot be discounted. Nor can reports of similar emigration from Balochistan be denied. Nobody should be surprised to learn that some Hindu activists have started knocking at the doors of foreign missions. The idea of appealing to the world outside is catching on.

While all minorities including Ahmedis, Shias (the Hazaras in particular) and Christians, too, are suffering as a result of the majority community's creed of intolerance and the state's negligence, at the moment we are concerned with the plight of Hindu citizens, though the practical steps suggested here will embrace all minorities.

While the more vocal among their leaders have consistently protested against the discriminatory provisions in the constitution and the law, Pakistani Hindus have, by and large, displayed great qualities of forbearance by resigning themselves to their status as second-class citizens as long as they are allowed to pursue their vocations and live with some vestiges of dignity. It is the inability to realize even these modest expectations that has driven them to despair.

Of the numerous Hindu grievances one need pick out only a few. They were hurt when their shrines and the attached properties were seized by the state or influential members of the majority community. Their needs were ignored while new housing colonies were planned and their right to buy plots in officially sponsored colonies was denied. Members of scheduled castes were either driven off the lands they had been cultivating for decades, maybe centuries, or turned into bonded labour. They put up with discrimination in access to state employment and educational opportunities in the hope of being left free to run their private businesses. This too has become increasingly difficult.

Worse, they began to be targeted for abduction for ransom, threats to their lives and property became more common, and the forced conversions and marriages of their girls took the form of campaigns organized by well-known clerics and political figures. On top of everything they got the feeling that the state did not even listen to their grievances.

What has perhaps deepened the frustration of non-Muslim citizens is the realization that no good can be expected of a government that did not have the courage to condemn the killers of its governor and minister or those responsible for the massacres of Shias in Balochistan, Kurram Agency and Gilgit-

Baltistan. They are not the only ones to believe that at the speed with which religious extremists are encroaching on public space and gaining acceptability by the elite, Pakistan could become unliveable not only for minorities but for a great many Muslims too.

Notice may also be taken of the view that stories of Hindu emigration are being played up with a view to increasing their fears and thus accelerating their exodus. This only increases the media's responsibility to be careful in reporting minority affairs.

Here is another noble soul, again from Dawn:

War against bigotry
Huma Yusuf
Dawn, 14 Nov, 2011

A week ago, three Hindu doctors were gunned down in Shikarpur. While the details of the incident remain unclear, the discriminatory aspect of the killings cannot be denied. The Eid day violence followed the release of a report in September by the Human Rights Commission of Pakistan (HRCP), which documents how minorities in Balochistan, particularly Hindus, are increasingly being kidnapped for ransom, forced to convert to Islam, and persecuted to such an extent that Hindu families fear sending their children to school.

In this context, it is not surprising that a recent study by the Pew Research Centre Forum on Religion and Public Life ranked Pakistan as the third-least tolerant country in the world in terms of social acceptance of religious diversity.

The reasons for heightened intolerance and violence towards religious minorities are multifaceted and well known....

And here is a superbly narrated true story of a Hindu girl, one of the twenty-five being abducted and force-married every month, going by the official record in Pakistan. As usual, the actual figure is likely to be much more. Fate of many a Hindu girls in India a decade or two hence could be seen in this story.

Memoirs of a Hindu girl
Faiza Mirza
Dawn, 20th August, 2012

I grew up in fear – every face around me depicted nothing but fear. I am sure that the first expression on my parent's face on my birth as a female child born to Hindu parents living in Kandhkot would have been that of fear also. Why did I bring so much fear into the lives of my parents? I grew up always wondering what is it about me that continues to terrify. But I always drew a blank. How naïve I was.

Before I knew it, the time to attend school had arrived. School was comfortable; however, there were times when I felt like an outsider, finding it difficult to gel in with rest of the majority. Perhaps the snide remarks and incidents of discrimination led me to believe that I am not one of 'them'. Of those incidents, I still vividly remember no one eating with me and refusing to sip from the cup I drank from.

Home wasn't very different either. My mother asked questions about my life at school and otherwise looking for answers that would somehow relinquish her from the unknown fear. Afraid to disappoint her, I decided very early in my life that my mother could not be my confidant.

Growing up was not easy.

And then it happened. The fears of my mother and many Hindu mothers like her materialized. I went out to one of the largest markets of Kandhkot and was abducted by a man I knew very well. He was none other than the guard who was responsible for safeguarding our temples.

Knowing his face well prompted me to sit with him in his car without protest, however, instead of taking me to my house he turned to an alley that I wasn't too familiar with. Scared and unsure about what lay ahead I started screaming just to hear my abductor scream louder and threaten me. Astonished and unable to comprehend the gravity of the situation I sat still until it was time to step out of the car to a small house which looked abandoned.

We entered the house to find a large room devoid of any furniture and other bearings except for a carpet that covered the floor. I was made to sit down on the floor.

Uncertain about what was going to happen to me; my mind raced with thoughts of the recent news of the abductions and forced conversions of Hindu girls. I sat there shuddering. The realization struck me and I could see my entire life in front of me in kaleidoscope. My mother's fears, my father's warnings, the alienation I felt, the yearning to be a part of the circle of friends, the search for a confidant, a friend.

My worst fears were reaffirmed when a man wearing a turban entered the room to teach me about a religion which I grew up hearing about, however, felt no urge to practice or embrace. He kept sermonizing me for hours but was unable to get me to listen to him, realizing that he left asking me to ponder about the true religion.

His departure did not ignite any fire for eternal glory inside me but only made me wonder why did my parents not relocate to another country when they had the chance to do so? Why did they continue to live in fear waiting for the inevitable to happen instead of making a move to safer pastures? And, what made me think that I am any different from countless girls who are forced to change their faith?

Each passing day appeared to be more and more surreal. The ritual of preaching continued for days, I lost track. Eventually, when preaching did not do the trick, my abductor threatened me....

Somewhere along this relentless persuasion, came that horrifying threat of harming my family – I gave in. My approval followed a small ceremony in which I was forced to embrace Islam and later married off to the man who will always be remembered as the 'messiah' who for saved me from the unknown territory of sin and infidelity I was treading on.

After the ceremony, instead of receiving blessings for a happy and prosperous life ahead, I was immediately escorted to a local court where a Muslim magistrate declared my conversion and marriage in accordance with the law.

The news of my conversion and marriage to a Muslim man spread like wildfire. I dreaded the moment of meeting my parents. I never wanted to see pain and agony on their faces let alone be the reason for all their grief. Sure enough, one look at my mother made me yearn for my own death.

I wanted to tell her that I love her and that her safety was all I had in mind when I converted. I wanted to tell my father to keep my sisters safe. I wanted to tell my brothers to leave the country whilst they still could. I wanted to say much more but their silent pain and suffering made me wish if only I wasn't born a girl, if only I wasn't born in Pakistan, if only I had the right to be myself and practiced my faith without being herded into a religion that I failed to comprehend, if only I could make them all understand that there is just one God for all, if only I could give us all an identity that we rightly deserve.

Looking at all the faces that once seemed familiar; I wondered: who am I?

I am one but share the pain of many. I am Rachna Kumari, Rinkle Kumari, Manisha Kumari and the many more Hindu girls who will be forced to convert in Pakistan. I am the fear of their families and the agony that they undergo. I am the misery of those girls who die a little every day for the injustices done to them.

I am a minority living in an intolerant society.

And the Hindus won't be alone to suffer at the hands of the Wahabi brigade. No consideration for the *'People of the Book'* appellation or the like. For, by now, everyone except those adhering to the strictest version of Islam have been turned into kefir and, therefore, *wajib-ul-katl*. With the rate they are getting purer and piouser (so to say), and coming closer to their 'Most Merciful and Compassionate' God, perhaps only one or two percent of the humanity (Quaraish of Arabia and a few others) would retain the right to be alive. Anyway, Christians stand no chance, whatsoever. Here is Irfan Husain again, a blessed soul, if there ever was one:

Muslims and minorities
Irfan Husain
Dawn, 28th January, 2012

IMAGINE the following scenario: a complex housing a mosque, a madressah, a girls` school and a home for the elderly being run by a Muslim charity is broken into at dawn and bulldozed by officials. No notice is served, and no documents challenging ownership are produced. Yet, within hours, the buildings are reduced to rubble, residents are made homeless, and copies of religious texts destroyed. Supervising this operation is the top local bureaucrat who pays no heed to the protests of the ulema in charge of the complex. Think of the outcry across the entire Muslim world. Demonstrations outside the embassies of the country that allowed this injustice to happen would have broken out instantly.

But when the Punjab government recently carried out a similar operation against Gosha-i-Aman, a Christian charity in Lahore, everybody in and out of Pakistan stood by silently. The chief minister, no doubt eyeing the two acres of land his minions had so brutally seized from the Catholic church, had nothing to say.

In the wider context of our vile treatment of our minorities, I suppose this incident fades into insignificance.

The hapless residents of Gosha-i-Aman should count themselves lucky that they weren't killed by the Punjab government goons. Had there been any bloodshed, possibly no action would have been taken against the killers: Pakistan has an appalling record of not convicting zealots who have killed so many non-Muslims in the past.

However, we treat our minorities neither equally nor fairly.

Indeed, we don't even pretend to. Almost every other day, I get some fresh evidence of our prejudiced attitudes towards non-Muslims. Even within the dominant religion, there is persecution. Shias are regularly targeted: just the other day, three Shia lawyers were gunned down in Karachi.

According to human rights organizations, Pakistan is among the most brutal countries when it comes to the treatment of minorities. Year after year, the Human Rights Commission of Pakistan issues reports highlighting a wide range of crimes committed against non-Muslims by individuals and the state.

In the recent Punjab government action against Gosha-i-Aman, no functionary has explained why this extreme step was taken without warning, especially when the church has documents proving its ownership of the property since 1887. But when the state is itself a party to what comes across as a blatant land grab, there is little ordinary citizens can do to resist, especially when they belong to a minority community.

Across the Muslim world, Christians are under attack from Muslims. In Nigeria, an extremist Muslim organization calling itself Boko Haram has killed hundreds of Christians and attacked dozens of churches. In Iraq, nearly half a million Christians have been forced to leave their homes, and scores have been killed. In Egypt, the ancient community of Christian Copts has suffered repeated attacks by Salafists.

And yet when these appalling acts of violent intolerance occur, there is scarcely any protest from either our clerics or our politicians. Nevertheless, we are constantly and deeply sensitive to all real and perceived wrongs meted out to Muslims in the West. `Islamophobia` is regularly trotted out in our criticism of foreign countries Muslims have opted to settle in.

But the reality is that Muslim immigrants in the West don't face a fraction of the injustice and intolerance native non-Muslims have to put up with in Muslim countries. In almost every western country, laws protect minorities from open racism. In the Islamic world, even where anti-discrimination laws exist, they provide scant protection, as show our daily acts of open discrimination and violence against our minorities.

Practice of untouchability by the Hindus is a well-known phenomenon for which they have been rightly excoriated the world over. Not only that, the Hindus have been condemned for practicing a kind of untouchability against the Muslims too. And for that reason, they never tire of praising Islam for its egalitarianism and humanitarianism...Well. The above article by Irfan Husain is suitably enlightening on this account too.

> I still recall a TV programme in which a Pakistani Sikh recounted how he was sitting by a stream, cooling his feet on a hot day, when a passing Muslim insisted he pull them out of the water because he was polluting it. Similarly, for generations, Christians and Hindus have been served in separate cups and plates at roadside eating-places across the country. Sweepers in homes are always given water in glasses nobody else uses.

> We don't think twice about these nasty acts of daily discrimination, having grown up with them as part of life's rituals. But consider for a moment how deeply insulting and wounding they must be. If Muslims were similarly treated in the West, imagine the outcry, not least among citizens of the country concerned.

Among all the minorities of the world, the lot of Ahmadis of Pakistan is perhaps the worst (it is another matter that they too hate the idolater Hindus as much as their 'pure' Muslim *'bretherns'*). It won't be wrong to conjecture that in a frank poll, 99% Muslims may be reduced to denying them the right to exist upon the face of the earth. And it is a sure bet that had the world not been there to watch over and take note, not a single Ahmadi would have escaped alive out of Pakistan. But, pray, what is their crime! It is that much like the Hindus, Christians, Jews or the Muslims of whatever dispensation, they were born to and keep practicing the faith their ancestors had bequeathed them. They can no more help it than the Pope his Catholic faith, Grand Mufti of the Grand Mosque of Mecca his Wahabi legacy, or the sundry Shankracharyas their Brahminism. But the rising tide of Islamic-Wahabi intolerance is not into that kind of thinking or logic. Yet, there remain many a noble and humane souls among the Muslims, otherwise the goose of Islam would have been cooked by now.

Why this kolavari di?
Murtaza Razvi
Dawn, 3rd February, 2012

What have the Ahmadis done to deserve this treatment in this Islamic republic of ours? The latest bout of hate speeches against the Ahmadi community and threats hurled at them was witnessed in Rawalpindi's Satellite Town last Sunday. Thousands gathered near a community centre on the call of banned militant outfits like the Sipah-i-Sahaba Pakistan and the Jamat-ud-Dawa, flanked by local leaders of the PML-N and trade unions.

They demanded not only the closure of the Ahmadi community

centre but also that all Ahmadis be expelled from Pakistan. The country's Christian minority also came in for a shock when the hate rally's meeting point, the Holy Family Chowk, was rechristened as the Khatm-i-Nabuwat (Finality of Prophethood) Chowk.

The rally itself was organized by a minority group of Muslims who also regard the celebration of the Prophet's birthday as unacceptable, according to their sectarian leanings which are similar to those of the Taliban; similar groups have attacked Friday congregations of rival Muslim sects and bombed many shrines across the country, killing and maiming innocent citizens. Such groups have also targeted girls' schools and colleges, even a women's bazaar in Peshawar. So basically, according to their ideology, it is kosher to kill anyone not subscribing to their particularly rigid view of Islam. That makes it the majority of Pakistanis, and possibly of Muslims everywhere in the world.

Thus, in a country where on the eve of Independence, Jinnah had proclaimed "You are free to go to your temples ... mosques ... or any other places of worship", Ahmadis were barred from calling their places of worship mosques; the kalima of Islam was removed from such buildings' façade; holding prayers and congregations similar to those held by Muslims inside a building that resembled a mosque and keeping copies of the Quran in such places, were proscribed. An official declaration defaming the Ahmadi creed and its religious leader was henceforth required from citizens to acquire basic identity documents or even to open a bank account if you declared yourself Muslim. The kalima and Quranic verses were also ordered to be removed from Ahmadi gravestones. Pakistan's anti-Ahmadi apartheid thus had the full force of the state behind it...

And when Ahmadis are there, can the Shias be far behind? It is another matter that the Shias, wherever they happen to be a majority, hate and persecute their minorities with as much virulence (perhaps more) and cruelty as they are being subjected to in Pakistan. And among the Muslims, they would be far more prompt than the Sunnis in denying the Ahmadis the right to call themselves Muslims or even to exist. Still it is nobody's case that they are any the less human than Sunnis, Hindus or Christians. Their human rights too need to be protected and security of their lives and livelihood guaranteed as that of any other community or race. Here is an anguished cry of a true humanitarian soul:

Minority report
Irfan Husain
Dawn, 21ˢᵗ April, 2012

A FEW months ago, somebody emailed me a chilling audio clip of a conversation between a journalist and a Pakistani Taliban.

When the interviewer reminded the terrorist that he was a Muslim too, and recited the kalima to prove it, he was told bluntly that the Taliban did not view anybody who did not subscribe to their extreme vision as believers.

When the Taliban was reminded that the founder of Pakistan was a peaceful, tolerant man, he replied that Jinnah had 'Ali' in his name, and so must be a Shia. "We do not accept the Shia as Muslims," he insisted.

From considering the Shia to be non-Muslims, it seems there is only a short step to declaring them wajib-ul-qatal, or deserving of death, preferably by violent means.

Indeed, this extreme view has been around for three decades in Pakistan....

The ongoing slaughter of Hazara Shias in Pakistan is yet another reminder of the inhuman nature of extremism. While individual Shias have been targeted for years, the recent mass killings of ethnic Hazaras is probably happening because they can be so easily identified. According to a Hazara website, 700 of the community have been killed in recent years without a single terrorist being brought to justice.

An article 'Who kills Hazaras in Pakistan and why' on the website, Outlookafghanistan.net states:

Since the declaration of religious extremists as 'strategic assets' by the ruling elites of Pakistan, the religious militant groups like Lashkar-i-Jhangvi and the Taliban have been given free hands [sic] to do anything they like.

The cold-blooded massacres of Shias in Kohistan and Chilas seem to indicate that either the local law-enforcement agencies were asleep or complicit. Gilgit's lockdown and the evacuation of foreign tourists showed the world yet again what an anarchic and violent place Pakistan has become.

In a recent army-led operation, several of the alleged killers have been arrested, and Shia and Sunni mosques in Gilgit sealed to forestall further tension. But the real test will come when these terrorists are brought to trial: thus far, the record of our judiciary in sentencing such criminals has not been very reassuring.

More often than not, they have been released on bail, or let off on grounds of insufficient evidence. Judges have been reluctant to grasp that witnesses are too scared to come forward. Repeated postponement of hearings also deters people from giving evidence.

Apart from the LJ and the SSP's anti-Shia violence, the Jundullah is a latecomer to Pakistan's sectarian slaughter.

Understandably, hundreds of Hazaras have fled, many to Australia. They are only the latest wave of persecuted Pakistanis seeking sanctuary in safer places. Those Christians, Hindus and Ahmadis who could have already left the country Jinnah saw as one where they would have equal rights.

Steadily, the space for anybody not hewing to the mainstream school of Islam is shrinking. Indeed, the Taliban spokesman I quoted earlier was clear that all those who did not actively oppose the state were non-Muslim and therefore wajib-ul-qatal. This is the inexorable logic of the takfiri philosophy that underpins the global jihad: anybody can be dubbed a non-Muslim and thus a target.

Sadly, the response to all this violence among the Pakistani ruling elites remains muted. There is little of the anger directed towards the Americans for the drone attacks that have killed far fewer innocent people than sectarian terror has. And yet, the media, the political class, and civil society seem oddly disconnected with the fate of our unfortunate minorities…

But Pakistan is not alone in this sectarian madness. Across large swathes of the Islamic world, non-Muslims are being targeted with increasing frequency and ferocity. More than half of Iraq's Christian population of around 1.4 million has fled in the face of extremist violence.

The ancient Egyptian Coptic community are regularly targeted by the country's Salafi fundamentalists. Nigeria has witnessed a wave of church bombings from the Boko Haram anti-education Islamist movement.

And yet Muslims demand ever-increasing freedom to pray and spread their faith in the West. Whenever permission to build yet another mosque is denied, authorities are blamed of Islamophobia. Any real or imagined slur against symbols of Islam results in demonstrations across the Islamic world. Yet there is silence in the West over the treatment of minorities in Muslim countries.

The recent edition of Minorities Concerns of Pakistan carried a moving article about the difficulties Christians face every day in dealing with Muslims. Apparently, they are forever being asked to convert to Islam, and made conscious they are living in Pakistan on sufferance. If Muslims in the West were subjected to this kind of rudeness, there would be protest demonstrations that would include western liberals.

But we in Pakistan have become so hardened to the plight of Shias and non-Muslims that we take their daily suffering for granted. However, we should remember that for the Taliban, we are all wajib-ul-qatal.

And this from I.A. Rehman

The Suicide Path
The Dawn (29th September, 2011)

A series of atrocities recently committed against members of minority communities shows that the (threat) canker of sectarian violence is posing for Pakistan is much greater threat than is generally realized, especially by the establishment.

The killing of 29 Shia pilgrims near Mastung set some kind of a record in bestiality; the innocent travelers were forced to alight from the bus, lined up and cut down in cold blood...

These incidents should be seen in the context of the killing and harassment of the Hazara community in Quetta, that have been going on for years, and the excesses being committed against Shias in Kurram Agency.

Three conclusions are obvious. First the size of the population threatened by the wave of sectarian violence has increased by a wide margin. Secondly, the targeted groups are no longer threatened with loss of job or property; their right to life itself is denied. And, thirdly, the addition of minority-bashing to the Al Qaeda's agenda has generally enhanced the strength of the forces that are challenging the state of Pakistan in this regard.

Discrimination including violence against communities that are non-Muslim by choice (Hindus, Christians, Sikhs et al) and those put in this bracket against their will (Ahmedis) has been on the increase for several years. That meant about five percent of the population, or nine million people, were threatened. Even that was not a small number. The addition of Shias to the people earmarked for extermination should raise the figure of endangered Pakistanis to 15 to 20 percent of the population—27 to 36 million people. Does it not put the need to combat sectarianism at the top of the national agenda?

Traditionally, attacks on minorities were limited to demands for their purge from services, denial of promotion or recruitment, exclusion from housing colonies and similar forms of economic and social discrimination. Now the target groups are threatened with physical liquidation. In some cases, the possibility of escaping death by 'conversion to Islam' is not even mentioned. Such threats carry seeds of pogroms that no sane person can possibly contemplate with equanimity....

The danger of the anti-Shia drive being made into a duty under jihad cannot be ignored. That could increase sectarian prejudices among the government personnel. The religio-political parties that do not oppose militants and inwardly support them are unlikely to protest against Shia killings (as they do not condemn killers of Ahmedis or those who defend the blasphemy accused), leading to a wider acceptability of Shia killings...

The increase in anti-Shia sectarian violence is fuelling intolerance in other areas. The excesses against the Ahmedis are on the increase. Every now and then an Ahmedi is killed for his belief. The latest is a movement for a complete social boycott of Ahmedis in Pachnand, Chakwal district, that includes expulsion of Ahmedi boys and girls from schools, boycott of Ahmedi shops and refusal to allow them seats on buses...

Mr. Mujahid Husain, who we have quoted earlier, has this to say about persecution of Shias in the same article:

It is difficult not to mention a group aligned with Tahreek-e-Taliban and Al-Qaeda which is getting successful in killing Shias in Baluchistan, Sindh and specially Karachi, Khurram Agency and northern region. This organization has many members of Sipah-e-Sahaba, Lashkar-e-Jhangwi and Jaish-e-Mohammad who have the support and help of many powerful institutions of Punjab government. In Baluchistan this group is assisted by Jundallah which provides all kinds of facilities and in northern regions it is supported by Punjabi Taliban and Tehreek-e-Taliban for sectarian killings. Main aim of this group is to bring Shias under their attack from Manasara to Gilgit and Askardu....

Another very important thing which Pakistani media could not bring to light out of fear for their own lives is that these killers attack small Shia populated villages, kill their men and kidnap women and children. It may be mentioned here that Tehreek-e-Taliban and such other sectarian groups have issued various fatwas during the last ten years that making Shia women and children their slaves and maids after killing their men folk, is not only a rightful but virtuous deed.

And now this news item for the Islamic mainstream which this chapter seeks to address; those who not only live smug in the belief that Islamic extremism and jihadism is for the kefirs and the apostates, but wish to see it triumphant in India, extending it their moral-psychological support:

Editor of Pakistani English newspaper beaten up for watching TV, PTI Sep 3, 2012

Islamabad: An editor of one of Pakistan's leading English dailies was beaten up by four men outside his home in the port city of Karachi for watching TV and listening to music.

Though the incident occurred on August 27 and Zainul Abedin, op-ed editor of The News daily, reported the matter to police, no action has been taken by authorities so far, journalists in Karachi said. The men who attacked the journalist are members of a proselytizing group.

According to Abedin, four men kicked open the gate of his house in the in Gulshan-e-Iqbal area at 11 pm on August 27 and began to abuse him.
When Abedin went to the gate to talk to the men, he was surrounded and grabbed.

One of the men objected to Abedin watching TV and listening to qawwalis.

When he asked them who they were and why objected to whatever a person did in the privacy of his home, one of the men reportedly said: "We do have a problem with these things but we will solve your problem today." The men beat Abedin and one of them punched him on the face and broke his glasses.

As they kicked and slapped Abedin, the men warned they would not let him go unless he repented and said he would not watch TV or listen to music...

The protagonists and supporters of jihadism could do well to refer to this supremely poignant and instructive confession regarding the passivity of German intellectuals following the Nazi rise to power and purging of their chosen targets, group after group.

First they came for the communists, and I didn't speak out because I wasn't a communist.

Then they came for the socialists, and I didn't speak out because I wasn't a socialist.

Then they came for the trade-unionists, and I didn't speak out because I wasn't a trade-unionist

Then they came for me, and there was no one left to speak for me.

As one can surmise very well from the progress of jihadism in Pakistan, the scenario described in the statement is being played out to perfection there. First it was the Hindus, then Ahmadis, then Christians, then Shias, and then the Sunni core. However, here in India, but for a blast here and a riot there targeting the Hindus, the things are likely to progress in exactly opposite sequence to that. Since it would be too dangerous to begin with force-converting or killing the Hindus, Christians, or even the Shias, they would fall to taking up purging activity among the Sunnis (lying at the core of their ideology) and moving on, by and by, to the periphery. 'First we must consolidate the ideological core and forge unity by purging the corrupting influences and the dissidence from our core-community,' would get to be the strategy. Supposed non-conformists, renegades and the traitors among the Sunnis, that is, all those opposed to their ideology and the goals (either out of conviction, or purely for the sake of long-term good of Islam and the Muslims), and refusing to yield to their moral-policing would be suitably disciplined or, if the need really arose, declared takfir and weeded out.

Bareilwis, especially those given to visiting or looking after the shrines and dargahs would be the first in the line of fire. Next would be the turn of the Deobandi Sunnis…those refusing to grow beards, watch TV and cinema, observe rules of prayer and fast, dissociating from the Hindus, and the like, and (in case of women) putting on veil, wearing jeans, carrying mobiles and studying or working alongside men (especially the kefir men). Then it would be the turn of the Shias. Their crime? Well, why they are not Sunnis? The turn of the Hindus and the Christians would come last. Though they would be getting killed in terrorist attacks all along, but grand project in wholesale pogroms and conversion would begin in perhaps two decade time when they had grown to be around one-third of the population of India, brought Pakistan under their heals, united the Indian Sunnis in a solid whole by firing their imagination with clear possibility of force-uniting the three Sub-continental nations (along with such minnows as Nepal, Bhutan and Sri Lanka), getting to be a majority and turning the united whole into an Islamic Caliphate.

That is not an altogether apocryphal scenario conjured up by a particularly scaremongering scalawag of an author. Even more than half century ago, when the wounds of the Partition had yet to heal and the Muslim population of the truncated India had been reduced to well below 10%, they had been so determined about their goal and confident of their own fecundity and the prowess, and the cowardice and spinelessness of the Hindus, their leaders and their state, as to be declaring from the rooftops: 'Ladke liya hai Pakistan, Hans ke lenge Hindustan' (We secured Pakistan through struggle and fighting, we will take over India peacefully).

Well. In the heart of his heart, even the most avowed Hindu secularist can't say that, half century down, they are not more than halfway down the road to that goal. Yet, it is more than likely that in comparison to the Hindus, the Muslims as a whole would turn out to be manifold greater sufferers of the emerging scenario.

✸

6

COULD THEY HAVE DONE IT THEN

Two of the greatest and most intractable problems destined to put India to interminable turmoil, and thence to disintegration and subjugation are laid out. All other problems destitution, illiteracy, water, housing, energy, and the like facing the nation may get to be solved ultimately, if its economy managed to clock, a la China, 10% growth rate for three decades running. It may get to be a real (and not merely in the imagination of ignorant and self-deluded idiots) superpower, ready to match China chip for chip, and the US stealth-fighter for stealth-fighter. What it is not likely to escape is the two nemeses (and the third) standing just two decades away down its path and ready to waylay it to its permanent disability or doom.

And great irony lies in the fact that, whereas, 10% growth rate will help India solve most of its quotidian issues, it will only serve to hasten the advent of these two scourges. On the food front, while it is likely to yank land away from agriculture and raise demand for meat, milk and fruits among the prospering sections, thus taking even essential cereals off the plates of the majority, on the population front it is likely to enhance the rate of destabilizing of the demographic equilibrium further. For, whereas, in the case of the Hindus, rapid development is likely to pare their population growth rate further as they came up the educational and developmental ladder and in keeping with the imperatives of modernism and nationalism, in the case of the Muslims, determined to outnumber the Hindus in the cause of Islamic suprematism (Kerala being an example), whatever the cost to the society, nation and the humanity as a whole, it will decline far too anemically.

Thus, even if, beginning tomorrow, the majority Hindus stopped producing babies to solve the approaching Nemesis No: 1, India is not likely to escape the approaching apocalypse. Rather, sooner they had put halt to their population growth, earlier the Nemesis No: 2 (and the third in the tow) is likely to grow mature enough to strike.

So, two decades or four, 10% rate of economic growth rate or not, India is well set on course to a future of mass starvation, internecine riots, communal holocausts, disintegration and doom. It is not a revelation of some prophet or crazy rant of a Cassandra. Everybody is dimly aware of the approaching nemesis. So dire however is the likely scenario and mind-numbing the implications, that one fears contemplating or even acknowledging the thing in all its aspects for fear of undergoing mind-bust or heart-collapse. So better to bury one's head in the sand and live, than think of the approaching doom and die every moment. Like the proverbial elephant in the room, nobody wants to acknowledge or mention it and a kind of omerta (oath of silence) has come to prevail over the issue. However, no amount of silence, sophistry or political double-speak can either refute the presence of the elephant, nor stop it running amok when the situation became ripe enough for it to go 'musth' (horny).

The issue however is not only to bring people to acknowledge it, but to drive out the elephant swaying and snorting ominously over the heads of the ceaselessly growing 1200 million. And here we have yet another elephant in our room that only a few want to acknowledge in so many words. It is that the political parties we continue to vote, and the political leaders we gullibly put our national-societal affairs in the hands of, are not of caliber that they can even begin to deal with the first elephant. Let alone possessing caliber or capacity, they don't even intend to do anything meaningful about that. They can't (or don't), because besides being responsible for bringing the things to the current pass, they are not ready to deal with even the first stage of the three stages involved. The three stages could be summarized as:

1. Acknowledging the thing in all its aspects.

2. Taking steps to stem the rot.

3. Stemming it not in the leisurely Indian fashion, but as fast as possible...before the proverbial 'moment of reckoning' struck.

Is the political system we suffer under, with the kind of politicians it breeds, even remotely up to the task? That is a million dollar – nay billion lives – poser that needs to be pondered over by everyone even slightly concerned about the nation's heritage and the future. The situation doesn't look encouraging, to put it mildly. Reasons are multifarious, fundamental and seemingly impossible to be addressed.

Reasons we shall have occasions to discuss, but the cruel fact is that the expectations or the premise, that the people who have brought the things to the current pass and remain engaged in dragging these further down, would, for no good reason, take a U-turn to cut the branch they are perched merrily upon, is like the proverbial hope that burns eternal in fools' hearts. Asking the people to reverse the trend they have made their careers upon, and are busy exploiting and enjoying it to the hilt is like advising a fit and strong octogenarian to abjure alcohol because it might damage his health.

One can very well see that very first thing one would expect to see in a person charged with finding solution to a societal evil or crisis is acknowledgment on his part of the gravity of the situation, as also empathy for the people suffering its fallouts. Now here are eight hundred million hovering permanently on the verge of starvation and an ancient nation hurtling towards doom, and there are our dear leaders, wearing a permanent celebratory grin more worthy of a hyena who just stole the lunch of a lion, than leaders entrusted with the task of solving the most intractable and momentous problems decked out by history to any nation or people.

One would be more than happy to believe the claims and pretensions of the present set of our politicos if it could be established that in the matter of such things as character, vision, wisdom, patriotism, empathy, dynamism, grit and the like, they fare even a shade better than our national political icons such as Nehru, Indira or even Rajiv (notwithstanding the fact that they are the ones under whose watch the things have come to the current pass).

And, here, we don't even intend to compare India with nations, such as Korea, Malaysia, Indonesia, Thailand, or, finally, China – where they had been on socio-economic scale as compared to India and where they are now? For, if one began doing that, these darlings of the masses would begin appearing more like confirmed villains than national heroes.

Moreover, we also intend to ignore the fact that even if there has been some growth on some of the measurable or perceptible parameters, it has been more than compensated by huge decline in those imperceptibles and unfathomables that are infinitely more indispensable for individual evolution, national competitiveness and the societal future. For, there could be no denying the fact that the things like honesty, probity of public conduct, work-ethics and bureaucratic efficiency took severe beating under the watch of our aforementioned national-political icons. After all, it takes some effort to drag a system down into the muck of sloth, corruption and degradation.

Argument is often extended (obliquely by the politicians and boldly by their apologists) whose essence runs along these lines:

> Nation's politicians, hugely sagacious and caring as they had been, able to charm and govern millions, would have solved nation's problems long ago had the albatross of periodic elections not been hanging around their necks. Elections return before they are able to put even their own houses in good repair and well-stocked. And the frustrating need to pander to the peoples' base desires – roads, hospitals, electricity, and the like which these blasted elections entail -- gives them no respite to even think of something of greater national and societal good. Under the conditions, a stint of despotism of some sort (of course of a benevolent kind and only till the `things had been set right` and `more glaring of the evils of the society and the system tackled`) would do a world of good to the nation and the people, especially in view of what the nations like Singapore, Malaysia, S. Korea and, above all, China have achieved.

Now even this argument can be swallowed if it could be proved that the acme of our post-Independence leadership, had it been enabled to brush the exasperating and constraining nettle of democracy, along with its malignant daughter (the elections) aside, would have pulled the nation out of the rut it had been stuck in. That would indeed be the gold standard to judge whether there exists even a remote chance of our nation thwarting the dire fate awaiting it a couple of decades down.

The idea or sentiment that democracy exacts a heavy recompense in terms of good governance and economic development is not something novel and none but Nehru, frustrated with the way it prevented him from giving full reign to his fancies and plans, had given voice to it. Likewise, despairing of the conditions in India that refuse to get better for its overwhelming majority, many people (and staunch votaries of democracy too) have sighed and wondered: 'Wouldn't a dose of *'benevolent despotism'* in the initial decades of Independence have done a world of good for the fortune of India and its people?' It is argued – and cogently – that the very leaders, looked upon now as only mildly successful in delivering, would have worked wonders had they been not hamstrung by the constraints and compulsions that electoral politics subjects the leadership to. The self same Nehruvian Socialism which has come to be held in great contempt nowadays, would have served the country and its people very well in that case. Admitted, that by itself the ploy wouldn't have made the nation great or very rich, for the ills were too many and people too conservative, fractious, illiterate and numerous to be made to 'behave' by some 'benevolent' kind of despotism, but the situation couldn't have been so bad and a solid foundation for modernization of society and development of its economy would sure have got laid.

It goes without saying that the leaders who presided over the helm of our affairs in the initial decades of independence (that is, Nehru & Co.) were the best candidates to be released from the constraint of electoral politics. Enjoying extremely high legitimacy quotient, they hardly needed to undergo the test of election process to validate their mandate to guide the nation's affairs as they deemed fit. That (i.e., not needing validation through the election process) would have proved to be more salutary and disciplining than the grind of elections (which they won repeatedly in any case), with its obligations of pandering to all kinds of rogues and putting up with the filibusters of parliamentary processes. Indeed, it can be argued that the contrivance would have worked well in the case of the later set of leadership too. Awareness, that they were there to deliver and deliver only, with no other claim to rule, would have exerted huge pressure upon them, prodding them to think and act in the right direction. Only the forward-ticking economic and social indicators, and not elections won on less than honorable platforms and by questionable methods would have been their validation and the alibi to rule.

As things stand, in a land where the sentiments of caste and religion, along with fat and liberal purses (and not larger societal and national good) continue to deliver votes banks, repeated electoral victories take the pressure to perform off our politicos, making them feel confident and justified in their waffling ways and roguish conduct. Earlier there used to be the fear: 'If our performance is bad, people won't elect us.' Then it came to: 'Had our performance been bad, people wouldn't have elected us repeatedly.' That has now degenerated into: 'If we are non-performer and corrupt, our rival claimants are worse than us and so people have no choice but to keep us in power.' Or, still more reprehensibly: 'It is all a game of musical chairs; this time out, next time in…all in a day's game. Anyway, since power is about money and not service, and it is money that delivers power and money that rules, we should not deviate from our political dharma of screwing the society and the nation for whatever we are worth.'

That logic and justification wouldn't have been there to condone incompetence or insensitivity, or both. A pressure to act, to perform and to deliver, pressure unrelieved by the safety valve of election process, would have forced them to act in real earnest. A sense of urgency not usually seen in parliamentary democracies would have reoriented their dismal and dawdling attitudes towards the fundamental needs of the country's overwhelming majority. Do not perform, go to the people, sway their opinions by old reputation, personal-charm, clan-loyalties, caste-considerations or demagoguery, and get fresh mandate and make merry -that attitude wouldn't have done. Absence of elections as a barometer to gauge the level of public anger and frustration would have kept them firmly on their jobs. Fear, as to how the public could react in the absence of the valve of elections to let its steam off, would have kept them on their toes. In the absence of an ideology to keep them opiated (as in many Islamic nations or the Communist nations of the yore), only the pace of economic progress could have kept the people suitably contented and quiescent. It is the same kind of pressure the ruling junta in China, now without the opium of an ideology to keep people in a state of idiocy and delirium, works under and delivers. And it is the situation keeping the Middle East Sheikhs and dictators on their prayer-mats 24x7. And though the mythology created around 'Freedom Struggle' and the Independence 'won' kept many people in thrall to the Congress for many decades, India carried no great or universally acceptable ideological opiate that could be deployed to keep people drugged and dumb for too long a period. It would have been a situation of perform-or-perish, with no safety-valve of democracy and elections for the people to vent their anger out.

When talking of such a course of action (that is, benevolent despotism) only the Dynasty (Nehru, Indira and Rajeev) comes to mind. Vajpayee was only a 'C' copy of Nehru and Shastri can't be imagined to have accepted the appellation of 'despot'. Of the rest, only Narsimha Rao showed flashes of brilliance, but he was constitutionally crooked and hopelessly compromised. All others could be said to have been a blot upon the fair name of wisdom, governance and sobriety. Managing to damage India a great deal during their tenures, they would have wreaked havoc in any another system or with longer tenures. Indeed, if the Indian democracy carries the stigma of not throwing even a single great leader or statesman on to the political firmament, it has a good account in its credit side too, in that it hasn't allowed out and out rascals to have free run for too long a period.

Now the inevitable question is: Could these leaders, all coming from a single dynasty and therefore carrying unique charm, authority and power, have, had they been allowed to rule without the 'mandate to rule', succeeded in pulling the 'teeming millions' of the land out of their hellish existence and putting the nation on to a secure future the way the more illustrious of the *'benevolent despots'*, namely, Lee Kuan Yew, Mahathir Mohammad and Deng Xiao Ping succeeded in doing to their people and the nation?

Extremely doubtful, one is forced to conclude with a heavy heart. For, to begin with, they (i.e., leaders belonging to the Dynasty) already enjoyed almost despotic powers, in that there had been little constraint upon them to put the nation's destiny on the right path. No one stopped them from pursuing compulsory education, neither any one forced them to put million obstacles in the way of industry and the enterprise. Contrarily, the opposition constantly goaded them to free peoples' energies from the controls that had been hindering nation's growth and making the bureaucracy and the political system progressively venal, slothful, obstructive and anti-growth and anti-people. Nobody forced them to make the elections obscenely costly, nor stopped them from taking action against the burgeoning corruption that had been doing in the people and the nation. People were illiterate and generally believing; their own party absolutely fawning; opposition divided and weak; judiciary largely compliant and the military loyal: What else a benevolent despot could have wished for? Yet the Dynasty – first Nehru, then Indira, and to a lesser extent Rajiv – failed to deliver. What gives?

They failed to deliver because, unbelievable and outrageous though the assertion might appear, they had no feeling for the people. Despite many assertions and slogans to the contrary, neither they carried empathy for the *'teeming millions'* (mostly low-caste Shudras and Untouchables) of the land, nor did they feel much discomfited concerning their state of degradation. That the problem of destitution, hunger, illiteracy and exclusion existed (as anyone setting his foot in India would know in an instant,) they had been aware too well. That the problem could be solved, they never bothered to bring themselves to believe. It could rather be said with definitiveness that they didn't even think it needed to be solved. Traditional Indian mindset of casteism and fatalism (which was given great lease of life by Gandhi by his intrepid glorification of the caste-system and poverty, as also relentless denigration of advancement the West had been making) had infected their minds too in some measure. The problem was compounded manifold by the virus of aristocracy and the noblesse oblige that had infected their genes. That being the case, utter destitution of their 'subjects' was no more than an old eczema; nagging irritant that one had to put up with, and not pay much attention to except scratching it in a while.

Meanwhile, real goals lay elsewhere: International glory in solving the Suez problem or the Korean War; preaching disarmament and international peace that had nothing to do with the starving millions of Kalahandi, Telanaga or Vidarbha; spewing fire, day in and out, on Diego Garcia or Palestine; or leading, in the name of NAM, a rag-tag band of idiots, bastards and cannibals like Gaddafi and Idi Amin. It could rather be said that poverty was a huge asset for the likes of Nehru and Indira, enabling them to project themselves as leaders of an arch-poor nation and therefore fit for assuming leadership of all the nerdish nations of the world.

It could be said now, with all the advantages that the hindsight provides, that grinding poverty of hundreds of millions of their charge didn't exercise their minds or goad their consciences unduly. Only mass starvation – discontent it was certain to cause – was to be kept at bay. Other than that (as regards Indira and Rajiv), playing chess on the domestic chessboard (shifting chief ministers and setting one politician or interest group of their own party against other), rubbishing rival political parties, riding roughshod over institutions, and devising catchy slogans and launching wasteful schemes to influence vote-banks was the alpha and omega of their ideas of governance and statesmanship. If those ends were met, all the questions related with poverty and good governance – ensuring education, nutrition, health, employment and good infrastructure for their subjects and keeping venality, apathy, arrogance and oppression of the public servants under control – be damned. Genetic urge to preach and moralize consumed them. Pretense to moulding the international order never left them. When one had so heavy a burden to carry, where was the time left to think or do something really meaningful for the children dying of starvation and diarrhea in the boondocks of Bastar or Bidar?

A bedraggled pauper manages to sneak into a seven-star hotel to beg, and finding corporate Moguls squabbling there, jumps in to mediate, lecturing them on the virtues of peace and admonishing them for their unbecoming conduct. That was our Nehru (and partly Indira and Rajiv too). The sight would have been hugely hilarious had it not been so pathetic. One is forced to cry out in horror and embarrassment: 'Oh God! Didn't we have misery and shame enough already that you had to inflict upon us this `Dynasty`!'

It would however be dishonest to insinuate that they didn't appreciate the need to remove the worst features of poverty, or the absolute essentiality of economic strength for a nation for its voice to be heard. But, sadly, though their minds couldn't have failed to realize the imperatives, patently brahminical-aristocratic hearts and the instincts willed something else. Even a beggar appreciates (in fact, he is best placed to appreciate) the gorgeousness of riches or the loveliness of being a millionaire. However, it requires deep sense of shame, stupendous resolve, unwavering focus and ceaseless hard work to come out of the morass of destitution and get to be a millionaire. Millions had been dying of starvation or defecating on roads and railway-tracks behind their very backs, as it were, and here were our exalted PM-ships pontificating on India's spiritual mission to teach the world the principles of humanity to save it from certain suicide. Fact is that the sense of shame or the faculty of appreciating the irony of it all hadn't even touched our Dynasty. Or, perhaps, they were super actors, able to disguise their pain behind smiling faces while their hearts were bleeding all the while. One can't however avoid having a lurking suspicion that the most essential ingredient for success in whatever venture one takes up, namely, consciousness of terrible essentiality of succeeding, was missing from the whole aspect of their being.

And as already discussed, other than apathy or insensitivity, it was a case of spreading their concerns, capacity and the time too thinly and without discrimination on virtually every subject under the sun. In any case, they failed to realize that those empty earthen pots on millions of cold hearths were writing a silent story for the posterity to read about the hollowness of their pretensions, vacuity of their minds and sterility of their hearts.

So, the answer to the hypothetical question, whether they could have delivered even if they had managed to become 'benevolent despots', is a big resounding NO. Why?

Because, ideal was not there. Vision was not there. Theory detailing the path of action was not there. Unity of purpose, subsuming all little goals and objectives was not there. Above all, sense of urgency born out of sense of loss of time and realization of approaching disasters was not there.

And if indeed these all were there, as their apologists – and there is never any dearth anywhere of people ready to defend any indefensible – would claim, pray, where is the outcome? We don't need their arguments. We need concrete evidence. Facts are there for everyone to see. Had the case been otherwise, so many hours wouldn't have been spent on writing this apology of a book.

People say that the nation has progressed much and fast but the population has run faster, nullifying all the gains, and it is reckless loins and fecund wombs that should bear major blame for the sorry state of affairs. That may be true. But, then, why the dispensation (political leadership and the higher bureaucracy) was there for if not to conceive plans commensurate with the ills and exerting to see them brought to fruition? Nehru launched grand schemes dams, steel mills and all that. However, these were not the most urgent things then and even not all that grand, if you come to think of them. Those steel mills and dam things the Tatas and Birlas and Walchands could have done much more efficiently and fast, with perhaps a little help and encouragement from the state.

Indira Gandhi could take credit for the Green Revolution, but she acted in real earnest only under intense pressure on the domestic front and after suffering inordinate amount of humiliation on the hands of the US. And as soon as that pressure was off, with the specter of mass-starvations receded, she was back to her ways – politicking, abusing and undermining every institution she could lay her hands upon, subverting democracy and liberty, tightening control-quota Raj and killing enterprise, and exposing the hateful family disease (preaching and moralizing) at national and international forums.

'But wasn't that an illustrious scion of the Dynasty who opened up the economy and initiated related reforms, enabling it to break the ancient curse of *Hindu-rat-of-growth* for the first time?', one is apt to ask.

Obvious rejoinder is, 'Who got the economy locked up in the first place, if not the Dynasty? Moreover, if indeed Rajeev opened up the economy or reformed the administrative set up of the country (as his apologists would have us believe), what did the (in) famous duo of Narsimha Rao-Manmohan do in 1991 for which they are so much feted (or reviled) to this day? And, pray, what about the pending reforms, said to be really crucial for releasing the economy and the enterprise of the land from many of the negativities still burdening them and for which the economists and the business community keep crying, day in and out?'

Essential fact is that whatever the economy achieved in 1985-89 was due to spring action. If you are sitting on a spring and release it, is bound to bounce up big and long. Another naked truth is that it was the growing fear of China, pulling ahead with escape velocity, and not the wisdom or the instinct of Rajiv Gandhi which forced them to relax some control stifling the economy. As soon as the things became a little tough on the political front, his nerve gave way, basic instinct took over, and he was back to his family ways of trying to control economy, industrialists, media, et al.

'But he brought IT and computer revolution…whose fruits we are savoring till now', so runs the argument of Gandhi-Nehru clan aficionados.

Well, the experience of Narayan Murthy, founder of Infosys, who, right during the Rajiv era, had to wait for years for a telephone line and permission to import a basic computer system so that software could be exported, should be instructive. And if really Rajiv brought computer or communication revolution, then what of the nations, ranging from Madagascar and Mali to Panama and Philippines, where neither computer awareness, nor mobile connections are any the less than India? Rather, India remains at the bottom of the nations in the matter of computer penetration or adoption of IT in its day-to-day governance.

Fact is that Rajiv was not in the least bit different either from his famous mother or the illustrious grandfather, in that, after attending to the unavoidable domestic drudgery (i.e., doing just enough to get the things crawling enough to preempt open discontent and revolt), he would go global glory hunting: Proclaiming relevance of NAM as panacea for world's ills, drafting schemes to make the world N-weapons free.…

It goes without saying that these grandiose, highfalutin things were not what the *'teeming millions'* of the land needed. Plans and action on the front of food, health, education and shelter were what the people and the posterity expected of them. Where were they? Raising impressive buildings to house science labs and earn accolades in return as great lover of science is one thing; solving basic problems of hundreds of millions quite another. They couldn't have failed to realize that every child not enabled to attend school was turning into a weed set to multiply faster than even the main crop and lay the entire field waste. Yet, to the abiding misfortune of the nation, they did precious little to address that.

As things stand, their reign, spanning forty most formative and precious years of India's freedom, can't fill up even a single foolscap paper by ideas, thoughts or concrete plans of action meant to strike at the root of the fundamental issues roiling and undermining the nation. At its most basic, economic and political empowerment of the excluded and the emasculated of the land by way of meaningful land-redistribution, and extension of education and health services to reach even the lowest of the lowlies were the only things the benighted land required of them.

That however was not to be, though platitudes, exhortations and alibis never ran short on supply. Never short upon ranting against 'anti-national' and 'scheming' Opposition, or the exploitative and sinister industry-wallahs and businessmen, ultimate hero of their demonology however was 'foreign hand', which, as per their version, was out to rob the gullible Indians (of their loincloths apparently). And their remedy for all the ills bedeviling the land: Applying ever more socialism to the economy (Translation: more controls and more tightening of the noose around the industry and the enterprise of Indians) and exhorting people to strengthen the hands of patriotic and progressive forces (Translation: vote for us).

It was the story, more or less, of the entire Nehru-Gandhi dynasty. Launching barren slogans and wasteful populist schemes was their idea of solving the problems of poverty. Garibi hatao, control lagao, five, ten or twenty-point programmes, Ganga action plan, Pulse Technology Mission, Navodaya Vidyalaya, and the like – all fake, puny or half baked ideas that elicit nothing but contempt and ennui. Either they all died well-deserved death, or were killed by corruption and apathy germane to the system for which no one else but the Dynasty had been responsible. Only Nehru could be said to have set for himself the task of nation-building in some sense of the word. Due however to some defect in his genetic make up, he mistook image for reality, mistaking nation image-building for nation building proper. Indira got busy in clan building and Rajeev in crony building.

So, even if they had been given absolute powers to do whatever they thought like, there is not the slightest possibility that abandoning much more glamorous and glorious projects of global dimensions, their hearts would have started beating for those who their exalted ancestors wouldn't have deigned even to look in the direction of. Considering the fact that prestige attached with their clan (due primarily to its close association with the Mahatma and its fortuitousness in acquiring the surname Gandhi), along with crushing majorities they continued to enjoy in the Parliament, had already put enormous power in their hands, there seems little chance that further power would have extracted anything novel or more beneficial out of their vaunted leadership. Contrarily, it is not unlikely that absolute power would have corrupted them absolutely and their incorrigible aristocratic pretensions and the superegos, combined with caste-engendered paucity of empathy for those lower in the social order, would have served to turn the country into still greater wasteland. Emergency, when despotic powers Indira acquired were enough to make the likes of Mao and Stalin drool, stands ample proof of the contention. Forced sterilizations and complete censure of the media were one aspect of the thing. But what grand plans this 'best' PM (in many an idiot's view) thought up for taking the land's six hundred million (then) out of the mire of utter deprivation could well be glimpsed in their condition even after more than three decades lapse.

Or, for that matter, the initial years of Rajeev rule...when he had more power in hands than perhaps Lord Curzon, and was more fawned upon by his besotted countrymen than even Lord Nehru had been in his heydays. His ideas for the nation: Ganga Action Plan (which he soon forgot), oilseed mission (which everyone soon forgot), reclaiming millions of acres of wasteland (which only those with their hands in the till remember fondly), and Navodaya Vidyalaya (pray, what is that?) and the like. Thus, things that should have been conceived and accomplished by any dutiful government in a routine sort of way were the man's grand ideas to rejuvenate a nation of eight hundred million!

Other grand plans of the man were, as CG Somiah, a former Union Home Secretary and Comptroller and Auditor General of India tells in his book, 'The Honest Always Stand Alone':

> He wanted us (The Planning Commission) to plan for the construction of autobahns, airfields, speedy trains, shopping malls, entertainment centers and big housing complexes.

That is, whatever he had seen in Europe and the US, entirely disjointed from the then Indian reality.

Thus, it stands beyond a shadow of doubt that democracy or not, even scores of Nehrus, Indiras and Rajivs wouldn't have been able to solve the problems of India. That is because they had been politicians, rulers, kings, aristocrats, diplomats, democrats, lovers, or family persons – that is, anything but empathizers and problem-solvers. Alleviation of poverty for them was a routine job; all that it needed was creating another government department, requiring, perhaps, a joint secretary level bureaucrat to handle it. If the problem got worse, the department could be upgraded to principal secretary level and more World Bank loans arranged to recycle back to Swiss Bank accounts. How simple their solutions and how ingenious!

Launching schemes in the name of children, women, the old, widows, the pregnant, the lactating, the crippled, slum-dwellers, foot-path dwellers, landless peasantry, goat-herders, kiln-workers, *dhaba*-boys, dalits, minorities, backwards, more-backwards and still more backwards, along with fudging data and squabbling about the statistics of poverty has been the name of the game in the entire post-Independence era. How many came out of the rut of destitution, ignorance and ill-health, and how many sank into it afresh needs no elaboration. When one feels pained by, or is serious about a malady, he exaggerates to highlight it and draw everyone's attention towards it. He doesn't fudge data to prove that the malady had been receding... which is what they have been doing all along.

All said and done, there has been a grave poverty of belief; belief that hundreds of millions of the excluded, disinherited and the disenfranchised (dalits and tribals, as also the most backwards castes from all the communities) needed to be properly fed, housed, clothed, educated, and empowered to turn them into proper citizens of a just, equitable and modern nation. Lack of resolve and commitment on the part of the ruling junta, together with everything the nation has been witness to in the last six decades is logical outcome of that primal poverty of belief. Suffice to state at this point that as the population of the country booms unabated, arable land shrinks, environment gets degraded, polity becomes progressively corrupt, institutions corrode, social trust evaporates, vital insecurities begin to bite hard, and hundreds of millions strong cohorts of ill-literate or ill-employed (but full of carnal knowledge and desires all the same) youths roam about ready to join the latest Mao, Hitler, or Bin Laden promising moon or deliverance, that elemental poverty of belief and lack of resolve on the part of the Indian State's title-holders would begin paying really handsome dividends within two decades times. That would be the beginning of turning of the vaunted nation into a haunted land.

Dry arguments apart, it is certain that had they felt and believed in what was required and expected of them, sincerity of purpose would have been getting reflected in billion-plus faces across hundreds of thousands of villages and towns of India. *'Yatha Raja, tatha praja'*. A nation inspired, rejuvenated, ennobled and galvanized into action would have been the natural and noticeable outcome. Does anyone sense something like that? They would have found moral power emanating from their own personality echoed million-fold off the personalities of their countrymen and rising up in a crescendo. Even if the country failed to boost the economic indicators to the requisite level, at least the social indicators (equity, harmony, probity of public life) would have improved vastly, instead of going downhill as they have been. That alone would have washed all the sins inherited, acquired and imposed of our motherland. But, alas, that was not to be!

✳

7

CAN THEY DO IT NOW?

Now, if even the acme of our leadership failed to address the problem in more innocent and congenial times, wielding manifold more power than is possible in the present coalition era, can we expect the present breed of leaders (mere apologies of those of the yore, with much diminished intellectual caliber, moral stature and political authority) to deal with, what without doubt is, an infinitely more fraught situation? Growing lumpenization and criminalization of the society; milling, exploding and seething towns and villages; environment degrading fast and agriculture turning unviable; corruption gone mainstream and things like honesty, ethics and morality completely evaporated; casteism gone more blatant and assertive, and communalism seeped down to the DNA levels; and all round decline in the standards of the institutions of governance and public service: Can even a Cassandra-incarnate wish for more grist to feed her alarm mill?

Even an eight year old boy, carrying elementary commonsense could tell, whether, with the intellectual capabilities and the public commitment of our ruling elite gone down precipitously even as its venality grew exponentially, the things are set to look up or go down further? If previously a CM of UP (say, N D Tiwari or Veer Bahadur Singh) made 10 crores a year, the present crop of chief ministers is minting at least 10,000 crores annually. The election process – bedrock of democracy – though apparently getting better, in that the voting and counting processes have become non-coercive and transparent, has become infinitely more expensive and rotten, relegating those not enjoying access to slush-money completely to the margins. If the things didn't improve much in the decades when the moral fiber and the commitment of those responsible for public good was many times strong and the level of their venality and concupiscence considerably less, what hope could one entertain now when the 'terms of trade', so to say, have stiffened beyond repair or redemption, what with the overwhelming majority of the political class and the bureaucracy appearing to have waged an all out war against the Indian society and nation?

A kind of *'passionate intensity'* seems to have gripped the political and bureaucratic elite of India, making it possessed with, what could be termed, *'obsession of cutting deals'*. Forget simple commissions or briberies of the yore; wink-wink, under-the-table kind of things. It is *'cutting deal'* all the way now, designed to cut at the very foundation of the nation. Hitler may have had his hated SS Brigade, but India has got more fearsome and indefatigable force, capable of not only demolishing nations but digging up the very foundations of the societies, at its disposal. Yes Sir, it indeed has! You could any day see the soldiers of the SSS (Sumo, Safari, Scorpio) brigade in a state of frenzied earnestness, entering secretariats and departments as if they were going into some armory to fetch arms and ammunitions to defend national borders. No such noble mission lies behind their possessed demeanors, however. As anyone with even a rudimentary knowledge of the workings of India's democracy and the character of its political class knows, they are on to some other mission, more vital and urgent. They are, in the Eastern UP and Bihar parlance, on mission *'jugglery'*: Get some 'project' cleared, arrange 'funds' for their phony NGOs, grab public resources and government contracts, get suspension of a particularly corrupt official revoked or have some conscientious or non-compliant officer removed. To wit, they are out to wage their daily battle against honesty, integrity, democracy, Law, justice, governance, society and the nation; and everything in the very names of the aforementioned.

It is beyond the power of realization of their fetid minds that damaging institutions and imperiling the national future in this manner, they are not enriching themselves in particularly edifying or enduring manner. For example, Lalu can't be expected to realize that by his acts of knavishness, cloaked in socialism-speak and cunning tomfoolery, how much has he hurt the interests of one hundred million of his state; not enhancing, even by a remote shot, his own happiness by a sum equal to their resultant misery. He would perhaps have been much happier man had he applied himself sincerely to serve the people of his state, setting standards in frugality and probity for the others to follow. Instead of contempt and ill-repute that he earned as his abiding legacy, appreciation, affection and gratefulness on the part of his people, indeed the entire nation, would have been his recompense. What would have been a thing of greater worth or happiness? Would Gandhi, Nehru, Patel, Subhas or Jinnah (even as in great need of money they too had always been, having great organizations to run) have been happier men had they accumulated a few lakhs or crores in their personal accounts, having filched it from the party coffers or earned as illegal commissions? Incidentally, Patel had only Rs. 262 in his account at the time of his death and Gandhi never had a bank account to begin with, and they were none the poorer for that.

Sadly, that is not the line our 'Maanniya Saansads and Vidhayakjis' and 'Netajis' – Gowdas, Reddys, Yadavs, Mayawatis, Paswans, Pawars, Patels, Sonias, Shielas, Singhs, Jaylalithas, Kalmadis, Kodas, Kamalnaths, Karunanidhis, Yeduruppas, Gadkaris, Sushmas, Katiyars, Nishanks, and the like – think along. Getting more powerful, bold, ruthless and insidious with each passing day, their tentacles have reached every scheme, their hands are on every businessman's' neck, their henchmen are extorting rangdari on every roadblock, and the site of every crime and sin committed upon the land reeks of their trademark smell. And things are not likely to stop even if the likes of Tata, Premji and Narayanmurthi began to be kidnapped for ransom and killed, or the likes of Harshad, Ketan and Telgis polished off not only the lowly co-operative banks, but the Reserve Bank of India itself.

A more ominous turn the democratic polity has taken lately is that now the Indians no more enjoy the luxury of respite from the shenanigans of the soldiers of this SSS brigade. Somebody said something to the effect that in democracies people had the power to change governments and that was enough for him. Even that wry solace or recourse is not open to the Indians any more. A few decades ago, if a particular regime got specially exploitative and oppressive, they had the option of replacing it by voting another political party in. Anti-incumbency they termed it. Incoming ministers and other beneficiaries took some time to get into the groove and get going with the speed and efficiency of their predecessors. Next elections were far away and there was no pressing need for big money to commandeer them. That was the proverbial, *'Age of Innocence'*, compared to what we face today.

That is because now there remain no more the political parties with a semblance of ideology, but only political clans with seamless nests to feather. Political ideologies are dead; only the whore-ideal making as much money in as short a period as possible prevails. Direct upshot is that they are prone to change or support parties with as much ease and brazenness as a slut does its partners.

What is more, now replacing one regime with another – Mayawati with Mulayam, or Jaylalitha with Karunanidhi – turns out to be still less satisfying or rewarding exercise than replacing a Tweedledum with Tweedledee was supposed to be. Rather, in the topsy-turvy land that India has become, democratic process of regime-change has grown to be a fraught exercise, turning the aforementioned smug logic in defense of democracy on its very head. For, forced to keep away from the trough for years and impatient to make-up for the loss, the waiting set of swine sets out to establish new records in screwing the nation right from the day one. Try bringing in the BJP in place of the blighted UPA, and you will see the contention proved in all its naked glory.

Finally, and yet more portentously, now they don't need money merely for running the party machinery and contesting elections– that is, money just enough for replenishing the party coffers, with some saved discreetly for their own election expenses. Now they need it to feed their insatiable lust which is completely independent of the party or the election thing. That is why they now set out to do the *'raping the society and screwing the nation'* job right from the day one, and with vigor and assiduousness that would do the termites or badgers proud. Not unlike the sex-starved Conquistadors, who, besides raping even pregnant native Indian women and little girls as soon as they happened to set foot on the Caribbean, set to ripping open their bellies and private parts even, so filled with passion and frenzy they had got, our honorable ministers too commence ripping open the belly of Mother India the moment their oath-taking ceremony gets over.

Is there no hope left then? Is India destined to sink deeper into the mire of corruption and crime and hunger and holocausts? Are we all doomed? Or, are there still left some silver linings in the dark clouds hovering over the hoary land–that is, a few good politicians we can latch our collective billion hopes on to?

There could be no two opinions that some of the political leaders are still doing their jobs in a fare manner, by and large. Question however is: To what avail? Can they deliver what is really required? Can they, with their time-worn and staid ways, and given the constraints germane to the system (which they are loathe to more than tinker with, being themselves the products of), beat the Time racing against the nation?

Beating the Time racing against the nation…that indeed is the crux of the matter. Do our politicians (or even a few of them) have it in them to enable the nation, carrying greatest set of negativities and deformities ever suffered by a nation, beat the time to reach the shores of survival, peace and happiness? Given the criticality of the issue, we can't afford to answer it in an unthinking or casual manner.

No two opinions that it would be a great mistake to tar every politician with the same brush. Though exceptionally corrupt in practice, they are as corrupt or honest in heart as the rest of the society; only difference being that they have managed to grab or create opportunities for corruption that the rest only aspire to. And they are not some undifferentiated specie like, say, water-buffalos, who all seem to have a similar character, but humans...as loving, emoting, empathizing, aspiring or lusting as any mother's son of them. One of them might be as different from another as, say, Hitler from Chamberlain. If most of them have come to be looked upon (and not wrongly) as insensitive, self-seeking and corrupt rascals, it is not their constitution, but our social and political system (and the entire society is responsible for that) wherein only the most unsavory or reprehensible characters manage to survive and rise.

Muddled and indiscriminating as the thinking and the attitudes of us Indians have been (All brahmins are Gods and worth kowtowing; all untouchables are...well, untouchables and liable to be shooed away), we tend to brush all politicians and bureaucrats as venal and avaricious rascals. Normally, that may have a good therapeutic use in taking out our frustrations, but, in the matter of evaluating leadership dealing in lives and the future of 1200 million, nothing could get more damaging. The world of politics is no more crooked or straight, or devilish or saintly than, say, the world of *babas*, padres or mullahs. There are good, bad and ugly as usual. It is only that while the latter set misleads and screws our Hereafter that nobody knows anything about and so feels but little pain, politicians and the state apparatchiks (in our *mai-baap* dispensation) screw our 'here and now', whose fallouts we feel every day in our wallets and the tummies.

The inescapable fact remains that we can't do without politics or the politicians. Therefore greatest fault – graver than even what we allege these politicians of committing – would be to mindlessly tar every politician as an avatar of the devil and be done with him. Besides overlooking the fact that in a big nation like ours, replacing khadi can only mean bringing in jackboots and unbridled *inspector-raj*, what we do by turning our faces away from politics or the politicians is to undermine a few good men left among them and, by default, let the bad have entire field to them. Discrimination is the word here. Picking the good and the able among them, and then supporting them to the hilt and encouraging them to be still better…that is the only way out for us. It therefore gets incumbent upon us to categorize and sift the good, OK and the ugly.

If the drift Indian public life has taken lately could be imagined to be a mighty but easy-flowing stream, those involved in it (or just about everyone, for that matter) could be placed in three distinct categories: Those swimming against the current; the ones floating along the current; and those not only swimming with the current but engaged in establishing ever new records, desperate to reach destinations they themselves do not know of, or haven't given much thought to. The concept could be understood with examples from another domain…

An executive engineer of PWD department joins his new posting. He is what they call a 'good officer'. He works diligently and within 'norms', that is neither does he feel any hesitation, nor he protests collecting his commission in the works amounting to, say, 5% of the total payments. He neither indulges in, nor does much countenance fraudulent works or outright embezzlement. That is our *'floating along the current'* class. It used to constitute the majority of government departments in the initial decades of Independence.

Another executive engineer refuses to take any cut or commission, takes some pain to prevent others from doing the same, ensures quality of work, and puts strict halt to fake works and phony payments. That is the second set, always swimming against the current. Minuscule minority at any time, he doesn't get the field postings anymore. Nor does he aspire for 'working divisions', for the *'interesting times'* we live in, endeavoring to stop commissions or fake works means clear danger to the life of his own or his family members. Net result is that this class has to spend almost entire life in pushing files at the headquarters and growing into bitter recluse. This set used to constitute the majority of government departments in the pre-Independence era.

It is the third set, given to swimming to establish daily new records which is ruling the roost now in every government department. Oppressing, obstructing and rampaging, filled with *'passionate intensity'* and drowning the *'ceremony of innocence'*, it is painting India red, literally. Filing of charge-certificates over, the first job of our hero is to summon the divisional accountant to tell him that, thenceforth, his share in the cuts shall be doubled. And that, when he is full aware that doubling his cut means it shall get doubled down the line, bringing the already bad quality of works down to abysmal level.

Not content with mere commissions, he proceeds to indulge in fake tenders, phony payments and outright swindle, making so bold as to steal and sell departmental assets even. He is engaged in devising ever new ways to make as much money in as short a period as possible. Swimming with the current to set ever new records, or, in cricket parlance, playing five-day series the 20-20 style, is the motto of this usually politically well-connected set.

Politics is slightly different ball game. Here the blacks and whites of public conduct can't be so sharply delineated. It is more akin to the world of international diplomacy where intentions or the end-purpose is everything. A diplomat indulges in all manners of lies, doublespeak and subterfuge for the sake of his nation, without the fear of perjury charges brought against him or anyone taking much umbrage. That doesn't however mean that he does, or is entitled to do the same (like lying to, or cheating his wife, friends or the tax-people) in his personal life too. Likewise, during a war, a soldier is expected to kill enemy soldiers... as many as he can. But that doesn't give him license to kill them in the peacetime too, or kill his enemies back home to settle personal vendetta. Trustees and custodians of Church organizations, Hindu ashrams, madarassas and charity organizations collect donations to run these, as also to meet out their personal expenditures. These donations do not always come from impeccable sources, nor is their account keeping transparent always. Yet these custodians are not deemed to be corrupt until they live lavishly, fly first class, build private mansions, or stash money in their private accounts.

Similarly, probity in political life means collecting just about enough (and not always from 'clean' sources) to keep the wheels of party organization moving... and then some extra as war-chest. What is of value here is keeping one's conscience and the house clean. After all, manager of a whorehouse needn't be a womanizer, nor that of a pub a drunkard. And politics is not a whorehouse even, but supposed to be a duty towards the society and the nation. Further, the party funds should come through donations (voluntary, even if some quid pro quo is involved), and not commission or extortion. In Indian context, conduct of Gandhi, Patel and Nehru could be deemed ideal in this regard. Big traders and industrialists, whose business ethics had been rather dodgy, were big contributors to the Congress coffer. And they in turn turned blind eye to their shady doings. Party was run, great movements were launched and elections were fought. Of course, they were accused (and not without reason; and here could be discerned germ seeds of corruption and sin that has grown into a banyan tree that doesn't let even small blades of grass of honesty and virtue grow under its shade) of profligacy, as also making the elections way too costly to let an honest opposition compete. Yet, despite essential truthfulness of the charge, even their worst detractors or political enemies never dreamt of branding them self-indulgent or corrupt.

Thus the triumvirate of Gandhi, Nehru and Patel (had they belonged to a government department) should have been put under the rather dodgy category of those floating along the current. But the politics being what it is, they have to be put into the most desirable class of the ones *'swimming against the current'*.

Context laid out, we can now proceed to classify some of our more well known and powerful political leaders as per the classification discussed above.

We may place the leaders like Manmohan Singh, Pranab Mukarjee, Shivraj Singh, Advani, Arun Jaitley, Mamata Banerjee, Divijay Singh, Naveen Patnaik, Khanduri and a few others in the *'floating along the current'* class. They neither try to stem the tide of corruption deluging the public life in India, nor work to exacerbate it in a willful manner. Thus, they are open – and wide open at that – to the charge of omission, and not commission. Though a few of them may not be as clean as their public image, they are not known to be personally greedy... amassing wealth to satiate their lust or for the, proverbial, *'seven generations'*. Yet, they have never sought to put spanner in immoral and criminal dealings of their party men, ministerial colleagues, or even their subordinate bureaucrats. More significantly, they have never expressed more than performa outrage at the corruption eating into the vitals of the society and the nation. So, even if one can't accuse them of being engaged in establishing records, by no stretch of imagination could they be put in the class of those swimming against the current.

The second domain (of those swimming against the current) is a desolate place really. And that is understandable. If even Gandhi, Patel and Nehru are included into it only by putting our belief in a state of *'willing suspension'*, to expect anyone to be surviving in that rarified atmosphere now, when the Sabarmati has run completely dry and the Kalyug has advanced far too much, is unfair, to put it mildly. Straining one's eyes hard, one spots a solitary, benign figure of Nitish Kumar...or, perhaps, there is another rather podgy looking guy going by the name of Raman Singh. Among the entire breed of politicians swarming over the country's political landscape, only these two could be said to have taken some steps (and that too extremely halting and anemic) to stem the tide of corruption in their respective states. That doesn't at all mean that have earned direct tickets to the Pearly Gates; only that their consciences clear and personal record blameless, they would be let in ultimately after serving only brief stints in the purgatory.

Overwhelming majority, in effect, the third category comprises of either reigning, or wannabe record holders. If some of them are not here, that is not for want of intentions, but because they are unlucky or incompetent to carry it off. A few of them are utter hypocrites desirous of keeping their cake and eating it too...that is, they want their billions, simultaneous with preserving their 'image'. Among the previous generation of politicians, Pratap Singh Kairon, Gundu Rao, Bansi Lal, Bhajan Lal, Kamlapati Tripathi, Hemwati Nandan Bahuguna, Chimanbhai Patel, Vir Bahadur Singh, Jagannath Mishra, Arjun Singh, Vidya Charan Shukla, Ramlal, Sukh Ram, Antulay, etc. earned their place in the record books. Likes of Kamal Nath, Kalmadi, Praful Patel, A. Raja, Yeduruppa, Madhu Koda, Rajshekhar Reddy, Pramod Mahajan, Sheila, Nishank are some of the recent additions to the records books. Likes of Sharad Pawar, Lalu, Mulayam, Mayawati and Jagan Reddy too belong to the list, though they are not done yet with screwing the nation. They are not merely corrupt but, what could be called in modern-speak, 'corrupt-plus'.

Categorization done, we think it wise to leave the answer to the question, *'Can They Do it Now'*, and the supplementary poser laid out at the beginning of the chapter, *'if the acme of our leadership failed to address.... could we expect the present breed of leaders....an infinitely more fraught situation'*, to the judgment of our readers.

✳

Part-II

TWO HOPES

1

TWO HOPES • Rahul Gandhi

Whatever has been discussed in the previous chapter is not a novel insight or piece of wisdom. Everyone is well aware of character, capabilities (or limitations) and the potential of the political leaders categorized. That is the reason as to why the names of politicians such as Gadkari, Shiela, Naveen Patnaik, Chidambaram, Sushma, Mayawati, Mulayam, Pawar or Advani for the premiership of India are looked upon but warily by everyone except their respective partisans, nursing, in many cases, less than noble intentions. General public is veering round to the view, and opinion-making brigade of the country is unanimous, that only Rahul Gandhi and Nitish Kumar carry character, capability and credentials enough to guide the affairs of the country in a fair and competent manner – that is, whenever the Dowager Queen decided to dispense with the services of the current incumbent or the Opposition was able to make a comeback.

We have seen as to how our nation and its 1200 million denizens stand at the cusp of a defining moment, wherein any failure or delay in breaking the status quo ante is certain to take them to the point of no return. As things stand, our collective failure to look deep into the character and the capabilities of our supposed destiny-makers has already cost the nation dear, being the major factor in bringing the things to the current pass. Anymore laxity on the account is sure to turn out to be absolutely fatal. It becomes, therefore, our highest patriotic duty to scan and scrutinize, in all possible details, the persona and the record of all the principal claimants to the throne. Being the first in the line of succession, we take up the case of the person regarded heir-apparent by everyone first.

Like father, like son. Resembling his father, he is handsome with a charming demeanour, carries a great lineage (OK, may be not so great, but most well known, without a doubt), and...and...well, leave it.

And again like his father, he carries great prior record of executive efficiency, public service and clean conduct. Before getting to be the Prime Minister of India, Asian Games of 1982 had been organized under his father's supervision; what greater credential or CV could one have required to lead a nation? Likewise, Delhi Commonwealth Games of 2009 were organized under the son's supervision...err, OK, under his watch, with his handmaiden party ruling in the state as well as at the Centre. He was in Delhi throughout and his word was the rule. As for the charges of corruption in the Commonwealth Games...well; the cussed rascals hadn't spared his father – epitome of probity and rectitude, who the admiring and grateful nation had anointed 'Mr. Clean' – too, dragging his name in the swindle that the Asian Games too had been, though in the absence of private TV channels, it had failed to gain the CWG-like fame.

His father suffered untimely loss of one of his parents and, in its aftermath, led his party to a landslide victory – such as it had not seen in the days of his illustrious grandfather even. Our heir apparent too has led his party in two of the principal states of India from the front to great landslides, albeit in the sense that the land has literally slid from under its feet.

After getting to be the Prime Minister of his nation, his father didn't waste much time in getting himself and his party hit with a road-roller (field-gun, to be exact) from which it took a decade and a half to recover. Our hero too, keeping with the fast times we happen to live in, watched it hit with another road-roller called 2G, even before he has come of age to claim his family inheritance.

So, ladies and gentlemen, meet Rahul Gandhi, the new white hope of the ancient land of India and its 'teeming millions'. A man-boy, if there ever was one, who has all the right credentials to lead the milling, starving, ailing, whining, squabbling and doom-ward bound sea of humanity to a future of virtue, plenty, security and peace.

Many a democratic soul bristle at the very idea of Rahul being groomed, projected, aspiring to and ultimately getting to be (Inshallah) the prime minister of a democratic republic. 'A particular brand of loins determining the fate of 1200 million people; that would be a shame of highest magnitude and negation of the spirit of the principles our Constitution is based upon', is the sentiment of this mighty indignant set. 'Besides announcing to the world how deficient in talent we Indians are, it will also tell it that we have still to shed the colonial-slavish mentality... not ready to embrace the democratic spirit that the evolved nations had internalized long ago', is the main burden of their logic.

To tell the truth, we are not on to morality or ethicality of Rahul Gandhi being projected as, or getting to be the chief honcho of our nation. Environment and upbringing is said to be ninety percent man and he has been brought up in an environment literally dripping with prime-ministerial fumes. No other man on the face of earth, not perhaps even Alexander the Great could be said to have received so sustained and quality training and apprenticeship to the throne of a nation as Rahul has. Sages such as Vishwamitra and Plato and Aristotle, and political Gurus like Chanakya and Machiavelli would certainly be approving from the Beyond.

Our sole concern is saving the future of our nation and its 1200 million denizens, and we would care two hoots if the savior came from the loins of Rajiv Gandhi, Ramlal Halwai or the very Devil. We would just bow to him in reverence and gratitude, taking him to be our new God. In this regard, question one must really ask himself is: 'Who should one take to be the real God: Entity 'above there', looking calmly upon the pain and the privations of 1200 million of its Creation, or the one below here, working like mad to relive them of their misery and securing their future?'

Parameter therefore is not loin or lineage, but credentials about capability and the will to deliver. We all know as to how Rahul Gandhi's immediate ancestors, suitably able and well-meaning though they all had been, failed not only to lift the nation out of the mire of destitution and ignorance they had been languishing in, but left it more immoral, demoralized, demeaned and depressed at their death than they had chanced upon at the commencement of their respective reigns. Thus his great-grandpa, Nehru (Tibet debacle, economic stasis, specter of famine hovering continually over the land, humiliating rout at the hands of China, and all-time low national morale), his grandma, Indira (Emergency, rapid expansion of control-quota Raj and erosion of nation's ethical-moral fiber, Punjab and Assam problems bringing the nation to the verge of another breakup), his dad, Rajiv (sowing the seeds of Kashmir Intefada, beginning of crony-capitalism and, most of all, Bofors, the grandma of all scams, providing great justification to the succeeding generations of rascals), and finally the mother, Sonia, under whose watch India has become the byword for corruption and the surname Gandhi a definite slur.

Does Rahul possess the qualities, namely, intelligence,

uprightness, sagacity, empathy and dynamism any more than any of his ancestors under whose watch the nation has sunk to the bottom of all the markers – moral, ethical, social or economic – that mark out modern, happy and progressive nations from the ones suffering a pathetic present and hurtling towards an uncertain future? Is there any chance that with the situation likely to get more fraught by the day, what with the supremacist China and Jihadi Islam breathing down its neck, Prime Minister Rahul won't leave the nation much more down on the selfsame path it is hurtling down along, with perhaps five or ten years wasted?

To find that out, very first thing we must appreciate is that it won't really be a rule by Rahul per se, but that of the clique grooming him for and scheming to see him occupy the coveted position. Whether this clique works to serve the interests of or is supported by the movers and shaker of the country, namely, the World Bank, MNCs, P-note investors and defense contractors, or works autonomously as regular power-broker, we shall never know nor attempt to speculate about. One thing that needs to be kept in mind is that even as snakes and scorpions, which have a habit of lurking in shadows, can't be a force of good for anyone, any person or clique working in shadows, like the infamous *Rasputin*, *'Gang of Four'*, *'Opus Dei'*, or (perhaps apocryphal) *'Elders of Zion'* can't help being sinister in its intent and extremely damaging in praxis.

True to the pattern, this cabal, when it sensed the UPA-I under Manmohan Singh succeeding beyond its brief, turned the knife in to turn it into static, pathetic, despised and shameless UPA-II, never mind the cost to the nation and the society. That way, it robbed the nation of the sliver of hope engendered at the beginning of the new millennium that here was a chance at last of ridding itself of its shame of chronic poverty and hunger, miring it, thereby, yet deeper into the pit of cynicism and despair then it had ever been before.

This exactly is the clique grooming Rahul Gandhi under close and loving gaze of his mother and would be the real force behind him when he finally came of age. With a few remaining specks of wisdom and experience set to leave the party or fade into oblivion, rest of the older set rotten beyond redemption, and the young set failing to show (or not daring to show) any spark, there is little hope or chance that Rahul Gandhi's regime, if it ever came to fruition, would turn out to be any better than that of Mir Jafar, the Nawab of Bengal (1757-60), of whom V. D. Mahajan, eminent historian, had this to say:

> He was neither brilliant nor active. He had not the capacity to carry on the administration of the province with his own hands.

Throughout the period, he was merely a figurehead and the real power was in the hands of Clive. Moreover, he was surrounded on all sides by difficulties...

Now does that ring a bell in your ears?

It is getting increasingly clear that the Prince has but little mind of his own. Through ten years of grooming and tutoring, we have not heard even one word from him which could be said to be infused with sincerity or wisdom enough to engender any hope. Coming into adolescence, every person not congenitally hardwired to be obsessed with himself only (me, my chocolate, my dress, my computer games, my cell-phone, my car, my home, my entitlements and my life) spares some thoughts (how can he help that; such thoughts come crashing on their own) for his society, nation and the environment. He nurtures day-dreams and devises plans, howsoever naïve, for their betterment. One would surely have liked to hear from our king-designate what dreams he dreamt in his excruciatingly long adolescence phase for improving the lives of his future subjects, or what schemes he thought up to rid the kingdom he was going to lord over of some of its abiding shames. Surely, this much his future subjects have a right to know, given the quasi-democratic times he is going to reign in.

Yet, not one piece of writing or speech from him which could give us an inkling of what he makes of this country of million mutinies or his plans for it, even if they be in embryonic form. Of course, some excellent pieces could have been arranged to be published in his name to give his CV some leg-up and address the widespread criticism, but, clearly, they – and you know who they are – know well that the ruse would blow away in the face of the first set of questions likely to follow in the wake. Fact is that whenever this Prince has been forced to speak extempore, he has stumbled badly and hurt himself, forcing his mentors to keep him off the public gaze for a long time to allow the dust of ridicule and doubts to settle down.

Thus, the Cabal and the Congress apparatchiks are perched on the horns of mother of all dilemmas. More they hide their Prince from exposure to media and public scrutiny, more questions about his intellect and the ability to lead a nation of 1200 million, carrying the greatest set of problems among all the nations of the world, crop up. And moment they expose him to the open air, those questions grow ten-fold. Their lot is pitiable indeed, for the eye-candy they had been weaving their dreams around and feasting their eyes upon has almost melted down and soured even before they could savor its taste.

He had more than a decade – entire life, rather – to learn. Import a young person of average intelligence from Somalia or Sudetenland. Tell him that he had five years to go through the history, economy and sociology of India and get acquainted with the principal issues facing it to as to prepare himself well to preside over its affairs. In three years flat the man will begin giving you lessons and instructions dripping with wisdom, insights and commonsense. Awareness of responsibility one was going to be burdened with serves to expand one's intellectual horizons and problem-solving abilities like nothing else does. Rahul Gandhi had been made aware of his past legacy and the future responsibility more than any other person in the world. He enjoyed best upbringing and had best brains at his beck and call for tutoring or consultations. And he has enjoyed indulgence, love and understanding of his countrymen more than any other person in the world. What has he got to show for that?

Justification is proffered that security concerns in the wake of his father's assassination kept the unfortunate boy away from the normal influences of life for far too long and, therefore, he came quite late upon the societal-national scene to commence his learning process in right earnest.

The alibi doesn't stand up to scrutiny. Firstly, the schools and colleges he went to and the friends he gathered around him would have been the same, exceptional security concerns or not. It was only a little different from what his father enjoyed (or suffered) in less insecure times. It is inconceivable that even without the security concerns, he would have been allowed to (or would have liked to) come into contact or fraternize with the slum-dwellers of Yamuna-paar or even the middle-class boys like we people. Further, he had access to all kinds of material and guidance necessary to prepare himself for taking over the throne. After all, the lesser mortals like us too gather most of our knowledge about our society, environment, politics and the nation through class-room, books and the media, and not through personal experience.

By the logic proffered by the apologists of the Prince, the scions of all the rich and the powerful should turn out to be late-learners or ignorant idiots. Far from it! Excellent nutrition, fine upbringing, best education, company of the intelligent and the successful, and the freedom to think ahead and far because their quotidian needs had all been taken well care of, makes them, on an average, outstandingly sharp, fast and smart (though not necessarily honest, sensitive or ethical). That there are persons that had been able to overcome their limiting circumstances, outsmarting even the best talents brought up in best environments, doesn't at all mean that one had better be born in a slum or lower-middle household for making his mark as intelligent, worldly-wise or commonsensical leader of men.

Bare truth is that the kind of child, who one never gets sure about that it had learnt enough to face life even after growing into the middle-age, is a problem that many unfortunate parents and exasperated mentors face. Just how many things could a person be tutored after all? And here is not an ordinary child, but one that is supposed to inherit a great kingdom. What even Aristotle or Chanakya could have done for a young prince that failed to learn simple and obvious lessons from life and the environment around him? Just how long and from how many people can you shield the eternal adolescent, unfortunate to be gifted with – and we are forced to speak the unspeakable here – below par critical attributes?

Even after a decade of launch into public life, they haven't allowed even one 'un-embedded' interviewer to come anywhere near the young prince. Talk of shielding from bad influences! Question, however, remains as to how a person unable to speak coherently and confidently to even one interviewer despite receiving more than a decade of best tutoring in the world, shall be able to face the high and mighty of the world politics, business and the media who shall not be as indulgent, circumspect or afraid of fallouts as the domestic set? Evidently, not satisfied with making it an object of worldwide pity and contempt on account of its continued destitution, illiteracy and evil social practices, they want to turn India into greatest joke too of the new millennium.

Already, the US Congressional Research Service Report (*Economic Times*, Sept. 15, 2011) has this to say about the king-designate of India:

> This heir-apparent remains dogged by questions about his abilities to lead the party, given a mixed record as an election strategist, uneasy style in public appearances, and reputation for gaffes.

Of course, they were polite enough to refrain from saying that the boy is a little thick!

This we shall have to accept: Our Prince Charming is charmingly deficient in the IQ domain. Outcome of more than a decade worth of grooming leaves no room for according him the benefit of doubt. First there was, and appropriately, sanguinity mixed with sympathy that an unfortunate lad, who lost his father and had to be kept shielded from normal influences and exposure due to security reasons, should not be judged too harshly and be given time to find his moorings. That excuse has worn off completely by now. After all the lad is not even a young man anymore, but a middle-aged man of 42.

In any case, and whatever the background or the alibis, his deficiencies – slow learning ability, glaring gaps in thought processing and articulation, fear of facing questions and deliberate, almost criminal, silence in the face of even most burning of issues; in short, rather low acuity, lack of essential commonsense and weaknesses of personality – have become more than apparent to one and all. And as singular lack of spark or success even on a single front is proven beyond a shadow of doubt, there stands no reason as to why a nation, which already carries more than its quota of sufferings, should suffer yet more only to oblige the imperial aspirations of the Dynasty or the designs of a clique scheming in the shadows?

However, had acuity of the young prince been the only problem, this unfortunate nation could still have put up with it. In fact, what this country requires is not people of high IQ (which only helps the people loot this country even more efficiently; not serve it) but high EQ, that is, possessing high ethical and emotional quotient; given more to conducting themselves ethically and caring for their country and the compatriots, and less to sucking them dry. If Rahul Baba's deficit on the crucial front is compensated duly with high EQ, the nation would welcome him with open heart to preside over its affairs. Economy, foreign policy, defence, home and the like could be well taken care of by people with high IQ and low EQ; Pawar, Chidambaram, Sibal and the like. What the nation needs at its helm is a person who cared for the country and its people, and didn't countenance the insensitive and wayward ways of his ministers and other subordinates. Does Rahul Baba possess that EQ? Ahem...er... well. Extremely unfortunately for the country and its *'teeming millions'*, the record here is even more ambiguous.

And, sadly, things like commonsense, commiseration, empathy, awareness of responsibility, sense of shame, governance and the like can't be taught like nursery rhymes, nor can these be purchased in open market like so many kidneys and livers. Had that been so, it was but a matter of enacting a mini-Bofors or Tatra to arrange these.

'That is a malicious innuendo having no basis to it. Rahul has done nothing that could even remotely be termed unethical or insensitive. Fact is that neither has he held any official position to be able to do anything wrong, nor has he ever invited allegations of the kind. Insinuations of this nature are completely mischievous and unacceptable', one can envision the entire Congress junta erupting in indignant rage.

First let me tell you a real story. I know of a person who has amassed tens, if not hundreds, of crores working in a state department. His son got good rank in the IIT and was duly interviewed by newspapers. Nothing unusual there, but surprising piece was boy's statement that what he hated most was corruption and the corrupt people, and his life's cherished mission was to fight this national scourge. So far so good; it would have been too much to expect an Indian boy to ask his father to desist from corrupt practices and to disown his past to begin life anew. But what would have made him live up to his noble sentiment was living a frugal hostel life, befitting the son of an honest government servant. Yet, his hostel life was far from being that. Plane and not train was what he always traveled by during his hostel days and, presently, he has gone to do his dad-funded MS in the States.

Yet the boy would like to think himself clean and ethical, even though he nurses no qualms benefiting from his father's ill-gotten wealth and can't be imagined to renouncing it when the time to inherit it came. And technically he is clean, for he has neither earned, nor had the opportunity to earn sin-money. As for the inheritance part, neither it is illegal or immoral for a son to inherit his father's wealth, nor it is expected of the sons to investigate the real source of their ancestral wealth.

Or, for that matter, Vikas Yadav (Nitish Katara Murder) or Manu Sharma (Jessica Lal murder); you could call them murderers but otherwise honest and clean, for they may not have done anything wrong on the corruption front. Conceivably, they had no need or time to do anything on the issue, busy as they had been painting Delhi red on the strength of their father's wealth. Their father had been on the job for them. What if it all was ill-gotten...bootlegging, extortion, land-grab and the like? Sons can't be called to account for their father's sins.

And, by that yardstick, Rahul Mahajan is an epitome of ethical-moral living. He hasn't committed a murder even!

Our Rahul Gandhi too has been brought up in luxury; what if the money for it comes through less than transparent means? And he continues to live as a king-designate should live, with planes, helicopters and caravan of SUVs at his beck and call. What if this money comes by way of 2G, CWG or any other goddamn G? His own hands are clean and his life an entirely Christian life, literally.

He may or may not have been leading a Christian life, but the most revealing and ominous part of the thing is that the man is not even claiming! His mother and the Cabal know the dangers of doing that, i.e., claiming a thing that he (they, rather) doesn't intend to live up to and which shall be held up against him if something fishy came to be exposed in the future. Myopic advisers of his father had tried to create an aura of *'Mr. Clean'* around him, with the result that a single revelation brought him crashing down. Those who do not covet the title or the accolade (Lalu, Maya, Mulayam, Pawar, Badal, Karunanidhi et al) enjoy much longer shelf life, for their acts do not attract as much attention and invite less opprobrium. But, then, these kinds of politicos are no longer considered prime-ministerial material, having lost the stature necessary for the top post.

Little wonder then that when it comes to the most burning issue blighting the nation and its billion lives, we have the silence of galaxies from this Pole Star burning bright on the nation's political firmament. 2 G, CWG, Lokpal Bill, black money in foreign banks, Tatra affair, Coalgate or gross misuse of CBI – Rahul Gandhi's ability to do a vamoose, and not allowing even a shadow to cross his face, as if he had been living in another world all that while is deeply unsettling, if not indicative of some sinister aspect of his character. (And here we do not intend to talk about his own *Jijaji* and the 'National *Damaad'* even; assuming that he was entirely unaware of the goings-on in his sister's home) It serves to show that in certain matters of self-interest he is not all that dense as the world thinks of him. Evidently, he doesn't want to commit himself to anything that neither he, nor his party or the clique behind him has any intention to honor or live up to. But like all simpletons that display surprising acuity when their vital (but in fact petty) interests get involved, he too is being too clever by half. If instead of simply evaporating from the scene, had the man-boy chosen to intervene decisively in the matters agitating the national conscious, that would have enhanced his moral stature and the political standing manifold more than what the million advices from the likes of Digvijay Singh, Satyavrata Chaturvedi and Ahmed Patel did. But, again, how could he, for neither does he intend to keep his conduct clean (when, ultimately, he inherited his family crown), nor is he innocent of the fact that most of the funds from the mega-scams roiling the nation had been channeled to his party coffers, that is his family concern, that is him, in the final analysis?

It won't be too much to say that the people, even the staunchest supporters of the Congress, have all but lost all hopes from the man-boy. Otherwise nothing explains appearance lately in *The Times of India* of the kinds of blogs that would have been thrown into the trashcan only a year ago. We can sample this one from one Monobina

Gupta (*'Rahul Gandhi's Ode to Silence'*, 14 September 2012):

One striking thing about the Congress leadership has always been their silence. From Manmohan Singh to Sonia Gandhi, and now the prince-in-waiting, Rahul Gandhi. Prodded from all sides, sometimes even by his own party leaders like Salman Khurshid, and badgered by his opponents, Rahul doggedly continues to be a 'leader' of few words. He is untouched by criticism now pouring forth from all quarters, at home and abroad. Will he or won't he join the cabinet? Will he or won't he accept a greater role in the party? Will he speak on the crucial controversies at hand – Coalgate, FDI in retail, the Kudankulam nuclear plant? Or do we have to read his silence to get an idea on all these issues that have taken centrestage in politics? Will he take Narendra Modi head on? Or will he save himself the embarrassment of leading the charge of his feeble party in Gujarat?

The answers are not 'blowing in the wind'! It's as if the entire nation is duty bound to guess the prince's thoughts, his opinion.

Congress veterans like Digvijay Singh rubbish The Economist's latest unflattering assessment of Rahul Gandhi as being of little relevance. Here is what the magazine has to say about Rahul : "Nobody really knows what he is capable of, nor what he wishes to do should he ever attain power and responsibility. The suspicion is growing that Mr. Gandhi himself does not know".

You may ignore the cutting remarks made by a foreign publication. But what about the growing cynicism about the 42-year-old's political capabilities, his reluctance to speak his mind in and outside parliament? Congress veterans spent years, even when Rahul was well into his mid-thirties, holding out alibis for his silence, his lack of people skills, taking the plea that the prince was grooming himself for the larger battles ahead of him.

Well, the larger battles are now being played out in all their diversity, every day, in every corner of the country. Yet Rahul doesn't speak. True, you can't hold his introvert disposition or his shyness against him.

Like Manmohan Singh, Rahul too seems to believe that some, or plenty of waving of hands, is enough to inspire confidence; enough to gain credibility as Congress' future prime ministerial candidate.

And, much like the fame of another prince (Prince Harry), the fame of our own prince too has reached far and wide. Reviewing a biography of Rahul by one Aarthi Ramchandran, the venerable *The Economist* has this to say (*'The Rahul Problem'*, Sep 10th 2012):

WHAT is the point of Rahul Gandhi? The 42-year-old scion of the Gandhi dynasty, which has long dominated India's ruling party, is still the most plausible prime ministerial candidate for Congress at the looming 2014 election....

Promoting Mr Gandhi now would in theory make sense for Congress. He has long been presumed the successor-in-waiting to Sonia Gandhi, his mother and the party's president. He needs time to start showing some skills as a leader before campaigning starts in 2014. And for as long as Mr Gandhi does not rise, it is hard for other relative youngsters to be promoted without appearing to outshine him. That has left Congress looking ever older and more out of touch.

But he has long refused to take on a responsible position, preferring to work on organizing Congress's youth wing, and leading regional election efforts, both with generally poor results. The problem is that Mr Gandhi has so far shown no particular aptitude as a politician, nor even sufficient hunger for the job. He is shy, reluctant to speak to journalists, biographers, potential allies or foes, nor even to raise his voice in parliament. Nobody really knows what he is capable of, nor what he wishes to do should he ever attain power and responsibility. The suspicion is growing that Mr Gandhi himself does not know.

The latest effort to "decode" Mr Gandhi comes in the form of a limited yet rather well written biography by a political journalist, Aarthi Ramachandran. Her task is a thankless one. Mr Gandhi is an applicant for a big job: ultimately, to lead India. But whereas any other job applicant will at least offer minimal information about his qualifications, work experience, reasons for wanting a post, Mr Gandhi is so secretive and defensive that he won't respond to the most basic queries about his studies abroad, his time working for a management consultancy in London, or what he hopes to do as a politician.

Mrs Ramchandran's book, along with just about every other one about the Gandhi dynasty is thus hampered by a lack of first-hand material on its subject. Mr. Gandhi can only be judged by his actions, his rare and halting public utterances, and the opinions of others who work near him.... "Brand" Rahul, she suggests convincingly, is confused. A man of immense privilege, rising only because of his family name, struggles to look convincing when he talks of meritocracy.

The overall impression of Mr Gandhi from Mrs Ramachandran's book is that of a figure who has an ill-defined urge to improve the lives of poor Indians, but no real idea of how to do so. He feels obliged to work in politics, but his political strategies are half-baked, and he fails to develop strong ties with any particular constituency…..

Opportunities have presented themselves to Mr Gandhi in the past couple of years. One was the Anna Hazare anti-corruption movement. Mr Gandhi might have intervened at some point, and tried himself to tap into public anger over corruption and inequality, and drawn some of the sting of the Hazare camp's efforts…. Instead he flunked the test in hiding, not daring to speak out, other than in one ill-advised intervention in parliament.

Cruel fact is that our Rahul is not even a bit unlike the pampered scions of corrupt politicos, bureaucrats, middlemen and contractors of different shades and denominations that Delhi's five-star hotels and night-clubs run choc-a-bloc with: Manu Sharmas and Abhishek Vermas and Sanjeev Nandas and Shahid Balwas, and the like. It's only that he didn't get opportunities to cultivate more unsavory friend circle and getting to be that arrogant and foul-mouthed. That appears to be the only distinction and the saving grace. Otherwise, he seems to be moving around in the same ethical-moral universe, thinking of entire India to be his oyster. He (and his sister, even more than him) is afflicted with the same sense of entitlement and noblesse oblige that the breed of all such heaven-borns usually is. And instead of nursing authentic empathy and sensitivity towards his compatriots, or sense of shame for nation's degradation and infamy, he seems to carry the same *'throw schemes and slogans in their way and capture votes'*, or *'manage emotions of poor to manage elections'* attitude that all his ancestors were specially given to.

What is absolutely clear is that he has shown no inclination of getting down from the tiger that his ancestors – great grandfather, grandmother and the father – had first ridden. The tiger is huge cost of running party apparatus and fighting elections which they all had willfully contributed to raise to astronomical levels. That tiger eroded the moral authority of his grandma; devoured the PM-ship (and his life too, as a direct consequence) of his father and gave permanent stigma to his otherwise fair name; and has brought his mother's name under fresh scrutiny. Now clearly is the turn of him, latest scion of the Dynasty, for which he seems to be preparing rather well. Before long, he would get inextricably bound with (and would have to allow his ministerial colleagues, the chief ministers, party-apparatchiks and the bureaucrats to do likewise) an unstoppably widening gyre of corruption fated to come crashing one day. That would bring him down with a huge thud and ineradicable muck on his face, but, much more sadly and consequentially, leave the nation a yet greater ethical-moral desert than it had been at the commencement of his career.

In your author's view, the most depressing part of the entire Rahul saga up to now is that though he has made all the politically-correct noises about the poor (any rascal is obliged to do that), he has never uttered a word (let alone moving his little finger) about the need to reign back the steeds of corruption pulling the country towards a future of stasis and doom.   Never a word of advice to the Congressmen about the need to show rectitude and thrift so that the tide of corruption deluging the ancient land could begin to be rolled back and a beginning to instill some morality and decency in the public life made.

And author's considered and unshakable view is that in a dirt-poor nation like India, where at least one hundred million people remain perched always on the edge of starvation-death, a person carrying low ethical quotient can't claim to be strong on emotional quotient. Thus, one supporting or getting involved in a system that loots money which comes, in the ultimately analysis, off the plates of the poor, can't be truthful in expressing empathy and solidarity with them by visiting their huts, partaking meals with them, and throwing manifestly phony and leaky state schemes in their way to give some rotten crumbs to them. Prophet (PBUH) had termed such people hypocrites and Allah has reserved most desolate part of Hell for them.

If an opinion poll were to be taken in India asking people about the greatest curse (besides corruption) that continued to undermine the socio-economic well being of the Indians and subvert democracy and justice, a good majority would unhesitatingly vote for the caste-system. Along with the God-Devil, Heaven-Hell, Kefir-Faithful kind of Manichean dichotomies that served to divide the humanity into great and permanent *'either with us or against us'* camps, caste-system has been the most sinister, invidious and inhumane artificiality ever devised. Gender, racial features, skin-color and language have at least some identifiable (howsoever flawed or reprehensible) markers to support discrimination; religion and caste have none. Yet, despite recognizing too well the illogicality and perniciousness of it, the Hindus continue to live, vote and…well, milk their caste.

Happily born a non-Hindu, our king-designate was entirely free of the caste thing (or so one thought). One could have fairly hoped him to be a great agent for ridding the Indian political system (and therefore the social system too by association and influence) of the caste blight. But, alas! That hope too lies shattered. In one fell stroke, the Prince lost the only clothes he had managed to cling on to up to now.

Manifestly deficient in the matter of intelligence, ethics and emotional quotients, the young prince made it clear, gratuitously and unprompted, that he is not at all lacking in that quintessentially Indian bigotry of caste.

Thus speaking in an election review meeting post-UP debacle, Rahul had this gratuitous declaration to make: *"I am a Brahmin...and general secretary in the party."*

Now, what does it tell about not so young or naive Prince who couldn't have been unaware of the implications of this smug assertion?

It is that he is either one ungrateful reprobate who has no qualm in rejecting his Zoroastrian (Parsee) ancestry (his paternal grandfather was Zoroastrian), or an ignorant whelp who doesn't know that caste is inherited from one's paternal side and is not like religion that one could convert to as a matter of choice. Or, that he is a petty imposter who, though knowing full well that he was Zoroastrian by ancestry (and perhaps Catholic by faith), lied about his caste in the hope of swaying the politically and intellectually powerful community of Brahmins. That also shows what low opinion he carries of even this most intelligent section of the country, thinking of them as casteist-emotional fools.

And that unsolicited comment is in stark contrast to his reply when someone asked about his religion. He thought about it for a while and replied: *"The Indian flag is my religion."* (*Outlook*, Aug 27, 2012)

Again, what does it tell about the man? That whereas he is cynical enough to flaunt unprompted his (presumed) caste credentials for political gains, he is equally cynical about the religion thing, hiding it from the majority Hindus (if he is a non-Hindu), or to court favor from the Congress's targeted vote bank, the Muslims (if he is a Hindu).

Yet, despite running low on the vital quotients, despite nothing to recommend him except his lineage (and we have seen that there is nothing really great about it), despite his manifest eagerness to adopt the first refuge of an Indian rapscallion politician (caste), and the first refuse of a secular Hindu politician (eagerness to show that despite being a Hindu by birth, how he hates Hinduism from his guts), and against all evident logic, he may get to rule the country. And further, Godwilling, he may turn out to be not so....well, what we have railed against him anon, but rather a successful PM (as success in India is defined or understood). Miracles do happen after all and India is nothing if not a land of miracles and miracle-makers.

The issue, however, is not one of merely carrying on. For, if you merely carry on, you are carrying the country on the same path it had been hurtling along all along. Question is to reverse the path, and that too with double quick speed. In addition to full comprehension of the quotidian problems (and their solutions) of food, water, power, education, health and crime facing the nation, what India expects of its supreme leader is willingness to acknowledge the presence of (not to say the ability to deal with) the demons conspiring to rob the peace and well-being of 1200 million of the land's denizens. Is Rahul even remotely up to that?

Is he more erudite and sagacious than his great grandfather Nehru, more spunky and maneuvering than his grandmother Indira, commands more initial goodwill and credibility than his father Rajiv, or is more feisty and scheming than his mother Sonia? Or, for that matter, is he more anything than anyone?

And, if indeed he has anything worth writing home about, pray, why it is that even once during the last eight years the UPA has been in power, the waiting suckers out there have failed to espy even a glimmer of it emanating from the persona of this putative saviour of India? Do not tell us that he had been merely an unpaid apprentice, having nothing to do with either the government or the party, and, so, cannot be judged on the basis of their alleged deeds, lapses, decline or the infamy. Here is M.J.Akbar, a fairly perceptive and conscientiously impartial observer of the political scene in India (*India Today*, September 17, 2012):

> .... When in the last eight years has Rahul Gandhi ever been out of power? He has been the working president of the Congress whenever he has chosen to work.

> Whenever he has taken a decision, it has been implemented, either at Government or party level. He pushed, where he could, for a younger generation of chief ministers; and got them in Kashmir and Andhra Pradesh. He sought to revolutionise Congress through the Youth Congress. No one stopped him. He wanted to lead his party's campaign in Bihar from the front, selecting candidates from a personal template. He did so. He chose to stake everything in his kitty on the prospect of a few seats more in Uttar Pradesh. He went ahead.

> Each time the consequences were disappointing, if not disastrous. He was never held accountable. Rajiv Gandhi was

never so powerful when his mother, Mrs Indira Gandhi, was prime minister. Dr Manmohan Singh began his second term as PM by offering to step down the moment Rahul Gandhi wanted the job. There has been some depreciation since then, and Dr Singh only expects Rahul Gandhi to join the Cabinet. Every senior or junior Congress leader ritually anoints Rahul Gandhi heir and pride of Congress; it is the current version of an oath of loyalty. Rahul Gandhi can pick any portfolio he wants. He could become home minister this week and use his abilities to sort out Assam and Telangana, both of which will be at the top of his agenda if he becomes the PM. Is there a single wish of Rahul Gandhi in these last eight years that has been thwarted?

It is an important moment in a young MP's life when a prime minister invites him to join the Government. But such an offer is quite meaningless to anyone who controls the Cabinet, either directly or through a mother's proxy.

Yet, one is constrained to ask, what has been the outcome?

Be that as it may, one thing can be averred with near conviction... Even if he came to acquire the premiership of the country by a stroke of good luck, incompetence of the opposition, or the continuing misfortune of Indians, and managed to cling to it for five years or ten, at the very best, we can expect no more than more of the same from Rahul Gandhi. By that time India would have advanced much more on its downward spiral, with the window of escape fast closing upon it.

So, sooner the nation, and also the Congressmen (that is, if they still carry a modicum of responsibility towards society and the nation, and have not sold the last scraps of their meager consciences to the devil of self-aggrandizement) accepted the fact that this Prince has absolutely nothing to show expect his dubious lineage and compulsory modesty, better it would be for the long-term future of everyone around.

The thing is not for Rahul to ponder over or decide, for not even a confirmed moron or nincompoop thinks of himself in those terms. It is for the self-styled custodians of the nation's well-being, that is, intelligentsia, media, academia, opinion-makers and professed custodians of public good to ponder over and ask themselves.

✳

2

TWO HOPES • Nitish Kumar

He is personable, suave, well-meaning and hard-working. He is personally honest and beyond such things as avariciousness or venality. And he is entirely free of that characteristic affliction of Indian politicians: caste-chauvinism. That makes him stand out among almost the entire crop of Indian politicians.

Above all, he is a veritable knight-in-shinning-armour who slew the 'Demon-King' almost single-handedly and released a state of nearly one hundred million suffering souls from its decade and half long night of willful philistinism, cultivated loutishness and calculated stasis. He thus set it on to the highway to progress and prosperity whereof it can, Godwilling, hope to join the national economic mainstream (whatever it be worth) in a decade or so.

Meet Mr. Nitish Kumar...only hope of the benighted state of Bihar and one of the two white hopes being projected as new-millennium saviors of India.

However, saving a state from the tyranny of, what could be termed, *'Lord of the louts'* is one thing, pulling it out of muck of ignorance, crime, casteism, overpopulation and destitution is quite another. And the issue here is not merely nursing the invalid back to normal health, but make it sprint to make up for many lost decades. If the record here turns out to be not as bright as it should be or is made out to be, it impinges directly upon this hoped-for saviour's supposed ability to lead the nation. And, as the question before the nation is not merely running its affairs in a business-as-usual manner – lurching from crisis to crisis; keeping things like downright starvation, energy crises and balance-of-payments under precarious control; and keeping the mortal enemies at the borders at bay by a combination of obsequiousness and colonial-style trade – but saving it from the two agents of doom (and the third) lying in wait to waylay it and club it to death or debility, anything less than the best shall turn out to be positively fatal.

For, it must be acknowledged here that any person aspiring and jostling to lead the country, but not carrying requisite competence to save it from the impending doom, just muddies the waters and wastes precious time, even as the window of survival closed fast upon the nation. He thus becomes an unwitting agent of those agents of doom.

Does Nitish have that level of competence...that is the billion-souls question.

One thing we need to understand at the very outset... If only they freed the energies and the enterprise of people from million controls and demands and delays imposed by brigades of *lekhpals* and *tehsildars* and inspectors and *'bada-babus'*, nothing much would be left to be done by the governments. And if they were unable or unwilling to do that, what else they did – launched million schemes, distributed bicycles and mobiles and laptops, and gave out stipends and pensions and *'dhans'* (purse) of hundred kinds – shan't be of any avail. Has Nitish freed Bihar of these sharks and piranhas battening upon its denizens? Significantly still, does he even intend to do that?

We have seen how the spring effect – taking the load of negativities off – freed the nation's economy of its *'Hindu rate of growth'* syndrome during Rajiv's time for which he earned deserved acclaim. Of course, here we need to ignore the bitter truth that his own mother, who he had anointed the 'mother of the entire nation', had been responsible for most of those negativities. Fact is also that it was not a particularly reformist heart or some kind of epiphany striking Rajiv, the Congress, or the Indian economic-bureaucratic establishment in general, but rather the fear of rising China – way it had been reaping the benefits of letting loose the talent and the enterprise of its billion-plus and threatening to pull light-years ahead of its hated enemy to the south – that made them go easy on some the worst features of the accursed *'control-quota raj'*.

As discussed earlier, releasing a spring from its compressed state is one thing. We all know how easy it is to take a weight off a thing. Real measure of prowess comes when the spring has to be stretched hard to its full length. In practical terms, it requires inspiring people to realize their full personality and the potential, in addition to taking the obstructing, oppressing and battening dirigisme off them. It requires moulding their outlooks in a way to make them keep comparing their status with only the best in the world. Regarding Indians, it meant enabling them transform their utterly third rate lives fashioned by Hinduism-moulded casteist-fatalistic, Gandhi-inspired *'Hind-Swarajist'* and Nehru-Indira created Third-Worldian mindsets.

Further, the inspiration imparted must not be theoretical preaching merely, but must run in tandem with hawk-eyed vigilance and Sisyphus-like patience and hard work. Translated, it means keeping strict check upon the corruption-brigade of *lekhpals* and inspectors and *bada-babus* and section officers and secretaries and ministers who won't move even a paper-weight from over a file without first exacting their share of rangdari. Of equal importance is the aptitude and the inclination for thinking up and putting in place policies, ranging from the domestic ones of agriculture, industries, infrastructure, education, health, crime-control and speedy-justice, to foreign, defense and, what could be termed, power-projection...of soft as well as the hard kind.

Well, in Bihar it was a double spring effect, for the spring had been suppressed by double weight. First it was the chief custodian himself of the state (and not merely his minions). Interested only in clan-building and looting the state, reveling in his own philistinism and vulgarity like a swine rolling about in muck, and instinctively hostile to any idea that smacked of progress and well-being of the people, he began projecting things like electricity, irrigation, roads, industrialization and education as upper-caste fads and abominations gravely injurious to the health of the non-upper-caste majority. He thus turned the state into the biggest enemy of development and the people. In one fell stroke, replacement of that anti-people regime with the pro-people Nitish Kumar led dispensation took that one great load off the spring.

The second thing weighing upon the people of Bihar and their enterprise which the regime-change took off was state sponsorship of crime. Yes, you have read that right. It had been state sponsorship all the way, for nearly all the criminals of the state found an enthusiastic patron in the robber-baron perched at the helm of the affairs who felt no qualms in bestowing prime positions to them in his party hierarchy; greater the criminal tendencies and lengthier the crime record, bigger the post given. It took some (OK, great; for organized crime was getting entrenched in the state since at least the L.N. Mishra-Indira Gandhi days) effort on the part of the new chief minister to take that incubus off the people. That helped release the pent-up energies of the people and has been the greatest spur to state's growth. For, it is little use applying your brains, or slogging your butts off to get rich (even by Bihar standards) when you are in perennial danger of losing your new-found wealth, with your kidnapped brother or murdered son presented as a ghastly kind of bonus.

There is no gainsaying the fact that the act of taking these two negativities off the chest of the benighted state is sufficient to earn Nitish Kumar a gold-lettered tribute in the annals of Bihar. It would be churlish to quibble about that.

There is little doubt that Lalu's departure itself was a big relief and image makeover for the state of Bihar. Though Bihar had long ceased to provide security of life or livelihood to its denizens, it was during the period of Lalu that the terms Bihar and Bihari came into their own as terms of derision and ridicule. And even as every industrial and metropolitan area across the country thrived upon and acknowledged the native industriousness, intelligence and grit of the Biharis, all round scorn and ridicule, thanks mainly to the loutish buffoonery of Lalu, came to be their sad lot. 'People who continued to elect people like Lalu can't be up to no good', so ran the subconscious reasoning. Biharis too lost confidence in themselves. By consigning Lalu to cleaners and choosing to elect and reelect Nitish, they have changed their image in the perception of others and regained confidence in their own capacity to be good.

On his part, Nitish Kumar has repaid the hopes and confidence placed in his leadership by the people of his state in an equal measure. More than any other thing, Bihar was notorious for its organized crimes and kidnappings for ransom. While the mafias cornered almost every sector of state's economy, distorting its very shape and running it aground, kidnappings removed all incentive on the part of the people to work hard and excel. Additionally, it forced the talent and enterprise to flee the state, beggaring it in every which manner. Nitish had his primary task cut out for him and he took up the gauntlet in full earnest. Scrapping of 'Local area development fund', great source of corrupt income for the MLAs and MLCs, was a clear signal that he intended to come down hard upon the corrupt practices of politicians too.

Bringing in clean (comparatively speaking) bureaucrats and police officers, he forced the Mafiosi to call off the more glaring and pernicious of their operations and lie low. Speedy trial of criminal-politicians – Anand Mohan, Shahabuddin, Pappu Yadav, and the like – that had thrived under full protection of Lalu, helped restore the fear of God and law in their hearts and confidence in the state-machinery among the general public. His constant harping upon the theme of punishing the corrupt bureaucrats and seizure of their ill-gotten gains by the state too kept the venality and depredations of the higher bureaucracy under some check.

On the economic-infrastructural front too, Nitish had his task cut out for him. Roads and bridges are the arteries of an economy and they had gone next-to-absent under the Lalu Raj, since the funds, as were made available, were siphoned off by the politician-mafia-bureaucrat-engineer nexus even before they had touched the ground. Nitish took up the task as a man possessed. 33,000 kilometers of roads, connecting even some of the most godforsaken villages, along with innumerable small bridges came up in eight years of his rule. Bihari, along with his goods, implements, enterprise and hope was on the move again.

Even though an average Bihari's hunger for knowledge and his capacity for putting in long hours in study are legendary, Bihar ranks (as in every other field) lowest in the matter of literacy rates. In contrast to Lalu, who was positively hostile to the idea of Biharis receiving education, seeing in it, much like Indira Gandhi, a threat to his disgusting politics and fraudulent regime, Nitish Kumar took keen interest in education, especially the girl education. Besides making trudging easier for the girls in a poor state like Bihar, distribution of free bicycles to school-going girls by the government injected a new energy and confidence in them, for it was an affirmation that the state cared for them and was interested in their education and uplift. Recruitment of 2.3 lakh teachers too helped give a backbone to the 'Sarva Shiksha Abhiyan' scheme for universalizing of literacy.

Little wonder then that, within a few years, Bihar became cynosure of all eyes, posting, year after year, highest growth rates among all states. Thus the rate of growth of its GSDP (Gross State Domestic Product) was 11% between 2004-05 and 2008-09, and 14.5% in 2009-10 alone; an awe-inspiring figure indeed.

Fittingly, winning respect and love of all patriotic Indians (and not just Biharis), Nitish became the darling of the media and toast of seminars and conferences everywhere. Delegations from wonderstruck lands far and wide came to see the unbelievable with their own eyes and high and mighty of the world (such as Bill Gates) paid court. Within no time, Nitish Kumar acquired the persona of a statesman, and the harried and oppressed Indians, disgusted by the doings of the ruling party at the Centre, constant squabbling and small-mindedness of the leaders of the main opposition party, and hopelessly corrupt and casteist honchos of regional political outfits, began to perceive in him their future prime minister and savior.

But, alas! There is always a flip side to a coin and, Nitish has turned out to be no exception. To put it bluntly, replacing Lalu and earning goodwill by removing some of the negativities associated with his regime is one thing and transforming the mindset of people and the economy of an entire state quite another. It has been eight years since Nitish ascended to the helm of affairs in Bihar...pretty good amount of time by any reckoning to effect meaningful change. In eight years (that is from 1978 to 1986), Deng had made China, a nation of billion coolies, explode like a supernova, even as the world stood quaking in wonderment, envy and fear. There is nothing even remotely comparable to that in the case of Bihar, a state less than tenth in size and population as compared to China. Rather, as we shall see, progress Bihar has made is seriously lopsided, if not altogether dubious. Let's look a little closer:

It must be admitted that though nowhere being great like him, honeymoon Nitish has enjoyed with his people (and the nation too) compares well with Nehru in the matter of duration. Things however were too good to last. As Lalu became progressively a caricature of even his clownish-sinister self, and the threat of him making a comeback receded, people began to take a closer look on Nitish's persona and the performance. Many acts of omission and commission they had ignored as initial hiccups and worth giving benefit of doubt to, began acquiring distinct salience. Data and figures that had appeared wonderful initially and not given second thought to, came to be scrutinized closely and began looking a little wan and tweaked, if not actually doctored. Truth that has emerged out is that apart from the general air made somewhat salubrious to allow people to breath easy, hopes for an average Bihari (and almost all Biharis are...well, average Bihari) even after eight years of Nitish rule have remained just that: unrealized hope, with little to show in his plate, farmstead, bank account or the electricity pole. The thing needs a little elaboration:

Bihar's rate of economic growth is said to have clocked 14.5% for the Y 2009-10 alone, and 11% as a whole for the entire duration of Nitish rule. That puts Bihar easily at the top of the states of India in the matter of economic growth. However, the growth-rate conceals as much as it reveals, for given an abysmal base, even a small increment in the GSDP (gross state domestic product) in absolute terms results in an impressive rate of growth. Further, at 14.8%, the inflation suffered by Bihar was highest among the states. And it is no secret that in a capitalistic economy, while increase in the rate of economic growth benefits the empowered sections the most, inflation affects its poor disproportionately. Needless to say, the poorer sections (and that means ninety percent of Bihar) of the state are worse off than ever.

The lopsided nature of growth and the sufferings of Bihar's majority are accentuated by the fact that agriculture and allied sectors, upon which about 80% of the Bihar's population depends, has registered only 1% yearly growth during Nitish rule, suffering negative growth rate thrice in the last six years. And it is more than compensated by almost 3% population growth rate being posted by the state. The secondary sector (manufacturing, construction, hospitality etc.), has recorded 12.9% and the tertiary sector (services) 6.9%. To make things worse, most of the growth in the secondary sector has come from construction, while manufacturing (which constitutes only around 5% of Bihar's economy) has stagnated. Thus, according to state economic survey, the construction sector grew by 23.3% in 2004-05, a huge 83.58% in 2005-06, 30.2% in 2006-07 and 43.85% in 2008-09. It now contributes 13.4% of state's GDP compared with 4.2% in 2003-04. Hotels and restaurants grew about 17.71%.

No one can dispute that electricity is a sine qua non of modern civilized life and the most obvious and accurate marker of progress of a people. From agriculture to industry to education to health to service industry – nothing can advance without electricity. Obviously, besides curbing crimes, first priority of any ruler really concerned about the wellbeing of his subjects would be arranging power to move the wheels of every which sector of the economy. The thing was truer still for Bihar, what with an average Bihari getting only about 100 units of power in an year, even as all-India consumption was about 800 units, that of Delhi 1600 units, Punjab 1200 units and Gujarat 1100 units. Given that electricity is modern citizenship for all practical purposes, it clearly meant that a Bihari was eight time less of a citizen than his average Indian counterpart. Yet, even after seven years lapse, what was the situation like in Nitish's Bihar? Here is a news item *(IBN Live, 30.05.2011)*:

> In Bihar, it is only the capital city Patna which seems to have no crisis as it gets over 90% of the total power supply leaving rest of the state with power cuts, which sometimes extend to three to four consecutive days....

> Of the total 800 MW supplied to Bihar, 375 is for essential services, of the remaining 425 MW, Patna gets 400 and rest of the state gets only 25 MW...

> The power scene is grimmer since the state owned generation units at Kanti and Barauni are under up-gradation and contribute

just 50 MW against their installed capacity of 1200 MW.

It must be repeated here that seven years is not too short a period to alleviate, if not totally address, some of the worst ills of just about any thing. It must also be remembered that Nitish had remained a prominent part of the dispensation that had prime role in bringing things to the disgusting level. Further, for the rest of the period, he was the star opposition leader of Bihar, yet one rarely heard him leading agitations against the crime of forcing the people of the state to lead a mediaeval existence. Recently he has laid foundation of a new power plant but the fruits of it lay in the future; we are on to miracle that Bihar has been and on the basis of which he wants to lead India to a future of prosperity and security.

Now what does all of the above tell about Bihar's economic miracle under Nitish rule?

Firstly, that agriculture, on which more than three-fourth of Bihar's population still depends, didn't grow at all. And, pray, how it could...without electricity, without expansion of irrigation facilities, without agrarian reforms, without a determined and imaginative push from those sitting at the helm of affairs? With barely 1% yearly growth in the face of 3% population growth, it is a no-brainer to surmise that eighty percent of Bihar has sunk 20% below where it had stood at the end of Lalu-Raj.

Within seven years of opening up, China had begun to emerge as the manufacturing hub of the entire world; manufacturing hasn't progressed even a whit in Nitish's Bihar. Contrarily, the share of manufacturing in state's economy has dropped to 5.45% in 2008-09 from 5.63% in 2003-04. As manufacturing is the real economy, all else being frill and froth, it means that Bihar has not progressed even an inch. Clear indicator is the fact that let alone the outsiders, even Biharis are loath to bet their money on Bihar. And why would they? Power-position remains as grave as ever. Things on the law and order front relapse ominously, and given Nitish's unconcealed national ambitions, promise to revert fully back to the Lalu-times. And as for that greatest impediment in the way of enterprise (corruption) thing is concerned, it marches on relentlessly, at least at the lower and middle level where it means and affects most. Can Nitish's genial face alone be deemed incentive enough by a sensible person to bet his money on Bihar?

Building of roads and bridges across the state is one bright thing for which Nitish Kumar has earned well-deserved encomiums. That, his detractors attribute his special interest and achievements in the sector to the fact that he has utilized it to keep the MLAs and other bigwigs of his party off the organized crime by offering them lucrative contracts, is irrelevant to our theme. In any case, denying big civil contracts to criminal mafia would serve no purpose. Firstly, it is impossible for a straight person to get any work done in most parts of India. If not a strongman himself, he would have to feed so many local strongmen, policemen and state and ruling party apparatchiks that what to talk of profits, even his basic capital will get eroded within no time. Secondly, way the governmental-political machinery runs in our country, anyone getting big contracts is bound to turn into a Mafiosi himself or risk turning out dead.

It isn't irrelevant however to our theme that much of the money for road-building is being provided by the Union Government, mainly under Prime Minister Gramin Sadak Yojna (PMGSY). According to state's economic survey, Bihar's dependency on the Central Government for meeting its expenditure is quite high. From around 40% in 2003-04, the ratio of gross transfers from the Central Government to aggregate expenditure has increased steadily to as much as 72% in last two years. In addition to the state's share of divisible taxes from the Centre, grants-in-aid have increased from 13% of total expenditure in 2003-04 to 26% in 2008-09. For example, at 3043 crores, allocation for Bihar under Indira Awas Yojna for rural housing for the Y 2009-10 stands highest among states, even though percentage utilization of funds has been 67%...almost same as the all-India average of 68%.

Clearly, Bihar's construction boom, which is nearly all Nitish has to show in the name of Bihar's economic miracle, is direct outcome of Central schemes and special consideration shown by the Centre to Bihar. That, it is reflected disproportionately in Bihar's rate of economic growth is due to the fact that it comes on the back of very low economic base of the state.

And that is not all. Even the figures of growth-rates doled out by Nitish media managers have begun to come under serious question. That is eminently understandable. People were bound to begin wondering that if indeed the state had been experiencing 11% rate of growth for six or seven years in a row, income of an average Bihari should have doubled (in real terms) at the very least. As the ground realities told quite a different story, reappraisal of the growth figures became overdue.

Thus, whereas, the figures dished out be the Central Statistical Organization (which takes its figures from the state governments) put the rate of growth of Bihar's state domestic product at around 11 percent during six years of Nitish rule, Bihar's economic survey puts it around 7.3%. To solve the conundrum, experts have taken another, and much more reliable, route to arrive at the truth. According to them, given that the agriculture and manufacturing sectors have largely stagnated in Bihar and the services sector has grown below the national average of around 7%, the growth in the construction sector (which constituted 4.2% of Bihar's economy in 2003-04 and 13.4% in 2010-11) alone spiking the overall rate of growth of the economy to 11% is more than the case of tail wagging the dog. They have taken data from the Reserve Bank of India, showing that Bihar's share of bank deposits between 2002 and 2009 remained unchanged at 2.2%. Bank credit, surest indicator of growth of business, agriculture and industry, too remained unchanged at 0.9%.

Now nothing can get more reliable than that. If Bihar's share in overall national deposits and credits remains unchanged, Bihar's rate of growth can't exceed that of the nation overall at around 7%. Even Nitish can't argue that Biharis have got special penchant for stashing their surplus income as gold, or that they had been sitting over piles of gold which they have now taken out to invest in industries and other enterprises (to be run without power).

Little wonder then that even the *Outlook*, a long term ardent supporter of Nitish, had no recourse left but to revolt in the face of the glaring ground reality of Bihar. Claiming to *'dissect'* the Bihar story to ascertain its *'success'* under the heading, *'How to Build A Reputation'*, it brings out some native truths lurking behind Bihar's 'miraculous' growth. Thus, about the *'Myth'* that *'Bihar became the fastest growing state in the shortest possible time'*; it tells that *'Bihar clocked double-digit growth even in the 1990s, fluctuating wildly'* and that *'Growth numbers mean little when starting from zero or negative growth'*.

About the *'Myth'* that *'Agricultural policies are progressive in Bihar'*, it tells that, according to statistics doled out, agricultural and animal husbandry growth fluctuated between -9.1% in 2005-06 to +30.2% in 2006-07; manifestly impossible figures.

Concerning the myth that *'Bihar will be a dynamic industrial state soon'*, it reveals that only Rs 62 crore – yes, sixty two crores; there is no typographical error – worth of investments came to Bihar between 2008 and 2011, though over Rs 1 lakh crore (!) were approved.

And about the great myth that *'Bihar is building roads at breakneck speed'*, it holds that *'84% of Bihar's roads are in rural areas. But 82% of rural roads are washed away in rains'*.

It further tells about the views of the critics that:

Nitish's growth is a `chimera`, the result of an overly critical eye on the previous regime's failings. They compare the last four years of Lalu's time, when growth averaged 5.87%, with Nitish's first four years of 6.35% growth, and see no `miracle'. At times, indeed there's no explaining how Bihar adds up. Agriculture declined 9.1% in 2007, only to grow 30% next year, an inexplicable variation that, experts say, highlights instability.....

Actually, grants from the Centre, which grew six-fold to Rs 24,000 crores last year, could be the real secret of Bihar's growth, not agriculture, not entrepreneurship, not even services....

But what explains the irreconcilability of growth figures or the claims and counterclaims? *'Outlook'* has the answer:

The Bihar government has outsourced a number of services. For instance, the state's annual economic survey is brought out by a private think tank, the Asian Development Research Institute, since 2006. Since the move, it is regularly pointed out, data on critical performance indicators is selectively included or excluded in these reports. So the problem, says Santhosh Mathew, a senior bureaucrat in Bihar government, may lie in "faulty, unreliable" data in "spin".

All said and done, what does one have to make out of the fact that even after seven years of Nitish rule, Bihar's per capita income remains unchanged at 30% of the national average? Had Bihar been progressing at the rate of 11%, even as the nation stuttered at around 7, the figure would have jumped to more than 40%.

Another thing Nitish is much feted about is his determined drive against corruption and organized crime which, along with unspeakable poverty and horrendous inequities, had come to be seen as principal attributes of Bihar. Closer scrutiny however reveals that here too Nitish's record is more than a little mixed.

While it is a fact that Nitish took many resolute and bold steps to clean up the Augean stable, but, at the same time, he left many – too many in fact – gaps to allow people to doubt his commitment to rid the politics of Bihar (and that of the administration and the society, as natural and inescapable corollary) of the cancer of crime and corruption. Thus, while mafia dons like Shahbuddin, Anand Mohan and Pappu Yadav were put behind bars to all round acclaim, many others like Gopal Narain Singh, Rajan Tiwary, Anant Singh, Munna Shukla and Rajan Pandey (that is, all those expressing allegiance to him) were not only spared but promoted and rewarded by giving big contracts and party tickets. According to National Election Watch, 58 of 141 Bihar MLAs having criminal cases pending against them belonged to Nitish's JD(U) and after the 2005 assembly elections, 39 of 86 JD(U) MLAs faced serious criminal charges. After a landslide victory in the assembly elections of 2009, having got 206 of 243 assembly seats under his belt, he had ample opportunity to sideline them but, sadly and revealingly, he has shown little inclination to do that.

A story by Dan Morrison (*Al Jazeera;* August, 08, 2012) under the title *'The dark side of India's `Mr. Clean`'* may be found illuminating here:

> At a time when many Indians hold their politicians in contempt, Nitish Kumar stands out as an object of veneration.

> Even Bill Gates and Robert Zoellick, when he was president of the World Bank, came to witness the Bihar miracle up close. Kumar, The Economist effused in Janurary 2010, "has uprooted the Jungle Raj, restoring law and order".

> Despite a reputation of personal probity and an apparently bona fide zeal for governance and development, Kumar has long kept silent on one bit of cognitive dissonance. Violent crimes may have declined during his tenure, but as a recent political assassination reveals, Bihar's "Mr. Clean" is himself surrounded by reputed gangsters.

> Like many an Indian states, the power structure in Bihar rests on a pillar of violence a nexus of racketeers, landlords, contractors and ward-heelers that bring out the right voters and suppress the wrong ones at election time. Kumar governs with a strong hand; no one gets on the ruling party ticket without his approval.

> In 2007, one of the state's leading reputed politician-gangsters, Anant Singh, was implicated in a grisly rape and murder. This didn't prevent Kumar from allowing him on the ballot in 2010, or from campaigning for his re-election. Kumar did allow justice to take its course in the murder conviction of Munna Shukla, another criminal politician, but he also allowed Shukla's wife to replace him in the assembly.

> Kumar's political reliance on accused killers doesn't appear in the well-polished narrative of rising Bihar. The mask fell last month after the murder of the popular leader of a militia of wealthy landlords.

> On June 1, Brahmeshwar Singh was gunned down in a dirt alleayway in Bihar's Bhojpur distict. Police officials said the

main suspect is Hulas Pandey, a reputed ganglord and a local political rival who also happens to be an appointed member of the upper house of Bihar's legislature. Who appointed him?

Kumar's ruling Janta Dal (United) party. Hulas Pandey has declared his innocence.

The suspect's brother, Sunil Panday, is an elected member of Bihar's lower house, also with Kumar's party. Sunil's criminal record includes pending charges of murder and kidnapping. Both brothers were members of Brahmeshwar Singh's militia, the Ranvir Sena, which massacred more than 270 landless peasants during feudal land wars in the 1990s and early 2000s....

Nitish created much brouhaha around seizure of ill-gotten gains of bureaucrats and others. But, clearly, that was only a populist move, for apart from sending a proposal to the Centre and making a show of seizure of the property of a bureaucrat or two, he has not taken any concerted or meaningful action on the front. Far better the Lokayukta of MP who has undertaken at least twenty raids in the last couple of years, unearthing billions worth of ill-gotten money. Had Nitish been serious about ridding Bihar of corruption, he would surely have established specialized cells working under his direct supervision to undertake raids to instill fear of God and the Law in the ranks of the corrupt. Why, he hasn't even got laid down a meaningful Citizen's Charter or some other kind of norms for putting some pressure on the government employees to do their job (under pain of punishment) in a time-bound manner, reducing thereby the avenues for corruption. On the other hand, his unstinted and almost instinctive hostility towards Anna Hazare serves to show where do his actual sympathies lie.

And the scam in Bihar Industrial Area Development Authority (BIADA), in which huge plots of State-acquired land were parceled off to the loin-begotten of party-men, matches in scope and brazenness any of those enacted by Mayawati or Yeddurappa. Thus Urvashi Shahi, daughter of state HRD minister Prashant Kumar Shahi, got 87000 sq. ft land in Vaishali; Rahmat Fatima, daughter of Social Welfare Minister Parween Amanullah and Water Resources secretary Afzal Amanullah got 87120 sq ft in Bihiya near Patna; MLA Rahul Sharma, son of JD(U) MP from Jehanabad, Jagdish Sharma, got 15,500 sq ft near Hajipur; and Saurabh Agrawal, son of Ashok Agarwal, BJP MLC and Sushil Modi's confidante got two plots measuring 13 lakh sq. fit and 246000 sq ft in Fobesganj in Araria district.

Matching that brazenness was the transfer of SP Patna on a direct order from Nitish. The crusading SP had dared to raid establishments manufacturing and selling adulterated or counterfeit sweets, medicines and cosmetics; little prize for guessing the party affiliations of people owning those establishments.

An impression was sought to be created that due to its dependence on Bihari labor, sowing and reaping activities in Punjab had begun to suffer gravely. That was (so we were told) because the Bihari labor had stopped migrating outside his state because Nitish had managed to make MNREGA a great success. It now transpires that utilization of MNREGA fund in Bihar in 2010-11 stood at a stately 7.38%! Given that Bihar virtually bulges with cohorts of starved and the unemployed, how much labor the MNREGA (whittled further down by the inevitable 'leakages') could have absorbed back in the state itself could be anybody's guess.

And in a state where millions die of hunger and ill-nutrition every year, but which now has (thanks to the God Almighty) come to have great good fortune to be ruled by an epitome of sincerity, painstaking hard-work and good governance, diversion of PDS food grains stands at another princely 40%.

We had stated at the outset (and no one can dispute the essential verity of the premise):

> One thing we need to understand at the very outset... If only they freed the energies and the enterprise of people from million controls and demands and delays lekhpals and tehsildars and inspectors and 'bada-babus' nothing much would be left to be done by the governments. And if they were not able to do that, what else they did launching million schemes, distributing bicycles and mobiles and laptops, and giving out stipends and pensions and 'dhans' (purse) of hundred kinds shall not be of much avail. Has Nitish freed Bihar of these sharks and piranhas battening upon the people?

And we had posed a question: *"Does Nitish have that level of competence?"*

Well, there is little doubt that Nitish would have proved to be a successful 'Head of the State' of nations like Iceland or Norway where personal integrity and amiability seem to be top qualifications, and not more than little tinkering with the socio-economic system is what is really required.

Thus *The Economic Times* of Oct 20, 2010:

> Every answer to question on Nitish Kumar's performance in the last five years as Bihar's chief minister begins with the phrase

"Kam se kam itna to kiya…(at least, he has done something.)".

By any index of growth and development, Nitish's five-year reign has unleashed no miracles….. Its recent growth has been predominantly driven by a construction boom which has a limited life.

Industrial growth is far lower than the national average and agriculture has stagnated. Yet, by the lowered expectations of Bihar's electorate, the Nitish era has brought change….

In the desperately poor Dalit village of Rattu Bigha, 60 km south of Patna in Jehanabad, expectations are even lower. "Life in this village hasn't changed even one bit for the better in five years of Nitish's rule", says Sudama Paswan (40), a landless farm worker. But it has not got any worse either, and the paved road is now only 10 km away. It is this harvest of lowered expectations that Nitish could reap.

And this *'kam se kam kuch to kiya'* man nurses ambition to become, and is being projected as, the next Lord Krishna come to slay the oppressors and mischief-makers from the face of the Earth and save the beleaguered Bharatbhumi from the *'ghor kalyug'* visiting it! Even as Bihar was not much better – better fed, better educated, better electrified, or better industrialized – than it had been at the commencement of his rule eight years ago, this man has cheek to think that Bihar had become too small for his ambitions and the national stage was the right arena to put his Napoleonic acumen to full use.

What in fact nearly four decades of his political career and eight years at the helm of the state have served to prove is that, much like the other white-hot hope of the nation, Nitish too has got little imagination and less feeling for the people of his state. That is apparent from his failure to think 'long and deep' about their problems and come up with possible (which are too apparent to be missed by anyone) solutions. And, since, he has failed to develop a grand idea or vision, or even less-than-grand road-map for the development of his state of only around hundred million, talks of him making a success of his premiership of entire India, which, along with the quotidian issue of feeding, educating, clothing, housing and employing 1200 million in a satisfactory manner, carries the uncertainty of bare survival even in an increasingly intolerant, supremacist and Darwinian world, can't but evoke contempt.

The hard truth is that people are wasting their energy and muddling the issue by juxtaposing him with some other serious contenders to the premiership of India. Besides the reasons outlined above, there are hard political issues involved too as to why he can never get to be the PM (or at least an effective PM) of the country:

1. Not even Nitish's strongest protagonists claim that he can ever come to power at the Centre on his own. All he happens to have is a small regional party in a state that carries less than 8% population and 3% area of the country. In the state too, his party would find it extremely tough to come to power on its own. And to make matters worse, his bete noire in the state is not only not politically dead, but waiting eagerly in the wings for either his alliance with the BJP to break up, or the public to get fed up of feeding on its broken dreams. What to talk of exciting the imagination of the country in the way a certain other chief minister does, he can't pull excited crowds anywhere in the country the Rahul way even. As things stand, one needs a strong party in a Westminster model of democracy (which India is), and charisma in the presidential system (like in the US), though there is some trade-off between the two (that is, one can compensate to some extent the lack of one with more of the other). Neither Nitish has, nor has he any chance of ever having a strong all India party of his own. And though he exudes charm, he clearly lacks charisma. That being the case, coming to power on his own must remain a pipe-dream for him or his enthusiasts.

2. There is little chance of him making it with the support of his alliance partner BJP. BJP supporting him in the state is one thing; in the Centre quite another. At the last count, the BJP had at least eight serious contenders of its own to the coveted post.

3. It is almost a certainty that, in the next elections, neither BJP nor the Congress can notch up sufficient numbers to cobble up a government on their own. Pressure may mount on the BJP to lend support to Nitish Kumar to enable him elicit support of other regional parties (and may be the Left Front) to keep the Congress at bay. That may prove tempting to many BJP leaders but is unlikely ever to happen. That is because there is an eight hundred pound gorilla out there in the BJP who would never let that happen. Besides the fact that Nitish has taken to attacking him rather gratuitously, he would rather have another UPA government, yet more unstable than the previous and failing miserably with Rahul at its helm, to take advantage of the public disgust, than let the Congress do it to the BJP. In any case, even if Nitish managed to come to power, his tenure is likely to be too

brief, for the conditions facing him are likely to be even more fraught and unresolvable than they had been concerning the previous Third Front experiments. And, after that, it would be political oblivion for him the way Morarji, V. P. Singh, Chandashekhar, Dev Gowda and Gujral faded into ignominy and oblivion.

4. Even if the Congress supported him to keep the BJP at bay and to yank him away from it, it would be more insecure this time around than it had been at the time of Gujral, particularly when it had a Prince of its own to enthrone. It is not likely to let Nitish rule for much amount of time to let him do any good to the nation. Simple reason being that any good happening to the nation through his acumen would be poison to the Congress and the Dynasty. That too would end in dismissal and disgrace for Nitish.

So, one way or the other, and even if it was assumed that Nitish had it in him to not only rule the nation efficiently but to save it from the dire future awaiting it, it is unlikely that he may come to power, or, coming to power, may get to rule for more than a couple of years. Such being the case, it is sheer waste of cogitative and argumentative energy to promote him or speculate about his chances.

And, as we have seen, the question before us is not merely cobbling up a government or running the national affair in a tolerable sort of manner. Even if Nitish had personality and the credentials needed for the job (which he evidently doesn't) and managed to become the PM (which is a dicey proposition, to say the least), no political permutation/combination can make it possible for him to wield the kind of authority and power needed to pull off the *'Bhuto na Bhavishyati'* (never before, never after) kind of feat the nation urgently requires.

As things stand, Nitish's long honeymoon with the people of his state is drawing to a close and the window of opportunity is closing upon him fast. Tentative nature of his governance is becoming more than apparent. More interested in politicking and nursing national ambition, he clearly intends to sit on his laurels (whatever they be worth) rather than immersing himself into state-building and taking hard decisions for the long term good of the people of his state. Little wonder then that unlike a certain other chief minister and his state, nobody seems willing to place his long term bet either on Nitish Kumar or Bihar. One more tenure with no real change, and his goose shall begin cooking real fast.

✸

Part-III

HERE COMES MODI

1

HERE COMES MODI

We discussed Rahul and Nitish. Rahul is not only completely untested concerning his executive-administrative capabilities (politically he has been tested and has been found out to be a pathetic failure), but shies away (or shielded) from any position of responsibility, lest his taken-for-granted capabilities and acumen got exposed in all luridness even before he got opportunity to get his name included in the (not so) illustrious list of India's prime ministers. In other words, he would be crowned the King in one go, lest the worst doubts and fears of his would be subjects about the abilities of their Prince Charming had turned out to be well-founded. Whatever little peek preview they have been allowed to (or managed to) glean inspires but little confidence. After a decade of peek-a-boo that the boy-man has been allowed to play with his indulgent subjects, only clothes they have managed to espy on his persona is his lineage; very thing (as we have seen) responsible for the ills that we want to get rid of through his agency. As of present, he has shown absolutely no inclination for wanting to do anything but bring more of the same to the table…that is, the selfsame culture of nepotism, sycophancy, corruption, sloganeering and drift that the Congress stands for and has practiced since Independence.

And we discussed Nitish, second of our two leadership solutions for the million woes of India. He certainly is eons ahead of Rahul, in that he built a party of his own almost from scratch; kept locking horns with Lalu, who, it had seemed, was here for eternity; established himself in the badlands of Bihar with (by and large) gentlemanly techniques and never stooping to the level of his uncouth and devious opponent; and managed to suffuse the land of mother of all ills and hopelessness with a lot of optimism. Further, he managed to prove that the promise he brought was not a fluke and he was not a fraud in the likeness of Digvijay Singhs and Ramkrishna Hegdes of yore. Applying himself sincerely and diligently to the task at hand, he managed to establish his credentials through a goodly amount of accomplishments.

But, that is as far as he can go. May be, it is because the ills facing the state he made bold to take into his hands are too entrenched or, perhaps, relentless and uncritical adulation has gone to his head, making him think that his work in the state had been accomplished, more or less, and time had come for him to take a shot at a bigger dream. Greater possibility is that he has realized that whatever he had accomplished in Bihar was as much as he (or anyone else) could achieve there. For, clearly, the next requisite steps to take Bihar out of the rut it has been stuck in (that is, altering land relations for agricultural growth, creating eco-system for attracting industry, and ridding it of the four 'Cs' of casteism, communalism, crime and corruption) appear to be beyond anyone's capacity to achieve in a reasonable timeframe. It is better therefore to move on to the next logical stage before the chickens began returning home to roost. Be that as it might, it is a fact that though the people of Bihar have got roads to move upon, the general air has got a lot more breathable and there is a definite sunshine of expectations, not much has been achieved on the level of the fundamentals. One other undeniable is that Nitish has failed to disseminate fear (fear of his authority and the law in the hearts of rascally politicians and bastardly bureaucrats) which is essential to make democracy a genuine success in the kind of milieu prevailing in India. In short, after eight years of rule, while he has begun to be taken for granted by those who must stand in terror of him, fear and cynicism has begun to set in again in the Bihar street.

As such, let alone tackling the two agents of doom (and the third) standing in wait to waylay India, Nitish has shown himself to be less than qualified in dealing with even the 'normal' ills and issues facing a state fifteenth its size. And that has begun to show...not only on the ground but also in the perception of people who took to pelting stones at many places during the last of the many of his 'yatras'.

That leaves the nation with only one option...and that is, like it or not, Modi. Yes, yes...Narendra Damodar Modi of million encomiums and billion opprobriums.

Now whether one liked or not, Modi is all over the place, and for good. Love him or hate him, fear him or feel safe with him around, curse him or sing paeans to him, associate images of doom with him or visions of deliverance, you won't be done with him till either you had hanged him, bumped him off, anointed him premier of the nation, or made him hang around till at least the age of seventy five. It would be no exaggeration to say that after Gandhi, Nehru and Jinnah, no sub-Continental leader has been discussed as much as Modi. And even as Gandhi is debated reverentially, Nehru lovingly, and Jinnah's case is all mixed up, with Hindus and Muslims of the sub-Continent nursing exactly conflicting views of him, Modi's case is akin to Jinnah, with positions of majority Hindus and the Muslims completely reversed. With dust largely settled upon the phenomenon of Partition, Gandhi and Congress role in formation of Pakistan has begun to be exposed and the formation of Pakistan is beginning to be looked upon by informed Hindus more as blessing in disguise than an unmixed disaster, leading them to take more favorable view of Jinnah. Likewise, with somewhat cooling down of passions, growing number of Muslims too have begun to revaluate Modi in the light of new developments. Thus, rather than his alleged response in the face of, what could be termed, mother of all Catch-22 situations that had been thrust upon him a decade ago, they have been reassessing his persona in light of his almost blemishless record since, as also what he can achieve for the nation and, therefore, for them too.

Yet, incontrovertible fact remains that despite possessing astounding capability and character, bolstered with matching achievements on the ground, the middle ground remains pretty thin, as far as the site of Modi-debate is concerned.

And the grand cleavage is not restricted to the general public or the politicians belonging to political parties other than the BJP. While the Indian public opinion is divided right down the middle, and the rival political parties hold an extremely dim view of him naturally, Modi's own party too is cleft hopelessly and unevenly on the issue. While around 80% of the party cadre and supporters could be said to be strongly enamoured of him, more than that percentage of the top leadership stands fearful and hostile to the idea of him graduating to the national stage, so much so that they would gladly give their right hand away to see the threat of Modi eliminatedeither politically or by any other mean.

In all surveys done by the news media and the survey agencies over the past decade, Modi has ranked best among the chief ministers and with an unfailing regularity. As a prime ministerial candidate too he comes on top of the list, ahead of all other real or perceived rivals such as Rahul Gandhi, Nitish Kumar, Advani or Sonia Gandhi. A recent survey puts his approval ratings as high as 24%, leaving all of his rivals distinctly behind.

However, 24% approval rating means that the other 76% might not only be neutral, undecided or benignly opposed (as may be the situation with those ranked lower like Rahul or Nitish), but fiercely opposed to Modi. So, let's not go with that 24%. In any case, even 90% approval rating can't validate a Hitler, or 20% economic growth-rate a Stalin; two historical evils his detractors love to compare Modi with. Modi is said to be a polarizing and authoritarian figure. Some hail him a Messiah and others demonize him as worse than Satan and would settle at nothing less than a life-term for him. Mighty peeved at the encounters of confirmed terrorists that took place under his watch, and now that the highest court of the land has all but exonerated him, these advocates of human rights, 'rule of law', and liberal-democratic values would break into joyous frenzies if, perchance, some terrorist succeeded in taking him.

But why this seemingly inordinate infatuation or irrational *kolavari*? While the loathing directed at Modi within his own party could be traced to the fear of being rendered irrelevant in the light of his nature of giving no quarters to the corrupt, inefficient or obstructionists, in the opposition parties to getting wiped out of the political map of the nation, disquiet and resistance among the general public, media, academia and chatterati could be pinned down to three reasons in the main:

1. Very first reason (though largely unacknowledged, lodged as it is deep in the typical Indian psyche) is that he doesn't fit into any of the recognized categories of political leaders or even an average Indian. His incorruptibility, immunity to the pleasures of senses, absolute lack of nepotism or clannishness, and absence of buffoonery, garrulousness and sloth appear so unreal, unsettling and...and...well, so un-Indian. And he is a celibate in truest sense of the term. Even his worst detractors have never accused him of showing even slightest deviation from his chosen way of life. If all that was not enough to render him so unworthy of being the denizen of this land of idiots, bastards and hypocrites, there is horror of all horrors: He is so free of caste! (and not merely casteism or caste-bias). Now, they (that is true Hindus) can forgive anything in a person – lecherousness, murderous tendencies and even visceral hatred of India and the Hindus; persons like Arundhati Roy, N. D. Tiwari, Zakir Naik or SAR Gilani. All of them are secular after all, going by their definition of secularism. What they can't stomach is a Hindu conducting himself in a way as if he had no caste.

They are not to be blamed however for that. The disease is genetic. In the ancient times too, the Hindus got defeated by Huns, Shakas, Kushans and innumerable other hordes descending down on the plains of India, but accepted and assimilated them as true sons of soil as soon as they consented to join the caste-hierarchy. Brahminism hated Buddha and Buddhism from its guts only because the prime target of Buddhism was the institution of caste (or *Varna*; its biological mother). A person or group without caste baffled and exasperated them no end; reason they failed to include the aboriginals of the land into their fold. Somewhere in their subconscious, a caste-free Modi baffles and exasperates many of them, engendering unknown fears and forebodings in their hearts. He has no personal axe to grind, no desire to amass trillions, no son or son-in-law to show indulgence to and promote, no family or friends to allot prime plots to, no caste-men to give lucrative postings to, and no love-interest to negotiate deals on his behalf or made director in companies. Only hard work and public good…that man sure is a genie or *'bhoot'* and therefore positively dangerous!

2. Second reason is their infatuation with Congress and the Dynasty; pathetic love of muddling-meandering ways of the nation's democracy; and high comfort level with the prevailing status quo. Fear of change, especially if it happens to come faster than the comfort level of their Nehruvian 'Hindu rate of growth' mindsets, too is a factor. If it is development, it must be anti-people, anti-democracy and utterly violative of 'traditional Indian ethos'. And though they carp incessantly about India's hunger, crowds, filth, corruption, nepotism, red-tape, crimes, and lack of even most rudimentary of the civic amenities, they love nothing more in the heart of their hearts, so much so, that they would die of anxiety and asphyxiation if made to live in the crowds, corruption and stench free air of Denmark or Canada. They fear nothing more than efficiency and fast pace of development – that is, as long as poverty, hunger and lack of access to water or electricity kept affecting others, not them. But, again, nothing wrong in that, for they are being true Indian in their hypocrisy. They dislike Modi from the depth of their guts because he is so un-Indian in wanting India to develop fast. Slurs like 'authoritarian', 'autocratic', 'insensitive' and 'intolerant' they hurl at Modi are all euphemism for the crime he has committed against the people of India by showing them that possibility of developing at breakneck speed did indeed exist here.

And one other crime of Modi for which they anoint him with Hitlerite slur is that he neither suffers idiots nor spares the bastards. That is, neither does he persecutes honest, no-nonsense officials on the recommendation of party MLAs and other functionaries, nor spares venal or slothful officials. His alleged authoritarianism and 'lack of tolerance' is reserved for those supposedly democratic souls for whom democracy is but a means to feather their personal nests. Once he has judged a person to be avaricious, self-serving and up to no public good, he refuses to waste his precious time upon him and works to cut him down to size, however high and mighty he might be in others' esteem. He doesn't distribute red-lights or prime plots as so many *mansabdaris* that used to be doled out in the feudal times. Had he shown but little laxity on this front, BJP, VHP and RSS functionaries would have been running riot all over the state, battening upon public money and singing paeans to him, instead of conspiring against him and trying to bring him down as many of them have been doing now. Further, he desists from attending marriages, funerals, birthdays, 'mundans', 'akikas', and the like of every little party man and his kin. It is a very important distinction, for it is a thing which, though yielding them great political goodwill and opportunities, takes up more than half of our politicians' time that had better been utilized to devise, review and reconfigure schemes meant for starved, illiterates and the sick of the land. However, unlike many of the past or present political leaders, he has neither rebuked, slapped or got his shoes cleaned, nor suspended or dismissed any public official or party functionary publicly.

3. Gravest charge against him however is that he is a Muslim-hater...that under his regime the Muslims may face discrimination, exclusion and worse. This indeed is a grave misgivings and can't be dismissed just like that. If the accusation carries even an iota of truth about it then Modi gets to be absolutely unacceptable. For, far better a poor and underdeveloped India whose inequities and injustices were an outcome of combination of historical factors (and, God-willing, may get to be solved, by and by), than a prosperous and developed India where discrimination against a section of its citizens was practiced or encouraged by none other than the State itself.

The charge is so grave indeed that it becomes almost a sacred duty for one claiming to be non-partisan observer of things to look into it with all the requisite thoroughness. So, here we go....

Entire case against Modi is based upon the incidents of those fateful three days beginning 28ᵗʰ February 2002, a few encounters of the likes of Sohrabuddin and Ishrat Jahan, and the hostility and boycott the Muslims continued to face for a couple of years in the aftermath of the riots. Presently however, the Muslims, even by their own admission, suffer no discrimination whatsoever in the state and are busy making strides in every domain of life. That can't however be a defense of Modi. Let alone being complicit, if indeed he had been a silent spectator to the post-Godhra riots, he deserves nothing less than public hanging from the first tree at the gate of *10 Janpath*. Indulgence, which a scion of Nehru-Gandhi family and also a (deemed) Brahmin got, for first instigating a pogrom against Sikhs across entire country and then delaying relief, can't be extended to a lowly Ghanchi pretender to the premiership of the nation.

What was the situation like when Modi was given the charge of BJP in Gujarat? On the political front his party had been staring in the face of certain defeat in the elections due soon. Picture at the Centre was none too rosy, what with terrorists making daily strikes, even as the nation got resigned to watch its home-minister giving bland under-secretary like ex-post facto briefings on the outrages, rubbing his palms all the time in what appeared to be excited smugness. Advani rubbing his hands while recounting terrorist strikes (as if these were things of pride and glory rather than national shame) is the image that has got etched permanently in the subconscious of the nation and has contributed to make BJP's national-level leaders look like a bunch of self-indulgent and insensitive poltroons that couldn't be entrusted with the job of running the troubled nation.

To revert, potential electoral defeat in Gujarat, which had come to be looked upon as its bastion by the party and the cadres, was sure to demoralize its rank and file beyond repair and make the Congress, otherwise down in the dumps nationally, smell blood. The combined talent of leader like Keshubhai, Kashi Ram Rana and Suresh Mehta, working under watchful eyes of such stalwarts as Vajpayee and Advani, not to talk of the entire Sangh-Parivar, had brought things to that pass.

On the economic front, the economy of the state had shrunk by 5% in the previous year, even as its CM was as aware of things like economy or administration as Kapil Sibal is of lifting the standards of education in the country or running of IITs. Rehabilitation work in the aftermath of Kutch earthquake, which took more than twenty thousand lives and flattened four lakh homes, destroying the towns of Anjar, Bhuj and Bhachau completely, was going nowhere. Though relief had poured in from across the world, stage was set to replicate the selfsame story of apathy, mismanagement and loot that has always been the lot of the land's excluded, traumatized and the displaced.

On the social front, Gujarat was a vast cauldron simmering with fears, complexes, hubris and resentment. For denizens of many localities with mixed populations and those bordering them, arson, kidnapping for rape or ransom, and knifing and murder had become a way of life, with absolutely no possibility of reconciliation or relief. Official curfews remained in force for months in a row and people's curfew, so to say, had become a permanent feature of the urban landscape. So, before discussing Modi's complicity, apathy, incompetence, or otherwise, we would do well to delve a little into the history of riots in Gujarat, with particular reference to Ahmedabad; epicenter of the post-Godhra riots of 2002.

As far as the city of Ahmedabad was concerned, riots (it would be a gross travesty to call most of these incidents, particularly the pre-Independence ones, riots; for they were naked exercise in rape, pillage and massacres of Hindus to show them their appointed place in the Islamic scheme of things) went hand in hand with rapid growth of the city. Historical records tell that riots occurred there in 1714, 1715, 1716, 1750, 1927, 1941, 1946, 1953, 1965, 1969, 1980, 1982, 1985, 1990 and 1992

An article in www.countercurrent.org, an avowedly anti-BJP site (it must be mentioned here that all the Modi-related quotes in the book have been taken from virulently anti-BJP or anti-Modi sources) has this to say:

> When communal riots broke out in 1941, curfew had to be imposed for over two and a half months. Justice Reddy Commission (set up to inquire 1969 riots) identified as many as 2938 instances of communal violence in the state between 1960 and 1969, that is, an average of approximately three riots every four days during this ten-year period...

> During this period, riots began to spread over a much wider geographical area of the state, affecting towns like Veraval, Junagadh, Patan, Godhra, Palanpur, Anjar, Dalkhania, Kodinar and Deesa, all of which have been hit by ongoing violence.

> ....But violence of a different, more systematic and sustained order was inaugurated in 1969. The Hindu-Muslim riots of that year mark a major break with the hitherto prevalent pattern of

steady if unspectacular social conflict..... A riot of this magnitude, unprecedented in both scale and duration, had a foundational significance for the politics of the state and the techniques of mobilization and orchestration that increasingly came into use... Most importantly, the riots of 1969 took Gujarati society past the psychological threshold of normally tolerable public violence, and this not just of the communal variety. Once the barrier to the use of violence in inter-party conflict was crossed, its repeated use acquired a tacit legitimacy as the social conscience became gradually more immune to the incremental doses of it that the polity administered.

An article in *The Hindustan Times* of 1969 said that the official death toll in the 1969 riots was around 5000, but it was actually three to five times the number.

Vadodra was engulfed in riots in 1982 and again in 1991 when riots began with a boy getting hit accidentally by an autorickshaw and ran for three months. In 1990 alone, about 1400 communal incidents took place in whole of Gujarat, with an official toll of 224 dead and 775 injured. Surat's turn came in 1992 when six-month long riots left nearly 200 people dead.

Godhra town, with its Muslim population more aligned (and declaredly so) psychologically and emotionally with Pakistan rather than India, has always been a hotbed of riots. Post Independence, the riots took place in 1965, 1969, 1971, 1980, 1981, 1982, 1988, 1989, 1990 and 1992. The town remained under curfew almost throughout the year in 1980 and also in 1985.

About Godhra, Gandhi's article titled *"What are We to Do?"*, published in his paper *Young India* (October 11, 1928) is particularly illuminating:

Two weeks ago I wrote in 'Navjivan' a note on the tragedy of Godhra, where Shri Purshottam Shah bravely met his death at the hands of his assailants and gave my note the heading 'Hindu Muslim Fight in Godhra'. Several Hindus did not like the heading and addressed angry letters asking me to correct it (for it was a one sided fight). I found it impossible to accede to their demand. Whether there is one victim or more, whether there is a free fight between the two communities, or whether one assumes the offensive and the other simply suffers, I should describe the event as a fight if the whole series of happenings were the result of a state of war between the two communities. (By that definition Jew Holocaust was Nazi-Jew war and enslavement and rape of whole of Korea was Korean-Japanese war). Whether in Godhra or in other places, there is today a state of war between the two communities. Fortunately, the countryside is still free from the war fever (no longer now) which is mainly confined to towns and cities, where, in some form or the other, fighting is continually going on. Even the correspondents who have written to me about Godhra do not seem to deny the fact that the happenings arose out of the communal antagonisms that exited there.... A volunteer from Ahmedabad who had been to Godhra writes:

You say that you must be silent over these quarrels. Why are you not silent over the Khilafat and why did you exhort us to join the Muslims? Why are you not silent about your principles of Ahimsa? How can you justify your silence when the two communities are running at each others throats and Hindus are being crushed to atoms? How does Ahimsa come there? I invite your attention to two cases:

A Hindu shopkeeper thus complained to me: Musalmans purchase bags or rice from my shop, often never paying for them. I cannot insist on payment, for fear of their looting my godowns. I have, therefore, to make involuntary gift of about 50 to 70 maunds of rice every month.

Others complained: "Musalmans invade our quarters and insult over women in our presence, and we have to sit still. If we protest we are done for. We dare not lodge a complaint against them".

What would you advise in such cases? How would you bring your Ahimsa into play? Or, even here you would prefer to remain silent!

Little wonder then that Godhra was the scene of the most shocking diabolical in design and appalling in its audacity carnage of Independent India. Worst part of it was that though the conspiracy, as brought out in investigations and the court-judgment, was known to thousands of Muslims in the Godhra town, but the level of their belligerence and insensitivity, and the culture of impunity that the previous feckless Congress governments had spawned, was such that not a single Muslim tried to intervene or bothered to inform the authorities. It shows how the growing Islamism all across the world had been affecting a sections of the Muslims, filling them with the sense of suprematism and conceit to the level than could be ignored or tolerated by the civilized world. Even after the carnage, reaction of the Muslim leadership was appropriately grudging and delayed. Condemnation was backhanded and came with many ifs and buts...only out of fear of repercussions on the fellow Muslims, not genuine shock or contriteness. To make things more infuriating for all the right-minded persons, but particularly the Gujaratis, not a single self-styled 'secularist' person or the entity squealed. Besides spawning accident theory, they stooped down to insinuating that the pilgrims returning from Ayodhya (children, women et al) had either committed a collective suicide (choosing Godhra, of all places to do so), or, worse still, in a conspiracy of satanic dimensions, Modi-government had got them killed to engineer riots all across the state so as to raise communal passions with the elections in view.

Congress leaders like Amarsinh Chaudhary, the erstwhile CM of Gujarat, 'national leaders' like Lalu and those from the left, and the whole of the secular intellectual-media kept adding fuel to the fire and won't let the embers of the conflagration die out. Even the virulently anti-BJP, *The Hindu* (May 7, 2002), and the Justice Tewatia Committee report surmised that Narendra Modi's charge, that the Congress was instigating violence in Gujarat in April 2002 to make the NDA allies withdraw support to the Atal Government, could well be true.

By the way, based upon the statements of witnesses, scientific investigations, and circumstantial and documentary evidences, the court has found clear evidence of a conspiracy behind the Godhra carnage, convicting 31 accused, all Muslims. Gujarat High Court too backed the conspiracy theory and quashed the Banerjee Committee report, declaring its formation as *'illegal, unconstitutional, null and void'*, its conclusions a *'colourful exercise'*, and its arguments of accidental fire *'opposed to the prima facie accepted facts on record'*. Now, these revilers of Gujarat should either apologize to Modi, the fifty-eighty departed souls and their relatives, and the people of Gujarat in general, or they should denounce the judiciary as complicit in the sinister designs and crimes of Modi government.

What came in the wake of Godhra carnage was yet more reprehensible and mind-numbing. Horrendous riots followed the next day and raged in full ferociousness for three long days. In all, 790 Muslims and 254 Hindus were killed, with a total of 223 people missing (figures given by a Congress Union Minister), though a figure of more than 2000 Muslims killed (with nary a mention of Hindu casualties) has been taken as gospel truth by the 'secular' entities.

Even if we discounted the Moplah and Kohat riots of the twenties, the Great Calcutta Killings of 1946, or the Partition holocaust of 1947-48, even far greater post-Independence riots (in terms of virulence, causalities and duration) have failed to evoke the kind of publicity, outrage and aftereffects that the Gujarat-2002 did. Reasons are many and varied. Of course, the big reason doled out, and now held as self-evident truth, is that the riots took place in the age of satellite television, bringing the blood-curdling scenes bang into the air-conditioned environs of people's drawing room. Thus Ashish Nandy (*Outlook*; April 23, 2012):

> The 1984 anti-Sikh riots were larger than the Gujarat riots, but they were not televised. There too justice came very late, actually much later than it is coming in Gujarat now. But because it was not televised, perhaps because people did not see the riots themselves but only read about it, there was some distance. In the case of the Gujarat riots, that distance is not there. So, unlike Maliana or Meerut or the Sikh riots, or any massacre for that matter, the Gujarat riots are etched in the minds of very large number of people. And every person who has seen that considers themselves a witness to that riot.

Yet, there are other equally portentous (thought ignored, due either to ignorance or deviousness) reasons as to why the embers of Gujarat riots won't die out, even though events such as the crimes of Partition and the accompanying holocaust, wholesale expulsion of Hindus from Kashmir, Nellie massacre of Muslims in Assa, and many greater or longer durational riots like those of Ahmedabad, Moradabad, Meerut, Aligarh, Bhagalpur, Bhiwandi and Surat have were either been brushed under the carpet or (almost) forgotten.

First reason, of course, is that all of the above riots or events took place under Congress regimes. And even though the Congress pointed out its fingers at the RSS or BJP (or the then versions of it), neither could it afford to go to the town with that, nor would the media stretch it any more than what was absolutely necessary to keep its credibility with its clientele intact. For, the very first question involved was that, if really the RSS people (and not Congressmen or general politically neutral public) were responsible for the riots, what prevented you from crushing them and do your appointed duty of protecting lives and the property? Another great reason was that though begun usually as green-on-saffron things initially, these deteriorated soon into khaki-on-green affairs. For example, in Meerut/Maliana case of 1987, while 51 people, all of them Hindus, were killed in the first three or four days of riots, in the next four days at least 295 Muslims were killed – almost all by, or under the active supervision of police and the PAC (*Rivers of Blood*; Brenda K. Uekert). Congress was the ruling party, both in the state and at the Centre at the time.

And here lay the great harm in stretching the thing too long.

Gujarat case was exactly opposite of that.

Second great reason was that our intellectuals, academicians, journalists and the media, political animals as they all are despite pretensions to intellectualism and impartiality, sensed early on that here was a man that had it in him to graduate to become a true leader of men. Modi's record on the Kutch earthquake front and the growing realization that he was absolutely incorruptible didn't help matters, in that it served to validate their worst apprehensions about him. As if complete incorruptibility, stupendous administrative acumen, love of setting developmental targets and then working to meet them at all cost, and unhealthy obsession with improving people's lives were not enough, utter lack of traditional Indian virtues of casteism, nepotism, philistinism, superstitions, buffoonery, loquaciousness, time-wasting and obstructionism turned Modi into a fearsome ogre. He was so un-Gandhian and…and, well, so unlike Nehru, Indira, Pawar, Atal, Advani, Sonia, Lalu or Mulayam. Simply put, explosive combination of these utterly un-Indian ills served to land Modi straight into the category of a Fascist of the most fearsome kind in their leftist-liberal epistemology. Now, if the man came from the RSS background, and showed sickly symptoms of healthy nationalism, he was bound to be worse than Hitler and Stalin combined. He was to be prevented at all costs to stop the politics deteriorating into a public-service affair; thing which could result into the politicians left holding begging bowls, bureaucrats turning into development freaks, and the Indians jumping out of the comforts of destitution and ignorance to fall straight into the fire of development and enlightenment.

But the greatest reason that continues to rile a section of the Muslims and the secularist junta, particularly those nursing suprematism and dhimmitude respectively, is that the Hindus got angry collectively and decided to unite as a community to pay their tormentors in their own coin. Hindus had been dying at the hands of their Muslim 'brethrens' for centuries; what was new in Godhra to feel so outraged about? That the Hindus (and Gujaratis at that) chose to be vindictive and violent despite their shameful history, cowardice, dhimmitude, Gandhi, and all that was incomprehensible and unpardonable. The phenomenon could be tolerated concerning the uncivilized regions like UP and Bihar, but the Gujarati Hindus losing their traditional tolerance and deciding to retaliate that was intolerable indeed. Nothing really could get more galling, outrageous and ominous.

The Muslim sense of superiority and the secularist Hindus' self-image (as earthworms and cockroaches) had been hurt in the way it had been hurt in 1947 when the Hindus of Bihar had decided to avenge the continuing massacre of Hindus in the East Bengal. That led that ogre of a man, Suhrawardy, to embrace Gandhi in a bear hug and Gandhi consecrating him his brother. That set the pattern for the future, turning Hindu-hating Islamic supremacists and the equally Hindu-hating Hindu secularists into blood-brothers for all time to come.

To revert, disbelieving question on everyone's face and the lips was: 'Et tu Gujarati?' Had police or army killed the Muslims to avenge Godhra, that would have been understandable and so much consoling; who can after all fight the police, PAC or the Army? But ordinary Gujarati Hindu, who they bullied with abandon and whose girls they seduced, abducted and molested with impunity, rising in unison: that was unforgivable and unforgettable...

So, what is the root cause behind holding Modi directly culpable for the post-Godhra riots and never forgiving him for it? Argument runs somewhat like this:

> We know that the Hindus (particularly the Gujaratis) are idolatrous-idiotic slaves...utterly incapable of finer human sentiments of honor or righteous anger, and normal human craving for justice and recompense. That was the reason they had been swallowing without demur the worst humiliations thrown at them by their 'brother' Muslims for centuries. It was only the reassurance that mere presence of Modi accorded them that, instead of swallowing the Godhra carnage as just another serving of *shrikhand* and getting on with their *'dhando'* (business), they felt like declaring that enough was enough and fell to giving back as good as they got.

In the event, the conduct of Godhra Muslims was little different, either from their counterparts from the rest of the country, or the Hindu secularist junta which either gave them the benefit of doubt, or absolved them of their culpability on the plea that they had acted under grave provocation (a right firmly denied by them to the Hindus) from the pilgrims returning from visiting a kefir avatar of dubious historicity. Here is a Christian cry of anguish and reason which, of course, it would be futile to hope as giving some food for thought either to the jihadi-supremacists or the dhimmi-secular brigade:

Anon E. Moss (October 18, 2008):

Sir,

This is in regard to 1969 riots. I was one of the officers from the Indian Armed Forces called to restore peace in Ahmedabad with my troops. The information made available to us at that time was that the incident of 'returning cows' happened AFTER the occurrence of the root cause of the riots. It was on the previous night when in the area of Jamalpur an off duty inspector of Police from the minority community returning from work too exception to the Ramayana Katha going on in the street. He asked the Kathakar to stop immediately. The latter pleaded that he should be allowed to complete the chapter. This police officer was livid with anger at the 'disobedience'. He kicked the Ramayana and the paraphernalia to the horror of a large group of worshippers.

The news spread to areas where there were large settlements of migrant textile workers for whom the Ramayana is the most sacred book. They were angry and wanted to retaliate. To add fuel to fire, the 'cow incident' (some cows strayed into the Urs being conducted at Bukhari Saheb Dargah and, in retaliation, nearby Jagannath Mandir was pelted with stones) happened the following day. It was rumored that the Holy Mahant of Jagannath temple was assaulted by the people from the Urs. Inflammatory pamphlets inciting majority community to pick up any weapon that came to their hands were distributed urging violent retaliation for all the rapes and murders that had been perpetrated by the powerful minority community over centuries. I read it myself and it was indeed horrifyingly vitriolic. The result is a history....

After the riots in 1969, when peace was restored, I did some research in the history of riots in Ahmedabad. It transpired that the main causes have been when religious intolerance coupled with violent actions (arson, murder, etc.) was perpetrated on the peaceful local population. Before 1969, there never was retaliatory action from the mainstream community. I do believe that what happened in 1969 and later was the result of injustices and sufferings of the past and inhuman insensitive and intolerable actions on part of some people. The case in point was an incident in 1948. To quell the riots in the same Jamalpur area, two unarmed Congress workers, one Hindu and the other Shia Muslim went on a peace mission. Both were brutally murdered in front of a mosque. Photographs in the Congress House showed that their bodies were completely covered with knife wounds. That was the lowest point in the history of riots in Ahmedabad. In the same riots, a Jain doctor was falsely called out to visit a patient, and when he stepped out of his house his throat was slit. He died in pain. People bore these incidents without retaliation. These reports were archived in local newspapers when I did my study.

The 1969 riots gave vent to age old fury, elicited grave and sudden provocation and resulted in large scale killings. I cannot condone the violence, however, it did happen. The violence then, to say the least, displayed the nadir of human values. No one has a right to take the life of another human and that kind of violence must be abhorred.

The point I wish to make is simple: even after coexisting for centuries, people of some faiths cannot respect the faiths of other communities, label them as pagans, idolaters, "unbelievers", fundamentalists, and punish them or to try to convert them to "enlightened" faith, how long can people go on tolerating? There is a limit to internalizing justice, grief and violence. When, as the cliché goes, enough is enough, the result is like the eruption of a volcano. What happened in the past and is happening now in India is this eruption. It is up to the religious leaders of ALL faiths to have a dialogue and eliminate the battle lines of hatred and generate respect for each others' faiths. The religious leaders should ask their 'flocks' to leave each other alone as far as their faiths are concerned. Human lives are more important than the propagation of a faith or establish a faith as the only acceptable one in the universe."

After Keshubhai Patel had managed to make a complete mess of the things in his state and, at the national level, BJP showed all signs of sinking into a state that it could afford to lose Gujarat only at the cost of losing all credentials to rule the nation, Modi was appointed the acting-experimental chief minister of the state. Not that he was recognized a great political leader with proven administrative record, or had been a darling either of the masses or the party cadres in the state, but his organizational acumen, rock-solid integrity and no-nonsense approach to things were well acknowledged in the inner party circles. Modi was forced to continue as acting chief minister for six months; his entire time spent either in bringing the earthquake relief work back on the rails or ducking the daggers of his detractors in the party who looked upon him with unconcealed distaste as a low-caste usurper. He got sworn in as full-fledged chief minister only a day before Godhra happened on 27th February, 2002. After that, for three long days, many parts of Gujarat, but particularly Ahmedabad, resonated with cries of revenge and pleadings for help. Reverberations were heard not only in India but throughout the world.

We won't go into the territory that has been scoured and scrounged to death: Why didn't Modi get the bodies of dead *kar sevaks* buried then and there, instead of allowing these to be brought to their native town of Ahmedabad? Why did he allow VHP to call a *bandh* (as if all the *bandhs* called in our country carry the consent of the chief ministers or the Prime Minister, as the case may be)? Why did he call a meeting of his ministers or the police officers in the Godhra aftermath? (According to this piece of wisdom, CM has no right to call meeting either of his party or the police officers.) Didn't he call so and so, didn't Jafri phone him to save him from the rampaging mobs, what he said to whom, what he did (or didn't do) during those three momentous days. There is a legion of those engaged in digging out the 'real' truth, and just as many ready to expose the lies behind those truths.

That Modi said (after the riots, and not before or during) what had been on display in Gujarat was the adamantine law of action and reaction, or called the Godhra Muslims communal and accused them of indulging in riots and molestations in the past is uncontestable, being a thing of record. But it too is a fact that these were statements of fact. What in fact he said in an NDTV interview was, *'Kriya pratikirya ki chain chal rahi hai. Hum chahte hain ki na kriya ho aur no pratikriya'* (what is going on is a chain of action and reaction; we want this to stop). Now, pray, what is so exceptionable about that? No statement could get more matter-of-fact, to the point, secular, sincere and statesmanlike. But, no, they won't have it. Heartfelt desire of these elements is that there should be action alright, but no reaction; every victim or recipient of injustice (especially if he/she happens to be a Hindu) should be turned into Jesus-incarnate.

It can't however be denied that it was so very impolite, un-political and naïve of him that instead of shedding copious crocodile tears and letting the riots run for weeks and months as the Congress chief ministers did during Moradabad, Bhagalpur or Bhiwandi (and now Assam), he chose to give voice to an earthy, essential and universal wisdom. That piece of political incorrectness shouldn't however be allowed to bury the incontrovertible fact that he moved exceptionally swiftly to control the situation, bringing the riots to near-complete control in three days flat. Police authorities fired more than 3900 rounds, used more than 6500 rounds of tear gas and arrested more than 2800 people. Ninety Hindus got killed in police firing; not as many Hindus may have got killed in police action in all the post-Independence riots combined (running into, may be, tens of thousands). Modi's tragedy is that he can't articulate that fact in so many words. He had to bear all the assaults silently. Despite taking strong administrative action, evidenced in the fact that 90 Hindus were killed in police firing, 17,947 Hindus (3616 Muslims) were taken under preventive arrest, and riots were brought under control in three days, he couldn't assert from the rooftop: 'See, I got so many Hindus and policemen killed.'

An independent agency (Vishwa Sanwad Kendra) compares the Gujarat riots of 1969, 1985 and 2002:

In 1969, the incident of violence reported on 18th September at 3.45 pm. The army was pressed into service on 21st September at 16.30 pm in limited areas (three police stations only) while army was deployed in the entire city on 22nd September at 18.00 hrs. In 1985, the riot broke out on 15/4/85 and the army was requisitioned on 16/4/85. by then, 177 deaths had already been reported. Compared to this, the army was requisitioned (in case of 2002 riots) on the same day, i.e. on 28th February itself. It is very relevant to note that unlike the earlier occasions, army at this point of time is deployed on the border. Therefore, the deployment of army was difficult at a short notice. However, Hon. Chief Minister impressed upon the Hon. Prime Minister and the Defence Minister to deploy the army forthwith in view of the prevailing condition in the State. The Central Government also reacted very fast and army was airlifted to Ahmedabad the same night. The army was in action from next day of the incident, having completed all the formalities of nominating Executive Magistrate, allocation of vehicles etc.

The incident in 1969 occurred on 18th September 1969 but the situation was out of control, even on the 5th and 6th day. The violent incidents continued to be reported even after the 6th day. The disturbances in 1985 were spread over a period of five months from February 1985 to July 1985. However, in the present case, the situation has been brought under control within three to four days only.

www, geocities.com (another virulently anti-BJP site, which posts such gems as *'Bajrang Dal killed 2 lakh Sikhs in New Delhi in 1983-84'*) has this to say:

During the 1941 communal riots, the Hindus took a terrible beating and never forgot it... The year 1969 was a watershed in communal relations. The Hindu-Muslim riots killed more than 5000 people and Ahmedabad became a vast burial ground. The riots were aggravated because of the conflict between the Congress government led by Indira Gandhi at the Centre, and the state government led by Hitendra Desai of the Congress-O. Congress-O leader Morarji Desai was not personally communal, but he hardly did anything to control the situation. For the first time in the city's history, the labour areas were affected. The killings here were most brutal. Since then, Gujarat has never been the same.

And nobody can deny that provocation this time around was too great. Thus *'The Times of India'* (self-appointed crusader against BJP and Modi) on 12 April 2002:

> Ahmedabad: If it took a shocking massacre like Godhra to trigger off massive communal riots in the state in the 21st century, History shows that trivial incidents caused most riots in the 20th century....

We would do well here to look into at the matter from another angle to gain complete perspective of the issue: What if Modi had done otherwise, i.e., what they say he should have done and which no chief minister in any state ever did—that is, killing all the Hindus that came out on the streets to give vent to their anger on account of the Godhra outrage? Would that have been the end of riots in India (as has been the case, more or less, in India since the Gujarat-2002)? Would the Hindu have swallowed the outrage meekly and silently, accepting their dhimmi position as their divinely-ordained fate for all time to come? Wouldn't that have made, on the one hand, the Jihadi elements (in collusion with the ISI and funded by Saudi money) grow bolder and move on to enact yet greater Godhra like outrages and, on the other, the fires of retribution and hatred simmer in the Hindus hearts...readying to burst out into open like some super-volcano, taking entire nation into their ambit?

And, what would have been the outcome had Modi (as demanded of him by his unthinking detractors) not permitted the bodies of *kar sevaks* to be brought to their home in Ahmedabad (in a celebratory procession; as the perverts choose to term, not holding the Hindus human enough, capable of mourning their dead with dignity) but forced their cremation then and there post-haste (not even terrorists killed in encounters are buried like that; why should have the victims of violence been treated that way) as if they were dangerous criminals and their dead bodies were abomination upon the fair name of secularism of India? Further, what if, satisfying the third main conditions laid down by his secularist detractors, Modi had chosen to resist VHP's *bandh* call and declared open season upon the protesters all over the state as they stepped out of their homes to express their grief and outrage?

For starters, thousands if not tens of thousands Hindus would have been killed in police firing. Further, resisting an ascendant VHP's *bandh* call and taking strong police action was sure to bring down full fury of Hindu wrath not just upon the head of the wannabe super-secular chief minister but the entire BJP, and not only in Gujarat, but throughout India, making its reelection in any of the states or to the Centre next to impossible. It is well worth bearing in mind that the natural constituency of BJP is still to forgive BJP's Kandhar shame or expression of Jinnah-love by Advani. In the event, the BJP was not reelected to the Centre, but its million acts of omission and commission (failure to do anything on the Bangladeshi immigrant front, Kandhar surrender, resisting extradition of Dawood Ibrahim, going soft on Pakistan in the wake of Parliamentary attack, coffin scam, idiocy of shinning India campaign...just about everything, in short) in virtually every domain of national-societal life, and not Modi should be blamed for that. It is a sure bet that had Modi followed what the secularists never tire of telling him ex post facto, BJP could as well have forgotten Gujarat too forever. As for Modi, gaining enduring secular-administrative fame, he would have got his name clubbed with such historical Hindu greats as Vibhishan, Jaichand and Gandhi.

On reflection, that would have been the greatest calamity to befall the Indian polity. Massacre Hindus wherever a BJP government is, ask it to stifle public reaction on the point of machineguns, and eliminate the possibility of a non pro-Muslim government coming to power for ever– that would have become the mantra. By now, every single BJP government (or, for that matter any government not going along the Jihadi agenda) would have got removed by following the prescription the secularists hold out for Modi to have followed...

It could indeed be argued that along with the Ramjanam Bhoomi row, Gujarat riots have harmed the Hindus immensely and benefited the Muslims in even greater measure. Tired of more than a decade long kerfuffle over several non-issues created by the BJP, weary and diffident Hindus have all but thrown the baby of crucial national-societal issues along with the bathwater of Babri Masjid. Muslims on the other hand have got immensely wiser. Instead of indulging in 'riots after riots' to vent their frustration born out of living in a non-Muslim majority environment, they have used the peace time to work to educate and lift themselves up economically, and hone their skills to commandeer the democratic processes to their particular benefit.

Be that as it may, overall outcome is that Modi has become an ideal fall guyfavorite voodoo doll of all those for whom the idea of India is an idea shorn of all traces of saffron and permeated with Islamic green and Christian white, with Hindus living in even worse conditions then Christians, Jews, Ahmediyas and even Shias living in the (Sunni) Muslim lands (evidence Kashmir).

Ironically, more than even the Congressmen, more than the

socialists, communists or the various Janta Dal-wallahs, the Gujarat brouhaha suited the BJP leaders the most by shifting the focus of anti-Hindu secularist venom from the troika of Atal-Advani-Joshi and many others to a single focal point of Modi.

2

IMPLICATIONS & FALLOUTS

Chou-En-Lai, long time premier of China, when asked about the significance of French Revolution and its overall effect upon the course of history, is said to have stated that it was too early to tell (or something of that kind). Well, Godhra outrage and the subsequent riots fall in the same genre, for their implications and the fallouts too shall continue to resonate for an indefinite amount of time.

And as we all are aware, a coin always has its flip side and nothing in the world is wholly bad or good; only He knows best. Thus, while the Partition is deemed to be an unmitigated evil in India, which, in addition to cleaving the ancient nation, took enormous toll in terms of human lives, in Pakistan it is celebrated with unreserved fervor, even though hundreds of thousands of Muslims too were killed and many millions displaced. However, for the Muslims of the sub-Continent as a whole, it is turning out to be an unmitigated disaster, in that, instead of living in a failing Pakistan and horrendously overcrowded and destitute Bangladesh, and having to make do as a minority stained with an indelible stigma in India, by now, with a combined population approaching that of the Hindus, they would have been on the verge of taking over the entire sub-Continent, in case the Partition had not come about. For the Hindus on the other hand, despite the holocaust, cleaving of their sacred land, and a truculent and implacable neighbor on the border as a ghastly kind of bonus, it is turning out to be the principal reason behind their survival up to now. Without the Partition, which caused them and their darling Bapu so much angst, the heartland of India would have been turned by now into the Lebanon of seventies of fortified neighborhoods engaged in interminable war, while in the areas that constitute now Pakistan and Bangladesh, the Hindu minorities would have been entering into the pre-Holocaust Germany phase of the forties…of kidnapping, rapes, pornography of public humiliation, and beginning of mass murders.

Likewise, England's and Japan's waif like geographical location, combined with dearth of natural resources turned out to be blessing in disguise for these nations. Besides saving them from marauders' attacks and the continental turmoil, it made the denizens of these island exceptionally hard-working, innovative and thrifty, developing among them a proud nationalism which made the two nations world's premier imperial and economic power respectively. More recently, as the new millennium heralded, humbling of the premier Western power through 9/11 was rejoiced by most of the Muslims of the world (most gleefully by the Pakistanis) as clear omen that the new millennium was destined to belong to Islam. And, predictably, it was mourned deeply by the Americans and the Westerners with deep apprehensions roiling their hearts as to whether it didn't signal irreversible decline of the West. What the Muslim world, but particularly Pakistan gained from it is there for everyone to see. The Westerners on their part were made acutely aware of the threat of Muslim proliferation within their borders; aware that if not controlled forthwith, they would have to face the scourge of Islamism later, but in manifold more virulent and uncontrollable form. But again, and contrary to what one may surmise, that may turn out to be a blessing in disguise for the Muslim nations by tightening the export from their lands of that most precious commodity a nation or society could have: Its talent! It should hardly need detailing what technology, jobs and wealth a single Henry Ford, Bill Gates or Steve Jobs can create in half of his lifetime may not be generated by entire nations even in a full generation time.

Most of these inadvertent and unforeseen fallouts come of their own accord. Man's instinct for survival, innate desire for happiness and enormous capacity for progress turn the course of history into entirely unexpected channels. Normally, the history meanders through at its own pace, but, now and then, events happen that force sudden change of course by putting an entire nation or social group to severe stress, affecting a catharsis of sorts. It is forced to reflect hard, revise its dearly held assumptions and discard false ego, along with many of its pernicious, obscure and outdated beliefs and practices. Though, many innocent babies are thrown out with the bathwater in the process, it brings much good not only for the people affected or involved, but everybody around. Defeat at the hands of a lowly Asian country (Japan) in 1905 did it for Russia, defeat and humiliation in the First World War for Turkey, and Gunboats of Commodore Perry, WW II and 9/11 for Japan, Europe and the US respectively. Question is: Would Gujarat-2002 do the thing for India, in general, and its Muslims, in particular?

Though discussed in the previous chapter, we have not yet done with the Gujarat riots. How can we...or anyone, for that matter? In fact, more than the Partition riots that were forgotten quickly, more than the Ahmedabad riots of 1969 that took a toll of around ten thousand lives, Moradabad of 1980 in which more than two thousand Muslims were killed over months, Bhagalpur riots which the famous three-star general of the secularist brigade (Lalu) did everything to brush under the carpet, and even the anti-Sikh pogrom of 1984 in which more than three thousand Sikhs were killed within three days to the tune of *'khoon ka badla khoon'* chanted by the Congressmen right in the heart of the national Capital, the Gujarat-2002, which the Congressmen participated in with as much gusto as anyone else and which came in response to as grave a provocation as it is possible to imagine, carries exceptional import. For whereas on the one hand it has traumatized an entire sub-nation in a way neither the Partition nor thousands of riots happening since managed to do, and, on the other, it has been forged by his political opponents into a supremely useful tool to checkmate the only person who has established beyond a shadow of doubt that he has in him the character, spirit and the mettle to slay the demons lying in wait to waylay the nation in not too distant a future.

Godhra train carnage was not a sudden or spontaneous eruption. That at least a few days, if not months, of planning had gone into it has been proved beyond a shadow of doubt. However, given the system the nation at large has come to develop and Modi inherited, Godhra was something Modi government couldn't have helped. But he could sure have prevented the riots that went on for about three days and took about one thousand lives. Three steps would have been enough for him to preempt the riots, prove himself a great administrator and win secularists and Muslim hearts.

1. Burying the *kar-sevaks* then and there, without bringing their bodies to their respective homes or allowing their relatives and acquaintances the luxury of mourning.

2. Warning the RSS and the VHP to call off their proposed ban, and in case they failed to heed it, ban them pronto, even though that would have entailed incarcerating their leaders, including perhaps some of his own ministers and party functionaries, thus bringing down own government even before the riots had erupted and infuriating the outraged public further.

3. Imposing curfew all over Gujarat and instructing police to fire upon the violator of the curfew without giving them time or opportunity to indulge in mischief.

Not a few would counter the contention vehemently, arguing that refusing permission to bring the bodies of the *kar-sevaks* to their home town of Ahmedabad and issuing strict warning and making extensive preventive arrests and show of force would have been enough to instill fear in the hearts of the potential mischief makers. That may be so. Preventing and controlling riots in India may have been so simple an affair. But, then, would anyone please explain why Moradabad, Meerut, Aligarh, Bhagalpur, Bhiwandi or Hyderabad riots, that ran for weeks and even months, and happened in response to insignificant incidents (as contrasted with Godhra carnage), could neither be prevented nor controlled promptly? Or, for that matter, why Gujarat remained in the grip of riots throughout the early nineties, even though no official encouragement or protection (as alleged in case of Gujarat-2002) was supposed to be available then?

Be that as it may, the riots could have been prevented and the legendary reputation of Hindus for tolerance and secular 'ethos' protected if only Modi had shown *'whatever it takes'* attitude. Nobody can deny that. Administrative firmness, along with full freedom accorded to police with its rifles would have prevented not just the Gujarat riots but all the communal carnages, right from Moplah and Kohat to Great Calcutta Killings to Noakhali, Garhmukteswar, Sambhal, Mau and the like. That said, it bears reiteration that the Gujarat riots of 2002 were entirely different in character, in that they took place in response to an outrage that was unprecedented in its chutzpah and shock value. Imagine a bogey filled with Muslim pilgrims returning from Hajj being torched by Hindus in Bangladesh, Ahmediyas in Pakistan, Bahais in Iran or Christians in Egypt, Indonesia or Nigeria. All these minorities would get wiped out in seven days flat, with only a few of the nations that erupted in indignation and rage over the Gujarat riots taking notice or going beyond making performa protest. Fact is that in the whole wide world, it is only the Hindus that demand more Hindus should have been killed in response to Hindus been killed.

Now, Modi deciding to respond firmly and swiftly (in accordance with the wishes of secularists and the English media), declaring that Sabarmati Express pilgrims had mass-immolated themselves in response to earnest pleadings of their Muslim brethrens of Godhra; banning his own political party and the outfits; arresting his ministers and colleagues for declaring *bandh* and to stop them from giving effect to it; and giving police and the paramilitary forces a carte blanche to act, thus nipping the budding trouble in its very bud, what would have been the repercussions for him, his party, Gujarat and India as a whole...

1. Firstly, Modi and the BJP can't be imagined to ever returning to power in Gujarat. BJP's image as a party of Hindutva (whatever the truth or the worth) would have got finished and whatever little credibility it continues to enjoy would have got reduced to nil. However, it is inconceivable that either the Muslims or the secularist-leftist junta, or the ISI, Saudis, Ummah at large, or the Western nations would have deigned to adopt Modi as their icon or the BJP as their party of choice.

2. Moronic-obscurantist rabble-rousing organizations and people like VHP, Bajrang Dal and Togadias, instead of getting neutered as they have been now by Modi, would have emerged immensely strong on the wave of Hindu frustrations and sense of insecurity. As things stand, Modi has succeeded in defanging these elements, thus diverting rightist Hindu focus off the crude communalism, and its hopes and faith on to himself and his singular agenda of peace and progress.

3. Hindu sense of betrayal, abandonment and defeat (even during the rule of supposed party of Hindus), and the Muslim sense of smugness would have combined to produce an immeasurably fertile ground for the people of India to reap rich crops of riots and death year after year. The situation would have been akin to what obtained in the aftermath of Moplah riots when Gandhi and the Congress surrender gave the Muslims a great sense of triumph and the nation got awash in blood. It extended to the Muslims the necessary confidence about their ability to wrench away a separate nation, which in their imagination extended up to Saharanpur and Aligarh, and included Bhopal and Hyderabad states too.

4. It would have given great confidence and spur to ISI and the Islamists of India. The dissembling secularist brigade would have everyone believe that all terrorist attacks in India that came after the Gujarat-2202 were in response to those riots (thus justifying the terrorist attacks in terms of action-reaction theory; a right firmly denied by them to the Hindus), making it very convenient to ignore all terrorist strikes prior to that.

5. Great spur the Jihadi elements within the country, as also the ISI

would have got is only one aspect of the thing. Indian Muslims, in general, and Gujarati ones, in particular would have remained stuck in the selfsame mindset of superiority and belligerence that had been taking them nowhere. No defense of Gujarat-2002, but it is incontrovertible that the resulting quasi-catharsis has led them to decide to contest with the Hindus on educational and economic fronts, abandoning, by and large, the site of physical contestation where they had been stuck since the Khilafat fiasco eight decades ago. This can't but turn out to be a thing of immense good to them and the country in general.

6. The nation would have suffered immeasurably, with the main opposition party losing all credibility and the support of even its core constituency. Development, which has been turned into kind of premier national agenda by Modi, forcing all the political parties to swear by it, would still have been nobody's baby. Further, getting yet bolder, the Congress would have got yet more corrupt (if it were possible) and the nation would have been resembling Nigeria and Sudan by now. Condition would have been getting ripe for either a Fascist takeover, or turning the land into another Somalia (Somalia at least has a saving grace in being all-Muslim), only hundred-fold magnified.

At the risk of sounding blasphemous, one may dare say that Modi has proved himself to be free of any type of bias. Affinities of family, caste, clan or class, which have always been and continue to be greatest banes of men in pubic life, do not simply exist for him. What is of yet greater import – and here I speak with full sense of responsibility – he is entirely free of religious bias too. In any case, his actions as chief honcho of his state betray no bias. Whether he carries that kind of freedom from all manners of biases in his heart too, no one can determine or tell. Despite what the likes of Mr. Ashis Nandy may claim, no one can perceive the deeper promptings of his own heart even, let alone those of the others. Caste Hindus can't see the dark and hateful casteist spots of their hearts, nor the adherents of Abrahamic faiths acknowledge that consigning, in their hearts and the beliefs, the non-believers to the direst Hell, they turn into misanthrope bigots at the most fundamental level, becoming, thereby, the heir to the selfsame Hell they believe the non-believers to be heading towards.

Fact is that no one in the whole wide world is entirely free of bias, be it on account of religion, caste, language, class or color of skin. What to talk of others, even the 'Son of God' had proclaimed:

'Those who are not with us are against us'. Gandhi's attitude towards the blacks of Africa or the Jews of Europe had been...well, singularly short on empathy. Further, he too saw Muslims as fanatical and intolerant. Was he being biased or prejudiced in saying that? If one said that Jews used to harbor a ghetto mentality, Afghans have always been proud and warlike, Japanese had turned into inhuman rascals at the beginning of the twentieth century, or the West Pakistani attitude towards their then East Pakistani compatriots was extremely shameful – would that be a rant of a prejudiced mind or a generalized statement of facts? Consider some of Gandhi's statements:

'It is the question of the Muslims that pricks me like a thorn. I wonder how I am going to be able to win them over to love and non-violence. They are steeped in hatred.' (Gandhi, telling Mahadev Desai (1918).

'The Muslims are religious fanatics... They say Islam is the brotherhood of man. As matter of fact, it is a brotherhood of Muslims'. (Gandhi to Louis Fischer, 1946)

'The Muslim as a rule is a bully, and the Hindu as a rule is a coward.' (Gandhi, writing in the aftermath of the Kohat riots (1924).

'The Muslim being generally in a minority has as a class developed into bully...The thirteen hundred years of imperialist expansion has made the Mussalmans fighters as a body. They are therefore bullies and aggressive. The Hindu has an old civilization... The vice (docility) is, therefore, a natural excrescence of gentleness.' (Gandhi explaining away his *'Muslim as a rule is bully...'* remark)

'I have not a shadow of doubt that Islam has sufficient in itself to become purged of illiberalism and intolerance.' (Gandhi, while undertaking fast at the house of Shaukat Ali in response to post-Khilafat riots)

'...Hinduism will captivate Muslims by the power of its compassion, which is its very essence...We can win over the Muslims this very day if we are sufficiently imbued with the spirit of brotherly love.'

'The Musalmans take less interest (in their country's political life)...because they do not regard India as their home of which they must feel proud.'

Now, if Gandhi was not a bigot in terming Islam illiberal and the Muslims bullies and less than patriotic, Modi should be deemed a sterling secularist.

So it is better not to go into the issue as to whose heart is black and whose snow white. However, as far as actions are concerned, Modi has shown himself to be most fair and judicious political leader of them all. For, most charitable thing that could be said about Indian politicians is that their greed takes precedence over their biases and pet hatreds, and if they manage to keep the latter under control, it is because that best suits their agenda, whose alpha and omega is to loot the nation dry. Had Modi got busy in amassing wealth for himself and advancing his clans and cronies like Mulayams, Lalus, Arjun Singhs and Pawars of the world do, they would have anointed him a secularist icon long ago.

There is little doubt that the Muslims of India were subjected to great stress and angst by the Gujarat riots. Though there was nothing like a full-fledged catharsis (*'Islam is the Way'*, or *'Islam is The Solution'* mindset impedes, if not altogether closes, rational introspection and discourse) in their case, the anger and angst engendered a great deal of debate, leading to realization of their position, revaluation of their social conduct and reassessment of their political strategy. And entirely reprehensible and tragic even as the loss of life and property was, Gujarat riots have had some beneficial fallouts too for the Muslims:

1. It got rid the Gujarat Muslims of their irrational and ultimately unprofitable belligerence and superiority complex, setting them on to a path of education and industry. By making their *goondas* and criminal elements toothless, it rid their youth of false heroes and ideals.

2. It is common knowledge that curfews affect the Muslims most. Muslims mostly live in towns and out of, say, fifty neighborhoods in a town, it is only the dozen or so Muslim majority ones that have to suffer riots and the resulting curfews, even as life in the rest of town goes on normally, by and large. In Gujarat of nineties, declared curfews ran for months and the undeclared ones for years, hurting the Muslims grievously and disproportionately. Harassment by police became routine, freedom of movement was curtailed, business and industry got destroyed or hampered, education suffered and mindsets got distorted. There hasn't been a single curfew since and the effects are visible all around.

3. It made them aware of the real character of many Congress leaders who had been making fool of them by offering empty promises and keeping them embroiled in pernicious politics,

even as they carried murder in their hearts.

4. Muslims of entire India got wiser too. They know now how pernicious, and ultimately pointless, it is to keep testing the patience of the majority. That is the reason there has been no big riot since then (Assam has come just now). It could be said that though riots may yet take place, constant tension that kept the Muslims on the tenterhook and diverted their energies has largely dissipated. Thus, the Gujarat riot got entire India rid of the riots of Moradabad, Aligarh, Ahmedabad, Surat Meerut, Bhagalpur or Bhiwandi kind.

5. It brought enormous sympathy and support to them from all around the country. And though pooping of the Pakistan promise has much to do with it, it restored their faith in the fairness of Indian political system, judiciary and the democracy.

6. It rid the Hindus of Gujarat of some of their inferiority complex, thus attenuating this one of the root causes of their communalism.

7. It brought the entire Babri Masjid/Ramjanambhoomi saga to a resounding end, placing the case firmly in the realm of courts. Whatever appetite the Hindus had been left with after the demolition of the mosque, Gujarat riots finished it in one fell stroke.

8. It brought a leader of caliber of Modi to the fore. By making development the principal agenda of the nation, he, almost single-handedly, managed to throw the misleading and damaging rhetoric and campaigns of his party (thing that had kept the entire nation hobbled for more than a decade) into the dustbin of history.

Essential truth is that Modi has not made the Gujaratis communal...at least more than what they had already been. Rather, he has enabled them to come out of their communal mindset and think along secular lines. What the Gujarati Hindu had been before was not a secular but fearful beast, nursing million resentments in its heart. It is a fact that only a proud and fearless people can afford to be liberal and secular. Modi exorcised them of this constant, nagging, demeaning and communalizing ghost of fear, and along went their communalism too. And he has set them a golden goal, and laid down a clear and straight path to march on to achieve that goal. It would prevent them from lapsing back into the past of horrendous and debilitating communal discord.

Himself free of caste bias or communal prejudices, Modi has helped Gujarat too rid itself of the two perniciousness: debilitating riots, and the insidious and divisive KHAM politics invented and pedaled shamelessly by the rapscallion Congress leaders. Now, increasingly, the Gujaratis are just Gujaratis, though the Congressmen, as also the disgruntled elements within Modi's own party keep stoking the old embers. Greatest and noblest method of resolving cleavages is to unite the people into a common and forward-oriented resolve, and Modi has done just that.

✳

3

WHAT HAS HE DONE, WHAT HE CAN DO

Of late, as the Congress totters under the wait of its diarchy and scandals; its young white hope turns increasingly darker shades of grey; nation's economy falters and unchecked inflation, scarcities and economic woes begin to stoke fears of resurfacing of social tensions and contradictions; and the eyes begin to search desperately for an effective alternative, the gaze of the media, observers, experts and the well-wishers, both national and the international, reverts again and again to Modi whose achievements, after a decade-long probation, no one has been left in a position to ignore or deny as sham or fluke. Increasingly, and to immense consternation of his political opponents and detractor within and outside his party, the man is getting increasingly defined by his ability and accomplishments that are beginning to be viewed as natural manifestations of his extraordinary persona and the acumen, and not the tragedy of those fateful days which was beyond the control of human agency.

The result is that there is a veritable flood of articles in the international media (*The New York Times, Washington Post, The Economist, Forbes, The Guardian, Brookings*, and what not) that contrast the congenital defects of the Congress and the shame and misery it is fetching to the nation, with sterling qualities of Modi and the glory he has brought to the state administered by him. Of course, when Modi is there, Gujarat Riots can't be far behind, but these are now treated less as his introduction and chief claim to fame, and more as appendage or caution that one can't help mentioning for the sake of objectivity. Now the chief claim to fame is the man's personal integrity, his administrative acumen, sincerity, attention to detail, frugality, ability to maintain peace in his state, robust nationalism and passion for bettering the lives of his compatriots. His alleged complicity or complaisance in the riots is categorized as a blot that he can't possibly get rid of completely but which his co-nationals had better ignored in order to harness the million qualities of the man for the country's good.

Before going into the encomiums being showered upon him lately, we would do well to have a 'drone-pilot' view of some of the doings and achievements of the man, so as to form our own independent estimation of him. But, even before that, it is essential to have a recap of the fundamental ills or obstacles that have always held India back from achieving its full potential, leaving its overwhelming majority poor, hungry, excluded, exploited, ignorant and diseased, and rendering its elite progressively exploiting, self-serving, lying and cheating rogues.

Unlike many nations of the world, India has been extremely fortunate in being largely free of antediluvian sentiments like, 'Islam is The Solution', or 'Islam is the Way'...attitudes that hold back the Islamic societies from coming out of their mediaeval mindsets and grow into world-citizens. Likewise, it has been able to steer clear of the crippling perniciousness of Communism whose fundamental focus is upon redistribution of wealth, simultaneous with stymieing, expelling or killing the talent, enterprise and the systems necessary to generate it. Yet it failed to join the ranks of enlightened and progressive nations that have been similarly free of the two drawbacks. Reasons have been the selfsame three Cs we have harped upon again and again but to have a brief recap:

First 'C' of course is caste, whose underlying misanthropic assumptions, and social and economic destructive potential can't be overemphasized. It has denied access to resources like education to an overwhelming majority, distorted land and assets ownership pattern, compartmentalized occupations and skills to particular castes, raised a steel-frame of exploitation and exclusion, wrecked social-cohesion, and kept greater part of the society from enjoying the fruits of civilization and culture. Presently, it has made a complete mess of our democracy, leading people to support candidates on the basis of their caste, rather than character or performance.

The second 'C' is communalism, or, more specifically, the Hindu-Muslim thing. Apart from the memes of millennium long history, the watershed event of Partition kept the majority Hindus angry and the minority Muslims in a state of nervous belligerence. Exploited shamelessly for its electoral ends by the Congress, the communalism of both the principal communities has continued to warp the polity and the democracy of the land. However, greatest long term damage has been on the population front. While the majority community has always been appreciative of the need for strong and meaningful action, not excluding some kind of legislation implemented in a transparent and humane way, fear of fierce Muslim resistance (and therefore electoral loss) to all talks of population control has kept all the governments since Independence from treading the path. As direct fallout, the nation's population, which could easily have been kept below the billion mark, is set to touch twice that figure by the middle of the present century.

As for the third 'C' of corruption, though eating into the vitals of our society, economy and the polity for a long time, it has acquired really sinister dimensions and salience of late. Since the thing has already been discussed in necessary detail, it may suffice here to quote what United Nations' 'Convention against Corruption' has to say about the phenomenon:

> Corruption is an insidious plague that has a wide range of corrosive effects on societies. It undermines democracy and the rule of law, leads of violations of human rights, distorts markets, erodes the quality of life and allows organized crime, terrorism and other threats to human security to flourish.

Further, according to the Organization for Economic Co-operation and Development (OECD):

> Graft imposes costs in terms of human suffering that go far beyond the moneys lost to bribery, embezzlement or fraud.' And, 'Counterfeit medical drugs at best do no good and at worst can kill; bridges built with substandard materials at best cost more to maintain and repair and at worst may collapse, injuring and killing people...

> Corruption is not a victimless crime, and those most hurt by it are the world's weakest and most vulnerable. Child mortality rates in countries with high levels of corruption are about one third higher than in countries with low corruption.

Coming back to Modi, the man may not have been able to eliminate communalism, render caste a redundancy, and wipe out the corruption, but he certainly has taken the most essential step in that direction, namely, presenting himself as paradigm of what a leader entirely free of these evils or biases can accomplish. Presenting an ideal, he has made the public space of Gujarat considerably free of the three blights. Little wonder then that the eco-system of Gujarat has become considerably agreeable for leading a reasonably uncomplicated, happy and progressive life.

Unable to refute growing evidence of Gujarat's rise, and realizing that negating it completely would put their credibility to serious question, Modi's detractors have taken another line which runs along these lines:

> Gujarat has always been a progressive state, clocking, year after year, higher growth rates than the rest of India. Ideal location (opening up to the Arabian Sea) it enjoys has always been a magnet for businessmen and trade-adventurers. Its people have always been the most businesslike, (and therefore) peaceable and welcoming people of the world. Little wonder then that more than any other, the term *'dhando'* has come to be emblematic of Gujarati spirit. Modi's claim of making Gujarat the leading business-friendly state should be seen in that light.'

That is all true. But, firstly, as a perceptible observer has commented, Gujaratis, for whom the entire world, from Dholera (in Gujarat) to Durban is a playground, are under no obligation to invest their money in Gujarat if it didn't promise best returns. Further, the people arguing in these terms are either ignorant of, or make it convenient to ignore, the crucial difference between crude *'dhando'* and highly desirable trade, industriousness, development and progress. *'Dhando'* is not industry or progress; it is profiteering, crude and simple, taking advantage of one's experience, location and capital. Buying cheapest and selling dearest, with no regard whatsoever to any other aspect of the thing – that is *dhando*. For thousands of years they had been doing *dhando*, but did that help to make common Gujarati any the richer, or Gujarat's per capita income more than only a shade better than the rest of India as a whole, which includes such worthies as Bihar, UP, Orissa, MP, Rajasthan, Andhra and Assam? By its very nature, the *dhando* remains limited to a few people while the majority gets exploited yet more shamelessly because of this spirit of *dhando*.

Creating a culture of development, enabling just about everyone to have his share (as distinct from crude *dhando,* which carries a distinctly mercenary air about it and had been a preserve of a few) is what has been Modi's greatest achievement. His role has been like that of a village jinn who has prepared the fields of the entire village by ploughing, leveling and composting it. All that the villagers had to do was to throw seeds into it and reap rich harvest... no Rangdari levied or obstacle posed.

But you can do only so much with a prepared field. In the absence of right kind of seeds, scientific knowledge or proper irrigation, you may be able to reap only a middling crop and that too once in a year. To wit, taking care of not only the aforesaid macro-level things of the three Cs, but micro-level things too – health, electricity, irrigation, education and hundred little cares and attentions that went into making small and desolate islands of Singapore, Hong Kong and Taiwan into modern economic behemoths – Modi's range of concerns and the depth of sincerity is manifested in the fact that there is hardly anything he has left out of the ambit of his concerns and endeavors. It is as if he has got an obsession of removing even the littlest pebbles lying in the path of progress and happiness of his people.

At the very inception of his chief-ministerial career Modi identified the fundamental hold-backs keeping the people of his state from rising up to their potential, as also his strategy to tackle these. Thus he identified five energies or powers required to energize the potential inherent in the people of his state (or any other people, for that matter). He gave these energies (and his plans thereof) the name of Panchamrut (five necters). These were: Gyan Shakti (power of education to tackle illiteracy and abysmal quality of education), Jan Shakti (power of full developed human resources), Jal Shakti (power of water resources for his largely arid and drought-prone state), Urja Shakti (developing energy resources) and Raksha Shakti (providing security of life and property, so essential for sense of well-being and economic growth).

First things first…that is, Modi's thinking and the achievements on the water-front. To tell the truth, Modi can never be praised enough for showing that…well, as a commercial says, 'Impossible is nothing'. In this country of extremely low expectations and even less achievements, he managed to show that impossible could indeed be achieved within a short span of time and without making much fuss about. Thus, in this era of almost irreversibly deteriorating environment, drying rivers, dying ponds and dwindling water-tables, he has managed to heal the environment of his state, rejuvenate an ancient and iconic river (Sabarmati) caught in its death throes, reverse the decline of water-table, and not only refill the extant water-ponds but create thousands of them anew! If this is not miracle-making in our blighted land caught in deepest of kalyugs, pray what else could be?

To come down to the dry arena of statistics, about 2000 km of bulk and more than one lakh km of distribution water pipelines, and more than one lakh (yes, one lakh!) reservoirs and check dams have been created within a decade. As a result, not only the number of villages dependent upon water tanker supply for their water needs came down from a high of 4054 (out of Gujarat's 18000) in 2001 to 326 in 2008, but even in such a drought-prone state as Gujarat, yearly number of tubewells installed got reduced from a high of eleven hundred in 2001 to about sixty in 2008. According supreme importance to the scourge of water scarcity and the quality that had been wastelanding the Gujarat countryside and blighting in every which way the lives of its tens of millions, Modi took initiative to form Village Water and Sanitation Committees in nearly all the villages of the state to take up the water-management responsibility. These innovative and conservation efforts present a role-model not only for the rest of India, but the entire developing world.

Creation of hundreds of thousands of farm (individual level) and village (community level) water ponds under the state guidance and the monetary help, combined with drip-irrigation techniques which Modi is specially passionate about have helped recharge the ground water, so much so that in almost every region of Gujarat, relentless receding of water table has not only been halted, but the trend has got reversed at a miraculous rate. Thus, for Gujarat as a whole, whilst the average fall in the table during the period 1998-2002 was 2.5 meters, it surged by 4.0 meters on the positive side during the period 2003-07.

The result has been that in the areas where it was difficult to take even one satisfactory crop in a year, vegetables are being grown and orchards planted, and the yield of milch cattle has shot up due to year round availability of feed. Inevitably, the productivity of crops too has grown significantly. Thus the productivity of groundnut (one of the most significant crops of Gujarat) has shot up from around 700 kg/ha to 1500 in 2010, of cereals from 1200 to 1900, pulses from 500 to 750, oilseeds from 850 to 1350, and cotton (biggest cash crop of Gujarat) from 250 to 530 (lints). Little wonder then that as a result of successful completion of water projects (including Narmada Dam and the associate canal works), combined with missionary-like zeal shown by the Modi dispensation to empower the farmers with knowledge and tools, the annual agricultural growth rate of Gujarat has come to hold steady at around ten percent...feat unheard of anywhere in the world.

That, attainments of Modi on the front of water supply, irrigation and agriculture are extraordinary, doesn't mean that he has shown any slackness on any other front, be that energy (including renewable energy), education, environment, tribal uplift, infrastructure, industry or public security. State-wise gas-grid, piped-water supply to most of the villages, twenty-four hour three-phase supply to villages and eight hour assured supply to agricultural pumps, and broadband connection to every village are achievements of which even middle-income countries could justly be proud of. One exemplar of these efforts is that Ahmedabad, that had begun to show perceptible signs of decay that mark every other metro of India, has been designated as most livable – clean, and congestion and crime free – city in India out of the thirty five surveyed, and Gujarat as a whole has come to be declared as the safest state in India.

Instead of recounting Modi's achievements to prove the point, let's hear it from some of the people/agencies who have been (and continue to remain) Modi's bitter critics. We begin with a true Hindu (and not only Modi) hater, so much so that he holds that:

> The rage that burst through the fissures in 2002 was long seething. That explains why a Muslim mob could so readily set fire to a train with fanatical Hindu political volunteers on board and the bestial retaliation against Muslims that followed, probably with state complicity.

Welcome, ladies and gentlemen, Vivian Fernandes of CNBC-TV18, writing in IBN Live of March 02, 2012. According to this gentleman, 58 people (mainly women and children), who were set upon and burnt alive by the Muslims mobs while returning from pilgrimage to Ayodhya, were 'fanatical'. According to this man's holy wisdom (as indeed of all the secularists of this land), all those who visit Hindu temples or places of religious significance are either superstitious or fanatical (that is, 'up to no good', if not up to something devilish or sinister), even as those visiting Vatican or Mecca are all pious lambs imbued with the sentiments of piety, doing their pilgrimage in search of truth and peace. And even as giving state subsidy to Muslims to go on Haj to a country irreconcilably hostile to India and whatever it stands for is par for course, the ancient denizens of the land have evidently no moral right to visit the place of birth of even the most revered of the avatars of the land, and that too at their own expense. Further, the attack on them by Muslim mobs was due to 'seething' rage (holy rage; he refrained from saying) born out of some desperation, while the retaliation that followed was pure 'bestial' in nature, and not natural reaction of normal homo-sapiens to the previous day's carnage.

Having shown his colors, what even this gentleman has to say about Modi? Thus our Vivian Fernandes:

> There can be little doubt that Gujarat is India's dragon state. The past decade has been the best since Gujarat became a state in 1960. Average annual economic growth, at 10.5%, is two and half

percentage points higher than that of the nation. Achievement on the industrial front is to be expected: Gujarat is India's workshop along with Tamil Nadu and Maharashtra. The surprise is Gujarat's agriculture. At 12 percent a year, it has clocked to a Chinese rhythm, while the whole of India struggles to tick past the target rate of 4 per cent. All this has made the Gujarati richer than the average Indian by a third.

Gujarat has had 14 Chief Ministers. Narendra Modi is the longest serving since 2001. As the past decade coincides with his tenure, he deserves much of the applause. Industry leaders hail him as the Prime Minister India never had. Such encomiums grate on those who see India as a vibrant and compassionate society, not just a thriving economy. Gujarat reflects in abundant measure the 'Beijing Consensus', which the Economist described as `going capitalist, staying authoritarian`. Gujarat is the wrong place to look for social justice. It has been a schizophrenic society. The rage that burst through the fissures in 2002 was long seething. That explains why a Muslim mob…

Modi therefore had a solid base upon which to build when he assumed office. He has also been very lucky…

But Modi is also an unabashed liberalizer. When attacked for his port privatization policy, Modi is said to have remarked that `the people of Gujarat are very enterprising and they want minimum government`. Some of Gujarat's minor ports (as state-domain ports are called) handle more cargo than major ports (owned by the central government), so much so that minor ports are now called non-major ports! Rising from the devastating earthquake of 2000 and leveraging its reserves of minerals, arid Kutch has attracted cement, steel, power and chemical industries. It is a global hub for pipeline manufacture. This is where Adanis have set up a deepwater port with a large industrial enclave. Drinking water from the Narmada is now being supplied through a pipeline. Work on extending the Narmada canal for irrigation began last year. At one point people were fleeing Kutch. Now they are flocking to it. With 32 percent growth over a decade, Kutch was the second fastest growing district in the state after Surat, according to the last population census. It is a metaphor for Gujarat'

Modi can also claim part of the credit for the state's stellar growth in agriculture. A Supreme Court ruling early in the last decade allowing an increase in the height of the Narmada dam has helped. Modi's contribution is the 'Jyotirgram' program that assures farmers around eight hours of subsidized power at off-peak time for pumps through a separate Rs. 1200 crore electricity grid. Power rationing also conserves groundwater. This has by and large spared rural homes from power cuts, which were frequent when pumps were hooked to the same network.

A vigorous check dam movement provides insurance against weather shocks....As chief minister Chimanbhai Patel gave official support. Modi has put the programme on skates by cutting red tape and providing technological support like satellite images to locate the water soaks. He is also keen on converting farmers to drip irrigation. A focus on outcomes, rather than outlays, decided against housing the scheme in a government department. The Gujarat Green Revolution Company claims considerable success, though figures are not in the public domain.

Similar success is claimed for a five-year Rs. 15,000 crore tribal development programme aimed at doubling household income among 15 percent of the state's population living in hilly and forested areas....

Modi has also fixed the agricultural extension system, which is broken in most states. Led by the chief minister himself and braving the May sun, tens of thousands of officials traverse the countryside testing soil, supplying high-yielding seeds and exchanging information in a celebration of agricultural outreach during the so-called Krishi Mahotsav (farm festival). It is an exercise that other states should emulate.

Anyone who has traveled in Gujarat would vouch for its roads, only Tamil Nadu perhaps has a better network. The World Bank, which financed the road-building programme, has compiled its happy experience in a book as a lesson for states. Easier access to market and suppliers has flattered both industrial and agricultural growth....

Gujarat's strength in manufacturing has profited from Modi's salesmanship.... In the 1990s, Gujarat was low down on the list. But it has climbed up the rungs despite not being known for IT and financial services (that get much of the FDI) and falling short of the frills of life: good schools, non-veg food and booze. Prohibition is official policy, though liquor is available for a price.

By slashing red tape, providing an administration that is said to be low on corruption, making land easily available, and assuring industrial peace (despite occasional strikes as at General Motors), Gujarat has attracted marquee industries...

Modi's innovation in administration are also noteworthy. Administrators from the district collector down are encouraged to implement projects beyond their remitthe ambition of these programmes and the enthusiasm with which they are executed allows Modi to size them up. Feedback gathered through monthly grievance redress exercises over video links. An annual retreat brings chief minister and officials together for an exchange of experiences. Modi likes campaigns during elections and between them. There are campaigns to get the girl child in school, stop the killing of female foetuses, promote sanitation, provide nutrition supplements and encourage birth in hospitals.

Some of these campaigns may be high on hype. during a week long tour of Sauraashtra recently, I found the state buses in dire need of wash (though run on the hour and take you there). The bus depots were also filthy. Even a prime pilgrim centre like Dwarka had mounds of garbage. The road leading to Dholavira, the largest city in India of the 5,000 year old Harappan civilization, was deplorable. This experience is hard to reconcile with the claims made for the Nirmal Gujarat campaign launched in 2008.

Gujarat health attainments are way below its level of prosperity. The death rate of infants (under one year) is the same as the national average. There is a yawning gap between rural and urban areas; the death rate being 51 and 30 (for every thousand born). The rate and disparity is much lower in states like Tamil Nadu (25 and 22). This does not mean that economic growth has been futile. Gujarat has reduced the infant death rate by 20 points over the last decade. But Tamil Nadu has done better with a reduction of 30 points.

Even economic success must be tempered with caution. High growth in the farm sector bodes well for the state. The experience of Brazil and China shows that agricultural growth is two to three times more poverty reducing than growth in other sectors. But on the industrial front, Gujarat's growth is capital intensive, unlike Tamil Nadu, which leads the country in number of factories. A danger to watch out for is crony capitalism that can flourish under a charismatic and authoritarian leader who is convinced of his certitudes...

So, here we are. We had stated at the outset:

As far as our country is concerned, it has become more than apparent by now that the State and the System obtaining here have got a certain degree of malevolence about them, for they have been uncannily consistent in transforming the society's best most resourceful and the enterprising into its worst. Thus, as a direct consequence of the kind of electoral politics the country has come to be burdened with and under the approving gaze of the complicit State, potential heroes and deliverers of the society are being turned into social parasites and predators.

In this regard, i.e., 'society's best turned into its worst', the case of Pradeep Shukla, IAS, topper of 1981 IAS batch, is an apt exemplar. First the political dispensation uses him to indulge in NRHM scam, thus affecting millions of ill-fated denizens of the land, and when 'unfortunately' he gets caught, the new dispensation not only does not suspend him from the job, but the very uncle of the government (so to say) goes out to meet him in jail and the man is given charge of a department as soon as he happens to come out on bail, with his wife (also an IAS) getting a plum posting as damage compensation.

Or, take the example of the very pinnacle of the dispensation obtaining at the Centre. Willfully and shamelessly, overruling vehement protests of the Leader of the Opposition, it sought to appoint a man charged with indulgence in an iconic scam the Central Vigilance Commissioner of India, no less!

Well, here is a pleasant exception. As one can very well surmise from Vivian Fernandes's fulminations, in Gujarat of Modi, society's best are being groomed, cajoled or forced to do what they were meant to, viz., giving out their very best to the society.

Again, instead of taking the tiresome task of recounting Modi's acumen and the achievements upon one's suspected self, it would be preferable to leave it to the people and institutions that have been his harshest critics. Thus Brookings, oldest and most respected of the American research institutions:

Brookings (March 16, 2012)

Meet India's most admired and most feared politician: Narendra Modi. The world's largest democracy, India, could elect him Prime Minister. And the world's leading democracy, the United States, currently does not issue him a visa...

In person, Modi comes across as an effective administrator, a proud Indian nationalist, and a committed if not zealous Hindu. He also is a policy mavenintroverted, precise, and even passionate about the most technical of subjects. On almost all of these issues, his Gujarat is pushing, not following, New Delhi and India.

"I had never run anything before, and I had never run for elected office", he said. "And then the Godhra train incident happened."...

Modi has never apologized. "I was just installed in my position the day before." He had been formally elected and sworn in on February 26th, having been acting Chief Minister for six months, mostly overseeing response to Gujarat's 2001 earthquake....

Later he told me in general terms about his years in office, "I have made mistakes, and my government has made mistakes. What is important is that we recognize them, evaluate what we have done, and then fix them."

After the earthquake and the riots, Modi launched a "Vibrant Gujarat" conference in 2003 to market the state to Indian and foreign investors. He established simple rules: "We will not pay any incentive and will not accept any bribes. But I will provide single window facilitation, quality power and water, and will honor my commitments."

Unlike Chinese-style urban manufacturing that draws workers from the country side, Modi also targeted rural development. "If it does not work in the villages, it will not work in the city." His eyes light up when discussing infrastructure, agricultural colleges, solar energy, and climate change. "I prioritized four things," he said: "Water, electric power, connectivity, and distance education."

Against considerable protest by environmentalists both in Gujarat an in New Delhi Modi expanded a dam in Gujarat's north. The arid state's fields are now irrigated. In three years, he also did what no other state has done: provide reliable electric power. "We now have high quality power all day, every day, in every village." Modi simply started charging people for electricity's true costs. They were willing to pay, once they realized that it would be more reliable. "Once farmers had power, they wanted to buy electric appliances."

He also made sure all villages were equipped with roads and high-speed phone connectivity. He has placed special emphasis on rural schools, especially on "educating the girl child" to wipe out female illiteracy...

I came away thinking that this was a man America needed to know better. He may never be able to move past his role in the 2002 riots. But he is a talented and effective political leader, and will continue pushing New Delhi and not following. He has successfully tackled some of India's toughest problems, but also touched its most sensitive nerves. He is wrestling with major global challenges, with all the complexities that implies for a man with strong nationalist convictions. One thing is certain he will continue to be a force in Indian politics.

Within the nation too, a goodly proportion of the kind of people and the media, which had cultivated the habit of flying off the handle on mere mention of Modi's name, is feeling compelled to sing paeans to his manifold achievements and the vision. It must however be said that this grudging change of heart has as much to do with Modi's achievements as with the sordid acts of omission and commission on the part of the UPA and utter let-down that its king-designate has turned out to be. Had the not-so-young prince shown to be carrying even 10% of what was required or expected of him, they would have remained unflinching in their project-demonizing-Modi. They tried to latch their hopes on to Nitish, but the man's limitations are too apparent to inspire anyone who is in the know of things. Poor nerds have been left with no option but to veer around Modi, in spite of themselves. And they are not to be blamed in this. Culture of nepotism and corruption spawned by the Congress has made the nation run abysmally short upon talent and virtue. Talent, especially if it turned out to be carrying cardinal vices of self-respect and conscientiousness too, is one thing they (that is, the Dynasty and the cabal behind it) become immensely suspicious of and implacably hostile to, seeing in it a direct threat to their image and the position.

It must be clarified at the outset that in visual terms Gujarat will appear to be only slightly different from other (comparatively) well off states like Tamil Nadu or Punjab. Talking of big states, Gujarat's per capita income is comparable to Tamil Nadu and less than that of Maharashtra. Concerning developmental indicators like education, health, nutrition levels or social equity, it doesn't come close to even Malaysia or Thailand, let alone S. Korea, Singapore or the Western nations.

That doesn't however mean that Gujarat hasn't made much progress, or that thousands of articles, news-items, reportage and comments in the national and international media, or millions of individuals wowing Modi's achievements in unreserved terms are all outpourings of misguided idiots, or worse, paid rascals. For example, one would be hard put to attribute this article by one Shiv Visvanathan (a 'renowned social scientist' and a self-confessed 'social nomad') appearing in The Asian Age (certainly not a fan of either Modi or the BJP) to anything other than objectivity:

'Man in the Mirror' (*Asian Age*, Oct 14, 2011):

What are the plus points? First, Modi has survived. Second, he has more than survived. He has become a semiotic act which people can't refuse to watch. Modi's importance is not in doubt. He commands attention, he demands attention and the press and the diaspora cannot keep away from him.

We have also to acknowledge that the appeal of Modi goes beyond the ideology of BJP. The middle class, the younger generation, the professional see in him the future. They believe his achievements are colossal. If investment is an index of achievement, Modi has achieved a lot. He has created at Sanand a second Detroit where major car manufacturers like Tata, Ford,

Peugot and Maruti see, and invest in, the prospect of a state which is stable and believes in governance. Governance is a word that corporations love and international agencies see as their rationale.

Modi's achievements go beyond the car industry. Gujarat is a state which was impressive in its handling of the earthquake. The earthquake of 2002 became not just an act of rescue and rehabilitation, but an attempt to create new forms of governance, new ideas of standardization and new concepts of participation. One can be niggardly and say that Modi was not responsible for this. That would be ungenerous. Modi was open to ideas from the World Bank and even from NGOs and this created all sorts of recognition for his competence. He was seen as a leader who makes things work and allows things to work.

Modi has understood the art of governance, at least as a certain form of decision-making. The corporates and the diaspora feel he is effective, more importantly, he is seen as effective. Modi has become an icon of a middle class that sees masculinity as expressed in managerialism as a core character of a leader. Finally, Modi has given Gujarat some sense of pride. He has opened up the creation of not just of industrial corridors, but intellectual corridors, which could be the pride of any state.

Or, if one thought that Modi had indeed purchased the Asian Age or bribed the writer, what is one to make of this magazine from Great Britain:

'The Economist' (July 7, 2011):

So many things work properly in Gujarat that it hardly feels like India. In a factory packed with kit from Germany and China, slabs of rubber and bags of carbon black are turned into tyres. After being x-rayed for imperfections, they will be distributed across India or sent for export within three days. Sandeep Bhatia, a manager for CEAT, the firm that owns the project, says it took only 24 months to complete, including the normally fraught process of buying land. There is constant electricity, gas and abundant water. The state government, he says, kept red tape to a minimum, did not seek bribes, and does not interfere much now.

So, what has Modi done that the world doesn't seem to tire of paying compliments to his leadership and the vision, even though per capita income of an average Gujarati is only 40% higher than that of India as a whole, which includes such worthies as Bihar, MP, Andhra, UP, W. Bengal and Assam? And, that, despite the fact that due to its location and history, Gujarat has always been several steps ahead of its Indian counterparts in the matter of business acumen, opportunities and the enterprise. That said, it would be presumptuous to say that those returning impressed with Modi's Gujarat are all star struck idiots. In spite of the fact that Gujarat hasn't exactly turned into Singapore or Shanghai, there must be something that compels them to put aside their hostility and skepticism towards Modi and his purported achievements. There seems to be some fundamental changes happening there that aredenied to other parts of India. What are these?

On the industrial front, from arranging land and water for industries to speeding up grant of permits and licenses...everything is done without delay, hindrance or bribes. And anyone carrying a novel proposal, or willing to establish a big industry or advanced technological venture can demand direct access to the Chief Minister. Thus *The New York Times* (8.02.2011):

> When the Canadian heavy machinery company Bombardier won a contract to supply subway cars to the Delhi Metro in 2007, it needed a factory site, quickly. It found one in Savli, an industrial estate in Gujarat. Just 18 months laterwhen in many parts of India, the permit process might still be grinding awaythe factory was built and operating.

> "It was incredible," said Rajeev Jyoti, the managing director of Bombardier in India, "and it was a world record within Bombardiers."

> In India, where corrupt politicians often seem to be raiding the public coffers to benefit their offspring, Mr. Modi's success is sometimes attributed to his apparent lack of a family life....

> Mr. Modi's administration has brought novel solution to some of India's most tenacious problems. Corruption became less widespread after the state government put a large amount of its activities online, from permits that companies need to build or expand, to bids for contracts. To plow through a multiyear backlog of court cases, and prevent day laborers from losing income, Mr. Modi asked judges to work extra hours in night courts.

> Mr. Modi uses a chief executive style of managing the bureaucrats who work under him, according to associates and business executives in Gujarat. He gives promising people positions of responsibility, sets goals and expects people to meet them. nonperformers are pushed aside.

> It may seem an obvious way to administer a state with more than 50 million people and a budget in the billions of dollars.

But this approach runs counter to India's tradition of cronyism. In a recent reshuffle to India's national cabinet ministers, for example, the minister of highways who substantially missed targets for road-building was made minister for urban development, a crucial position for a rapidly urbanizing nation struggling to build livable cities....

At village and agriculture level, from arranging power, irrigation and road to even remotest of villages to righting the land records to arranging markets to ensuring presence of school teacher and doctors at their respective places of posting no sector is left to suffer for want of funds or attention.

Little wonder then that in complete lock-in-step with the industries, agriculture too has recorded a growth rate of 10-11% in Modi's Gujarat. Nobody can accuse Swaminathan S. Anklesaria Aiyar, eminent economist and a long-time columnist with the *Times of India* for decades, of being anything less than impartial and secular. And he has been a staunch critic of Modi. In a recent article in the paper (*'The XI that won the Gujarat Test'*, 9 September 2012), he has commended the recent court verdict sentencing the accused of Naroda-Patia to harshest terms possible, as also the team bringing the court case to fruition – Yusuf Muchhala Mallika Sarabhai, Teesta Setalvad, Harsh Mander, J S Bandukwala and others; bitterest Modi-haters them all – in strongest laudatory terms. Mr. Aiyar has this to say regarding miracle wrought by Modi in the field of agriculture:

Swaminomics (Times of India, July 2009)
Agriculture: Secret of Modi's success

Between 2000-01 and 2007-08 agricultural value added grew at a phenomenal 9.6% per year (despite a major drought in 2002). This is more than double India's agricultural growth rate, and much faster than Punjab's farm growth in the green revolution heyday. Indeed, 9.6% agricultural growth is among the fastest rates recorded anywhere in the world. That dries home the magnitude of Gujarat's performance...

Gujarat is drought prone, with 70% of its area classified as semi-arid and arid. Although journalists focus on Sardar Sarovar Project, its canal network is hopelessly incomplete, and currently irrigates only 0.1 million hectares. No less than 82% of irrigation in the state comes from tubewells, which have depleted groundwater. By the mid-1990s, groundwater extraction exceeded natural recharge in 31 talukas, and 90% of the same extraction yield in another 12 talukas.

The IFPRI study says that 10,700 check dams were build up to 2000, and helped drought-proof 32000 hectares. That sounds a lot. But subsequently, under Modi, Gujarat has build ten times as many check dams!...

Gujarat has promoted drip irrigation, badly needed to conserve water in semi-arid districts. Like other states, Gujarat offers subsidies and loans, but it also fast-tracks and simplifies procedures. Farmers contribute 5% initially. Then a state-owned company provides 50% as subsidy, and arranges a bank loan for the balance of 45%. One lakh acres have been covered by drip irrigation so far. Like the Sardar Sarovar Project, drip irrigation's total irrigation potential is far higher.

Research shows that rural roads are the most important investment for agriculture. Gujarat has one of the best rural road networks, and 98.7% of villages are connected by pukka roads.

Modi's Jyotigram scheme for power has provided regular, high-quality electricity to villages, greatly helping farming. Jyotigram provides separate electric feeder for domestic use and pump-sets. This permits the state to supply round-the-clock domestic supply, while limiting agricultural supply to eight hours a day (which is continuous and of constant voltage)

This has facilitated a switch to high-value crops like mango, banana and wheat, which need assured water. Constant voltage has protected farmers from damage to pump-sets earlier cause by fluctuating voltage. Continuous power to non-agricultural uses has spurred diversification into non-farm activities, vital for rural growth. The irrigated area has expanded at the rate of 4.4% per year.

New institutional arrangements like contract farming have helped improve marketing. Gujarat's famous dairy co-operatives have provided a stable basis for milk and livestock development. But the private sector is emerging as an important player too. Corporates have entered agro-exports, agro-processing, organize food retail, and rural infrastructure development...

At individual level, from the moment of birth of a child, to her education, marriage and employment, Modi is a cradle to grave jinn, if there ever was one. And, mind you, he is not your run-of-the-mill Mulayam, Mayawati or Sonia type of welfare maven: content with launching a scheme, making allocation, collecting his/her commission and let the rest of the scheme run into the coffers of state officials and down the drain. Most crucial thing about these yojnas is that these are not run like your million yojnas run in the name of Nehrus and Gandhis that go to feed only the NGOs; state minions like DM, CDO, SDM, BDO, tehsildar, and the like; middlemen and commission agents of various descriptions and levels; and gram-pradhans, Panchayat-adyakshas and the ruling party apparatchiks. No minister or public official – DM, CDO, or welfare department official – can dare to tinker with the scheme launched by Modi. Talk of an ideal socialist or welfare state! And they accuse Modi of promoting crass and predatory capitalism!

Of course, no force of police or vigilance, or the 'long arm of law' could have stopped all these dalals, gram-pradhans, bureaucrats and the party-apparatchiks from harassing the public and swindling public money, had the person sitting at the helm of the affairs carried even an iota of venality or blemish. Try taking bribe and simultaneously prevent your subordinates from doing the same! And the idiots wonder what prevents Manmohan Singh and Sonia Gandhi from stopping their colleagues and the subordinates from indulging in corruption and scandals!

Much like death or tsunami, Wikileaks came as a phenomenon that was entirely free of lies or bias. We have this about Modi:

Wikileaks
American Consul General meets Narendra Modi (2006)

Rajkot Congress leader Manoharsingh Jadeja said "Modi's accomplishments are undeniable," and admitted that the Congress would make little headway against the BJP I Gujarat anytime soon. Modi is extremely popular, Jadeja said, and even Muslims are now supporting him to some extent because he is viewed as someone who is completely incorruptible and can deliver the goods. Consul General asked if Modi could become a national BJP leader, and Jadeja said he hoped so because so long as he was the CM in Gujarat, Congress would face a tough challenge.

Consul General met at length with longtime former Congress party MP and former Minister of Environment Yuvraj Digvijay Sinhji. Asked whether Modi could become a national leader, Sinhji (himself the scion of the princely Wankaner family and a Cambridge grad) sniffed that Modi "lacks the polish and refinement" to become a national leader. But Sinhji raised another reason why Modi could face challenge in becoming a national leader: Modi's reputation for being completely incorruptible is accurate, and if he were to become a national leader he would crack down on corruption throughout BJP. There are too many BJP rank and file waiting to line their pockets once the BJP returns to power, Sinhji said, and the prospect of Modi cracking the whip on corruption is entirely unappealing to this crowd. Modi would have a hard time clearing this hurdle, according to Sinhji....

And that is what lays the ground for all round and sustained economic development and societal progress, rather than having great economists at the helm of the affairs or the crude *dhando* that they make much of regarding the Gujaratis. Alternatively, there is Mulayam-Mayawati-Rajshekar-Pawar-Vilasrao-Karunanidhi-Jharkhand type of development which is all about striking deals with assorted carpetbaggers and adventurers to hand them over mines, forests, rivers and farmer's land in lieu of hefty commissions, even as genuine industrialists and investors are sidelined to the eternal detriment of society and the nation.

The difference between the two extremes – what distance Modi goes to attract investment and facilitate business and industry, on the one hand, and the harassment, humiliation, delays and extortion sincere entrepreneurs are put to in other states – could best be evidenced in an article by Sitaram Yechuri (*Amar Ujala*; May, 22 2012) whose party all but wiped out industry from W. Bengal. This is what this patriotic soul has to say (translation from Hindi):

> Argument is being extended in favor of SPV that for establishing a power plant, permission is required from at least fifty-eight ministries and departments at Centre, state, and the local level. Plan is to make the SPV envision a plan, arrange all the requisite permissions at public expense and then auction that plan to the private bidders. It would be the responsibility of the SPV to identify a project, acquire land, finalize the design and obtain all the permissions and present the whole thing for bidding by the corporate players (sic)

> This means, in other words, that through the device of SPV, readymade plans shall be made available to the corporate players to just buy the projects and rake in profits. In this way, SPV could be termed the next stage of the PPP to maximize private profits...

Now see the hatred of the man for the investors and industrialists. He uses the terms 'public expense', knowing full well that when the thing is being put up for auction, that 'public expense' shall be recovered many times over. And the term corporate 'player'? If there are certain players in the corporate world, pray, who allows them to play their choice games in the first place? Clearly, he would rather that industrialists and investors were treated as pariahs... exploited, beaten and shooed away. He wants that an entrepreneur ran from pillar to post – 58 pillars and posts exactly – to obtain permission for a power plant or any other industry, and after unconscionable amount of harassment, perhaps millions (if not billions) of rupees spent in bribes, and a delay of perhaps a decade (and everything compounded by inevitable courts, police and pimps, and 'social workers', professional agitationists, do-gooders and bleeding hearts of a hundred sorts), he called it a day in sheer frustration, leaving all plans for investing in India for good.

And that is what is actually happening across the country. Why, this very day (19.08.2012), there is a news item that the industrialists of NOIDA have asked Gujarat government to provide them land to enable them to shift their industries there, so fed up they have got of the power position and other hassles in UP. Now this is the condition of the extant industries and in the so-called industrial heaven (NOIDA is an acronym for Naveen Okhla Industrial Development Authority). No prizes for guessing that no sincere investor or industrialist can even imagine establishing a new project there. As for what this man Yechuri has to say, no sworn anti-India element – Hafiz Saeed or Hamid Gul – can propose better than that to undermine and ultimately destroy India and its billion-plus people.

Modi government is certainly guilty of the sin — snatching morsel from the mouths of poor inspectors and officers and dalals of 58 departments (at the very least) outlined by Yechuri. However, unlike the Union or other state dispensations where they first make life extremely difficult for the investors and then exact a heavy price for making it somewhat easy, he extends this facility to the industrialists and the businessmen for free, extending a red carpet welcome as an added bonus.

Though placing a system in place should be enough to describe the mettle of leadership, everyone is aware by now of the strides Gujarat has made in virtually every socio-economic domain. These have become part of modern Indian folklore and it would be a waste of reader's time to recount these anew.

What Modi presents is an ideal, Plato's 'guardian' (of the society): full of acumen and foresight; free of vices and venality, with no caste, clan or dynastic axe to grind; and dedicating entire life and working relentlessly to lift his fellow countrymen, otherwise no relation to him, out of an innate sense of responsibility. He gives hope in this increasingly hopeless land of ours that there is at least one leader who is beyond fear and greed, knows his job exceedingly well, and is capable of eliciting good out of a rotten system and the milieu, triumphing against all odds and pitfalls.

In case of Modi came to power at the Center, the environment of cynicism, hopelessness and disgust that the Dowager Queen, the supremely blasé Regent and rather simpleton Prince have worked assiduously to create would be immediately lifted. After suffering decades of VP Singhs and Raos and Devgowdas and Gujrals, the nation would be galvanized as it has never been before. Besides transforming the domestic scene, that would send a clear signal to the world, that in choosing a real leader of men the Indians have at last decided to get rid themselves of the their...well, the Hindu way of life (and Islamic as well), characterized by casteism, superstitions, fatalism, sloth, divisions, corruption, grime and...the rate of economic growth.

To be more specific, if Modi takes political centrestage and gets to rule the nation the way he has Gujarat, the politics of the Mulayam-Mayawati-Mamta variety would become obsolete within a decade. That in itself would be achievement enough. If only the Indians began voting for development and against caste, communalism and corruption, there would be no stopping them from getting to be China and Malaysia, without shedding a wee bit of their democracy, liberalism and secularism. A sense of national purpose, where a sense of rudderlessness, listlessness and cynicism had prevailed, is sure to fill the nation's denizens. Fact is that a leader of men doesn't wield a magic wand. Making people realize their own potential and giving them a mission, and then guiding them ever so gently towards that mission is his way. And if Modi is not up to that, nobody else is, and India may well keep plodding on its journey towards self-destruction.

In addition to dealing with the quotidian problems, if Modi could come down heavily upon corruption at every level and manage to tackle the population-explosion, he would have saved India from a certain doom. And if along with these he could deliver upon social justice too...social justice for all, without favor or discrimination whatsoever, he is home and dry, gliding to the very top of the rank of all time greats. One can envision all the three hundred thirty million gods and goddesses of this god-soaked land showering flowers upon him.

Going by the look of his character and the record, one can fairly visualize him being showered with flowers dropping out of heaven. For, the fact is that he can't do otherwise even if he wanted to; for these things incorruptibility, impartiality, thinking deeply about and caring for the society seem to be part and parcel of his persona, even as sticking their rotten snouts in troughs full of filth-money seems to be the nature of almost all other politicians.

Widely nurtured expectations from Modi are not wooly speculations or blind hopes. When one puts his bets upon Rahul Gandhi, he does so against all concrete evidences... absolutely no flicker of hope to latch on to he has given despite decade-long grooming under India's best brains. When one puts his bets on Modi, there is a great body of proofinfinitely more weighty than the charge-sheets brought against the beleaguered man fighting a stupendous battle waged against him by just about every entrenched interest of the land.

If the Indians choose not to choose a leader that comes in centuries, thus doing manifold more damage to themselves than what they did to themselves in choosing Nehru over Patel, their future generation would have none else but them to blame losing out the Darwinian race to the unabashedly hegemonic China and Jihadi-supremacist strain of Islam.

4

HINDU HITLER, GUJARATI GOEBBLES

That Modi has been slandered for a decade running would be the understatement of the decade. Choicest printable epithets have been hurled against him in the national media (and to some lesser extent in the international) and most lurid labels pasted on his stocky frame. It is no exaggeration to say that no other political leader belonging to a democratic setup has been subjected to so much libel. It is a sure bet that any lesser man – even slightly less than Modi in the matter of character, intelligence, forbearance and grit – would have cracked up long ago and been buried, never to rise again, under the million ton pressure that was brought to bear upon him. It is a measure of the man that not only has he managed to stave off the unbearable burden of being Modi for an unforgiving decade, holding his poise and preventing himself from sliding into the cozy but self-destructive muck of cynicism, bitterness and vengeance, but succeeded in showing to the world as to how, if only he could keep his character, capacity for learning and the sense-of-mission intact, even a lowly party apparatchik born of a poor household of lowly caste could use extreme adversity and bitterest calumny to mould himself into a potential savior of a huge nation.

Yet, that Modi has proved a great fighter and survivor, or managed to become the darling of significant section of the populace, can no way subtract from the gravity of the charges leveled against him. For a man can't be exonerated of grave crimes such as rape or murder on the ground that reforming himself, he had managed to turn a new leaf in his life and had graduated to evolve into a great philanthropist or saint. If anything, the hammer of justice should fall more heavily upon him if only to preserve the purity of the terms and prevent the masses from turning cynical. Modi has himself averred in a recent, much-celebrated interview that he should be hanged on the town-square if indeed he had sinned. Well. The man is trying to prescribe for himself an easy, swift and painless denouement. He can't be allowed to escape just consequences of his sins that lightly. If proven guilty, he should be bound to a stake, put up for public ridicule and stoned mercilessly to death the Islamic way for sinning against the adherents of Islam.

So, what is the litany of charges against Modi? Mass-murderer, psychopath, misanthropist, congenital liar, constitutional fraud, an arrant knave, a gnome, a werewolf, a blot upon the heaven of religious harmony that India has always been, and a slur against the humanity and the fair name of democracy — the litany is long and bitter indeed, reeking end to end of toxic fumes. For convenience's sake, we could sum up the sentiments of his detractors by saying that Modi is a Hindu Hitler and Gujarati Goebbles.

Charges are grave indeed and can't be dismissed just so without examination and without logical and convincing rebuttal. Further, the task is of utmost importance either way, for at stake on the one hand are imperatives of justice, religious harmony and continued peace of the land, and, on the other, very survival of the nation of 1200 millions souls hurtling relentlessly towards precipice. The exercise can't be delayed anymore, for even as the moment of reckoning draws near inexorably, the moment of decision is right upon us.

Where should one begin? Standing there is the entire secularist junta that has howled itself insane over Modi. Let alone arriving upon a definite and fair conclusion, cross-examining each of them or even a few among them would take more space than a sane reader can afford to put up with. For that reason, we would cross-examine, and that too very briefly, one archetype (and one or two other) from each category...that is, one accusing Modi of being a Hindu Hitler and the other of Gujarati Goebbles.

Hindu Hitler. Ashis Nandy, without a doubt, is the archetype, very Godfather indeed – ruthless and relentless, with take-no-prisoner attitude – of all those raising Modi's stature to the Hitlerite levels. Right from the day Modi learnt to walk on his twos, to the present, when he has emerged inarguably the best politician-administrator in India's history, Nandy has been relentless in his tirade against him, refusing to see or acknowledge even one redeeming feature in his persona. It is as if the unfortunate boy Narendra had been born with a *'hamzad'* (an evil, congenitally born doppelganger sent with a mission to undo a man) in tow. Virtually everyone from the secularist-leftist brigade and interested in playing let's-spit-on-Modi game looks upon Ashis Nandy as his Dr. Johnson and Carl Jung combined.

To check whether the substance presented to you is genuine medicine-substrate, chalk-powder, cocaine, or even something more pernicious, you need to take only a couple of samples out of it and put them to rigorous test. Same goes for Ashis Nandy's oeuvre concerning Modi. Quoted below are two articles that best represent his views about the Gujaratis in general and Modi, in particular. The first article was penned less than one month after Godhra and the Gujarat riots happened. It has since become a beacon for an entire generation of dhimmis, pseudo-secularists and Modi-haters aspiring to dabble in the fine art of Modi-bashing and hoping to make a living out of it. And the paragraph about Modi's psychoanalysis has come to be the most celebrated and quoted piece in the annals of post-Independence Indian politics.

The second article is of recent vintage and excellent substantiation of Churchill's famous adage that a fanatic is a person who can't change his mind and won't change the subject. The world has changed, Modi has changed and the world's view about Modi has changed, but as this article bears out, this man Nandy, who has taken upon himself to prove the entire Hindudom to be swathed in bigotry and illiberalism, hasn't changed even a bit.

For the sake of convenience and clarity, the article has been broken down into pieces and italicized, to be followed with explanatory or confuting comments by the author.

Obituary of a culture

Ashis Nandy (21 March 2002)

Gujarat... is a state that has seen thirty-three years of continuous rioting interrupted with periods of tense, uncomfortable peace. During these years, a sizeable section of Gujarat's urban underclass has begun to see communalism and rioting as means of livelihood, quick profit, choice entertainment, and as a way of life. Riots have, in addition, ensured temporary status gains for this underclass; they are considered heroes in their respective communities during riots and for brief period afterwards an important reward for persons at the margins of society.

Rioting everywhere is pre-eminently an urban disease.... The icing on the cake is that the urban middle-class in Gujarat is now the most communalized in the country; it has become an active abettor and motivator of communal violence. Sections of it participate in the loot enthusiastically, as we have seen in the course of the recent riots; those that do not often participate in the violence vicariously.

For the last hundred years or so, the so-called non-martial races of the sub-continentBengali babus, Kashmiri Muslims and Gujarat upper castes, for instancehave had a special fascination for violence, particularly if someone else was doing the fighting and risking their lives. However, in recent years, this fascination and the search for redemptive violence, which bestows heroic stature by being expiation for one's own 'passivity' and 'effeminacy', have often found direct expression in public life.

By Ashis Nandy's own assertion, Gujarat has been witness to *'Thirty-three years of continuous rioting interrupted by periods of tense, uncomfortable peace'*. Congress obviously was at the helm during most of those thirty-three years. According to Mr. Nandy (next article), *'riots have been engineered by many politicians. Riots primarily are a professional job, professionally handled by politicians.'* Yet, there is not a word of criticism from him either for the Congress Party or the chief ministers that had been at the helm of the affairs in the state. He puts the blame instead on the *'urban middle-class in Gujarat'*, the *'most communalized'* one in the country. And who is that most communalized urban middle-class in Gujarat: Hindus, naturally...which Nandy won't say in so many words.

And, pray, why shouldn't that be so? It is Gujarati urban middle class that has suffered most in the riots since centuries; their women abducted, children murdered and businesses looted. *'Sections of it participate in the loot enthusiastically'*, Nandy alleges. Now what businessmen, government servant or other professional would go out to loot the ghettos and slums (that is where the Muslims have been cornered into, according to Mr. Nandy) of Muslims of Kalupura and Juhapura, and what would it get by risking its life foraying into those Muslim-dominated areas?

And if *'a sizeable section of Gujarat's urban underclass has begun to see communalism and rioting as means of livelihood, quick profit, choice entertainment, and as a way of life'* in addition to yielding *'temporary status gains'*, pray why should it not keep the pot of riots boiling, especially in view of the fact that it has four to ten children per family to spare for the sport. But no, keeping with the character of the 'intellectuals' coming from the self-hating middle class, it is only the middle class, having only one or two issues per family and that too either in schools or gainfully employed, that should be blamed.

In any case, Nandy's contention that a fearful people at the receiving end of violence of a long time become the most communalized of the lot serves to underscore author's contention in an earlier chapter. If the Gujarati urban middle-class, or other peace-loving people deemed non-martial by the British, grew into being most communalized section in the country, reason is clear and understandable. As for the Gujaratis, the redemptive violence of 2002 helped it overcome the age-old feelings of inferiority, fear and vengeance, and exorcised in a great measure the ghost of communalism out of its system. That, combined with purging of the sentiments of hauteur and superiority from the Gujarati Muslim system made the decade of unprecedented peace and harmony in Gujarat possible.

> ....The state has fifty cities, many of which have already become cauldrons of communal hatred and paranoia.... The state has not only been riot-prone but at war with itself. Even after the present riots die down – available data show that riots last longer in Gujarat than in other states – it would be at best a temporary truce. Tension and hatred will persist and both sides will remain prepared for the next round. Gujarat is and will continue to be an arena of civil war for years....

> The minorities of Gujarat are by now aware that, for good or worse, they will have to prepare to protect themselves. This is a prescription for disaster. It will underscore the atmosphere of a civil war and create a new breeding ground for terrorism. More than Operation Blue Star, the anti-Sikh riots spawned terrorism in Punjab in the 1980s; the two decades of rioting in Gujarat has by now similarly produced the sense of desperation that precedes the breakout of terrorism.

Now, so much for this man's social science-expertise and psychoanalysis. *'Gujarat is and will continue to remain an arena of civil war for years...'* Indeed! In light of the experience of the last decade, would it be too much to ask Mr. Nandy to eat crow publicly? In what thin air has vanished the *'sense of desperation'* that according to this national psychotherapist *'precedes the breakout of terrorism'*?

Reason for Mr. Nandy turning out so wrong is plain enough. Complete inversion, either willfully or out of ignorance (willfully, in all probability, for it is difficult to believe that living in India one can be that ignorant), of truth has made all his conclusions go wrong. His gospel-truth-like assumption (as indeed of the entire secularist junta), without giving any cognizance either to the tenets and the history of Islam, or contemporary events across the world, that the Hindus are aggressors and the devils incarnate, and the Muslims Mary's little lambs is as classical a piece of travesty as could be. Events have borne that out. Muslims were aggressors, not desperate victims. As soon as the sting of their aggression was taken out the things became completely quiescent. Had the reality been the other way round as our dear social scientist would have the world believe, by now the Hindus would have by now made life impossible for the Muslims of Gujarat, rendering them desperater (so to say), resulting either in break out of terrorism, as Nandy surmised, or their mass migration out of Gujarat.

Contrary to Mr. Nandy's analysis, minorities of Gujarat have become aware that the state as well as the Hindu majority is their best protector, provided they do not continue to behave as aggressors blessed with a superior genetics and faith. That exactly is the reason that no civil war or terrorism break-out has happened despite Mr. Nandy's prophesy and instigation.

> In the early 1960s.... Many Ahmedabad Hindus seemed afraid and suspicious of the Muslims, but they were afraid and suspicious mostly of non-Gujarati Muslims, many of them labourers in the huge textile industry of Ahmedabad. They took the Gujarati Muslims, a large proportion of them business castes, as a part of Gujarat's landscape, though there was a clear social distance.

> The 1969 riots began to change the city radically... The violence paid rich dividends. So did the imaginative hate campaign unleashed by the Vishwa Hindu Parishad and the RSS. Together they gave a kick-start to the process of ghettoization of the Muslims and the growth in the power of Mafia-like bodies in both communities, always itching for fight and acting like protectors of the Hindus and the Muslims at the time of rioting.

Mr. Nandy's observation that Ahmedabad Hindus were afraid and suspicious contradicts in a large measure his earlier contention that Hindus were aggressors and Muslims desperate victims. And his blaming Vishwa Hindu Parishad for unleashing hate campaign against Muslims ignores entirely the history of riots in Gujarat when VHP was nowhere upon the scene. He also fails to mention the visibly ambivalent response, even brazenly open expression of support by sections of Muslims to Pakistan during the 1965 India-Pakistan war; thing that had exacerbated suspicion and hostility towards the Muslims at that time and has been widely held to be one of main reasons behind break out of riots not just in Gujarat but all over India.

> However, the growth of this criminal sector was disproportionately high among the young, unemployed Muslims. Understandably. The existing social distance between the communities had already acquired another tone. Facing discrimination in job situations and housing, many among the

unemployed youth began to take to professions in which slum youth everywhere in the world specialize illicit distillation, drug pushing, protection rackets and petty crime. And they always seemed ready for street violence. The situation worsened once Ahmedabad's famed textile industry collapsed. The changing political culture of the city ensured that this collapse too, affected the Muslims more.

Mr. Nandy professes to understand the disproportionate rise of criminal sectors among the Muslim young. But here too, either he has got it completely wrong, or (as is the wont of the secularists) he is trying to mislead. For, he would never elaborate as to how disproportionately higher number of children per family is always a big reason for higher unemployment and spare children left free to indulge in criminal things. Unemployment and poverty was unbearably high in India – and not just among the Muslims – in that decade. New jobs were as good as non-existent for anyone, Hindu or Muslim. In any case, the state-sector (where the alleged discrimination takes place) employs not more than 5 to 10% of the populace. Even if there had been discrimination on account of religion, it couldn't have affected more than 5% of the potential job-earners. What about other 90 to 95%? How were the Hindus responsible for their unemployment?

Further, Nandy's averment that collapse of Ahmedabad's textile industry impacted the Muslims more gives a lie to his earlier contention that Muslims were discriminated against in the matter of jobs. Why would they suffer to disproportionately higher extent from the collapse of industry if they hadn't been employed with it in disproportionately higher numbers to begin with?

And discrimination in housing? Pardon me, do you mean to say that the Hindus were responsible for the Muslim housing problem, or that every Hindu should take one or two Muslims in his home to throw cow-bones around, lure or abduct his girls away, and teach him Islam, unsolicited and under threat? We have seen the humiliation Zainul Abedin, op-ed editor of *The News* of Pakistan had to suffer in his own home in Karachi for watching TV and listening to Music. And that was not an isolated instance by any means, or not confined to Pakistan. Considering the fact that huge riots have erupted over playing of music, throwing of color during the Holi festival or even kite-flying, reluctance of the Hindus to take kindly to the idea of sharing neighborhood with the Muslims won't appear to be that outrageous or intolerant a thing.

Obvious give away is why would Muslims want to go and live in the Hindu areas and not the other way round? Clearly, Muslims expand too fast to be accommodated in their own traditional areas and letting Muslims in means for the Hindus being crowded out before long from their own areas, as indeed has been happening in virtually every part of the country. Further, would any Muslim look upon the Hindus venturing to reside in their traditional areas with anything but hostility, silent or overt? Far from it. Then why only the Hindus are sought to be made to feel guilty on the account?

Further, as far as the sixties were concerned, the state too can't be held to be discriminating against the Muslims in the matter of housing, since, unlike the last three decades when myriad of state agencies and development authorities have come up to develop housing schemes, it was completely out of the sector to be able to discriminate on the basis of religion.

That is not to say that there has been (or continues to be) no discrimination against the Muslims from the Hindu side. But, firstly, it is considerably less than what the Muslims practice against the Hindus whenever the occasion to do so arises. Secondly, the discrimination indulged in by the Hindus is not gratuitous, or without valid or inexplicable reasons, but carries sound psychological logic behind it. Discrimination, if it doesn't have a doctrinaire basis (like it had been in the case of Savarna discrimination against the Untouchables, or the dhimmi/kefir laws enunciated by Sharia), it usually has two logics: Either it is born out of the feeling of overweening superiority (displayed by the conquerors against the subjugated), or it is an outcome of the sense of nagging inferiority or fear. Now, no one can say that the Gujarati Hindus (or most of the Hindus, for that matter), subjugated, humiliated, converted, raped and killed for over eight hundred centuries, and then worsted time and again in the riots (till the police comes to their rescue) even in the Independent India, could have nursed a sense of overweening superiority against the Muslims. So, fear it is – fear of being worsted in confrontations in the short term, and being overwhelmed by sheer numbers in the long term – that lies at the root of the discrimination. Now can you really accuse a fearful creature of being....well, fearful and discriminatory, especially if it had valid historical as well as contemporary reasons for being fearful?

Essential fact is that Nandy's argument is part of a larger conspiracy to keep pressurizing the Hindus every which way and prove to the world that Hindu is the aggressor party at every site of Hindu-Muslim interface. After all, which sane person would believe that even Javed Akhtar and Shabana Azmi could have faced discrimination when they went out to take a house on rent (that is, if they didn't already have dozens of flats of their own)? But that story is doing round since decades and is waved in the face of the Hindus as supreme evidence of their diabolicalness. Hindus of Bombay are gladly letting their only daughters cavort with and marry Muslims, but won't rent their houses to them! Canards like this have been spread by the secularist media as horrific truths; evidence of untold miseries being inflicted by the devilish Hindus upon the Christ-like Muslims.

> Almost nothing reveals the decline and degeneration of Gujarati middle class culture more than its present Chief Minister, Narendra Modi. Not only has he shamelessly presided over the riots and acted as the chief patron of rioting gangs, the vulgarities of his utterances have been a slur on civilized public life. His justification of the riots too sounds uncannily like that of Slobodan Milosevic, the Serbian president and mass murderer who is now facing trial for his crimes against humanity. I often wonder these days why those active in human rights groups in India and abroad have not yet tried to get international summons issued against Modi for colluding with the murder of hundreds and for attempted ethnic cleansing.

Till the Gujarati Middle Class was mighty *'afraid'* of the Muslims and harbored *'special fascination for violence'*, but was held down by its *'passivity'* and *'effeminacy'* (Nandy's words and analysis), it was high noon of culture in Mr. Nandy's esteem. When it took the job of *'expiation'* – driving out centuries old fear and redeem its honor by giving as good as it got – upon itself, it became *'decline and degeneration'* of that great culture. Wonderful logic Mr. Nandy, one is led to exclaim.

As for *'ethnic cleansing'* thing was concerned, does one need reminding our erudite converted Christian analyst that it is an Abrahamic sisterhood (Jew-Christian-Muslim) specialty, completely alien to the Hindus. Jews were as intolerant of even the presence of non-Jews in their stronghold as is possible for human beings to be. Jesus' view, *'those who are not with us are against us'*, too is an open call for conversion, expulsion or extermination of the non-believers. And there is clear injunction in Koran that there shall be no two religions in Arabia; command which led to complete extermination and expulsion of non-Muslims from the core areas of Islam. Holocaust, Armenian genocide and Srebrenica, or the apartheid that continues to be practiced against the Palestinians in Israel, serve to prove that the holy injunctions and commandments of the Abrahamic sisterhood hold good in our times too.

As far as Hindus are concerned, they have assimilated – and not ethnically cleansed – hundreds of races and nationalities over millenniums. Further, as Pakistan, Bangladesh, Kashmir, and Assam and other North-East experiences so evocatively show, Hindus specialize in being ethnically cleansed, rather than ethnic-cleansing the others. Had Modi carried even one-hundredth part of the traits of Slobodan Milosevic in him, Nandy wouldn't have been spreading this canard across the world.

> More than a decade ago, when Narendra Modi was a nobody, a small-time RSS pracharak trying to make it as a small-time BJP functionary, I had the privilege of interviewing him along with Achyut Yagnik, whom Modi could not fortunately recognize. (Fortunately because he knew Yagnik by name and was to later make some snide comments about his activities and columns.) It was a long, rambling interview, but it left me in no doubt that here was a classic, clinical case of a fascist. I never use the term 'fascist' as a term of abuse; to me it is a diagnostic category comprising not only one's ideological posture but also the personality traits and motivational patterns contextualizing the ideology.

> Modi, it gives me no pleasure to tell the reader, met virtually all the criteria that psychiatrists, psycho-analysts and psychologists had set up after years of empirical work on the authoritarian personality. He had the same mix of puritanical rigidity, narrowing of emotional life, massive use of the ego defense of projection denial and fear of his own passions combined with fantasies of violence all set within the matrix of clear paranoid and obsessive personality traits. I sill remember the cool, measured tone in which he elaborated a theory of cosmic conspiracy against India that painted every Muslim as a suspected traitor and a potential terrorist. I came out of the interview shaken and told Yagnik that, for the first time, I had met a textbook case of a fascist and a prospective killer, perhaps even a future mass murderer.

So, here we are. This paragraph has come to be the most celebrated paragraph used by the army of Modi-bashers to deny him even elementary humanity due to a man by virtue of him being born to the specie of Homo sapiens. Admitted that the Hindus as a whole are considerably less than full human being in the eyes of the followers of Abrahamic faiths, but Mr. Nandy has really gone too far in this exercise of taking out his visceral hatred for the heathen race. Besides, there are some crucial questions crying out of the paragraph for answers, putting the verity of the entire exercise to serious doubt.

Question is: Why did Mr. Nandy choose to interview a *small-*

time' RSS flunkey and a *'nobody'* like Modi, and that too in the exalted company of Achyut Yagnik (a classical exemplar of dhimmi Hindu)? And if indeed he had found out a *'textbook case of a fascist and a prospective killer, perhaps even a future mass murderer',* why didn't he publicize this sensational finding in any of his studies? Discovering that Hitler had taken rebirth in the form of Modi – wasn't it a sacred duty of this Savior of the world to inform the world of the dreadful event to enable the sentinels of secularism and humanism to nip the trouble then and there? What otherwise had been his purpose in going to visit a *'small-time'* man, complete *'nobody'* rather? Clearly, Mr. Nandy is lying through his teeth and the entire paragraph is an afterthought striking him in the aftermath of Gujarat riots. Yet, it is a measure of the extent to which the self-styled secularists have stooped to, and the others so cowed down into unthinking submission, that nobody has ever dared to put this most obvious of posers to this godfather of dissemblers.

> The very fact that he has wormed his way to the post of the chief minister of Gujarat tells you something about our political process and the trajectory our democracy has traversed in the last fifty years. I am afraid I cannot look at the future of the country with anything but great foreboding....

Well, if Mr. Nandy describes a man dedicating his entire life to an organization and working his guts out to bring it to power, rising by the dint of his talent and grit to become a national level secretary of the ruling party and never wasting even a moment on things like foreign vacations, glamour-parties or other frivolities, as worming his way to the post of chief minister of a state, what would he say to Rajiv Gandhi's ascent to the premiership, Manmohan Singh soiling the exalted throne for a full decade, and Rahul Gandhi hoping to be crowned soon?

> The forces Gujarat violence might have released are a different kettle of fish. They have seem to have done what the Partition riots did. Also, given that they have been arguably the first video riots in India riots taking place in front of TV cameras their impact will be pan-Indian and international. The minorities all over the country have seen the experiment in ethnic cleansing and the attempts to break the economic backbone of the Muslim community. The sense of desperation brewing among the Gujarati Muslims is likely to be contagious.

> I wonder what we should do with 120 million bitter Muslims, a sizeable section of them close to desperation. Will it be another case of Palestine now onwards, at least in Gujarat? Prima facie,

Modi has done his job. The Sangh Parivar's two-nation theory is genuine stuff and has already initiated the process of a second partition of India, this time of mind. We, our children and grandchildren above all, the Gujaratis will have to learn to live with a state of civil war. The Gujarati middle class will have to pay heavily culturally, socially and economically for its collusion with the recent pogrom.

Can a social-scientist or 'psychoanalyst' turn out to be more wrong than Mr. Nandy? Gujarat suffering *'civil war'*! The *'sense of desperation brewing among the Gujarati Muslims'* likely to become *'contagious'*! Lurid dreams of yours and the heartfelt wishes remain entirely unrealized Mr. Nandy! What we have been witness to instead is a decade of unprecedented peace, education and growth among the Muslims — direct outcome of realization, consequent to Godhra and its aftermath, that unnecessary show of belligerence or remaining perpetually on a short fuse has done them immense harm over the decades by diverting their focus and energy away from issues more relevant to their lives.

It is clear from Mr. Nandy's writing that he is more interested in exacerbating the feeling of anger and alienation among the Muslims and provoking them to yet greater misadventures, than analyzing the root cause or bringing out the truth. Allusion to Palestine, two-nation theory, civil war or initiation of process of second partition of India is plain seditious-sinister stuff in the garb of analysis and commiseration.

'Sangh Parivar's two-nation theory'? We won't elaborate who was the real founder of the two-nation theory as it played out in the thirties. Do we need to inform Mr. Nandy that Abrahamic ideology, dividing the mankind at its very core in 'we the darling of our God and natural candidate for Heaven', and 'they the camp-followers of Satan and obvious clients for Hell', or, simply 'we the faithful' and 'they the kefir or heathen, and therefore fair game for rape, rapine, force-conversion and slaughter' is the grandma of all the two-nation theories roiling the world, and not pathetic organizations run by certified half-wits and confirmed nincompoops?

PS. Mr. Nandy has this footnote to his article above:

The Godhra incident, which precipitated the recent riots, was partly a product of this larger process, not a conspiracy of the ISI, as the Sangh Parivar claims. Nor was the incident the result of a provocation by karsevaks so severe that the Muslim victims of the provocation had to burn alive scores of train passengers, most of them women and children, as some politically correct secularists have begun to insist. For the moment, I am ignoring the even more inane attempt to explain away the Godhra episode as a non-event. In some ways, the episode is typical example of the chain of events that have characterized a huge number of communal riots in recent times in slums and ghettos, followed by fully organized, large-scale attacks on Muslims in general.

As we all are aware, the Hindus of Godhra had been harassing, raping and killing their Muslim brethrens for centuries. Not only that, and as is their wont, they had been indulging in wholesale ethnic cleansing, that is why despite the Partition and all that, the ratio of Muslim population of Godhra had dwindled to 65% at present, from about 40% post-Independence. Not only that, and as we have seen, not content with harassing, raping, killing and converting the Muslims not only in India, where they are in majority, their fanaticism has led them to abducting, raping, killing and converting the Muslims even in Pakistan...and not only the Sunni Muslims, but the Shias, Ahmediyas and the Christians too.

And, truly, their diabolicalness knows no bounds. Contrary to the trends obtaining in the world, in general, and the Islamic nations, in particular, they are doing the unspeakable to their minorities. They have forced them into becoming their supreme political leader, presidents, prime-minister, chief justices, army chiefs and what not. Most powerful woman of their only country a Catholic, Prime Minister and the Chief of Army staff Sikhs, defence minister a Christian, Chief Justice a Zoroastrian (and now a Muslim), and their 'own' supposed political party first rooting for a Muslim to be made president as well and then voting a tribal Christian for the post – if that is not an evidence of mindset intolerably intolerant of its minorities, pray, what else could be?

And tolerating incessant ridicule and denigration of their gods, goddesses and the way of life by Missionaries and the Mullahs, and the tele-evangelists like Zakir Naik, and none of them retaliating by doing similar things to their prophets – that sure is evidence of fanaticism...of the peaceful-timid kind, but fanaticism nonetheless.

That is perhaps why that interviewing Indian Muslims on his recent visit to India, an insightful Pakistani journalist has felt compelled to write this (*Dawn*, Sept 21, 2012): *'Some years ago, they would have expected to commiserate with them on their plight as stranded Muslims. Now, they pity you for being marooned in Pakistan.'*

We should however be thankful for crumbs of little mercies thrown the way of us lowly Hindus by this secular God. For, the provisional verdict of this secular icon of India is that the provocation the kar sevak gave to the Muslims of Godhra was not *'so severe'* as to demand their wholesale burning. Also he doesn't consider the Godhra event a complete *'non-event'* (but a little more than that) and terms the attempts to so explain it away as *'inane'* (and not devilish).

But that is as far as he goes. For, the onus of the blame, in the considered view of this social-scientist, lies with the Hindus only. The pattern runs somewhat like this according to this man's timeless wisdom:

'First the Hindus engineer the atmospherics and a larger conspiracy aimed at ethnic cleansing of Muslims (That perhaps is the reason behind Muslim population of India dwindling from 3 crores post-Independence, to 25 crore now, while that of the Hindus grew from about 30 crores to 80 only. Why, the rascals are even behind flocking of Muslims from Bangladesh and even Pakistan to India). Then the devil-incarnates give gratuitous provocations to the Muslims, who are absolutely quiescent by definition, their history throughout the world being a saga of boundless peace. Currently too, the latter do not indulge in any kind of violence in other parts of the world: Neither do they abduct, force-convert and marry Hindu girls (at the rate of 25 a month in Sind only), nor do they kill Christians in Sudan, Nigeria and Indonesia by hundreds and thousands, or their co-religionist Shias and Ahmediyas in dozens.'

'India however is a different kettle of fish. Here, sometimes, after receiving gravest provocations at the hands of hated idolaters, the legendary Muslim patience cracks and they are forced to slap a particularly mischievous passing Hindu boy, more with reformatory intents, as an expression of sibling love for a wayward younger brother, than in actual anger. But that is what the devils had been engineering and aiming for all along. Massacres, genocides, holocausts, pogroms and what not is let loose upon the poor waifs. But, then, what could you expect from idolatrous and polytheistic kefirs that even the God Almighty had forsaken, reserving direst Hell to punish their dark rotten souls?'

Commemorating a decade of the aforediscussed iconic article, Mr. Nandy published an article in the *'Outlook'* of 23 April, 2012. And though as soaked in venom as the previous one, the article failed go gain the same level of virality. The reason seems to be that, by now, people have got a little wiser – about Modi, as well as the nefarious games the secular fanatics of the kind of Mr. Nandi have played to undermine the nation and its true leaders.

Out Damned Spot!
Ashish Nandy

Narendra Modi may have got a clean chit from the SIT in the Gulberg society case but this is a small peg on which the case for and against Modi rests... So what can he do to redeem himself? Can he outlive his past? Narendra Modi should do what Pakistan's deputy attorney general, Muhammad Khurshid Khan, did as penance. On his visit to India, Khan spent hours cleaning and shining devotees' shoes at a Delhi gurudwara as penance, so upset was he by the killing of a Sikh man by a Taliban group in Pakistan two years ago. Modi needs to make a gesture of spectacular repentance and apology for 2002.

The man accuses Modi of being a fascist par excellence. Modi may be that or may not be. But, as the above para shows, this man Nandy is a true fascist in a liberal hide. Contrary to all cannons of fairness and justice that liberals like him measure others against, he has kept accusing Modi of being complicit in the post-Godhra mayhem even before the court had turned its verdict. We should let that pass however, for, it is one of those necessary evils of the world from which there can be no escape. For unless one had been suspected of committing a crime and charged accordingly, how could he be proceeded against even?

But, what about his attitude now? Damned be the highest court of the land, damn the weight of evidence become available since then, damned the rational opinions that have begun to see the events in the light of limitations and the compulsion of a fledgling chief minister, and damned the coruscating and spotless record of a decade, he won't waver from his belief even if very God appeared to declare Modi's non-complicity in the post-Godhra riots. If that is not fanaticism of the worst kind, pray, what else is?

Mr. Nandy's hero, Muhammad Khurshid Khan, unreservedly praiseworthy and touching though his act is, is doing penance for the murder of a Sikh committed two years ago by his co-religionists. Obvious question is 'why now'? On his part, Mr. Nandy should have advised him to put the energy of his piety and remorse to better contemporary use. For example, Mr. Nandy could have advised him to take vigorous measures to protect 25 Hindu girls abducted, converted and force-married every month in Sindh alone, or work to alter the blasphemy law (Mr. Khan being one of the main custodians of the law, being deputy attorney general of Pakistan) wreaking such havoc upon innocents of every religious denomination, or try to mould the Pakistan public opinion as a whole against and persecuting and marginalizing the unfortunate Ahemadiya and Shia Muslims in so shameless and inhumane a manner.

Be that as it may. Muhammad Khurshid Khan knows best what touches him most, what his heartfelt desire is, and what manner of penance avails him spiritual satisfaction. Hajj works for one, Jerusalem for another and silent prayerful contemplation at home for yet another. No person can know the workings of another's heart and should therefore refrain from offering unsolicited advice. That would be so self-righteous, presumptuous and insensitive. That attitude is the seedbed for fanaticism to sprout. But, apparently, the thing is not applicable to Mr. Nandy. Since he has done some stupid course in psychology, he will only advise others and not be advised. But to proceed:

> To some extent, there has been an apology for the Sikh riots from the Congress party. Manmohan Singh is the prime minister partly because of this. Modi can in fact learn from the Gandhis. The Gandhi dynasty, after the Sikh riots, has ensured great security for itself by apologizing for the violence, because they know and understand the transience of power. They know that desperate people cannot be stopped by security. So they have shown humility and bought their security.

Now, what are the implications of the above? Primarily, that Modi should apologize if only superficially...to buy his physical security as the Gandhi dynasty did with the Sikhs. In short, this man accusing Modi of being a violent fraud, is advising him to commit a greater fraud to cover up his previous sins...only to buy physical security like those pretending cowards. Secondly, this man is encouraging *'desperate'* people to take on Modi, telling them that if you were desperate enough, no security can stop you from targeting 'my' pet object of hatred.

And, what is that about the Gandhis being more knowing and understanding of *'transience of power'*? Pardon me. I thought permanence of power was the thing they are more acquainted with. Transience of power is for the Gujrals and Guljarilals of the world, not the Gandhi-Nehru 'dynasty'. In fact, use of the term 'dynasty' by Mr. Nandy itself connotes permanence of power. Why does our celebrated analyst slip so easily on his own assumptions?

> If I was Narendra Modi's psychotherapist, I would have told him: my dear friend, if you wish to play a larger role in national politics, you need to reflect. You cannot go directly from the chief minister's office in Gujarat to the prime minister's office in New

Delhi. Buy peace in the interregnum. He should go to a dargah. Go to Ajmer Sharif and apologize. The Khwaja is supposed to be benevolent and very forgiving.

Why would Narendra Modi appoint this babbling baboon his psychotherapist? Rather than being in need of therapy of any kind, he has become rather adept at giving seizures to the likes of Ashish Nandy and his entire pseudo-secularist clan by going from one success and glory to another and gathering strength with each passing day. And what is this thing about *'You cannot.......office in New Delhi'*? Confirmed morons could be deemed worthy of going directly from their mothers' laps to the prime minister's office in New Delhi and an immensely successful and feted person cannot? One is led to say to Mr. Nandy: Either you have gone senile, or have got this bad habit of thinking others as suckers for your warped arguments.

As for going to the dargah of Khwaja to buy peace…well. That won't buy Modi peace or security, for the Salafists or Deobandis, who hate fekirs and spiritual middlemen like Khwaja from the depth of their guts and hold visit to their *dargahs* as nothing less than blasphemy, form the overwhelming majority of the Muslims and won't be placated even a bit by such a show of contrition (if not actually alienated further). In fact, being such a 'Catholic' adviser, why doesn't Mr. Nandy advise Modi to convert to Islam like Malik Kafur of the yore, go to Mecca for Hajj and, upon his return, begin the job of conquering India for Islam and slaughtering Hindus to expiate his past sins and get to be an instant and enduring hero to the Muslims?

> But politically it is different kind of game. Even if Modi wins all the cases and goes scot-free, the stigma of the riots will not go. The stigma will remain. Neither these cases, nor his internet presence, or being on the cover of Time, will matter in the long run. In Modi's case, even without analyzing his personality, one can say that his chances of being a major presence in national politics are doomed by his past. He can make space for it only by a very abject apology and by really, truly giving a public demonstration of his ability to renounce and disown his past self.

As for washing off the stigma thing is concerned, it depends entirely upon those stigmatizing; perpetrators, and not the victim. Was it the fault of the (so-stigmatized) outcastes of India that they continued to be not only stigmatized, but also subjected to untold oppression and exploitation for three millenniums running? Jews too had been stigmatized through two millennia and continue to be stigmatized even now; should they too go to Khwaja to expiate their purported sins? Hundreds of people, their presumed crimes not even brought to see the dark lights of courts, are being blasted away across nations through drones under direct supervision of Obama, but nobody is stigmatizing him. Ahmedinejad keeps calling for destruction of Israel, even as the entire Muslim world (and the Indian left-liberals) applauds and admires the man for his noble sentiments, instead of stigmatizing him. If Modi is held to be complicit in any way in the Gujarat riots, Rajiv Gandhi was at least ten times more complicit in the Sikh genocide, yet nobody stigmatized him. Stigmatizing is a weapon of the powerful, articulate and the selfish against the weak and the cornered. By no reckoning it is proof of guilt or a matter of shame. Should a girl feel shame and offer *'abject apology'* to her tormentors to exorcise her stigma? But that exactly is the line pedaled by the likes of Mr. Nandy for past ten years against Modi.

As for Modi's *'chances of being a major national presence in national politics'* being *'doomed by his past'*…well. Clearly, Mr. Nandy doesn't much care for what he writes. Modi is already a major national presence…in fact bigger presence than anyone else out there, though he has yet to make a formal appearance upon the national political scene. What tectonic shift will take place whenever he decided to actually come to the national stage, the likes of Mr. Nandy can't even dare to contemplate.

According to Mr. Nandy, Modi *'can make space…..disown his past self.'* That is so nice of him showing his bete noire the way out of the impasse. If Mr. Nandy could guarantee the premiership of the nation to Modi by offering an *'abject apology'* and *'disown his past self'* (that means, clearly, trashing his RSS background and abjuring the Hindu faith), I, for one, would try to persuade him to work on Mr. Nandy's suggestion.

> Modi fits the description of the cult of the 'dictatorial democratic' leader. In politics, masks do work. If you wear a mask long enough in politics, it becomes your face. But I am afraid that Narendra Modi has not even worn the right mask. I may applaud his administrative skills but I cannot applaud his intelligence and his long-term vision. I say this because riots have been engineered by many politicians. Riots primarily are a professional job, professionally handled by politicians. But all politicians, when promoting riots, take certain precautions. They do not as blatantly use the riot as a campaigning device to win elections, then gloat over the killings and create a whole atmosphere of hysteria which then can be beamed to the whole country and seen by millions.

And now a truly Machiavellian piece of advice from this secular-liberal icon! Apparently, entire generations of Congress leaders – Rajiv Gandhi, Arjun Singh, V.P. Singh, Arun Nehru, Sharad Pawar, Madhav Singh Solanki, and the latest, Tarun Gogoi – have apprenticed under him. Wear the right mask, engineer communal conflagration in a *'professional'* way at one place and make great show of putting it off at another, shedding crocodile tears all that while...everything in the service of secularism and *'long-term vision'*. Sorry gentleman, keep your precious tutorials reserved for the Congressmen; Modi is not game. That he suffered a near-fatal accident learning to drive doesn't at all mean he enjoys adventure sports. A decade of safe and skillful driving is proof enough.

> After Gujarat, riots have become politically very expensive in India. And now you will see a decline of riots not because of better ethics or because Indian politicians have suddenly become saintly or because Indian laws have become strict.... India has no shortage of laws. I am following the legal cases against Modi and the riot cases because I want to see where they go as that gives an inkling of how much the system is complicit how much it is not.

Only a few years earlier, this chief social-scientist and 'psychoanalyst' of India had been predicting that the nation was certain to be engulfed in interminable communal riots, for the Muslims were not likely to take Gujarat lying down. Yet, the years since his dire prognosis have turned out to the most peaceful ones (barring the Pakistan-originating attacks) ever experienced by the country. And now three months have not elapsed for his present assessment (*'After Gujarat...decline of riots...'*) to be turned out completely off the mark. Clearly, Tarun Gogoi, a fine specimen of Congress culture, has been following his advice to a dot. Clearly too, riots remain politically fruit-bearing as far as Mr. Nandy's darling Congress is concerned. Consequences and the expenses are for Modi only, even if the riots that occurred the day after his confirmation in the chief minister's post were natural and unavoidable outcome of the Godhra outrage and by no means engineered.

And, yet again, in true fascist fashion, Mr. Nandy has declared Modi fit for hanging even before the trial is over and intends to declare even the Supreme Court of the land complicit if it failed to turn out verdict in consonance with his long-formed (much before the Gujarat riots even, when Modi was *'a nobody'*) prejudices about the man.

Beside the Hitler-Holocaust theme, another line the tribe of Modi-haters has taken to demonize Modi is Stalin-Dictator theory. And they seem entirely unafraid or unmindful of the fact that the kind of dissimulation and chicanery they take resort to in support of their logic serves only to put them directly in the league of the Devil they are trying to prove Modi the avatar of! Thus, though detesting RSS and the BJP men from the depth of their guts, who they would like nothing more than to throw into the Arabian Sea without even an iota of remorse, they suddenly turn mighty solicitous of their political and other interests, accusing Modi of being thoroughly illiberal and undemocratic in making them politically irrelevant. The real grudge or worry underlying their carp however is that unless Modi had let them (RSS, VHP, Bajrang Dal, and the like) run riot and screw the state to their heart's content (like they did in Karnataka), how could their heartfelt desire of seeing the Congress make a comeback be fulfilled?

The theme is brought out beautifully in this rant of one Rajiv Shah (of whom later). Writing in the *Times of India* (5 May 2012) under the title, *'Centripetal undercurrents of Gujarat's No 1'*, thus Mr. Shah:

> ....Take, for instance, the Cabinet he heads, Modi is not just Gujarat's chief minister. As some one who matters in Sachivalaya put it to me, a little jokingly, `There is no No 2 in his Cabinet, not even No 3 or No 4. You have only No 9 and further on in Cabinet. There is no one in between!

One is led to say that Modi is such a giant (no.1 to no. 8) is exactly the reason that much more than any other politician, old or young – Advani, Sushma Swaraj, Rahul, Sonia, Nitish, Naveen, Mulayam Singh, Lalu or Sharad Pawar – he is being seen as future Prime Minister of India and the only hope to pull it out of the mire the extant crop of leaders has landed it in. To say that anyone could be Modi's no. 2 or 3 in the state-level politics is naïve and holding it against him cussed.

Mr. Shah won't of course tell that even the Prime Minister of India doesn't hold no. 10 post when put alongside Sonia, or even the India's Simpleton No. 1.

> Narmada which is considered the 'lifeline of Gujarat' does not have any minister, let alone Cabinet minister. One has only to recall days when powerful politicians with strong convincing powers were asked to head it, as it involved frequent talks with neighboring states as also the Centre. The predicament is the same with ports, so important for a state with 20 percent of India's

coastline, where many private ports are operating and many more are coming up. They get more traffic than anywhere else in India.

Now who could possibly be more *'powerful politician'* than Modi to persuade the neighboring states to do Gujarat's bidding? In fact, it was Modi's resolve, heft and the 'convincing' power that made first the successful completion, and then passing of the plan for raising its height further possible for the Narmada Dam. Apparently, here Mr. Shah is barking up the entirely wrong tree.

As for the ports, again, successful completion and operation of private ports is due in part to Modi's vision and perseverance. Mr. Shah's argument, *'they get more traffic than anywhere else in India'* is in itself testimony against his contention that Modi is doing a disfavor to his state by holding on to the ministry of ports.

It is not that Modi is insensitive about the charges about the style of leadership brought against him. In a recent interview (*The Economist*, 27 September 2012), he replied to the charges:

> The Economist: Tell me about your style of leadership, because it is sometimes controversial. One of the criticisms of you is that you are not a team player.

> Narendra Modi: The success story of Gujarat, credit goes to team Gujarat. If I would not have been a player, Gujarat would not have given this success. This success is because we are all team players. In the political system we are a team, politics and bureaucracy we are a team. The politicians, bureaucrats and the people we are a team. And this is the result of the team. So these allegations are absolutely baseless allegations. This type of person can work for one year, two years, not 12 years. Impossible.

> TE: So you are not a dictator? You are not pushing your style?

> NM: You cannot do that. Unless and until you inspire the people, you will not get results. Imposition will never give you the results. Inspiration will always give you the results. Our progress is because of clarity of thoughts, faith and conviction, character to act. These are the basic things, that is why we are getting success. We are a policy driven state. In my state, we are the only state, we put our policy draft on the net, we invite the people, go through our draft policy, give your suggestion, then we discuss, then we finalize. You will never find a draft policy from any government. We circulate the draft to the people.

Convincing, by and large, one must say. But to proceed with Mr. Rajiv Shah and his tirade:

With BJP, things have been equally bad. Ever since Modi managed to politically finish off his main competitors in the party, including former chief ministers Keshubhai Patel and Suresh Mehta, and former Union textile minister Kashiram Rana, the state party has a BJP president whom few know RC Faldu. Former BJP chief Rajendrasinh Rana is merely a member of Parliament with no clout in the party now. Ministers, MLAs and MPs have become so dependent on Modi that they openly say, without a slip of tongue, that they can't win an election without Modi.

This man's solicitousness for the former BJP chief ministers and other functionaries is touching indeed. Its however a sure bet that had these people been at the helm of the state affairs, he would have been fulminating against them too for their bigotry, incompetence and worse. Things have been bad indeed, not only for these BJP deadwoods but much more so for the Congress, for unless Modi gets to be less 'dictatorial' in his attitude, letting scores of these 'stalwarts' run riot across the state and make life difficult for him and the general public, Congress has little chance of making a comeback to power

> Over-centralization is not just confined to the Cabinet and the party. It has become a key to all government programmes. Over the last two years, Modi held exactly 863 Gharib Kalyan melas at districts, taluka and village levels, where the poor were handed over the doles at one go, allegedly 'without any intermediaries'. Here too Modi ruled at each of the melas... Modi's over-centralized ways, interestingly, has put the entire babudom on tenterhooks. A senior state official quoted a collector of a North Gujarat district to say, 'We have no other work to do, except organizing melas for Modi's functions. We cannot do our routine work, which keeps piling up'...

Poor man's bailiwick encroached upon by a political usurper and he rendered unable to lay his hands upon what he looks upon as his traditional due: The grief of *'senior state official'* is heart-rending indeed. What is not comprehensible however is Mr. Shah's fervent wish that the job of handing out doles (Center's schemes in the main) be handed over to the 'intermediaries' and NGOs so that (much like other states) the schemes were run down into the mud. Apparently, he doesn't want Gujarat standing out like a sore thumb amid quintessentially 'Indian' other Indian states.

The said official's angst regarding *babudom's* inability to attend to routine work is also very touching. The babudom of UP and Bihar (or most of the states for that matter) has not been burdened in the manner Gujarat's is, and see how fast and efficiently it carries out its 'routine work' and how best it serves the honored citizenry of these states!

In other ways too, Modi's dictatorial ways seem to know no bounds (*Along with centralization of power, Modi seems to show scant regard to democratic institutions*). Most fascist in its implications is his desire to see that, unlike the villages of Bihar, UP and other states, the focus of village-level democratic processes in his state remains peace and development, and the elections to village panchayats don't degenerate into engines of games of one-upmanship and feud. How undemocratic indeed! Thus Mr. Shah:

> ...Modi rewards those village panchayats which are elected unopposed in the name of creating a 'samras' atmosphere. Working towards undermining competitive elections at the village level ever since he came to power, he has been progressively increasing the prize to the panchayats declared samras. And who would give prize to these 'samras' panchayats?

OK, admitted, Modi is a fascist in rewarding the villages that elected their *pradhans* uncontested. However, is that fascism any the worse than the unbridled democracy about which *India Today* (October 1, 2012) has this to report: *'Political murders in Bihar have found a new constituency: The Panchayats. At least 34 mukhiyas have been murdered in less than two years in Bihar'.*

As always, Mr. Shah catches holds of an angst-ridden soul:

> A district Panchayat chief belonging to BJP complained, `The effort here is to undermine the constitutional requirement of 72nd and 73rd amendments which gives more powers to local bodies. The state Panchayat department has prepared a list of 15 items whose powers must be progressively transferred to the local bodies. However, here, under ATVT (Apno Taluko Vibrant Taluko), even the job which are with panchayats are being sought to be monitored by 100 plus class one officials, directly controlled by Gandhinagar`.

Again, concern of Mr. Shah for a district Panchayat chief of BJP, and the latter's for the constitutional imperatives is eye-watering. One can sympathize with the poor *panchayat* chief. For, whereas, district *panchayat* chiefs in other states may be earning Rs. 2 to 5 crores a year, our BJP man, for whose democratic health Mr. Shah is mighty concerned about, may have to be making do with a tenth of that, if any. That is the reason he wants everything to be left unmonitored to him so that he may milk the holy cow of *'constitutional requirement'* to his heart's content.

We had the pleasure of quoting from an article penned by a gentleman, Shiv Visvanathan, in our chapter titled 'What Modi has done...'. In the course of his article, Mr. Visvanathan had waxed eloquent about Modi's administrative acumen and developmental achievements. That however was not the end of the story. One may applaud a man's vision, acumen and the achievements, but if he carries, like Shakespeare's Hamlet, a fatal flaw in his character, everything turns to sawdust and therefore unacceptable. That seems to be this gentleman's view about Modi, who raises deep apprehensions in his heart:

> Gujarat is inaugurating one of the most profound acts of urbanization. In fact, it is going to be the centre of giant maglopolis, linking Surat, Bhavnagar, Ahmedabad, Gandhinagar, Mundra. This urbanization, which is impressive in its speed, may be built at large human cost. Gujarat is home of some of the greatest nomadic and pastoral civilizations. The question just not to Modi but to development experts is, what do we do with them. Do they have a say in history or is the logic of development indifferent to alternative lifestyles and alternative visions of the future? Will they disappear in the years to come?

That is so cruel of Modi – letting the population, along with its housing and development needs swell unchecked. Still more reprehensible are his attempts upon *'inaugurating one of the most profound acts of urbanization'* so as to fulfill those needs which would, of necessity, rob some of the great civilizations of their nomadic way of life by making them part of urbanization process. Would Modi be democratic enough to keep the rapidly growing population herded into their ghettos, or would he persist with his insensitive and dictatorial ways by making the herding communities part of the urbanization process, is for Modi to answer.

'What do we do with them?' Of course, we put them in zoos, which is what the people like you want. And, *'alternative visions of the future'*? Pardon me, if you don't want them to come out of their nomadic-pastoral 'civilization', what vision of future that pastoral community can have but to keep gazing into the bums of cows and goats?

Finally, the cup of man's sentimentalism flows over:

> Finally, how does one create a dream of justice that includes minorities? Where do Muslims fit as citizens? In fact, where do marginals and minorities exist in this dream? Do they get destroyed in a flat land of citizenship? If Gujarat's development is an act of culture, do Patel and Gandhi have a place in it?

'Do they get destroyed in a flat land of citizenship' that is the nub of the matter. They don't want the Muslim community to become Indian citizen like all others, but (mirroring the Hindi movies where veil, *adaab, mujra,* chewing of *paan,* and reciting of a *sher* at the drop of a hat is all that is to being a Muslim) a thing worthy of zoos, museums or exhibitions and...and a vote bank, with a permanent look of suffering, deprivation, grouse and anger on its face. Their greatest fear is that if the Muslims were *'destroyed'* in the *'flat land of citizenship',* millions of sociologists, journalists, politicians, middlemen and other assorted do-gooders would lose their livelihood. And their greatest grouse against Modi is just that, that he undertakes welfare measures, and conceives and implements schemes without thinking for a moment what religious denomination the intended beneficiaries belonged to. It is this flatland of citizenship that not just the bleeding hearts like Mr. Visvanathan, but the entire left-liberal establishment stands in dread of.

> If Gujarat's development is an act of culture, do Patel and Gandhi have a place in it?

If the man accuses Modi of trying to make development an act of culture...well, there could be no greater compliment than that. Every true-bred patriot would give his right hand away to cultivate such a culture among his compatriots. Gandhi being an enemy of development is alright but Patel? Further, is Modi alone in giving a short shrift to Gandhi, as far as the issue of development was concerned? Is Gandhi or his 'ism' being followed in, say, Haryana, Maharashtra or Tamil Nadu, or, for that matter, in the corridors of power at the Centre where another breed of Gandhi reigns?

> A regime that condemns dissent and treats human rights as a poor commodity eventually falls on its own assumptions. I admit this is a marginal view, as dissent today is a dying industry in Gujarat.

Why do you want to make dissent a full-fledged industry, instead of an honest, conscientious and normal thing? Dissent for dissent's sake, for love of argumentation, to gain recognition on the strength of exotic phrases and to show that you were a mighty great, secularist, sociologist, thinker and humanitarian...well, such dissent should surely be given a couple of slaps in the face, followed by a kick in the teeth.

> 'Amid the hosannas to Modi as a great manager, decision-maker, politician, let me insist on presenting this footnote as a critique of 10 years of a regime that refuses to go away.'

One is forced to say that much more than an honest critique, it is a meaningless rant from one of the tribe of leftist do-gooders which, in the name of people and liberal principles, has done everything in its power to do this nation in. And, by the way, no regime anywhere in the world has gone away gladly or of its own accord. Whether a democracy or dictatorship, it is the people that force the regimes out – through the power of ballot in the former, and through the power of unity or/and bullets in the rest. People it is keeping the Modi dispensation in power and shall force it out if and when it crossed the bounds of its mandate.

Gujarati Goebbles. The Times of India, leading and extremely influential (especially with the aging set, for their craving for sleaze and tittle-tattle grows as they pass increasingly into senility) newspaper of India has taken upon itself the job of demolishing Modi on his achievements fronts, seeking thus to rob him of his great USP. That doesn't however mean that it has left the 'Hindu-Hitler' job entirely to the care of others. But, since, *'Modi, the mass-murderer'* theme has begun to lose its sting, or sensing that the light of their torch on Modi has been countered successfully by him by throwing back the searchlight of his economic and governance accomplishments in his detractors' faces, it has changed track to throw missiles of *'True lies'* directed at the searchlight to fuse its very bulb. One Rajiv Shah, who everyone in Modi's party and the administration, right from cabinet ministers to the chief secretary, seem to have fallen in love with, so much so that they not only make bold to let him in their respective offices (despite being, according to Mr. Shah's own insinuation, mighty afraid of the Devil's legendary spy network crawling around every nook and cranny of the state), but also tell him every single 'truth' lying behind the abominable lies concocted on a daily basis by the Demon King.

We take some samples from the articles penned by this intrepid Sherlock Holmes employed by *The Times of India* to enlighten Indians about the sins and debaucheries going on in the benighted state of Gujarat. This man Rajiv Shah is a former Marxist, who, despite leaving the Communists (there was little money there and Mr. Shah is a Gujarati; that explains the thing) long ago, has shed neither his warped thinking and uncouth communist ways, nor the Hindu-hating dhimmi mindset germane to the Indian Communist thugs.

Writing in *The Times of India* of Oct 21, 2010 under the title, *'Modi used UPA funds, conned Congress'*, Shah alleges:

The BJP won 100 percent of the six municipal corporations seats,

68.37% of the 807 district Panchayat seats, 60.55% of the taluka Panchayat seats and 50.71% of the 1890 municipality seats… Modi is smart if he won this landslide victory by using the UPA funds.

UPA fund he alludes to is state's share in the taxes and duties collected by the Centre and allocations made under different Central Government welfare and dole-out schemes such as MNREGA. According to this piece of wisdom penned by Mr. Shah and promoted by *The Times of India,* which prides itself on being the premier newspaper of the nation (but aspires clearly to become a tabloid), all the taxes and levies collected by the Government of India belong to the UPA (ruling coalition of parties led by Congress). Modi, as is his wont, utilized these funds very wisely targeting the really needy and giving no quarter to corruption and won election to the local bodies. That in short is the way the lies and the deviousness of Modi have been exposed week after week by the venerable *Times of India*!

(But, perhaps, Mr. Shah is right after all. The money collected by the Central Government belongs indeed to the UPA, which in turn belongs to mummy Sonia. That is why they keep helping themselves to the central coffers ever so smoothly, without any care, fear, guilt or shame whatsoever.)

In another article, *'Lies, damn lies, and statistics'* (*The Times of India*, June 10, 2012), Rajiv Shah poses this innocent question for truth's sake, *'Does Gujarat government fudge figures to prove its success story? The suspicion is, indeed, not new…',* and proceeds to tell about a *'closed-door'* seminar held in Ahmedabad by a *'few senior experts'* who wanted to *'understand'* Gujarat's growth story to determine: *'whether it could at all be called a model for other states to follow, as Modi wants them to believe….'.*

What *'struck most'* this babe-in-the-wood (and he claims to be a veteran of a decade in exposing Modi's misdeeds) was that *'several experts seemed to feel that there is something fundamentally wrong with the figures Gujarat government has been officially disseminating. The scholars only fell short of declaring that the figures had been manipulated…'.*

Now, after a decade of stories doing rounds about Modi's accomplishments, these *'senior experts'*, rising from their slumber, as it were, deemed it fit to find out the veracity of the claims and that too in a closed door seminar in Ahmedabad! If their mandate was to proceed in secret and not expose themselves either in the field (where only the claims could be verified), or in an open seminar or hearing, they could as well have done it in New Delhi. And delay of a decade in recommending the Gujarat model (if it indeed had been successful) to the other states (they are imbeciles you see; can't see or learn by themselves) was indeed unconscionable.

And why did they need to hold a seminar to understand the growth numbers disseminated by the fraudulent Gujarat Government? Growth (or otherwise) in collection of taxes and levies of thousand kinds (income tax, sales tax, excise, custom and the like) would have brought out the truth more lucidly than any closed door seminar held by *'senior experts'* in various stages of senility.

Thus, Prof YK Alagh, a well-known economist, *'wondered why Gujarat was at all claiming a double digit rate of growth in agriculture when, even by global standards, a four plus percent of growth in the sector was considered very good.'*

Four percent growth in agriculture should indeed be considered very good if efforts are not that extraordinary — one million check dams built; Narmada Dam, an irrigation project of biblical dimensions completed; eight-hour regular supply made available to the irrigation pumps; extraordinary efforts made to make seeds, implements and technical know-how available to the farmers and introduce new commercial crops, with the entire government machinery made to descend down upon the countryside in the sowing season; and corruption, that most debilitating drag upon the enterprise and growth of just about anyone, and not just the farmers, eliminated.

Nothing against the erudition or integrity of Prof Alagh, but he is one of a piece with the elite that, having seen or presided over dispensations that paid only lip service to the farmers' cause (if not actually looted and beggared them) and witnessing only two to three percent growth their entire lives, can't bring itself to believe that double digit rate of growth could indeed be possible.

Mr. Shah has one Prof Leela Visaria telling on the status of health of children and women that she relied more on the data from large national surveys, as the other sources such as official administrative data were frequently not reliable. And *'while she agreed that the infant mortality rate (IMR) has declined from 69 per 1000 live births in the early 1990s to 44 in 2010, quoting survey data, she said, `Gujarat ranks poor in the rank in this decline among the major 20 states in India`.'*

Now there is no way of knowing about the record of Modi regime on the said IMR parameter, though, very cunningly, Mr. Shah would have us believe that it was lackadaisical at best. Though a decline from 69 to 44 in the IMR rate is not an achievement to be scoffed at, the figures presented by Prof. Leela Visaria relate to two decades time. We have no way of knowing whether the rate declined too sharply during Modi's time of impressive economic growth, decline in corruption, focused attention and strict supervision, or remained stagnant or even grew under his watch. Only a naïve would believe that it is a case of poor homework or oversight on the part of Mr. Shah or the *Times of India*.

Prof Visaria also revealed that *'the percentage of married women aged 15-19 suffering anaemia increased in the state, from 46 in 1992-93 to 56 in 2005-06. This incidence is particularly high among rural, illiterate, ST and poor women'*.

Even Bihar, with one-fourth per capita income, recording the same nutritional levels as Gujarat...phenomenon, is strange and inexplicable, to say the least. In any case, Modi has already taken listened to the criticism and taken steps. A doer if there ever was one, he is not one to brush the things under the carpet. And he has taken up the thing in his usual thoroughgoing manner by instituting a committed to undertake comprehensive study and recommend solutions.

Mr. Shah proceeds next to quote one Prof Sudarshan Iyengar about the status of education in Gujarat:

> Since the official method of calculating dropout rate is not specified by the Directorate Primary Education, the reliability of these data is questionable. There is no reason to believe in the official data on school retention. The reliability of the data is also challenged by other studies by scholars... Poor quality of education is a serious problem in Gujarat. Introduction of Gunotsav in 2009 was, in a way, recognition of the fact that quality of education is below the desired level. This annual event, however, cannot substitute regular machinery.

That indeed is a serious charge. However (if only to put things in perspective), we have this gentleman also saying about Gujarat (*Counterview*; June 12, 2012): *'...there has been substantial improvement in physical infrastructure and services for education during the past decade. Access to primary education has definitely improved in the state. However retaining SC and ST students in school is still a serious matter. The retention rate seems to have improved radically since 2006-07'*.

That of course Mr. Shah won't tell us. Modi's obsession with improving the quality of education, educational infrastructure and the issue of access to poor and the excluded sections is not only extraordinary, but something completely out of character with our politicians and other trustees of the nation. No chief minister or prime-minister in India (or any other political leader for that matter) has taken as much interest in educating his people as Modi has. Everybody is aware by now about Modi's obsession with primary education, especially of the girl child. And not one to miss out on anything, he takes equally keen interest in technical and higher education too. Yet, this interest is not the kind, wherein thousands of engineering and medical colleges and universities have been allowed mindlessly by the greedy chief ministers in lieu of hefty commissions. An entire industry of fleecing the gullible parents, making fool of students and destroying the future of the entire nation by churning out a vast crop of unemployable 'engineers' and other graduates has been set into motion by the anti-national dispensations obtaining in other states. Situation has come to the pass that more 'engineers' than technicians are being turned out now in India.

Of course, Modi, nationalist to the core and mindful of the interests of the students, the society and the industry alike, would have none of that. Thus, whereas, other chief ministers were busy in issuing permit to 'engineering colleges', Modi was engaged in opening institutes of technical education (lowly ITIs), so much so that the number of such institutes grew from 442 at the beginning of his tenure to 18000 (yes, you have read that right) now. Outcome has been that the industries from all over the India flock to Gujarat to recruit technical hands and the ITI pass-outs from Gujarat are fully employed, earning much more than the so-called 'engineers' of UP, Bihar and other states.

Comparing Modi with other political leaders of some substance (on the educational front), only Nehru comes to mind, as Indira Gandhi was positively hostile to the concept of the subalterns of the land getting any kind of education (and getting more aware of their democratic privileges, demanding of their rights, and wiser about the shenanigans of the Dynasty) and Rajiv Gandhi didn't have the caliber, vision or inclination to go beyond the idea of 'Navodaya Vidyalya', which remained a non-starter from the word go, besides being extremely limited in its reach and impact. Of others (including Atal and Manmohan), the less said, the better.

Now, our peerless Nehru was accorded the sobriquet of *'Chacha Nehru',* his birthday celebrated as *'Bal Divas'* (Children's Day) because he was extraordinarily fond of children and concerned about their welfare. He never tired of waxing eloquent about their welfare and the need for imparting them proper education. He therefore allocated – hold your breath – Rs. 12 crores for primary education, out of 2000 crores budgeted for the first five year plan (which comes to a princely share of 0.6%)! Though neglecting (willfully, one can't but conclude, and for the same reasons as his daughter Indira) this issue of most critical importance for a nation's evolution and development, especially during its formative stage, Nehru must nevertheless be deemed a visionary and Modi a lying cheat.

Reverting to the comments of this man Iyengar, quoted by Mr. Shah: Now, according to this man, introduction of *Gunotsava* (occasion for making special efforts to improve the quality of education) by Modi in 2009 was a recognition of the fact that the quality of education had been poor in Gujarat.

Modi is damned if he doesn't and damned too if he does. According to the logic, if a political leader, say Obama, takes special measures to improve the health of his subjects, that would be clear admittance of the fact that the quality of health services had been bad in the US, badder even than in such gems of nations as India, Somalia and Haiti. By that yardstick, the quality of education in the nations like Singapore, Taiwan and South Korea, where they never tire of emphasizing the need to improve the quality of education and the efforts on the account are relentless, trail way behind the Indian states like UP, Bihar, Bengal or Orissa.

Scanning Mr. Iyengar's remark, Mr. Shah *'instantly'* remembers what a state officials had told him about fudging enrolment data by Anandiben Patel, a former education minister of Gujarat who *'remains 'ideologically closest to Modi'*:

> "We collected data and gave it to the minister. The minister called for a meeting and declared the data were all wrong. She split the meeting angrily. Later, she directly called for more data from districts, which she got. She added these data to the data that we had given. And what she gave us a nearly cent percent enrolment!"

What clearly Mr. Shah seeks to imply is that notwithstanding superhuman efforts of Modi, and Gujarat's per capita income being more than two to four times of some of the major states like Bihar, UP and Assam, enrolment ratio in Gujarat remains not much more than fifty percent, even as the claims forwarded by the Centre suggest national enrolment ratio at around 90%. Nationally the literacy rate is said to be around 74% and that of Gujarat around 80%. Clear implication is that Gujarat's enrolment ratio under that arch-philistine is half of the national average and Gujarat's literacy rate is set to decline from around 80% now to around 50% a few decades down! That is Rajiv Shah and *The Times of India* for you.

PS: A Times News Network report (April 1, 2011) tells that in 2001, the male literacy rate in Gujarat was 79.66% while for female it was 57.88%. This saw an increase in 2011. Literacy rate for males had gone up to 87.23% while for females it was 70.73%.

In another blog published in *The Times of India* (13 May 2012) titled, *'Of hype, misadventure and Gujarat's powerdom'* Rajiv Shah tells about Modi calling an *'urgent press conference'* on June 25, 2005 to announce the *'biggest ever gas find in India'* by GSPC (a Gujarat state enterprise) at the KG basin off Andhra coast. The find was projected to yield a total of 20 trillion cubic feet (tcf) gas over the years, valued at around Rs 2 lakh crore. Subsequently, the find turned out to be bearing much lower gas than the initial estimates according to Mr. Shah, as he proceeds to tear into Modi for creating unnecessary hype around the find just to drive political advantage, even as his whim, irrational love for mega projects and craving for glory were responsible for flushing Rs 8000 crore worth of Gujarat money down the drain. Mr. Shah continues:

> In fact, Modi's officials tell me that it was the `biggest mistake ever' to have made the 20 tcf announcement. `Oil exploration nowhere in the world takes place on borrowed funds from banks. It is too risky a business. These should always be held after raising funds from public,` one official, an expert on issues of financial, told me, adding, `And this one at KG basin was more risky than any known one. It has taken place in deep sea, deeper underneath than anywhere, and at very high temperatures. All of it added to the cost. The risk of this kind wasn't worth taking for a commercial proposition, when PSUs are constrained by strict official rules and regulations. Very little expertise is available, that too at a very high cost, for exploration of this kind`.

So, here we are. Modi first forced the GSPC to undertake KG basin exploration on mere hunch or whim, poured in Rs. 8000 crore worth of public money in a project that was uniquely fraught and for which little expertise was available, and then proceeded to commit *'biggest mistake ever'* (crime rather, if we go by the tone adopted by Mr. Shah) by announcing on his own a gas find of, hold your breath, 20 tcf! No greater wastrel or monster was born in India, for eight thousand crores is certainly a much greater sum of money than one hundred seventy six thousand crores lost to the nation by way of 2G or more than 3 hundred thousand crores by coal-block allotment.

Mr. Shah won't tell his readers that it takes at least half a decade of survey and data-taking to arrive at the decision to explore a prospective hydrocarbons field. And, after the decision, another half a decade passes before everything is arranged and installed, and exploration results (not the actual output) begin to pour in. Thus, the survey activity of the KG basin must have begun at least a decade (if not more) and the decision to begin exploratory drilling half-a-decade before Modi committed his *'biggest mistake ever'*. Modi came to power in 2002, and he held the referred-to press conference in 2005, so Mr. Shah's attempt to show that the costly decision was an outcome entirely of the whim of that greatest enemy of the people of Gujarat is at least two to three years off the mark. Further, according to him:

> Soon after this announcement on KG basin, unconfirmed reports began to trickle in Gandhinagar Sachivalaya quoting sources in DG hydrocarbons, the Central regulator, that the gas find `is quite low`.' I thought, the DG was a UPA appointee, hence couldn't be relied. I asked a top bureaucrat, who knew the reality, and he told me, `it's not more than 2 tcf (just 10 percent of what Modi had claimed). Of this, less than two-thirds is recoverable`.' I did a story, saying the 20 tcf balloon had been pricked. Yet, two years later, in 2007, talking with mediapersons at a sumptuous lunch, Modi insisted, `it is at least 20 tcf, it can be 26 tcf, even more…`.

What Mr. Shah won't tell *The Times of India* readers that 2 tcf gas certification by the DG hydrocarbons was only beginning of the process as only a few wells had been drilled. The picture becomes clear, and the 'True lies' and the intent of Mr. Shah and his patron newspaper laid bare by this report from *'The Economic Times'* (a sister publication of *The Times of India*) of Sep 19, 2009:

> Director General of Hydrocarbon (DGH) has certified two TCF (trillion cubic feet) gas reserves in the western area KG-8 in the Gujarat State Petroleum Corporation (GSPC) prolific Deendayal blocks in the KG basin.

> Talking to mediapersons here after the board meeting of GSPC, DGH V K Sibal said, `in the GSPC's block in the KG basin, approximately two TCF gas reserves have been certified`.

> He said GSPC has made good discovery in the Deendayal block in the KG-8 field. `It is a very good discovery in the field wherein four wells have so far been drilled and 11 more are planned to be drilled,` Sibal said.

> He said the certified reserves is a very conservative figure of the huge potential of the block.

'We are very conservative in certifying the reserves but in reality when the entire block is developed, the reserve can be significantly higher,' he said.

So only four wells had been drilled, 11 more were planned to be drilled and 2 tcf certification regarding those four wells too was *'very conservative'*. Now, should Modi's (purported) whimsical decision to force GSPC to undertaken exploration in a uniquely fraught region, and then his announcement, way back in 2005, of 20 tcf of gas find be termed a 'hype' and *'True Lie'*, or (if, as insinuated by Mr. Shah, Modi made the announcement on his own hunch, and not on the recommendation of experts) a great piece of prophetic revelation?

Further, coming to think of it, 20 tcf was not so great a discovery and rather than boastfulness as Mr. Shah alleges, Modi could certainly be accused of small-mindedness on the account. To provide the readers some perspective, Russia's known gas reserves stand at around 1,600 tcf, of Iran 1,000 tcf and even tiny Qatar's at 900 tcf. Why, the recently explored Lolotan gas field of Turkmenistan is believed to be holding around 600 tcf.

But to proceed, how the KG basin exploration was risky? High temperature? Pardon me. From Malaysia and Brunei in the east, to Ankleshwar, Bombay-High, Qatar and Saudi Arabia in the west – are they any different from the Andhra coast in the matter of temperature? In light of the fact that exploration and extraction work is being done successfully in regions ranging from the impossible *'pre-salt'* Tupi fields of Brazil (situated 200 kilometers off coast and below 2000 meters of ocean waters, and then 5000 meters of sand, rocks and salt layer), to the most unforgiving arctic climes of Canada, Russia and the Arctic itself, where temperature goes down to minus sixty degrees, KG basin exploration must be regarded a teddy bear's picnic in comparison. Reliance undertook successful exploration in the same region and is earning huge monies off its fields. How did it manage to do that if technology was not available? (And please don't befool the readers by telling that Reliance had developed the technology in-house while the GSPC was not in a position to do that.) It is another matter that contrary to the estimates of the international as well as the Indian hydrocarbons experts, and the much-vaunted expertise of the DGHC (Directorate General of Hydrocarbons), the Reliance field too failed to match up to its initial hype (though, as in everything Reliance, there is alleged to be some hanky-panky involved in underestimating the potential). It is in the nature of the thing. Even the supremely capable Americans didn't know that they had been holding world's biggest gas reserves right under their bums; thing which, within a decade and a half, has transformed the US from being world's biggest importer into its likely biggest exporter.

But, no, it is Modi who must be excoriated for the estimates fed to him by the experts. It can't be that this sixty year old man Rajiv Shah, or the editorial junta of *The Times of India* is unaware of the truth behind *'True Lies'* fed to the unsuspecting readers. But when one carries political, ideological or monetary axe to grind, items like probity, conscience and sense of duty get to be the first in the line of sacrifice.

As for the (alleged) mindless business risk-taking in the matter, Shah's contention is that the GSPC (Modi, rather) should have used funds raised from the general public, and not borrowed from the banks. Clear implication is that it is alright to make fool of the public, play speculative games with their money and beggar them, rather than have it arranged from banks. A convoluted logic that, one must say.

The intrepid friend of the people of Gujarat goes again, picking on Modi for his enthusiasm and the achievements regarding something for which he has been rightly acclaimed across the nation and the world:

> Officials are now waiting for the day when Modi's KG misadventure would be repeated for several other projects which he has taken up to show up how he is different…

Mr. Shah then proceeds to tell of a mighty angst-ridden official of Gujarat (it doesn't require the brains of Rajiv Shah for one to see that the poor man failed to extract any commission in the deals) telling him that the Gujarat Government had signed up power purchase agreements (PPAs) for 960 MW, three-fourth of India, with tens of solar units, taking advantage of the offer of a very high subsidy. The offer was for Rs 15 per unit for the first 12 years and Rs 5 for another 13 years. *'The plants already put up 650 MW are producing 3 million units per day of power. It would mean the state would have to shell out on an average Rs 1,600 per year* (sic) *for next 25 years'.*

And…

> 'This happened at a time when the cost of solar power began coming down drastically', the official, who is an insider, told me. `The capital cost of solar power per MW has come down by half. Many of the plants were established on purchase of power equipment at a sharply reduced cost, for Rs 8 crore per MW.

Entrepreneurs would recover capital cost of power from government subsidy in less than seven years. As for the rest of 18 years, they would be happily enjoying on government subsidy especially when the actual cost of producing power is just 15 paisa per unit.` He insisted, `What a contrast! Reverse bidding in Delhi has brought down price of solar power to Rs 7.75 per unit. And we are offering Rs 15`.

It is very easy – criticizing a decision ex-post-facto and making a farsighted statesman look like a wastrel or a fool. Just about no one could foresee (not even the companies producing solar panels, otherwise they wouldn't have sunk billions of dollars in bringing up new capacities) that the cost of solar panel would reduce to less than half within a year. But it was no thanks to India whose 'officials', 'journalists', 'intellectuals' and politicians are all half-literate idiots mired in myopia, pettiness and corruption. Here too, as always, China upset all calculations of the men and mice.

However, this revolution, whose greatest beneficiary in the long-run India stands to be, has become possible solely to the vision and the venturesomeness of forward-looking persons like Modi. For, without people and the nations venturing into the high-cost zone of solar energy, no technological evolution and cost-reductions witnessed lately could have become possible. What Mr. Shah argues is that one should keep postponing the decision to purchase a TV, computer or mobile because prices were coming down all the time. In the absence of electricity, people, even destitute farmers, are being forced to take to capital intensive diesel generation that produce energy at the rate of Rs. 15 a unit even with the hugely subsidized, foreign-exchange-draining, environment-damaging and health-destroying diesel. Mr. Shah won't touch upon that point. And he doesn't bother to think over or elaborate that the issue of energy is not like your TV or the mobile thing, but that of very life and death for a nation and its people. Modi chose life for his people over stasis and death, whatever the cost.

And even regarding the matter of cost, the people of Gujarat don't stand to lose a dime more than the people, who, despite million advices from the likes of Mr. Shah, bought computers for their kids a decade ago when it cost at least four times as much. As in case of any other technological revolution, in the present case too, it is not the laggards, fence-sitters, or the me-too-China nations, but the people and nations who have prepared themselves well by bringing systems and institutions into place and developing skills, that stand to benefit the most from the unfolding solar revolution.

The grouse of the said fictitious official is that Modi government's offer for the solar investors was for Rs 15 per unit for the first 12 years and Rs 5 for another 13 years. And that the *'Entrepreneurs would recover capital cost of power from government subsidy in less than seven years. As for the rest of 18 years, they would be happily enjoying on government subsidy especially when the actual cost of producing power is just 15 paisa per unit.'*

Now, as any investor could tell you, prospect of recovering capital costs in seven years is not a terribly exciting idea. After subjecting to much harassment and bribe-taking, the banks charge an interest rate of close to eighteen percent which necessitates recovery of capital within four to five years. Close to two years is the time a commercial level solar plant requires to start yielding output. Add those two years to the seven years and you had the investors squeezed as tightly as possible. What did he do or earn after that should be nobody's concern really. Further, energy rate of Rs 5 a unit after twelve years is something for which one could even kill, literally. Reason is clear. With the coal dwindling fast, hydro disappearing, and the nuclear growing more intractable with each passing day, you won't get electricity at any rate whatsoever — that is, if you failed to take to the renewables in a big way as Modi has been doing. As for the rest of 18 years of *'enjoying'* by the entrepreneurs. Apparently this official (if there actually is one) can't swallow his grief that the buggers would be enjoying the fruits of their enterprise and the capital without giving a penny to the officialdom. It is exactly the kind of mindset that has scared away the talent, killed the enterprise and rendered India a stinking hell reeking of corruption and scarcities.

To give our readers still better perspective on the thing, we quote here a news report from *The Times of India* itself. Of course, one can't hope it to have any effect on the enthusiasm, either of the ToI or Mr. Shah, concerning exposing the truth behind Modi's lies.

Secret of Jindal's success: Cheap coal, costly power

Supriya Sharma, TNN, September 9, 2012

As recent revelations have shown, many gained from coal blocks by selling stakes in their companies. But a few gained by simply making and selling power at high prices.

A case in point is Jindal Power Limited (JPL), a subsidiary of Jindal Steel and Power Limited (JSPL), owned by Congress MP Naveen Jindal.

The company's 1000MW plant turned fully operational in 2008. Over the next year, it sold power at an average price of more than

Rs 6 per unit. By 2010, the high returns had not only covered its running costs but also investments of Rs 4,338 crore. According to infrastructure experts, it takes a minimum of 5-7 years to repay debt incurred for capital investment in power projects.

However, that's not the case with this project. A July 2011 report by the research firm Motilal Oswal notes, "Jindal Power has become debt-free within two years of operation due to strong cash flows on account of low cost." A big component of the low cost was cheap coal obtained from its captive coal mine just 10km away Gare Palma IV/2 and IV/3 with combined reserves of 246 million tones of coal.

Cheaper coal should ideally translate into lower power prices at least this has been the coal ministry and UPA's key defence. They have argued that coal blocks were given for free to private companies to keep power tariffs low.

The combination of cheap coal and high power prices explains why Jindal posted Rs 1,765 crore as profits, or 60% of its income, while Lanco made a profit of just Rs 155 crore, just 12% of its income.

Now, according to the above report, 'it takes minimum of 5-7 years to repay debt incurred for capital investment in power projects'. But the paper has no qualm pedaling this canard (or tolerating the fraudulent blogger spreading it) that Modi had beggared his state by extending a deal to the investors that would enable them to recover their capital cost in around 7 years. Further, while the Congress has facilitated a deal that allowed Jindal to sell power at Rs. 6 a unit even in 2008, Modi has arranged power for his state at Rs. 5 a unit after 12 years…and till a quarter century hence!

Mr. Shah isn't done yet with Modi or the solar:

Meanwhile, despite advice to the contrary from senior engineers, Modi's men have begun yet another misadventure. They have installed 1 MW of solar power panels, 750 meters long, atop a Narmada branch canal, at the unprecedented cost of Rs 17.50 crore, nearly double that of what the entrepreneurs are investing. Even Modi admitted, no entrepreneur came forward to invest, hence the government decided to do it on its own. Modi's aides now say that `2000 MW of solar power can be installed atop the Narmada canal network,` even as engineers say the project mean the canal network would be susceptible to rupture. The lining cannot bear the heavy load. And, how do you clean up the canal of the silt in that gathers naturally in the canal? By carrying them several kilometers in order to bring them out?

Mr. Shah won't tell the poor ToI readership that solar plants occupy an unconscionable amount of space...up to five to ten times as much as a similar-sized coal plant. For that reason, largely uninhabited deserts are deemed most suitable for establishing solar plants, but for two drawbacks: Big towns, industrial estates and arable land (that is, where the energy is really required) are usually huge distances away from the deserts. That necessitates not inconsiderable investment in erecting transmission network. Further, solar plants require water too – in huge quantum in case of solar-thermal plants (to generate steam and clean the reflectors) and in moderate amounts in case of solar photovoltaics (for cleaning of panels). But had water been available in the deserts, they wouldn't have been deserts in the first place. Transporting water long distances is again a hugely capital and time intensive job.

So here we are. We have two problems (though not insurmountable) with establishing solar plants in the wastelands (which Gujarat happens to possess in good quantum): transporting water to the site and then transporting electricity to the load-centers. And hence the solution (though only to the extent of 2000 MW) hit upon by Modi. The idea gets to be really brilliant in face of the fact that Gujarat as a whole gets unusually water deficit in the lean summer months, as also in the draught years of which it has more than the usual quota. That was why Narmada Dam was brought to fruition, overcoming almost impossible obstacles put in its way by the enemies of people masquerading as do-gooders. It has brought immense relief and prosperity to the people of Gujarat for whom every drop of water counts.

But, lamentably, the water has a bad habit of evaporating. And this bad habit gets aggravated exactly when it is needed most...that is, in the summer season. Now, if one could put a canopy over the waters to stop the sun's rays working to evaporate it (and to condense back the water evaporated), in addition to generating energy at the load centers itself and having inexpensive water for cleaning of the panels, that would be hitting three birds with a single stone. As for rupturing of canal-linings and cleaning of silt issues were concerned, that is just hogwash... as if the thing couldn't be designed to take care of these! Only a true son of the soil obsessed with the well-being of his people could have come up with the idea for the land where water is worth its weight in gold.

In another blog, *'The karmayogi device unplugged'* (*The Times of India*, 24 August 202), Mr. Shah claims that entire official machinery of Gujarat has come to a halt due to Modi's penchant for launching one scheme after another; his meddlesomeness and fetish for *kalyan-melas* and *vikas-yatras* to showcase his achievements; and the resulting overwork and loss of direction among the bureaucracy. This epiphany to Mr. Shah came when, as usual, he was sitting in the office of a *'senior-most state bureaucrat in Gandhinagar Sachivalaya'* and *'innocently wondered'*...

Now, when this bureaucrat told him, *'how the state administration, especially at the grassroot level, has come to a standstill'*, Mr. Shah was *'tempted to scan through recent documents prepared by Modi's administration for internal circulation'*. And what did he hit upon? That, *'The district collector's office is unable to cope with taluka issues because it, too, is burdened with work other than what it is required to do land management'*. And..

> Significantly, the report complains that the district collector's office is flooded with works which it is not supposed to do, and the staff doesn't know what to prioritize water supply, housing for the poor, development of polluted areas, development of tourism spots, government securities and assets, education campaigns like Gunotsav and Kanya Kelavani, krishi mahotsavs, village-level gram sabhas, jan seva kendras, Swarnim Gujarat sankalp jyoti yatra, implementation of National Rural Employment Guarantee Scheme and Suvarna Jayanti Rozgar Yojna.

So, here we are. Poor district collector, who commands unparalleled respect and authority in India, deemed a district-level god almost, drives this authority by 'land management' work only in other states. But here, in Gujarat, he is given charge of such lowly things as 'housing for the poor', 'development of tourism spots', NREGA and 'village-level gram sabhas'! Poor man has to build houses for the poor, level out land at the tourist spots, teach students in schools, disburse NREGA payouts with his own hands, do husbandry work and manage gram sabhas, even as his appointed 'land management' work suffered terribly!

The contention of Mr. Shah is that, firstly, the focus and the energy of district collectors shouldn't be deflected from (what obviously is the most important thing in the world) the task of 'land-management', burdening him with sundry developmental tasks. And if the thing became really unavoidable, these tasks shouldn't run concurrently so that the poor nerds didn't die of overwork. For example, there should be no job schemes for the rural poor till all of them had been provided with houses, perhaps in a century. Or that till the drive for school-enrollment of girls through Kanya Kelvani was in progress (a ceaseless process, for girls are born every year), there should be no Gunotsav meant for improving the quality of education in the schools. The argument of Mr. Shah is unexceptionable in its entirety.

As indeed is the carping of the bureaucracy...or, at least, the sections which are, for one reason or other, busy praying for departure of Modi and return of the Congress and find a commiserating soul in Mr. Shah to open their hearts to. For, these are not British times of slavery and slogging; India is free and democratic to the boot and if even the higher bureaucracy was deprived of the joys and benefits of freedom, pray who could hope to be happy?

Why, this very day I have this article (*Dawn*, 4 September, 2012) by a Pakistani bureaucrat regarding the torture and humiliation the bureaucrats had to put up with during the British regime:

> Several decades ago, some members of the public were kept waiting for hours under Jacobabad's scorching sun to see John Jacob, then the deputy commissioner of the town.

> They wanted to request the powerful government functionary to address some minor administrative issues that fell in his domain. In addition to being a British government functionary, Mr. Jacob was also an inventor and on that day, he became so engrossed in his workshop that he did not attend to visitors from the general public. Later, when he realized that he had failed to attend to his official duties, he was so filled with regret that the next day, he set up an office under the sun. The intention was to make the self-indulgent Jacob of the day before appreciate the suffering of the people who were forced to wait because of him.

> Perhaps, for this reason, when decades later it was proposed that the settlement's name be changed to something more 'pious', as has been done to many other cities in this land of the pure, the people of Jacobabad opposed it. Perhaps this is why John Jacob's grave in Jacobabad is generally afforded the status of a saint's mausoleum.

But, apparently, our bureaucrats do not cherish such ghastly and joyless things as mausoleum raised in their memory by a grateful public. Hard cash to buy insensate objets and properties and 'settle' worthless and ungrateful louts of progenies abroad are infinitely preferable to lasting affection of grateful millions. And that exactly is the difference between the slave race John Jacob came from, and the master race our Pradeep Shuklas, AP Singhs, Neera Yadavs and the Joshi couples belong to.

In any case, isn't it the Central Government that should be hauled over the coals first for over-burdening the bureaucracy? It has, perhaps, more than 100 schemes running simultaneously in the name of Gandhi-Nehru clan alone, most of them to be implemented through the state machinery? A possible way out could be to appoint additional officers to oversee implementation and monitoring work. But here too, Mr. Shah has a huge problem, which he has expressed in another blog, *'Centripetal undercurrents of Gujarat's No 1'* that we have discussed under the *'Hindu Hitler'* title. Complains Mr. Shah:

> ...Modi appointed 100 plus class one official all over the state to `oversee` the developmental activities which are under the purview of panchayats. These officials, with funds in hands, are answerable to none, except Gandhinagar Sachivalaya.

Finally, Mr. Shah comes to the conclusion that none of the bureaucrats has been doing anything, all have lost interest in work, and due to Modi's meddlesomeness, ineptitude and worse, the state of Gujarat has come to the verge of collapse. If the assessment is indeed true, another factor (apart from Modi's idiocy or cussedness), should be apportioned the blame. Bureaucrats of Gujarat are human beings after all. And, it is the fundamental nature of the humans to compare themselves with others, especially those from their peer group. When the poor Gujarati bureaucrats see that they are earning no *'worthwhile'* recompense for their *'public service'*, even as their peers in UP, MP, Maharashtra, Haryana, in fact every other state, were earning anywhere between Rs. 10 crore to 100 crores annually for their 'public service', they become disheartened and lose interest. Little wonder then that due to over-enthusiasm of their bureaucrats, states other than Gujarat have become models of good governance and development, while Gujarat totters on the verge of collapse.

A recent high water mark in the sport of Modi-bashing is a long blog penned by one Vinod K Jose under the title, *'The Emperor Uncrowned; The rise of Narendra Modi'*. Published online on 1 March 2012 in *'The Caravan'*, it managed to gain a good amount of virality. Though it concentrated more on the 'Hindu Hitler' theme, we choose here to discuss 'Gujarati Goebbles' aspect of the blog.

Picking on Modi's trademark Vibrant Gujarat summits, Mr. Jose carps that *'Vibrant Gujarat has been successfully marketed as a major global business event...'*. According to him, though five summits since 2003 have generated investments pledges worth $ 920 billion for Gujarat and Modi claims implementation rate greater than 60% for pledges made at the summits, *'an analysis of data from the state industry department suggests that only 25% of the promised investments have actually been made'.* Yet the man has good grace (albeit with a codicil) to concede that even that moderate implementation rate is not a mean achievement:

> While one-quarter of a trillion dollars is hardly small change, the considerable disparity between the image and the reality actually highlights the tactical genius behind the investment summits, which are the crowning achievement in one of the most extraordinary acts of reinvention in Indian politics....

But, according to Mr. Jose,

> Though Modi has presented Gujarat as the clear leader among Indian states in attracting foreign direct investment, it ranked fourth among states on this measure between 2000 and 2009, and in 2011 fell to sixth place, after Maharashtra, the National Capital Region, Tamil Nadu, Karnataka and Andhra Pradesh; Maharashtra has foreign direct investment inflows almost nine times greater than Gujarat.

Now, here is really something to chew upon...and a classic exemplar as to how the blessed tribe of Modi-bashers mutilates the truth, almost beyond recognition. A simpleton, taking the fact of Maharashtra attracting foreign direct investment inflows nine times more than Gujarat on its face, is likely then on to regard Modi a roaring fraud.

What this tribe of Modi-haters, in this case Mr. Jose, won't tell is that they always compare apples with oranges and proceed to declare from the housetop that the gains posted by Gujarat under Modi are nothing in comparison to the other state of India, including Bihar and UP.

Thus, in the present case, while the data for implementation rate in case of Gujarat has been gathered from the state industry department, the data for the Maharashtra is largely the fly-by-night equity flow in the stock markets (and less than transparent or beneficial real-state) and therefore of dubious value for the state's or nation's overall development. In case of Karnataka and Andhra, the inflow is in the IT sector and the real estate, concentrated in Hyderabad and Bangalore only, and though not of as questionable value as the equity money, is not at all comparable to industrial investment. In Tamil Nadu and the NCR it is a combination of IT, industry and real estate...again not comparable to pure industrial investment figures gathered by Mr. Jose from the industry department of Gujarat.

Like innumerable others, mighty afraid of any big or novel idea or speedy development (in the name of environment, the poor of the land, or for just being against Indian ethos or Gandhian values), Modi's latest and the biggest is giving severe heart-pangs to Mr. Jose too:

> About 30 km outside of Ahmedabad, on barren plains of dusty grassland, Modi's most monumental construction project is taking shape: an entirely new and singularly massive financial capitaIndia's own version of Shanghai, build from the ground up. Bearing the anodyne moniker Gujarat International Finance Tec-city (or "GIFT" city), the plans call for 124 skyscrapers nestled into an 886-acre plot, with more than 75 million square feet of office space, more than the financial districts of Shanghai, Tokyo and London put together. Modi's goal is to lure the financial companies now headquarterd in Mumbai to shift their operations to Gujarat by 2017. Between the capital markets, trading desks, hedge funds, software developers, and back-end operations of banks and insurance companies, India is expected to generate 11 million jobs and $ 425 billion in growth by 2020, and Modi's plan for the GIFT city are aimed at securing a large slice of that pie.

> To build his own Shanghai, Modi has recruited his architects right from the source: the city is being designed by the East China Architectural Design and Research Institute, the designers of much of the modern Shanghai. `Every bit of the drawing comes from China,` an architect who has worked on several of Modi's projects told me. `Mr Modi trusts thembecause he's clear on what he wants, because he has been to China and is in awe of Shanghai. He wants a copy, an estate of glass boxes`.'

> ..... When the final phase begins in 2013, more than a million workers will relocate to this site, making it the largest urbanization project in Indian history. That's also when most of Modi's supersized glass boxes will go upincluding centerpiece Diamond Tower, an 8plus story skyscraper designed to resemble the facets of a cut diamond, and the Naga Tower, so named because it resembles a coiled serpent.

> I was extremely shocked when I saw the design at one of the Vibrant Gujarat summits`, the architect continued. `it seemed to me like an awfully alien idea. I felt like it was the King asking, "Go and build a new kingdom for me"and someone just executing it`.

Now, pray, what is wrong if Modi thinks big or wants to take a slice of the pie of '11 million jobs and $ 425 billion growth' for the state he is in the charge of? Coming to think of it, 124 skyscrapers on 886 hectares of plot is not that big an idea even. Noida-Extension and Yamuna Expressway Authority, which were in much news recently for the way the then chief minister of UP duped the farmers to amass tens of billions for her personal coffers, are at least five times that big and not even meant to facilitate trade or industry. Modi is alleged to be besotted with Shanghai, as so many others had been with New York, London, Tokyo and Singapore in the past, and are with Dubai and Kuala Lumpur now. Only difference is that visiting these great and swanky cities, while the others think that these were built by the aliens and were, therefore, beyond the capacity of the lowly Indians to build, and the only yearning they return with is to loot the country even more speedily so as to be able to send their wards and buy properties there, Modi returned from Shanghai and Tokyo to build one for his people.

As for the architect of Mr. Jose getting his shock of life upon seeing the *'awfully alien idea'*...well, that is shocking indeed, coming from an architect. All modern towns are built that way — skyscrapers, glass and chrome and granite, and stuff. Is there any place left anywhere to build Champ Elysees or Lutyen's Delhi? Modern Shanghai or Manhattan too would have appeared to be alien ideas to the Chinese and the New Yorkers then. Or, does Mr. Jose mean to say that it was part of the history and the *'culture'* of Chinese or the Americans to build *'supersized glass boxes'*? In fact, every new and more-than-out-of-ordinary idea appears *'alien'* and *'against traditional Indian ethos and the culture'* to the people of this nation of third-raters.

One curious feature of this tribe of Modi-haters is that, whereas, on the one hand, they would want you to believe that Modi has not only done nothing for Gujarat, but has also taken it past the era when rioters, bootleggers, smugglers and assorted criminal mafias ran rampant on the coast of Gujarat and the streets of its towns, and rotten tomatoes like Chimanbhai Patel and nincompoops like Amarsinh Chaudhary and Keshubhai Patel sat at the helm, and, on other, they feel compelled to admit some essential truths, so as not to forfeit their credibility entirely. Thus, first Mr. Jose tells us:

> Even the headline figures for Gujarat's economic expansion in the past decade diminish under closer examination. The state's GDP growth has only slightly outpaced India as a whole over the past decade. But this is to be expected: Gujarat has long been an industrialized stateand, in fact, growth rates under Modi are not significantly higher than they were in the prior two decades...'
> And '...the state lags behind even Bihar, Uttar Pradesh, West

Bengal and Andhra Pradesh in poverty reduction. According to the 2011 Indian Human Development Report, Gujarat also scores poorly in several social indicators, with 44 percent of children under five suffering from malnutrition, worse than Uttar Pradesh.

And after making you believe that Modi had all but drowned Gujarat, he first proceeds to give a back-handed complement:

Ten years after the anti-Muslim pogroms that killed more than 1200 Gujaratis, Modi has managed to bury the past and resurrect his own extinct prospects for political advancement, replacing epithets like 'fascist', 'mass-murderer' and 'Hindutva fanatic' with a title of his own choosing: Vikaas Purush, or Development Man. For the first families of Indian business, Modi is 'the next leader of India', 'a visionary', 'the unstoppable horse', and the 'CEO who can lead the country', to quote just a sampling of the effusive endorsements from men named Tata, Ambani and Mittal.

And then gets rather effusive...

The transformation of Modi's image has been powered by a sophisticated public relations campaign, but the embellishments rest on a foundation of genuine accomplishment. His record as an efficient and capable administrator is undeniable. He appears to prefer power to money, which is a particularly appealing proposition for voters who regard most politicians as corrupt, ineffective and weak.

But, perhaps, they are the people who did Modi a great service by turning him into an exceptional man by the simple device of pouring exceptional venom against him. That no other leader has been subjected to so much calumny and scrutiny in India is perhaps the reason that no other leader has gained so much strength of character and personality. One can see the condition of Rahul to judge the verity of the contention by contrast. They have literally killed his personality. Fact is that so much indulgence and adulation and protection would have killed anyone. Or, for that matter, Nitish...After he had managed to mould his personality by long struggle and got successful in dislodging Lalu, they began the spoiling-job through a deluge of praise and encomiums for the initial good steps that any normal man would have felt obliged to undertake. Acting against daily kidnappings and the like, plank on which Nitish had won the electionwas there anything extraordinary about that? And he didn't go whole hog about that even...not only shielded criminals taking shelter under his party flag, but even promoted them, giving election tickets to them election after election. And except for road-building, which he found to be a good avenue to engage the mafia affiliated with his party, there has been no other great step or achievement whether on the front of corruption, industrialization, agriculture or power to write home about. But they feted him as if a savior had descended down from the heaven, not only for the state of Bihar but the whole of India. Direct consequence is that the growth of the man has not only stalled, but appears to have receded a notch or two. After the women chief ministers of India (who all seem to be suffering from some personality problem germane to female politicians of our country), no other chief minister seems to be as righteous, presumptuous and intolerant of criticism as Nitish.

So, perhaps (though it must be admitted that raw material must have already been there), these especially spiteful critics Ashis Nandy and Kingshuk Nag and Achuyt Vinayak and Rajiv Shah and Jose, and the like have made Modi what he has come to be. In fact, they must be thanked and cosseted by Modi as the particularly mordant well-wishers that the great poet Rahim had advised the people, desirous of improving upon their personality, to shelter in a hut put up at their own expense and in the very courtyard of their homes.

Be that as it may, the articles discussed above are the very acme of 'Hindu Hitler, Gujarati Goebbles' theme. Whether Modi is a particularly toxic brew of Hitler and Goebbles at their worst, as his detractors try to make out, or a potent mixture of Hercules and Gandhi, as the legions of his enthusiasts believe, is for the readers to determine for themselves. The author's take is that if indeed Modi is Hitler and Goebbles combined, it is all for the good. May the tribe of such Hitlers and Goebbles in India increase (as the popular saying goes), two-fold by the day and four-fold by the night, for, as Suhel Seth states in his article quoted in the next chapter: 'we may need many more like him'.

✳

5

WHY SHOULD EVERYONE WELCOME MODI

So, it is more than apparent that nobody is better poised (or poised at all) than Modi to rid the land of its ills, old and new, that continue to keep its overwhelming majority excluded, exploited, starved, diseased, ignorant and low, and have turned this ancient land of great civilizational past into an ethical, moral, cultural and intellectual wasteland. Choice before the majority Hindus is clear and easy. Letting alone growing into well-fed, healthy, well-educated, progressive, civilized and humane citizens of a post-modern world, if they want to survive even as a race of lowly nerds, just able to keep the vital insecurities of food, energy and defense from drowning them under, they would have to dispense with not only the present crop of leaders, but the entire weltanschauung spawned by the Congress and the Dynasty. It goes without saying that almost the entire BJP and the Left, not to say the likes of Mulayam, Mayawati, Mamta, Jaylalitha or Lalu are inalienable parts of that weltanschauung. However, not unlike Gandhi who, despite being an inalienable part of the Congress, was as different from the common run of Congressmen as chalk from cheese, Modi is not your run-of-the-mill BJP or RSS man. Even as a diamond stands out coruscating and distinct in a necklace of assorted stones, Modi, despite being a product and the part of the system, stands out among them all. No escaping the fact then that it's Modi only for the Hindus if they cared to care about their progress and survival.

Understandably, the choice before the Muslims of the land is not so unambiguous or apparent. Arraigned on the one side are leaders like...well, almost all of them, and manifold worse than those under whose guidance the nation has come to its present pass. And, thanks to their million acts of omission and commission, the nation continues to hurtle towards sure doom, major proportion of whose blame is, justifiably or not, bound to be credited to the account of the major minority community and (as usually is the case the world over) the major brunt of the fallouts too likely to be borne by them. Though the dire prospect is around two decades away, it is more than clear that up to that time too they are not going to have a great time, what with majority of them likely to keep leading a life which could only be termed as only a notch better than hellish; as full of (if not more) scarcities and anxieties as ever.

And on the other end is Modi, who, it would be dissembling to claim, that even a miniscule section of them has grown fond of by now, million paeans and positive evidences and reports notwithstanding. One can't however blame the Muslims for that. Gandhi too had come to be a bete noire to them after the Khilafat withdrawal (a conscious decision on the part of the consummate politician-Mahatma, as against a horrendous tragedy and the resulting beyond-control situation faced by the novice chief minister). However, they kept their opposition to him limited to keeping aloof from his political campaigns and never did actively oppose these. That was immensely wise and pragmatic of them. They knew that Gandhi was fighting for political liberty of the nation whose fruits, whether they came to have a separate nation or not, were bound to accrue to them too.

More positive fallouts came in the form of Gandhi wagering his life to stop their wholesale banishment from India. It was something even he can't be imagined to have done had they opposed his campaigns actively, entailing violent clashes at every stage. Muslim outrage at sudden and 'un-consulted' withdrawal of Khilafat by Gandhi was understandable. Opposing, decade after decade, him actively disrupting Congress meetings, beating the *satyagrahis* and enacting riots wherever the top Congress leaders went even in the project of universal benefit would have been uncalled for and positively harmful. However, had they come around to cooperating with him in his campaigns for freedom, their position and the status in the post-Independence India would have been elevated to an entirely different plane altogether.

Gandhi stood for political liberation of the land; Modi stands for its economic liberation. And even though the latter's positive fallouts can't bypass the Muslims, active cooperation would bring a sea change in their status within the country. In any case, opposing Modi vociferously can't be deemed to be a brilliant idea by any reckoning.

If they think that their interests inhere in the national interests, and their needs and aspirations stand in consonance with those of the non-Muslim majorities of the land (and not reflective of the faithful-kefir dichotomy and implacability that the ideologically hidebound among them like to believe in and preach), then Modi – and not those who seem to have nothing better to do than devise ways and means of looting the nation, and perpetuate their rule so as to indulge in yet more loot – is the man to make full use of.

To such Muslims I say: Your apprehensions concerning Modi-led BJP are entirely misplaced. Nobody would devour you, nobody can devour 20 crore people. Even in the age of considerable less political correctness, human rights concerns, international scrutiny and absence of mobile cameras and the citizen-journalism, they couldn't eat even 4000 Sikh souls without suffering serious attack of peptic ulcer which hasn't been cured fully even after three decades lapse. As for the Gujarat riots, they haven't been able to digest one-fourth that number even after a lapse of a decade and continue to pay through their noses as court verdicts begin to pour in.

Don't be misled by the thought that surge in Hindu support for Modi has anything to do with their love of Hindutva of the RSS-VHP variety – that is, even if Modi stood for the commonly understood strain of Hindutva, which he clearly doesn't. Yearning for good governance and economic progress, freedom from growing cancer of corruption, and mounting crimes, scarcities, squalor, societal breakdown and general sense of mayhem are the things leading them to Modi's arms. These are the aspirations and worries of the Muslims too concerning this life, and there is not a shadow of doubt that only a miniscule section of them harbors the view that this life counts nothing in comparison to the afterlife.

In many respect, Hindu is a very pragmatic race. Had it been really interested in Hindutva, it wouldn't have booted Atal government out and brought Sonia – a practicing Catholic, with Christian and Muslim inner-circle advisers – in when the Hindutva fad was still hot. Even the BJP coming to power...it was more than a decade-long outrages and crassness – first Rajiv's Bofors, then disgraceful VP Singh experiment, then the revolting Narsimha Rao regime, then the discreditable Janta Dal – that forced them to bring BJP, more specifically Atal, to power and that too seriously short of clear majority. Essential fact is that like every other person, with a family to take care and desirous of living with dignity, an average Hindu's growing support for Modi is no more than a cry for clean and effective governance, and for saving the country from falling into stasis and anarchy.

If one cared to go through the 'letters to editors' and comments and blogs upon the internet, he would have found out that, in addition to his record of governance, Modi's supporter root for him because they have lost all hope from the Congress. They never say that they want to bring Modi to the national scene because they want the Gujarat-2002 enacted everywhere. They defend their support to Modi on the alibi that he was not complicit in the post-Godhra riots…and not that he encouraged or organized these and was justified in doing so. Why, even the Gujaratis (though their support to Modi surged in the wake of the riots), hugely money-minded as they are (and I am not saying that in bad sense of the term), would have booted Modi out of power in the 2007 elections had his record and the conduct been anything less than extraordinary…something at par with the likes of Maya, Mulayam, Karunanidhi or Digvijay Singh.

I say for myself (and I believe that there would be only a few million Hindus who would refuse to endorse the opinion) that had a Muslim been there (belonging to whatever political outfit) exuding probity, selflessness, acumen, capacity for hard work, and good of the society and the nation at his heart, I would have unhesitatingly gone all out to support him for the premiership of the nation. The way the Hindus at large voted Sonia despite her being a staunch Catholic (and a foreigner with dubious nationalist credentials at that), I have little reservations about my aforesaid conviction. Their love of Abdul Kalam is instructive. Had Kalam been a political man carrying Modi's administrative capabilities, I have little doubt that they would have accepted him as their prime minister, without misgivings or hesitation whatsoever. To extend an example, had Antulay, a dynamic man who had become the chief minister of Maharashtra (birthplace of RSS) without any protest or heartburn whatsoever, shown the character of Modi and not turned out to be a petty crook, or had Salman Khurshid been even half of the Modi in the matter of positive attributes, Hindus would have gladly accepted as the prime minister of the nation.

Surging support for Modi among the Hindus across the country is not because he comes from a party of Hindutva, or because they expect him to establish a Hindu theocratic state in India. Rather the contrary. The way he has neutered the Hindutva bands of moronic thugs; kept his distance from assorted 'sants' and 'mahants' that begin crawling the corridors of power the moment BJP comes to power; and refused to fulfill the dream of many a RSS man to turn Gujarat into a 'laboratory of Hindutva' (combined, of course, with his exceptional character, and administrative and developmental record), is the thing that has endeared him to the average Hindu. They want a solver of the real-world problems – poverty, corruption, crime, environment and breakdown of services – at the helm of their affairs and not a reviver of brahminism or persecutor of minorities. And they have lost all hopes from Sonia or the Congress, either at the Centre or in the states.

So, I say to the Muslims, coming to think of it, not even one of your real world problems is different from those of the overwhelming majority of the Hindus (and vice versa). Poverty, ill-nutrition, venality of government machinery, crowded cities, squalor, crimes, accidents, breakdown of services, falling standards everywhere, inflation: how is anything different for the Hindus as contrasted with the Muslims? They rise and sink together. If anyone thinks that one can ultimately triumph over the other, or that any other nation might be of some help to them if the crunch came, he is living in a fool's paradise. And the path to that paradise is crisscrossed with mighty rivers of blood, designed to drown anyone trying to wade across to reach his imagined bliss.

And as you must have judged from the record of either the Congress and the Communists, or the assorted regional politicians in the mould of Mulayam, Maya or Mamta, Modi is the best item available in the political bazaar of India. It's nobody's contention that he is perfect or ideal; far from it. And, ultimately, he too may fail to deliver what is really required to save this unfortunate nation from the impending catastrophe, yet he is head and shoulders above the available lot. There is not even a second or third best.

Of course, all of the above the Muslims know too well. Yet no sane person can say that the Muslims, despite not denying that Modi's administrative record has been excellent and that he is the best person to deliver what is really required by the nation, are being unduly unreasonable or intractable in continuing to be hostile to the idea of Modi landing anywhere but in jail, and not the '7, Race Course Road'. Moreover, in face of the fact that even Gandhi failed to win back, despite a quarter century of groveling, the Muslim confidence after he had lost it in the wake of Khilafat, asking them to come around to accepting, let alone supporting, Modi could only be termed the height of naiveté.

Yet they could be asked to learn from the caste-Hindus, especially the Brahmins. No one could have imagined, particularly in the wake of BSP slogan, 'Tilak, taraju aur Talwar; Inko maro jutey chaar' (give good shoe-beating to Brahmins, Rajputs and the

Banias), that the upper castes of UP would come around so soon to supporting Mayawati, abandoning even the arch-brahminical Congress and the Savarna-darling BJP. Brahmins and the Rajputs had supported wholeheartedly many a Congress Muslim leaders throughout, but to think that they would 'stoop down' to support the abusively anti-savarna party of Mayawati was unthinkable. But such was the call of self-interest and the wonder of democratic-politics that they voted the BSP to power with a near-clear majority, coining wonderfully clever slogan (of course with the consent of the BSP supremo), *'Pathar rakh lo chaati par, muhar laga do haathi par'* (vote elephant, the BSP symbol, even if it meant having to put up with severe mental agony). They deserted it (though not completely) in the subsequent election only in the wake of belief-beggaring corruption indulged in by Mayawati.

Were they (that is, the supremely selfish Brahmins and the other upper castes) idiots in placing a big – really big – stone upon their conceited chests and extending support to their bete noire, Mayawati? Hardly!

The nation stands at such a juncture of history that self-interest of just about everyone cries for bringing in Modi. Till the time he had proven his credentials as the prime minister, they (the Muslims) may continue to regard him warily, even inimically, but comparing him with the second obvious (and imminent) choice, they must not forget the adage that an intelligent enemy is always preferable to a half-wit friend.

Do what Deng asked his fellow Chinese to do and the rewards, as the Chinese experience shows, would be immense. Antipathy of the Communists, particularly the Maoist-Chinese variety, towards the capitalist system was not any less than what the Muslims nurse towards the BJP, in general, and Modi, in particular. Yet Deng asked his compatriots to disregard the color of the cat till it kept catching the mice. And the rest is history unfolding before our very eyes.

I therefore say to the Muslims: Use Modi, take advantage of his skills and the drive to better your lot. If you could use the man to improve your lot significantly (even as the situation of Gujarati Muslims has improved even better than the Hindus), that would be your best revenge and reparation. A peasant doesn't discard one of his bullocks on the ground that he doesn't like its color or the look on its face, or because it had once shown symptoms of belligerence. He sets out to put it to yet more rigorous work. Keeping your distance from Modi and betting your future upon the likes of Rahul and Mulayam won't be in anyone's interest, Hindu or Muslim.

To them I say, even as the mind-numbing corruption, incompetence and chicanery indulged in by the likes of Sonia, Pawar, Mulayam or Mayawati harms you in the same way (perhaps more) as it does the nation as a whole, the crumbs thrown by them your way as emollients and bribes do not benefit you any more than the poverty-alleviation programs like Garibi-hatao and 20-Point Programme launched four decades ago did for the land's toiling millions. Likewise, Modi's integrity, vision, dedication and acumen can't but benefit you, as it would benefit the nation. It can't be held to be a wise or foresighted policy if you kept clinging to the hands offering crumbs even as the very ground beneath continued to slip away. If (as your author suspects it to be) the country is not already past the stage of being saved, only those caring and determined and capable, and not those not only incompetent, powerless or disinterested, but pushing it ceaselessly down the precipice by their deliberate acts, can save it. And if the nation is saved, you are saved. If the nation goes down under, taking one billion Hindus with it, no power on earth can save more than two hundred million who turned their back upon the possibility when it had still been there.

It's not counsel or warning, but a plea. In democracy, one can only plead and not warn; days of issuing warnings are long over. Even if you continue to oppose Modi tooth and nail, it's your choice which no one in the world can take exception to. Many Hindus – rather a majority of them – won't ultimately support or vote Modi; would that be held against them? Every one is free to choose (or not choose) a leader and government of his/her choice and savour the outcome. One can only put his viewpoint across and that too very discreetly. That everyone is intelligent enough to know what actually his self-interest is and where does it lie, is the assumption on which the concept of democracy and adult franchise stand. And that is non-negotiable.

To those infuriated with the suggestion I have this to say: Be true to yourself, step in Modi's shoes, cross your heart and swear that you wouldn't have conducted yourself in a far worse manner than what you allege him to have done – that is, had you been in a position of authority in a Muslim country like Pakistan, Iran or Bangladesh. That, let alone asking your police to fire on the tremendously outraged mobs comprising of your natural constituency across towns (as Modi indeed did), you wouldn't have ordered them to kill the beleaguered Hindus, Christians or the Ahmedis. To these Muslims I say: 'Separate a novice and badly cornered chief minister from a man who has proved himself to be above all attachments and corruptions, in addition to being a development man par excellence. Now there is a never-before-never-after chance to tread a true secular path to move lock-in-step with your Hindu counterparts to realize your material destiny. Forsake cheap gratification of being courted by thoroughly self-serving Mulayams, Lalus, Digvijay Singhs and the like who can do no real short or long-term good to anyone. Don't go with politicians and rent-a-cause windbags masquerading as secularist do-gooders.'

Many of the Muslims voted Atal, despite the fact that assorted Hindutva thugs had continued to receive his indulgence. Contrastingly, Modi has only contempt for these elements and has worked assiduously to neuter them. Even if they (the Muslims) choose not to give up their reservations about Modi, it would be a piece of good policy to hedge their bets concerning the ascendant star, instead of opposing him tooth and nail. Once even a tiny part of them begins to place its trust in him and vote for him, they have him bound, leg and foot, under the power of their trust and expectations.

To those unconvinced still I say: Complicity or otherwise of Modi in the post-Godhra riots has been dealt with. If you are not convinced by the available evidence (in case of Godhra carnage) and compulsions and constraints of a political leader (in case of post-Godhra riots), then go by what the highest court of the land decides. As things stand, the Special Investigating Team (SIT) appointed by the Supreme Court to investigate Modi's alleged role in the Gulbarga Society massacre has all but exonerated him, holding that there was *'no prosecutable evidence'* to proceed against him. However, Modi's intrepid detractors have not taken its findings in stride, imputing motives against it and, by implication, the highest court of the land. Now, using the judiciary to keep Modi unhinged and roiled, and then trashing it because the verdict didn't meet your political ends is just not on. Here is Rohit Pradhan (a bitter critic of Modi) in the *Outlook*:

> However, instead of accepting the findings of a duly constituted investigative body, many have attempted to put the SIT itself on trial. It appears that their faith in the legal process may not be as unshakable as they have repeatedly claimed especially if it yields results that they find unpalatable. In fact, lambasting the legal system in India and labeling it fundamentally unfair to the poor and the marginalized seems to have become an element of faith among the Left-liberal section of the Indian polity and civil society. Even the argument that SIT has `ignored` important testimonies is fallacious. Any investigative and judicial process rests on weighing competing narratives and evidences; mala fide

intent is not proven merely because the ultimate verdict favors one particular narrative over the other.

Finally, the legal options for Modi's critics have hardly closed. They can certainly contest the SIT's findings in a judicial forum, but casting aspersions on an investigative body constituted and monitored directly by the Supreme Court is hardly appropriate.

Naturally, Modi can and should be confronted politically. It can reasonably argued that Modi's administrative and moral failure in 2002 make him an unsuitable candidate for the highest office in the land.

Instead of launching a calumnious campaign against SIT chief R.K.Raghvan, Modi's opponents should let the judiciary adjudicate on the SIT report. If the SIT has indeed ignored important evidenceas critics like Teesta Setalvad allegethen surely the Supreme Court can be trusted to take the SIT to task and order a fresh investigation. Retaining faith in India's institutions is of paramount importance and is a concern Modi's opponents would ignore at their own peril. After all, it is the same SIT which recently secured the conviction of 23 accused in the Ode massacre case.

Now, if you are still not convinced or remain undecided, then ask the Gujarati Muslims if they face any manner of discrimination at the hands of the government and haven't they made substantial progress in every walk of life during the unprecedented peaceful decade. Would they prefer rollercoaster decades of interminable riots and stress to what they have seen in the last decade? Would they like to go back to the pre-Godhra Ahmedabad and Surat of perennial riots, tensions and turmoil, and the hostilities and discriminations that came in their wake?

And not to make light of the killings, see what the post-Godhra riots have done. Despite grave provocations purpose-made to plunge India into pogroms against the Muslims, and million other minor incidences of whom there is no dearth on any day in this land and which have potential to blow into full scale Bhiwandi and Maliyana, India has kept its peace. Whether it was because the constitutionally belligerent section among the Muslims has become enlightened about the futility of wearing its bellicosity on its sleeves, or the gratuitously provocative segment among the Hindus has worked itself to exhaustion is irrelevant to our discussion. And remember, unlike the peace of graveyard that is the lot of Hindus in Pakistan and Bangladesh, it is a peace that has brought equal (if not disproportionate) gains to the Muslims.

And now for some testimonials from eminent Muslims…

Here is an article by Suhel Seth published in *'The Financial Express'* of Oct 19, 2008. As patriotic an Indian as any out there, with not a single communal bone in his Muslim frame, no one can accuse Suhel Seth of being a Modi fan or one who has 'eaten' his *'namak'* (salt):

'Why India Needs Narendra Modi?': Suhel Seth

Let me begin with a set of disclosures: I have perhaps written more articles against Modi and his handling of the post-Godhra scenario than most people have; I have called him a modern-day Hitler and have always said that Godhra shall remain an enduring blemish not just on him but on India's political class. I still believe that what happened in Gujarat during the Godhra riots is something we as a nation will pay a heavy price for. But the fact is that time has moved on. As has Narendra Modi. He is not the only politician in India who has been accused of communalism. It is strange that the whole country venerates the Congress Party as the secular messiah but it was that party that presided over the riots in 1984 in which over 3,500 Sikhs died; thrice the number killed in Gujarat.

The fact of the matter is that there is no better performer than Narendra Modi in India's political structure. Three weeks ago, I had gone to Ahmedabad to address the YPO and I thought it would be a good opportunity to catch up with Modi. I called him the evening before and I was given an appointment for the very day I was getting into Ahmedabad. And it was not some official meeting but instead one at his house. As frugal as the man Modi is.

And this is something that the Gandhis and Mayawatis need to learn from Modi. There were no fawning staff members; no secretaries running around; no hangers on…just the two of us with one servant who was there serving tea. And what was most impressive was the passion which Modi exuded. The passion for development; the passion for an invigorated Gujarat; the passion for the uplifting the living standards of the people of the state and the joy with which he recounted simple yet memorable data-points. For instance, almost all of the milk consumed in Singapore is supplied by Gujarat; or for that matter all the tomatoes that are eaten in Afghanistan are produced in Gujarat or the potatoes that Canadians gorge on are all farmed in Gujarat. But it was industry that was equally close to his heart.

…. There is a clear intolerance of terrorism and terrorists which is evident in the way the man functions; now there are many cynics who call it minority-bashing but the truth of the matter is that

Modi genuinely means business as far as law and order is concerned.

I left Modi's house deeply impressed with the man as Chief Minister: he was clearly passionate and what's more deeply committed.... After I finished talking to the YPO (Young President's Organizations) members, I asked some of them very casually, what they thought of Modi. Strangely, this was one area there was no class differential on. They too said he was God.

But what they also added very quickly was if India has just Narendra Modis, we would be a great country. I don't know if this was typical exaggeration or a reflection of the kind of leadership India now needs! There is however, no question in my mind, that his flaws apart, Narendra Modi today, is truly a transformational leader! And we need many more like him!

(And does it need saying that the nation too needs millions of Suhel Seths.)

Full four years have passed since the appearance of the article. If anything, Modi's record has gone only better since. And in utter contrast to the Congress record since, and in spite of zillion attempts of terrified enemies of Modi to dig up something sordid and sticky, absolutely nothing has come up to take away even a word of what Suhel Seth wrote about him.

Very name BJP is anathema to the Communists of India, and they would have remained bitterest enemy of Modi even if he had got ten thousand Hindus killed to save one Muslim life in the aftermath of Godhra. And a Muslim Communist from Kerala! Things can't go more hopeless for Modi. An idolater and polytheist could perhaps hope to gain entry to the Muslim paradise somehow, but Modi receiving a word of appreciation from a Muslim Communist...God forbid!

AP Abdullakutty is a two term CPI (M) MP from Kerala. We have this report from him from *IBN Live* of Jan 17, 2009:

CPM MP defends Modi's development model

Risking disciplinary action from his party, two-term CPI (M) MP AP Abdullakutty on Saturday stuck to his stand that the development model being pursued by Gujarat Chief Minister Narendra Modi was worthy of emulation while outrightly rejecting the 'communal agenda' of the saffronite leader...

"I will not pardon Modi for his communal agenda. But I will give full marks to his efforts for development. I don't think there is anything wrong in that," Abdullakutty said.

"Some people say that Muslims in Kerala would react adversely against what I had said. But they were not aware of the changes that have taken place in my community. It is Muslims who wish for an investor-friendly climate in the state," he said.

He said, many of the Muslim friends had patted him for speaking about the developments in Gujarat while on a visit to an Islamic country.

On the reported comment by a CPI(M) leader that only `a mad man can heap praises on Modi even on development', Abdullakutty said his reaction to it was "God will not pardon you".

Curry King Sir Gulam Noon is a well known and respected figure among the Muslims (and Hindus) of India and England. Despite being a non-political person, he is no simpleton or gushing fool. During a business trip to Gujarat recently he met Modi briefly on the latter's initiative. Later he answered some questions regarding the meeting.

To a question, 'You met Chief Minister Narendra Modi at his residence. What discussion did you have with him', he had this to say:

"I actually responded to an invitation that he had given when he was visiting London. I met him at his residence in Gandhinagar; the conversation was short, but fruitful. He is a very friendly and courteous person... I am not a politician. But the image that I will carry about the state is that it has very good infrastructure and it is an extremely well-run state."

To the question, 'Is it at variance with the impression you carried about Chief Minister Narendra Modi in the past?', he answered:

"The past is forgotten. I have met him and believe that he is a very good administrator and an extremely good person."

Ghulam Ahmed Vastanvi from Vastan in Southern Gujarat should need no introduction. He was asked to head the premier Sunni Muslim seminary of Deoband, carrying unmatched influence not only among the Muslims of India but the entire Muslim world. It was no mean achievement for a Gujarati Muslim to be invited to head an institution dominated by people from Utter Pradesh. It came on the back of solid pioneering educational model that he had developed to modernize madarassa education.

So, the man was no bumbling babe and knew his apples from oranges better than any. What are his take and the message concerning Modi and the development story of Gujarat? Of course, no sensible Indian (not to talk of a Muslim) can condone the Gujarat carnage or fail to underscore the absolute essentiality of punishing the guilty; Vastanvi doesn't. But he refuses to fall into the trap of self-pity that the assorted do-gooders and the Congress have created for the Muslims to keep languishing and lamenting in. According to Vastanvi, it was time for the Muslims to emerge out of the past and move on. They must educate their children so that they do not take to crime or religious extremism and strive to flow within the national mainstream.

And the man, who, working in madarassa-education domain (and hence in constant touch with the most 'rooted' sections among the Muslims) knows the situation and the thinking of the Muslims of Gujarat better than any, gathered courage to utter the ultimate (but true) blasphemy:

> The relief work has been carried out very well by the government and the people... All communities are prospering in Chief Minister Narendra Modi's Gujarat and there is no discrimination against the minorities as far as development work is concerned.

Understandably, the Muslims of all hues were up in arms against him, though he was not completely lacking in support. He had to resign soon from the post – not because he had lied, or anybody found any ground to allege that he was on the payroll of Modi or carried some hidden agenda, but because the statement was so politically inconvenient for the people sitting away from Gujarat and wanting to keep up the canard that the Muslims of Gujarat continued to be a persecuted and discriminated-against lot.

Though unnerved initially, Vastanavi however refused to retract his statement and went out to aver:

> Development has undoubtedly taken place in Gujarat and we hope it will continue. I ask Muslims to study well. The government is ready to offer jobs but for that they need good education.

In Annexure at the end of the book is given the English translation of the recent interview of Modi given to Shahid Siddiqui of Nai Dunia. Such among them who have not read it in full may, if they so wish, go through it to judge things further for themselves – that is, if they don't hold the view that reading anything about Modi could cause grave damage to their spiritual and psychological health.

So, what is the final uptake for the Muslims? Firstly, that,

Gujarat riots were direct fallout of Godhra and couldn't have been avoided altogether. May be their scale could have been reduced with more prompt and tough action, but to say or hope that any Congress chief minister would have done that is to disregard the entire post-Independence history of communal riots in India.

Secondly, that even as the culprits of anti-Sikh pogrom are roaming scot-free even after twenty eight years lapse, verdicts are pouring in for the Gujarat riots and culprits are landing in jail. Supreme Court is relentless in its pursuance and if Modi is indeed complicit, he too can't escape his just comeuppance. But, then, keeping it both ways – trusting the verdicts of the courts fair in innumerable cases and unfair in case Modi was declared to be not complicit – won't be fair.

Thirdly, that, absent Modi and the things would be back to square one in Gujarat within a couple of years. As for the Muslims, with their energy dissipated in communal kerfuffle, discrimination against them resuscitated, and their youth mired once again in criminal-mafia activities, magnificent progress they have posted lately on every front would begin slipping back to the 90s era. And the effect of Modi's absence would be felt all over the country, and not just in Gujarat.

Fourthly, if overcoming their suspicions and the antipathy they came forward to support Modi, that won't just be the biggest antidote to his (alleged or imagined) mischief-making prowess, but would start a novel chapter in the annals of Hindu-Muslim relations and help lay a solid foundation to create an immeasurably prosperous and strong India.

At another level, it must be understood by the Muslims that despite making apparent progress, India is poised on an interminable decline, what with food, energy and water scarcities set to strike it with full force in another decade or two. Then there are Pakistan and China, ready to upset its peace and progress applecart and plunge it into deep internal turmoil. By all accounts, depending upon the quality of leadership it happens to be administered under, the coming decade is going to be a make or break decade for India. It could either break out of its historical weaknesses and deficiencies to enter a virtuous cycle of population-control, plenty, prosperity and peace for its people, reaching a position whereof it gets fortified against mundane worries of food, water and energy, as also the attempts upon internal destabilizing, or it could go down under, taking everybody down with it, but the Muslims more thoroughly and cripplingly than the others.

As they can very well see, though appearing benign and preferable to them, the present set of rulers offer no hope; are in fact tailor-made to push India deeper into the vicious cycle of corruption, over-population, starvation, intellectual and moral stasis, all round decline and apocalypse. Modi may not be perfect (and here we are not talking of the communal issue), but he is our best bet, eons ahead of the current run of politicians.

Only hypothetical fears based upon imagined scenarios lay behind the Partition. Yet more than a million died and many times that number got maimed, raped and displaced. There had been available a Gandhi then, who, almost single handedly, managed to douse the fires of hatred and violence incinerating the border areas, thereby stopping its extension to thousands of towns and hundreds of thousands of villages sprawled across the length and breadth of India. Fortuitously, no outside power was involved in the carnage or had any intention of baking its bread, as the saying goes, in the raging fire.

How the present situation compares with the foregoing? An average Hindu is certainly not the Hindu of the thirties and forties...swaddled in Gandhian inanities or Nehruvian nonsense and ignorant of the mortal danger that the Jihadi-Salafist strain of Islam holds for all the non-believers (as also for the majority of the believers). As things stood then, all the hostility and hatred of the Hindus was directed either against the British or their own coreligionists (i.e., all the castes above and lower then oneself in the caste-hierarchy). Muslims stood a clear third in the demonology, and here too, the hostility towards them was entirely reactionary in nature (natural response to what they were subjected to at their hands from time to time and not due to long-term existential fears). That was the reasons as to why despite gravest kind of historical atrocities and ongoing provocations, they refrained from going whole hog with the ethnic-cleansing thing in the manner the Muslims of Pakistan went about doing with the Sikhs and the Hindus.

The situation however is vastly altered now. Many a Hindu is convinced of Muslims planning a second Pakistan through proliferation route. And as the declaredly purposeful and deliberately brazen Islamism marches relentlessly on – beards, *burqas* and outlandish attires and caps of Arabic and Turkish variety proliferate; complaints, demands and peeve and hurt, real or imagined, are built into a crescendo so as to shame, blackmail and cow-down the state and the Hindus to do their bidding; proselytizing and conversion activities get ever more blatant; Muslims detach themselves more and more from their compatriot Hindus and align openly with the world-Ummah; and, finally, demand for a second Partition or open declaration of resolve to takeover India itself gets articulated by some millenarian demagogue – the ignorant or the skeptical among the Hindus too shall come around.

And that would be the beginning of the end. Muslims have to decide. Do they want to stick with their Sonias and Digvijays and Mayawatis and Mulayams and Lalus and the Nitishes whose policies and the actions are (designedly or inadvertently) tailor-made to make the situation hurtle towards the end outlined above, or will take their leave from them to join the truly secular and progressive leadership of Modi? Even as he has profited the Gujarati Hindus and Muslims alike, setting them firmly on to a path of true progress and enlightenment by neutering and banishing the fractious and antediluvian mindsets that had been warping their good sense and stalling the progress, there is not a shadow of doubt that he, if they but came forward to place their unstinted trust and support in his leadership, would be able to do that for India as a whole too.

Reverting to the Hindus, they have but little choice, as the alternatives available are either insipid, inspiring but little confidence or hope, or are positively deleterious. India is their only country and Modi the only man with appropriate credentials to save it from being destroyed by corruption and stasis in a Darwinian free-for-all which is sure to strike (at least this part of) the world within a couple of decades. Essential fact is that the Muslims may have reasons, however genuine or misconceived, to continue with their reservations about Modi, and many of the genuine, simple and patriotic Hindus might have had these in the initial years of his regime when the real worth of the man was still to unfold, but exceptions exist and miracles do happen. Modi came as a true revelation. Whether it was his innate genius, or the extremely difficult post-riot years forced him to grow into a genius through constant introspection and practice, should hardly concern us. The man stands before us gleaming as only a perfectly cut diamond does. Much like Deng, his genius took time to come to the fore but came it did dazzling and surefooted. Yet more creditworthy is the fact that man has been able to do things without the advantage of authoritarian set up Deng had enjoyed, besides suffering such all round and sustained attacks and calumnies in his own land that no democratic ruler has ever been subjected to in the human history. Yet, he never turned bitter or acrimonious; did instead get progressively more open-minded, liberal and...sweet. And here lies the true greatness of the man.

Be that as it may, the Hindus of whatever caste (it is the only distinction they suffer from and acknowledge) have no reason not to repose their full faith in and get united behind a man who labeling with a caste sticker would be as pointless as labeling Marx with the racial. Indeed, he could (like Marx did to many a nations regarding religion) be depended upon to completely de-legitimize caste among the Hindus. And he is as secular in his actions as one could ever get. Of course, he is not built in the mould of your traditional secularists whose secularism lies in the stand: 'I won't demolish one *mazaar* or (for that reason) an apology of a temple even if it encroached upon public land and hindered construction of a highway.' Modi's secularism lies in making absolutely no distinction, and giving no quarters to sundry temples or mosques encroaching upon public land or hindering development of a project. 'Developmental Nationalism' could be termed the only religion he seems to be subscribing and caring for.

And that is what should matter, and not whether he rejected a skullcap offered by a silver-bullet Maulana. If however they think that true measure of secularism lies in genuflecting before Ajmal Kasab or not hanging Afzal Guru, they can keep sticking with their Sonia, Rahul, Manmohan, Mulayam, Mamta, Lalu, or Nitish...

If they think that vastly inferior versions of Nehru (Manmohan), Indira (Sonia), Rajiv (Rahul) and Atal (sundry BJP leaders), or slightly superior versions of Digvijay Singh (Nitish), Mulayam (Akhilesh) and Mayawati (Jaylalitha) are enough to pull this country of 1200 million (and exploding all the time) starved, ignorant and diseased out of the mire of corruption, crime, sloth and moral and intellectual cesspool, as also to face the relentlessly advancing suprematism of China and Islam, and the dog-eat-dog competition created by the global capitalism and technological rat race, then god bless their blissfully ignorant Hindu souls.

Leave alone those fantastic figures of 10 % agricultural or industrial growth, or matching China chip for chip and bullet-train for bullet-train, if the man (Modi) manages to remain the way he is – splendidly incorruptible and focused only on improving the lives of his countrymen without a hint of prejudice or favor – that would be vast improvement upon anything Indians have seen in their lives and enough to let the country move lock-in-step with the galloping world.

I say to the Hindus, that having only one country, you have no two choices: Either pull your country up and fast too, or go down under...be written off the pages of history like so many dodos and dinosaurs. And as for pulling your country up (and fast) was concerned, again you have got no two choices: it is either Modi, or a bunch of carpetbaggers and morons at best, and confirmed rascals and anti-nationals, generally.

In any case, should India's development and future be held hostage to the memory of a single outrage (in a country that has suffered hundreds), or the ululations of self-appointed solicitors of Muslim interests who even the Muslims won't place their trust and affections in, if the push really came to shove?

Can a Hindu give me a single reason not to support Modi? Of course, they might have genuine reasons for not being terribly in love with the BJP or the RSS, but, it could safely be averred, that much more than his party or its ideology, Modi as a man belongs to none but his country and the countrymen...

As for the Congressmen, they could be put under three categories: People leading and running the party, those in the habit of voting it, and the ones intending to vote for it (particularly against the Modi-led BJP).

First set is the legion of Congress leaders, party functionaries and ordinary workers with their hand in the till, as per their respective heft and the capability.

Under the second category come 'khandani' (traditional) Congress supporters: those who continue to nurse pathetic attachment either to the Dynasty, or to the imbecile belief that only the Congress Party can run the affairs of the land in an efficient or passable manner; that without the guiding hand of the Congress, run under the tutelage of the Dynasty, this country would go to the dogs.

The last set is not really *khandani* Congressmen, but the people who harbor antipathy to the obscurantism of the BJP and the righteous, chauvinistic, meddlesome and extremely self-serving mindsets and the conduct of its leaders and the functionaries, particularly those coming from the RSS background. Further put off by its show of crass brahminism in the garb of Hindu religion and 'Indian culture' ('*surya-namaskar*' and '*kalash-yatras*' variety, which majority of even the upper caste Hindus have neither heard of nor practiced), and revolted by assorted '*sants*' and '*mahants*' doing round of the corridors of power and hogging limelight wherever it happens to come to power, they either refuse to come out to vote, or turn to the Congress or the casteist-regional parties to defeat the thuggish syndicate.

I have nothing to say to the first set. Like the greedy monkey that won't give up the pie so as to pull its fist out of the hole, they won't leave the Congress or the Dynasty, even if the very nemesis hovered right over their head. One can only bid good luck to them. It would rather be in the interest of the (Modi-led) BJP that they didn't cross over to it, for it may be possible for a leopard to shed its spots than for a hardcore Congressman to alter its crooked and anti-national ways.

As for the second set, it is a safe bet to assume that now that the UPA II under Sonia-Rahul tutelage is in its last leg, having squandered a great opportunity presented to it by the Indian electorate in 2004 and again in 2009, many of its pet beliefs and superstitions must have got nearly cured. I say to this set that whatever little probity, maturity and wisdom was with the Congress has either left it already (Pranab), or is in the process of leaving it (Man Mohan). It's only Sibbals, Digvijays, Kamalnaths, Manish Tiwaris and Narayansamis now on. And your Godmother is interested only in one thing: ensuring *rajgaddi* for your baby-god, even though he has all but failed himself even, not to talk of the party or the nation at large. Sticking to the Congress, you can have only a manifold worse UPA coalition than you had just a taste of.

To the third set I say: Does one need to say anything more than what has been explained throughout the book? Forget the BJP, along with its *sants* and *mahants* and *surya namaskars* and Ram Sene and Bajrang Dal, and the like. Modi is the man for you... as secular, liberal and modernist in his outlook and conduct as one could be. If some of you haven't already made up your mind, do it now. You can't afford to be in two minds as there are no two choices.

To the votaries of the regional parties I say: Keep supporting, for whatever reasons, regional parties of your choice at the state level. I hold no brief for the state-level BJP leaders (or for the other national parties, as far as the state-level politics was concerned) and ask you to switch to the BJP only if Modi had been able to develop his state-level clones in the matter of incorruptibility, dynamism, vision and the sense of mission. But I ask you to support only the national parties be that BJP, Congress or the Communists at the Centre. That is because the regional parties, as they have proved time and again, can do littler better than to muddy the waters there further, interested as they are only in extracting as large a pound of flesh as possible, whatever the implications for the nation and the society at large. I plead them to leave the job of running national political affairs to the national parties only.

As for the BJP-wallahs...traditional BJP supporters and the workers are already for Modi. Plea is to the BJP leadership...at the Centre and in the states. To them I say, the next election (or the one after that, if the widely assumed scenario of mid-term polls came to hold true) may be your last shot at coming to power. You enjoyed your only full-term at the beginning of the century and gave it the best you could muster. But even the best array of leadership you ever had running the affairs of the government, combined with the fact that the main opposition party, the Congress, had been in tatters at that time, couldn't save you from being booted out. That was because the public felt thoroughly cheated and disgusted by your chicanery, cowardice, hubris, and the evident contempt for people's intelligence and the aspirations. Further, one additional saving grace (besides having best leadership cabal) you had then was that you had been united behind Atal and the second rung leadership was quite young (by Indian political standards) and relatively uncompromised. Now you don't have second rung leadership of any capability or credibility (all have become first rung!).

So, the things for you (without Modi as your candidate for the PM-ship) pan out somewhat like this:

You go to the elections without your supporters or the grass-root workers feeling any enthusiasm in their veins, for even after enjoying long political careers, your extant top leadership hasn't given anything remarkable in the matter of ideas or vision for the 1200 million of the land to peg their hopes on to or alleviate their fears concerning their future. That the Congress leadership too has failed on that account may be a good argument, but hardly a tonic to rev up your extant workers or the potential supporters. You may have been filled with 'passionate energy' at the prospect of capturing power, and the coteries around you at the possibility to indulge in some scandals of their own, but except for his disgust with the Congress ways and the Dynasty's diabolicalness, an average worker or the existing or potential supporter sees no reason to feel enthused about the prospect. That may yet suffice to bring you to power somehow, but that is when your troubles – as against the merry games of parliamentary filibuster you had been content playing during the past decade – would have begun in the right earnest.

Even if you happened to form government at the Centre by going in for million compromises to secure power and to save and run your government (much like you did in Karnataka and Jharkhand), pray, what would you be able to do or achieve for the people and the nation that you hadn't been able to during the Atal government, which, as it turned out, was not enough to satisfy even the uniquely undemanding public of India? One could bet his last shirt that even if the so-called honeymoon wasn't over even before it got going (like the three Janta experiments, of which you were a part) because of your fractiousness, it shall be over within six months due to your incompetence.

The Atal government managed to bide its time and passed out somewhat honorably, but you managed to earn so much apathy (and considerable antipathy) in the period, and have failed so miserably since in redeeming your image, that you seem nowhere near making a comeback on your own even after a decade. Why, even now, after the UPA has managed to hurt itself almost fatally, you don't look capable of gaining worthwhile numbers to cobble up a stable coalition. Failing this time, or collapsing due to dissensions or disastrous performance in case you managed to raise a governing coalition...and your fate (in fact the fate of your entire party) is sealed for ever...the way it had for the likes of VP Singh, Chandra Shekhar and Dev Gowda, who no one ever again felt like talking of even.

And even if you managed to complete your term; what of that? What would that avail the people or the nation? Would that bring them any closer to being saved? Ideas, vision, character, competence, grit or the pluck: Has anyone of you got even one of these attribute (even as all of these were required and in extraordinary amounts) necessary to secure them something of lasting worth? Even Zardari is close to completing his term; has that availed anything for Pakistan except taking it closer to its own brand of comeuppance? And, mind you, Zardari is manifold intelligent than any of you, and even though his past has been despicable, sitting at the center of relentlessly prying eyes, he didn't have many opportunities to indulge in his favorite game of percentage this time around. That being the case, his stupendous acuity was free to run Pakistan better and save it from the doom it continues to hurtle towards. But he couldn't. He couldn't because neither did he have a sense of history, nor that level of detachment from power and the pelf which is essential to see things and trends in their true perspective and draw appropriate conclusions; thing from which flows everything else—ideas, vision and the courage of conviction necessary to guide the affairs of a people in a statesmanlike manner. Do some introspection and try to find parallels.

Or take our very own Sonia. Even if she came to nurse, by and by, genuine affinity and empathy for the people of India, she didn't patently have any visions or plans for them. How could she. Does she have any sense of Indian history? Even if she desired to have, is she intellectually equipped for that? And as for the detachment thing; even if one chose to forget Bofors or Quattrochi as aberrations, one overweening desire and obsession with her has been to keep the fire in the hearth burning somehow till her eternally adolescent son came of age to be able to preside over the dinner table. What has that availed the people or the nation?

Coming down to the brass-tacks, essential truth is that you are neither Nehru, Shastri or Indira, nor Rajiv, Rao, Atal or Manmohan even...that is, leaders under whose stewardship the things have come to the pass which by no reckoning can be termed as eductive of satisfaction with the present or confidence in the future. With much dismay and regret one is led to say that there is no report of anyone seeing in you that spark which could give even a sliver of confidence that you can even match one of these past premiers, letting alone better them.

But, perhaps, it is futile to make appeals to you. For, if indeed you had been capable of comprehending or open to advice, you wouldn't have insulted the countless millions of the land by throwing the slogan of *'India Shining'* in their wan and tortured faces. Your conduct past ten years has nothing to show that you have learnt anything since. And that is why you look even more clueless, cantankerous and pathetic than you had been a decade ago in the wake of losing power.

One may well ask: What Modi at the helm would avail the BJP except scaring away its allies (that is, if dissensions within the party had been settled amicably)? That may be so. But, does an organization live by and for its own workers and supporters, or those of its purported allies? Should BJP be concerned more that its workers and supporters remained energized and full of hope, or care for the interests of the leaders of its allies? Can a party survive long if it kept caring for its allies even at the cost of heartfelt aspirations of its workers and supporters, even though the prime requirement of its long-term growth and fulfillment of its (purported) mission was complete decimation of those very allies?

Modi may indeed scare away many people and parties, besides creating short-term mayhem within his own party, but how does that matter? A person striving to please everyone ends up pleasing none and can secure no real good. Modi may ultimately come to power or may not; that hardly matters. Modi as principal – and principled –

opposition would be nearly as good for the nation as Modi in power. As leader of opposition, with a solid record of character and governance behind him, and waiting in wings to seize power should the ruling party falter, he would be enough to scare the daylights out of the ruling dispensation and keep it on the straight and narrow path of probity and good governance. And the option and the hope, that there is a person out there capable of saving the nation if the crunch really came, would be a thing of priceless value for our democracy. In fact, without Modi as hope, Indian political scene would already have become too desolate and scary by now: Congress would have got yet more corrupt and insensitive, and people would have been looking for some drastic alternative.

Otherwise, Congress or the BJP-sans-Modi: what is the difference and who cares? See your own respective records as the Leader of Opposition, or patriarch and the president of the party? Why was the Congress not deterred from looting the country in a manner no party has ever done in a democratic dispensation anywhere in the world? Why was it so confident or unafraid? Why indeed? If the ruling party feels entirely dauntless about indulging in anti-people and anti-national acts, that can mean only one of the (or combination of) three things: The opposition is sleeping on its job; is either in cahoots with ruling party, doing similar things wherever it gets its opportunity, or intends to indulge in similar acts upon coming to; or the ruling party thinks of it, or it thinks of itself as having become electorally irrelevant. Little wonder then that with you at the helm of its national affairs, many people still continue to hold the view (and they might not be too off the mark) that, in many ways, Congress is far better any day than the BJP?

So, my appeal to the present crop of the BJP leaders is: It would count as greatest service of your respective political careers to the people (whose name you swear by and for whose sake you claim to run your politics), if heeding the heartfelt longings of your workers and supporters (extant, as well as, the prospective), you welcomed Narendra Modi wholeheartedly as your candidate for the premiership of the nation.

Had this writer not deemed Modi's record incomparable, or not regarded him the only available dude capable of saving India Hindus, Muslims and the others from the impending doom, he would not have rooted for him for all the gold in India. Further, even if Modi had proved himself to be Disraeli, Lord Curzon, Lloyd George, Churchill, Sardar Patel, Lee Kuan Yew and Deng bundled into one, he wouldn't have rooted for him had he believed that Modi was complicit in even one murder (let alone hundreds that perished in the riots). I believe that the fact that, let alone the Indian Army, no chief minister ever has called even the state-level paramilitary forces so soon after breaking out of riots in his state, and handed them over the charge of policing its towns, leading to killing of close to a hundred Hindus too in the firing (not a single Hindu was killed during the anti-Sikh riots and hardly any during innumerable Hindu-Muslim riots in firing by the forces) is incontrovertible proof of his determination to stem the mayhem. He may be carrying a streak of bias, but, besides the fact that no person in the world is free of bias against some people or the other on the ground of religion, race, caste, nationality or color, I believe that responsibility of governance subdues that bias in a considerable manner, forcing the man at the helm of the affairs to carry out, as Atal said, his *Rajdharma*. In author's considered view, Modi's record of governance is ample proof of that.

✳

EPILOGUE

We took a *'Google Earthview'* of India in the first part of the book. And as anyone not having (or choosing to keep) his eyes wide shut could see, it was not a pleasant, heartwarming or reassuring sight. Crime and grime and hunger and insensitivity and concupiscence unlimited: who but only cockroaches and maggots busy battening upon it can call the sight of a garbage-heap an artwork and the odors rising thereof frankincense?

We saw as to how the kind of secular-democratic polity the people of India have come to be burdened with has devastated their moral cosmos, robbing them of their innate innocence and goodness. And, as a return gift, they have got from it everything vile except a little, dubious and utterly transitory kind of prosperity available to only a miniscule section of the populace. As a result, this ancient land of wisdom, compassion and innocence has been plunging inexorably into a state of *'jahiliya'*...that is, land completely devoid of things like culture, morals, compassion, wisdom and social trust. By its acts of omission and commission, the Indian State has managed to segregate the Indians into two distinct and increasingly disconnected classes of perpetrators and victims. Direct upshot is that one is forced either to inflict million tyrannies and indignities upon his less fortunate fellow beings, or be prepared to suffer them; absolutely no middle ground has been left for him to lead an honest, dignified, noble and kindly life.

We brought out the axiom that every time a bribe or undue favor was asked in lieu of a legitimate work, or right denied on account of a person's birth-status (caste, class, color or creed), a poison-ivy came to be planted. And millions of such poison ivies were being planted daily in government offices, police-stations, and even in hospitals, schools and town-squares of the country, vitiating the very air doing the rounds of the ancient land.

Essential truth is that, thanks to the social safety net, an individual can yet manage to remain alive (though he would die as a human being) even with his moral fiber destroyed, but the nations can't. Dark forces within and without are always at work and there is no safety net except one woven from its own moral fiber. India has all but lost its moral fiber, and stands naked and unprotected in an unrelentingly Darwinian world.

As things stand, instead of joining the superpower league which its elite desperately craves for, India is set to face a crisis of *'never before in the human history'* proportions and, 'be forever a slave or face mayhem and anarchy' is the inescapable fate the corrupt and feckless trustees and the partisans of the Indian State have set up for the Indians.

And when even the great political leaders and 'statesmen' of the yore, brought up in far salubrious times and raised in the very best 'Gandhi Academy' (so to say), couldn't do anything about moral freefall of the polity and the society, could any hope be placed in the present crop of politicians, who, having come up in a milieu devoid entirely of things like morals or ideals, are singularly ill-equipped to deal with problems grown far more humongous and complex over the decades? Possessed with *'obsession of cutting deals'*, politics for them is but an arena to set ever new records in amassing *'greatest amount of wealth in the shortest period of time'*, and not the domain to work to effect *'greatest good of the greatest numbers'*. Political ideologies have become dead and only the whore-ideal – making as much money in as short period as possible – has come to prevail. Result is that getting more powerful, bold, ruthless and insidious with each passing day, their tentacles have reached every nook and cranny of the national-societal life and the site of every crime and sin committed upon the land reeks of their trademark smell.

It was a foregone conclusion then that as the population boomed unabated, arable land shrank, environment got degraded, polity became progressively corrupt and fractious, institutions corroded, social trust evaporated, vital insecurities began to bite hard, and hundreds of millions strong cohorts of ill-literate and ill-employed (but full of carnal knowledge and desires all the same) youth began joining the latest Mao, Hitler or Bin Laden that were sure to sprout out of the fetid environs, the vaunted nation of hungry and seething 1200 million souls was destined to turn into a haunted land.

Billion-soul poser before the Indians therefore is: Is there no hope left? Is India destined to sink ever deeper into the mire of corruption and crime and hunger and holocausts? Are we all doomed? Or, had there been still left some silver linings in the dark clouds hovering over the hoary land...that is, a few good men we could latch our collective billions hopes on to?

We had reminded ourselves that the greatest crime – graver than even what we blamed the politicians of committing – would be to mindlessly tar all politicians as avatars of devil and be done with them. That is because replacing khadi could only mean bringing in jackboots and unbridled *inspector-raj*. Democracy was the only way then and, in a democracy, all that was required of the people was to pick good and able leaders to preside over the national affairs, and then support them to the hilt and encourage them to be still better. If, however, for some reason, right kind of persons were not available for electing, it became absolutely critical to choose at least one right kind of person to sit at the helm of the affairs. If the man was indeed right, carrying right attitude and vision, he would naturally select right kind of persons to work to materialize his vision and the people's aspirations...

It couldn't be denied that there still were some good political leaders doing their job in a fair manner. But the hard fact was that given their time-worn and staid ways, and faced with the constraints germane to our system which they are loathe to more than tinker with, they couldn't be expected to beat the Time racing against our nation.

If his mother so wished, Rahul Gandhi could any day become the prime minister of India. However, and as the nation has seen all too clearly, he has utterly failed in showing the character, nerve, ideational prowess or mettle essential for pulling of, what without doubt is, most arduous and momentous job in the world, having in it to make or mar the future of more than a billion people. And the record of the other probable, Nitish Kumar, remains mixed, at best.

Now one of the two probable thoroughly ill-equipped and the other falling too short of what was really required, the urgent task before the Indians boils down to finding a leader who they could place their collective faiths in and extend all out support to enable him to extricate them from the mess they had been stuck in and save their future for them.

So the issue, whether one liked it or not, condense down to Modi...Narendra Damodar Modi, that is. He seems to be the only leader around worthy of latching our billion-plus collective hopes on to. That is not to say that Modi can indeed extricate us from the mess we are in, or save our future for us. What to say a Modi, not even a thousand Modis, aided suitably by hundreds of Gandhis, Nehrus and the like can save us from the consequences of the attitudes and the sins we have been nursing and piling upon us for three millenniums running – that is, if we failed to alter those attitudes and expiate our sins in a heartfelt manner. And if we indeed succeeded in doing that, we could merrily throw Modi et al into the Arabian Sea, without the nation turning out to be any the worse.

What do we hope from Modi, and what he seems to be capable of doing is what teachers of the old used to do for their students and were remembered lifelong for by the grateful nerds. Those teachers – panditji, maulviji or munshiji – were uniquely caring, but all the more strict and stick-happy for that, in addition to being men of extreme dedication and impeccable character. But they were no guarantee of success for a student in his later life. Success came only to the students who shed their recalcitrance and chose to realign their attitudes to take full advantage of their cares.

In utter contrast to Modi, the present crop of leaders is not only not caring, it is not even apathetic or neutral. Completely devoid of character or any other redeeming virtue, and knowing precious little about the subject it is meant to teach, it is engaged in exploiting and molesting its students 24x7. And we know that when the students begin loving such teachers, and hating, avoiding or protesting against those demanding discipline and attention, it is time to kiss good bye to the future of those students, as well as of the society and the nation as a whole.

Although obligatory, really crucial issue before the nation is not 4%, 6%, 10% or even 20% rate of economic growth. For, as has been discussed, though solving one set of problems, the ten or twenty percent rate of growth is likely to bring another and much more intractable and catastrophic set of problems bang upon the nation's head. Besides accelerating the rate of destabilizing of the demographic balance further, it will make almost entire Bangladesh and half of the Pakistan migrate wholesale to India, advancing the date of the feared Armageddon by a decade or so. Do two of our most hopeful and touted of the prime ministerial candidates possess guts enough to even mention the thing, not to talk of resisting or stanching it?

So the thing is not about effecting five or fifteen percent growth only, but also the integrity and the courage to say and do what is essential to save India and its people, Hindus and the Muslims alike, from the developments destined to see the two principal communities at each other's throats. Needless to say, among all the available supply of leaders, only Modi offers some hope on the account.

However genuine or misplaced these hopes, or whether or not they came to fruition ultimately, a curious and accelerating trend is clearly discernible. And it is that the people and the institutions that had begun as bitter and implacable critics of Modi, have all, without any exception whatsoever, ended up acknowledging (even if gradually and haltingly, and in spite of themselves) the sincerity, capabilities and the achievements of the man. At the very least, their worst fears and dire predictions have turned out to be entirely unfounded and, increasingly, they are admitting to that in the print, even if with customary ifs and buts. Contrary is the case with Nitish, for everyone who had begun by showering encomiums upon him, has grown a little cautious (if not exactly skeptical) in his opinion of the man. As for Rahul, things are more even, for the expectations from the man-boy had never been too great.

In any case, it is a fair bet that given the opportunity and time, Modi could be relied upon to deal with the historical blights and drawbacks such as casteism, communalism, corruption, socio-economic backwardness, the modern curse of rangdari, and the future demons of hunger, demographics and Islamism in an effective way...at least better than any other person in the line of our sight. Especially on the front of caste...no doctrinaire basis remains any more for perpetuation of the caste system; only politics and nepotism are keeping it alive. Being entirely free of the blight, if Modi could keep his politics free of casteism and eliminate the culture of nepotism (real sister of corruption), he would as good as have eliminated the cancer from the Indian bloodstream. The billion futures worth question however is: Would they give him the opportunity and the time to act out his state-level performance at the national stage?

Having proved his character, earned his spurs as politician-administrator and visionary of high caliber, shown breathtaking sensitivity towards the little quotidian problems of the people, and cleared his name from the highest court of the land, Modi may have emerged in view of many as the savior India desperately needs. It is not necessary, however, that a person, who a people look upon as God's son or messenger, wondering why others can't see the obvious truth (they must be under the influence of Devil), be looked upon by others too as such. Why, even in our own times, even such pacifist and harmless soul as Gandhi was looked upon with deep suspicion and wariness, if not outright hatred, by his non-believers. That being the case, what chance Modi carries of earning majority acceptance (not to talk of enthusiastic support) of his coreligionists even (let alone Muslims and the others) could be anybody's guess. 'Why can't you see that he is the messiah promised us in the scriptures', one may ask, much like the fanatics of Abrahamic faiths do in rising bewilderment and anger, but others may continue to be as lukewarm as ever.

And as far as the past credentials or the future promises were concerned, they prove just nothing. How much hopes the Janta Party in 1977, VP Singh in 1989 and BJP in 2000 had engendered in the heart of an average Indian and what huge letdown they turned out to be! And the Madam's men! Managing to earn some spurs in the UPA-I, what dirty rotten scoundrels they all turned out to be in its second avatar! With such a historical experience, what are the grounds to believe that Modi won't turn out to be only a slightly better version of, say, Rajiv or Musharraf? Admitted, that in utter contrast to the available political leaders, most of whom carry personal agendas only and not the nation's or people's good at their heart, Modi is probity and patriotism personified. However, as if to more than compensate for that, the mental makeup, character and the secret dreams of majority of the generals and foot-soldiers he hopes to inherit are no better than the thugs cramming the UPA or any other political party. Can even a lion win a battle with an army crawling with jackals, monkeys and skunks?

'But such speculative doubts and fears, or less than warm response (if not outright antipathy) of a section of populace can't be a reason to disregard a proven leader and performer. A Napoleon may ultimately turnout to be a failure, but that is no reason to continue to be led by self-serving bunch of gormless knaves and jokers,' is the likely rejoinder from the Modi enthusiasts.

Now Modi may have come to be recognized as the nation's best bet by an overwhelming majority of Indians, but not all those admitting up to the fact may be inclined to vote for his men there at the district or taluka level. There could be little doubt that he would turn out to be a clear winner in a Presidential form of political system. However, in the Parliamentary form of democracy that we have, a self-righteous schemer (Moraraji Desai), dissembling fraud (V.P. Singh), rootless swashbuckler (Chandrashekhar), greenhorn born of an appropriate womb (Rajiv), a jelly fish of a man (Gujral), an imposter humble farmer (Dev Gowda), or a gormless factotum (Manmohan Singh) may get to become the head of the government and a rather dense scion may be looked upon as a natural choice to lead 1200 million souls of an extremely fraught land, but a proven leader of men faces almost insurmountable hurdles to get there. It is another matter that 'overcoming the impossible' is the stuff true leadership is made of and Modi is nothing if not a fighter and winner.

Yet, it would be in the fitness of things to dwell at some length upon the types of obstacles Modi is going to face in his journey towards nation's premiership, as also the arrays of options available to him and the likely outcomes...

First hurdle of course is the forthcoming Gujarat election that may not be a cakewalk for Modi this time around. Anything less than the previous performance would be dampening. *Sadbhawana Yatras*, which turned out to be little more than ego-trips, may have done him more harm than good. These haven't certainly won over the liberal hearts or made public opinion more favorable to him. Further, his vision of growth and commensurate actions may have been entirely non-sectarian, but even otherwise non-partisan, non-left minds acknowledge that certain sections of the populace, such as dalits and tribals need special care and attention. Modi has done them a world of good, but in his own way. Nobody certainly looks upon him as a champion of dalits and the tribals. That is in utter contrast to Gandhi, who, though remaining implacably against the idea of the dalits gaining even elementary education, property rights or political awakening, managed to project himself in the eyes of undiscerning or the complicit Hindu masses a great crusader on their behalf. Though it is somewhat late in the day, yet if Modi could go whole hog about the thing, that would be a great service to the excluded-exploited sections, in particular, and the nation as a whole. And besides securing him gratitude and faith of these excluded-exploited groups, it would help erase the post-Godhra slur from the hard disk of many a liberal hearts.

As things stand, even a Gujarat landslide won't automatically lead to his welcome at the national stage. What to say of the others, the leaders of his own party, more anxious to preserve their portion of the turf (however shrunken or worn out the rug) than the party or the national good, are not likely to take kindly to his foray beyond the realms of Gujarat. Their likely reaction (as also the reason behind it) could be gauged best in the comments of Congress leader Manoharsingh Jadeja as brought out in the Wikileaks (quoted already). RSS leadership too remains more interested in asserting its own authority than furthering the BJP, Hindutva or the national good.

Under such a situation, projecting himself as a great champion of the dalit-tribal cause (besides being a thoroughly genuine and urgent thing) will come extremely handy to counter the negativities associated with his image and to put the political opposition on the defensive. Besides undercutting the Congress across the country, it would prove attractive to those Dalits of UP (indeed the entire Hindi belt) who have become aware that massive corruption indulged in by Mayawati may have done incalculable long-term harm to their interests, and not only in UP. Favorably inclined caste-Hindus have been put off and there is no conceivable reason as to why the Muslims will keep voting or supporting this arrogant lady whose level of corruption can fetch them no conceivable good. And, in view of the fact that the mistakes made by the Samajwadi Party in its Amar Singh phase may not be repeated so egregiously, thus diluting the chances of her making a comeback in the next elections, a section of dalits may consider ditching her, at least at the national level, in favor of a nationally ascendant pro-dalit Modi. Another possibility is that if Modi builds up an appropriately pro-dalit and pro-tribal image, a suitably chastened Mayawati may choose to support Modi at the national level in lieu of his support in UP (albeit with the condition of running a significantly less corrupt regime).

However, we are jumping the gun here. For Modi has still not marched to the Centre, or having marched there, hasn't managed to become a clear first among the equals. For that he may have to wait till the top leadership of his party had managed to expose and exhaust itself further in the Armageddon likely to follow in the wake of the next general elections. That is, when enough demoralization had set in among the BJP and the RSS mandarins to render them completely resigned to accepting the idea of him taking complete charge of the organization.

Gaining uncontested leadership of the party and overcoming its own provincial satraps carrying huge egos is only the initial of a series of battles awaiting Modi. Next great hurdle is political allies piggybacking the party. It is more than likely that a few of these turned out to be completely intractable. However, 'blessing in disguise' is not such an uncommon phenomenon and the essence of true leadership lies in turning every hurdle into a great opportunity. Essential fact is that aligning with few of these regional parties personalities has turned out to be an unmitigated disaster for the BJP. It has turned the party into little more than a brass-band for these regional Nizams. Stratagem that was meant to counter its avowed enemies has served only to lower the self-esteem and the fighting spirits of its cadres, and to put off its existing as well as the potential followers. More glaringly, it has turned its state-level leadership into little more than geishas dancing to the tunes of these wily personalities for plots, contracts and ministries, and inclined to scorn their own party-men and undermine the parent party.

Upshot is that refusal of support on the part of the regional leaders like Nitish Kumar, Mamta, Mulayam, Naveen or Chandrababu Naidu would be an opportunity to grind them to oblivion in an ideological pincer movement launched in (default) concert with the Congress. In any case, even if, motivated by political or material self-interest, all of them came to accept his (Modi's) leadership willy-nilly, his freedom to act shall be curtailed badly, undermining his personality and the image almost fatally. Rendered little better than a glorified Morarji or Dev Gowda, his chances of turning out to be an effective national leader shall be finished forever. That would be a great calamity to befall the nation. Far better – for him and the nation – an effective opposition leader forever, poking sticks in the eyes of the ruling party wherever it went wrong, than getting to be a Manmohan or Gujral.

Even if Modi managed to move to the national stage soon after the Gujarat elections (due in December 2012), general elections would be due in a few months. That would leave him little time to select a team of his choosing, build countrywide momentum in his name, and make the sickly and fractious party fighting-fit. In any case, a jittery Congress would not give him much time, preferring to time elections to preclude the allure of 'Modism' infect the entire country. To put it in simple terms, Modi won't have enough time to work to make the NDA (or whatever remains of it) reach a tally of unstoppable 200. And at 140-150 or so, the BJP won't be able to form government in the Centre, even if the Congress came a distinct second at 100-120.

That would still be a major gain for Modi and the BJP; near repetition of the Janta Dal fiasco in the closing years of the last century. It would either be a government by the Congress, with a certain simpleton at the helm of its sorry affairs, what with its stewardess increasingly ailing and paranoid; a few of the saner elements left with it descending into senility and decrepitude; and the allies grown manifold demanding, blackmailing and belligerent. Or the nation would have to suffer an X or Y Front once again, with such worthies as Mayawati, Mamta, Mulayam, Lalu, Stalin, Jagan Mohan, Kumar Swamy and Sharad Pawar at the forefront. No prizes for guessing that notwithstanding a Nitish here or Naveen there, things can go only from bad to worse, with each passing day enhancing the stature and the allure of Modi in the same way the moon grows strength to strength in the *'shukl paksh'* (bright-moon phase).

It is almost certain that no government formed in the wake of 2014 elections can complete its term. And it is just as much certain that the party choosing (or forced) to sit in the opposition shall have its chance next. As things stand, it is next to impossible for the Modi-led BJP to form the post-2014 government. If Modi plays his cards well, his chance for the ultimate prize could come as early as 2016 or 2017.....

However, all the above would require the wisdom of a Solomon and patience of a Job. Besides, there are many things one would like Modi to work upon or show greater commitment to:

Learning to choose a great team of advisors and workers, and reposing complete faith in and delegating substantial authority to them are said to the essence of true leadership. By all accounts, Modi has shown no especial inclination or aptitude for that. Nobody outside Gujarat is aware of even a single talent nurtured or promoted by him. Admitted, that it is next to impossible to glean even a few grains from the heap of rascals elected generally by the people, but, then, Modi had earned enough public goodwill to get a few good men of his choosing elected. 'Let deluge prevail after me' mentality lying behind the failing is self-serving, at best, and unpatriotic, generally. The scorched-earth policy in politics (that is, countenancing no one between one's own kingship and the general public), though immensely satisfying to the ego, puts immense burden upon one's resources and consumes up essential time in non-essentialities that had better been delegated. The approach could have sufficed him for a medium sized and generally better managed Gujarat, but India is much bigger and diverse than Gujarat; even Indira's attempts to run it according to her whims and the lights had fallen completely flat.

So, in author's considered view, failure to nurture talent, political or otherwise, could be regarded as greatest charge against Modi. There is no known name that could be said to have graduated out of Modi School, or termed his godson, alter ego, or intellectual or political heir. Contrast that with Gandhi or Deng. Nehru's cabinet too suffered on that account, but, all the same, that was also a failure and results are all too apparent. India is too big, complex and fraught, and the colleagues and lieutenants Modi is going to inherit are no better than their Congress counterparts. For being a national level and long term success, Modi would have to transcend his individualism and become a clone-making institution. He may be capable of delivering the good single-handedly but he is not immortal. Without at least half-a-dozen Modi-clones picked and nurtured personally by him, everything he has built up or is expected to build would begin to turn to seed even before his own eyes. Rightly or wrongly, preface to any of his future biographies can't be a pleasant read; if he fails to groom worthy leaders capable of carrying his legacy forward, the epilogue won't be a heartwarming affair either.

There is little doubt that more than any other leader in India, Modi has shown considerable sensitivity towards the deprived and excluded sections. However, it too is a fact that nobody identifies him as a champion of their rights or being unusually passionate about their welfare. If only he could put in extra (extraordinary, we mean) efforts to really really enable them to shed their historical disabilities and join the national mainstream, he would have done his state and the nation a great service, in addition to winning many a liberal hearts.

Though he has managed to reduce crime and lawlessness in his state, but hasn't shown the level of intolerance necessary to instill the fear of God and the Law firmly in the guts of criminals and the corrupt. His reluctance on the front is understandable though; laws and the courts being what they are and largely beyond his control, he could have done only so much. Further, he tried to show intolerance towards terrorism but got his hands badly burnt. And any talk of toughness on the criminals, even rapists, murderers, child-lifters and organ-traders would immediately be touted by the left-liberal brigade as another give away of his Fascist mindset. That said, one still finds something missing in his attitude that one would dearly love to see.

This should really have been at the top of the shopping list presented to Modi, but, of course, it is acknowledged that he can begin to act upon it only after the process of policy and consensus-building had been completed. If however he failed to do anything about it, either for want of courage of conviction or failing of nerves, whatever else he did shall come to complete naught within a decade or two, with the nation sinking into unstoppable chaos and mayhem. Yes, we are talking of population and the illegal immigration problem. Even as this chapter is being penned, the nation is being witness to a gory trailer of the things to come: Assam riots, followed by mass-exodus of the people of the N-E from even, what were considered to be, the safest and the most non-sectarian and communally 'untouched' metros and other towns of India. The trend only likely to gather further momentum, what would the situation be like a decade or two hence can't even be begin to be imagined.

And even as suffering cold, eczema, toothache, loose motion and peptic ulcer simultaneously, we won't at all mind if our doctor completely ignored or failed to relieve us of the first four ailments but succeeded in curing the ulcer, the nation won't mind if Modi chose to do neither of the above but concentrated upon ridding the nation of the blight of corruption. It would be no exaggeration to say that, now, when all the requisite tools – systems, information, technology, economic model and, most momentously, burning desire for improvement in material conditions, combined with renouncing of the Gandhian inanities and characteristic Hindu fatalism – are there, it is nothing but corruption which is holding the Indians back from attaining their rightful place among the well-regarded nationalities of the world. Following simple arithmetical formula, it could rather be claimed that if the corruption came to be reduced by half, just about everyone of India's woes poverty, hunger, ill-health, illiteracy and the ill-literacy, crimes, population explosion, and civic problems and the associated miseries too would be cut by half and the looming doom delayed by a factor of two.

So, the agenda and the expectations are there before Modi, as unmistakably clear as they could be. If he managed to roll back the rising tsunami of corruption threatening to wash India away into oblivion and doom, he would have to do nothing else but sit back and see his name entered into the annals as the man who (almost; for there still remain the agents of doom) saved the nation of 1200 million. And if he did everything else in the world – coined million slogans, launched trillion schemes, and brought zillion dollars worth of foreign investment – absolutely nothing shall avail the country and its people.

As things stand, administrative acumen and passion for development are inalienable part of Modi; nobody can take these away from him. Incorruptibility and principles, his USP in a land which runs abnormally low on the commodities, are fickle things however. He would have to preserve these even at the cost of the top job. They may tolerate massive corruption of the Congress and its leaders; they didn't tolerate lesser corruption of the BJP; and won't tolerate even a whiff of it from Modi.

In many way, tangible and subtle, Modi is still to better himself, even though he is not to be faulted for many of his shortcomings, for one can't even survive in India (let alone rise in its politics) without learning and employing some meanness. Modi's greatness lies in his ability to do serious introspection and reinvent himself, and he has achieved a lot on that score. Suffice to state that he has to keep doing that for some more time, especially on the forgive-forget front.

That said, Modi needs to be flexible only in the matters of

attitude and not principles.

Finally, but equally portentously, if he diverted even one inch from the straight and narrow path of nationalism and secularism (and there is not, as is sought to be proved by the myopic Hindutva as well as the Islamist proponents, even slightest dichotomy between the two; contrarily they are entirely compatible, indeed complimentary terms), his act of ridding India of corruption too shall come to naught. For, if one cared to dig but a little deeper, he would have found out that much like the blasted casteism, communalism too is greatest corruption ever devised or practiced, corrupting the very soul of the entire society and robbing it of its humanity.

And if he indeed did, that would be so cruel of Modi towards the author who has forgone many a pleasant evening for the sake of bringing out his case. He (the author) shall then be duty bound to forego many more precious hours to bring out another book, this time tearing him end to end…

ANNEXURE

Modi's Interview Given to Shahid Siddiqui of Nai Dunia

Recently (July, 2012), there was much furore over an interview of Modi conducted by Shahid Siddiqui of Nai Dunia. It had been ages since Modi consented to give such a long interview to anyone, particularly on the issues roiling the Muslim community of India. On his part, Shahid Siddiqui is the first Muslim editor to gather courage to do what could appear to be an act of blasphemy. He couldn't have been unaware of the hostility it would invite from many quarters, yet he proceeded to do what seemed to him a true-bred editor's call of duty. Mr. Siddiqui had told beforehand that the interview shall focus upon the Gujarat riots and other issues specific to the Muslims and refused to give an advance copy of the questions to be asked. On his part, Modi called for video recording of the interview to preclude distortion or misunderstanding.

As things turned out, Muslim reaction was ambivalent and watchful (and not hostile) at worst, and cries of pain and condemnation came from the traditional quarters, more interested in keeping the Muslims isolated and fearful so as to keep serving as vote-bank or case-study, and less in securing their rights, welfare and modernization, or joining the national socio-economic mainstream.

There is no doubt that the said interview was a landmark phenomenon. It is a fair bet that most of the educated Muslims have read it first hand – if not the detailed interview in Urdu or Hindi, then the excerpts in English. To the author's knowledge, full English translation is yet to appear in print or the internet. As things stand, any chapter dealing with Muslim-Modi interface shall be incomplete without this epochal interview. For that reason, an English translation (by the author) of almost the full text of the interview is being provided here to enable people to have their take. Only some portions not relevant to the present book have been excised. Effort has been to keep the flavor of the language and the conversation intact.

Detailed Interview:

S: Narendra Modiji, what is your vision concerning Muslims? Do you want to turn India into a Hindu nation? What kind of nation you want to make India in the next fifty years?

M: We want to see a flourishing India, strong India. That the 21st century comes to be the Indian century is our dream, which has to be realized.

S: It is alleged that you are using Gujarat as a laboratory of Hindu nation. If you came to rule at the Centre, would you want to turn India into a Hindu nation? What shall be the place of Muslims and other minorities then in such a nation?

M: First thing is that the situation of the minorities in Gujarat is lot better than what prevails in other parts of the country. Opportunities for their betterment here are as good as that for a Hindu. Muslim too should get equal opportunity for advancement. Even a homestead can't be run if there is friction. One daughter-in-law favored over another is not a recipe for a peaceful home.

S: Suppose that you have four children in your home. If one is weak and lagging for whatever reason, shouldn't it be paid more attention to? Shouldn't it be given more opportunities to come up?

M: Our constitution too holds that the weak and the left-outs should be accorded necessary leg-up. If it is not the society to help him out, who possibly will? If a child is mentally weak, entire life of its parents shall be spent in bringing it up. I am of the opinion that responsibility of a weak child falls on the entire society, and not just its parents'. Saying that born to you, it is your responsibility solely won't be kosher.

Reservation

S: All the surveys conducted in this country, whether Sacchar Committee or the Rangnath Mishra Commission, have brought out the fact that whether education or economic conditions, in every domain of life the Muslim is trailing by a wide margin. What are your thoughts about likely steps to correct the situation and ensuring their rights and dues? Shouldn't they get reservation when 50% jobs have already gone to reservations? Muslim is unable to compete in the rest of fifty percent too. All doors are closed to him. What should be done to make him come up?

M: That is not so. There are 36 sub-castes among the Muslims that come under the OBC category in Gujarat. They get all the facilities available to the backwards. I too come from a backward caste. We would have to find out how everyone gets his due share. Many continue to remain illiterate despite facility of schools and teachers. We found solution to that in Gujarat. We ran campaigns to ensure hundred-percent education for girls. In the month of June when summer is at its peak, all the officers, minister, indeed the entire government, visit every village and house to find out whether every single girl has been enrolled or not. Today 99% girls are in schools, belonging to every religious denomination. There used to be 40% dropout rate, which now has dwindled to barely 2%. Now, who is gaining? My philosophy doesn't run along Hindu-Muslim line. I only ensure that every child of Gujarat gets it due. Among all my endeavors, I draw special pleasure from the thing that when I call guardian meets in a Hindu school there is only 60% attendance, while meetings in Muslim areas draw 100%.

Muslims are getting more awakened

S: You have conducted such meetings in schools falling in Muslim areas?

M: Of course, a whole lot. My experience rather is that today there is greater awakening among Muslims concerning the issue of education. I would like to tell you that I went to a village in Danta carrying 70% Muslim population. Three girls asked to talk to me in private. I was unaware of their religious denomination. Girls belonged to 7th or 8th standard. Talking alone with them brought out the fact that all the three were Muslims. Their plaint was that they wanted to proceed with their education but their parents were opposed to the idea. I was touched that there were three girls in my state not feeling awed about the idea of asking for help for higher education from their chief minister even. I sent a word to their parents. That was two years back. Today the girls are continuing with their studies.

S: You are right in saying that Muslims were made eligible for backward reservations but it has become clear by the experience of 20 years of the Mandal that they still fail to secure their due. For example, if there are ten jobs and five hundred applications including those of Muslims; all the jobs are given to the Hindu backwards, with Muslims failing to get anything. That was why the Sacchar Commission had emphasized that the Muslims be given separate quota in reservations for the backwards.

M: Founding fathers of Indian Constitution had thought hard about the thing and arrived at conclusion that there would be no reservation on the basis of religion. That would be dangerous. That despite the fact that no RSS or Bajrang Dal had been in picture then.

S: Muslim leaders, even Maulana Azad had opposed reservations on the basis of religion. But we too should learn from the experience of the last 64 years. We have done many amendments to the Constitution. So, what is your problem if, after 64 years, we give reservations to the Muslims to address their backwardness?

M: No, no, this is not a matter of altering something. The issue is fundamental. There can be no alteration in the fundamental structure of the Constitution. But I am on to another thing; the states you call progressive or secular, Muslims have got only 2 or 4% jobs. Muslims constitute only 9% of Gujarat population but their share in jobs is 12 to 13%. Bengal has 25% Muslims but their share in jobs is only 2%. That is Sacchar Committee's version, not mine.

S: Muslim was already advanced in Gujarat. You have worked no wonders for them. Muslim was advanced in the domain of business as well as the education.

M: Ok, we accede to what you say. Gujarat has BJP rule for the last 20 years. Would they (Muslims) have been that advanced had we been working to their detriment? Wouldn't they have been lagging had we been anti-Muslim? Sacchar Committee worked during my government. Recruitment to state jobs in Gujarat was banned from 85 to 95. It was opened up during my time. Three lakhs out of six lakh government servants were recruited during my time.

S: Was Muslim share 10 to 12% in the recruitments done during your time?

M: No, I haven't calculated the thing. That is not my philosophy. Nor shall I ever calculate along Hindu-Muslim line. My mandate is to see to it that everyone gets opportunity on the basis of his merit and without discrimination. If he is Muslim, he should get it; likewise with a Hindu or a Parsee. You believe everything said in the Sacchar Committee Report. Then why don't you believe its report relevant for my time?

What happened during the riots

S: Now we come to Gujarat riots...what happened all that while. Why were the bodies burnt in Godhra transported to Ahmedabad? Couldn't you envisage the consequences of that?

M: I have given detailed reply to SIT as well as the Supreme Court...that a dead body would have to be returned (to relatives). Is it appropriate to keep the bodies at the place of maximum tension, and tension at the time was in Godhra. That is why it was important to remove bodies from there. The train was Ahmedabad-bound and the recipient of the bodies belonged to Ahmedabad. What other way of doing things you possibly had?

S: You should have transported these silently to some hospital to be handed over to the relatives. Why were these taken around?

M: Now listen to the truth. Godhra was not the place to keep so many dead bodies, so it had become imperative to remove them. The administration thought it fit to remove these in the night and did accordingly. Ahmedabad civil hospital was a possibility but it was a crowded area prone to tension. It was wise of the administration to remove these to Shola hospital which was at the outskirts of Ahmedabad at the time and a jungle. There was no procession in Shola. Bodies were handed over to the relatives in silence. 13 or 14 bodies were unrecognizable and were cremated behind the hospital itself.

Why didn't the riots stop

S: Riots erupted in whole of Gujarat after that. Homes were being put on fire. Being the Chief Minister of Gujarat, you should have been well aware of the happenings in Ahmedabad and other places. What did you do to stop the mayhem?

M: First thing we did was to appeal to people to maintain peace. This I did from Godhra itself. After my return to Ahmedabad I appealed on the radio. I told the administration to deploy all the police force available. It was a very big incident though; never before a thing like that had happened. There used to be times that people learnt about an incident through next day's newspapers; two days elapsed before the pictures appeared. You enjoyed enough time to take necessary steps and send force. Today you have the news and the pictures moments after an incident. Administration has to compete with the TV's speed. Phone call can be made from Ahmedabad to Baroda in a few minutes but it would take at least two hours to send force. Police force can't compete with the speed of TV news. Should I compare this riot with other riots that happened in the country? I am not concerned what happened in Delhi riots of 1984? Riot is riot. Not a single bullet was fired at any place during the 1984 riots nor was there a lathi-charge. The only lathi-charge incident was to control the crowd at the place where the dead body of Indira Gandhi had been placed. There was no lathi-charge to control the riots. At how many places bullets were fired, lathi-charge was resorted to, and curfew imposed and requisite action taken in Gujarat on the 27th February?

Hindus were given a free hand

S: But we have your party members and officers from your administration telling that you asked them to let the Hindus vent their anger for forty eight hours. Haren Pandya and Sanjeev Bhatt have brought this charge. What is your take about that?

M: You would have to believe someone; if it's not me then the Supreme Court. Supreme Court arranged an investigation. What was the report? What action was taken on my part? I am presenting entire facts about the thing: where bullets were fired and people killed. Today the media is proactive. Neither anything can be concealed nor some untruth pedaled successfully. I tell you a very important thing but please don't publish it (after that Modi told something about calling the army, but forbade me from publishing it). There is one more lie. Godhra happened on 27th, riots erupted on 28th and the army was called in on 1st March. Some people from the media say that army wasn't called for three days. They forget the fact that February has only 28 days. Means, we had handed Ahmedabad over to the army the very next day. Please think over before hurling abuses.

Riots were pre-planned

S: But riots happened as if they had been preplanned. Muslim homes and shops were picked for burning as if they had been marked beforehand; (as if) plan had been readied and Muslims listed already.

M: That's all a lie; propaganda, merely. Go through the news of the time to find out how many Muslims were saved. Who could possibly have been come out alive had we not acted to save? Detail of the actions taken is with the SIT.

S: Indian Muslims are grievously hurt and suspicious. That is why people want to know whether or not your ministers had been present in the police control room?

M: Lie, absolute lie! Every fact is with the SIT. Supreme Court has investigated. Wait for its findings. My explanation doesn't count.

S: You were well aware of riots occurring across Ahmedabad. Did you take a round of the city or visit the refugee camps?

M: I visited all the places, cared for everybody. Propaganda is run that the government didn't run refugee camps. Social structure is very robust in our Gujarat. We didn't run camps during the earthquake too. We had handed over all the arrangements, food grain, rations etc to the social organizations. Many of the camps were run by Muslims but all the essentials were being supplied by the government. What had been supplied and where; everything is a matter of record. Not only that, class 10 exam were imminent, we made all the arrangements. Muslim students took the exams and made grade. People went to courts over this too but were proved wrong. But some vested interests and the media have taken upon themselves to spread canards about me.

What had Vajpayee said?

S: What did Atal Bihari Vajpayee tell you at that time? He accused you of not carrying out the duty becoming of a ruler (*rajdharma*).

M: This is also a lie pedaled against me. The speech Atalji made said that one should adhere to his *rajdharma* and that he was aware that it was being adhered to in Gujarat. This is the very next sentence but the media makes it convenient to obliterate it. Video recording of it is available though.

S: Ten years have elapsed since the riots. What did Atalji say to you, what steps you took to stem the riots, what talks the prime minister held with you; tell something.

M: He said that we should join forces to do better and control the situation.

Hang me

S: Rajiv Gandhi apologized for the 1984 riots. Action was taken against HKL Bhagat, Jagdish Tytler and Sajjan Kumar. Their political career was finished. Sonia Gandhi and Manmohan Singh too apologized. Why didn't you apologize for the Gujarat riots or express regret, though the responsibility had been yours?

M: First go through my statements of the time. What did Modi say in the heat of the moment? I had asked in a 2004 interview why should I be forgiven? If my government had indeed lain behind the riots then it should be hanged at the town square. And the (barbarity of) hanging should be such that, for a hundred years, no ruler dared indulge in this kind of sin. People talking about forgiveness are encouraging sinfulness. If Modi has sinned then hang him. If however the motive is to abuse Modi for political reasons then I have no answer to the thing.

S: Do you feel any pain for the thing? Thousands died; do you feel sorry for that? I am a newspaper editor; I apologize for anything wrongly published.

M: What is the logic behind apologizing now? I took responsibility at the time; expressed regret, apologized. See what I said after the riots. (He handed me a copy). Shouldn't you write about the treatment Modi is being unfairly subjected to for the last ten years? We (they) should apologize to Modi instead.

Why didn't they get justice?

S: Ok, riots happened alright. But what happened after that? Muslims didn't get justice till now. Your administration let all the accused go scot-free. You did nothing till the Supreme Court forced you to by constituting the SIT.

M: You seem to have fallen victim to false propaganda.

S: We are also a victim of lies; whole world is.

M: There is a selfish cabal. The SIT you are talking about has carried investigations for 6-7 year. For your information, thousands of FIRs were recorded in Gujarat. Thousands were arrested. How many riots occurred in the country? Nobody was punished for the 1984 riots while people have been punished here in fifty cases. Two cases you talk about were taken out of Gujarat. Who probed these: Gujarat police. Whoever brought these to Goa: Gujarat police. Who framed the charge sheet: Gujarat police. High court pronounced acquittal. Cases were taken out of Gujarat. Same papers, same witnesses, same probe that had been conducted by the Gujarat police Maharashtra court turned guilty verdict. Three had been no fresh investigation. You have shown (by your actions) lack of faith in the court system, not the Gujarat police. Bilkis Bano case was investigated by the Gujarat police and handed it over later to the CBI. You would be shocked to learn that people Gujarat police had arrested received punishment. People arrested by the CBI were all acquitted. The policeman who delayed handing over of the papers too got punished.

S: Muslims were killed in fake encounters during the last ten years. Cases are in progress and your police officers are in jail. Your administration...

M (interrupting): Listen, listen! Mayawatiji advertised before the elections that she established peace through 393 encounters. Only 12 encounters were conduced in our case. Cases are under progress. No one has been punished till now. Human Rights Commission has said that 400 encounters conducted across the country were fake. Supreme Court has been petitioned to get all of them investigated. Why is that not happening? Only Gujarat encounters are being investigated. Why is there no investigation concerning the encounters carried out in other parts of the country?

S: And why is that?

M: Because Gujarat has been targeted. Mumbai is seeing encounters but there has been no investigation. Every party is busy in giving a bad name to Gujarat.

S: Is Congress behind it?

M: Every party interested in giving a bad name to Gujarat is doing that; I don't want to single out.

Modi is a dictator

S: But people from your party Vishwa Hindu Parishad, Bajrang Dal, RSS accuse you of being a dictator; that you silence your detractors. They are not your political opponents; belong to your own party.

M: I have no knowledge, but if somebody says so…well, its democracy.

S: It is said that you are preparing for the premiership of the country. You want to come out of Gujarat to assume national responsibility. If you get to be PM, what five issues shall be the focus of your attention?

M: See, I am an organization man basically. A special turn of events made me the Chief Minister. I didn't compete for a monitor's post even during my school days. I have never been an election agent even for someone. I do not belong to this world, nor do I feel any attachment to the things of the world. Six crore Gujaratis are my focus today; their welfare, their happiness. If I do good work in Gujarat, that leads to people from UP and Bihar getting employment. I shall serve India through developing Gujarat. If Gujarat happens to produce abundant salt the whole nation gets to consume Gujarat's salt. I have eaten Gujarat's salt and made entire India eat Gujarat's salt.

What was done for the Muslims?

S: Have you done anything for the benefit of Gujarat Muslims?

M: I don't think along the Hindu-Muslim line. I believe in supporting whoever is left behind. Muslims are more numerous in the coastal area. We have given a package of 1500 crores. We have opened IITs there (he meant ITI, perhaps: author); opened schools; have trained the children of fishermen to drive planes (meant fishing ships or trawlers, perhaps: author). Fishermen get work for six months only. We have introduced seaweeds culture to give them year-round employment.

Modi's kite

S: There are many Dalit and Muslim areas in Ahmedabad that are backward. They lack banks, hospitals...

M: Urban development plans are operative there. Computer education is being imparted. Banks are not there; job concerns the Centre...your darling Congress Government... Kite is a huge industry in Gujarat run 99% by Muslims. I have done a deep study of it, so much so that if I begin speaking on the theme, you would award me a PHD in *'patangbazi'* (kite-making). 34 steps were involved in making of a kite in Ahmedabad; bamboo-work at one place, gum at another and the paper-work yet another. The process was way too costly. I got research done into it. Previously worth only 8-9 crores, the kite-industry today posts a turnover of 50 crores. Previously there used to be three different pieces of papers for three colors. I asked the paper producers to print different colors on a single paper. Bamboo for kite was imported from Assam, I had it produced in Gujarat itself. Who benefited? Muslims, you would say. I would say my Gujaratis.

Modi's secularism

S: Modiji, would you like to keep India a secular nation? Do you have faith in secularism?

M: Entities professing to teach India secularism are insulting the nation. This country has been secular since its very inception. India was secular when it was a part of Afghanistan. Pakistan too was secular till it happened to have Hindus. Bangladesh had been secular. Kindly investigate what party wiped out secularism from the country?

S: You use a term, pseudo-secularism. What does it mean?

M: Pseudo-secular are people who are secular in name, not deeds; who preach fine but indulge in communalism. Now we had a BJP leader Shankar Singh Baghela. Today he has managed to become a great secularist leader with the Congress. One of you should ask him, where had he been when Babri Masjid structure was brought down? What platform had he been standing upon? Joining the Congress he has turned secular; every sin of his has been washed away. Now he asks Muslims to vote for him because he is fighting Modi. And we call this secularism!

Indivisible India

S: Do you want to recreate 'Akhand Bharat' (undivided India)? Is it your dream?

M: My dream is that India remains one from Kashmir to Kanyakumari, with everyone conducting himself ethically and flourishing. The suprematism minded are running campaign in Pakistan for an undivided India...that Pakistan, Hindustan and Bangladesh become one so as to create Muslim majority here. You people too are salivating today because you want to create a Muslim majority nation in the name of undivided India. Bring all the Muslims together and put the Indian Muslims on the frontline to create tensions. It must be your dream too.

S: My dream was for an undivided India. My father had opposed Partition and Pakistan. Our dream is for peace in entire Indian Sub-continent.

Hindu terrorism

S: Terrorism is on the rise these days. Terrorism has no religion but some Hindus too have taken to it; what steps are required to contain it?

M: Tough laws.

S: You have caught only Muslims under the tough law of POTA.

M: Whoever we arrested...cases ran up to the Supreme Court but not a single was found to be fake. May be POTA was badly applied in other parts of the country but that was not the case with Gujarat. Not a single case taken up by us turned out to be fake. Thousands were arrested under TADA when Congress had been ruling here. Makrant Desai had been the BJP president then. He organized a conference against TADA and managed to show to the world that 90% of those arrested under TADA were Muslims.

S: SIMI was banned. Why don't you demand ban upon Abhinav Bharat?

M: There is no clear picture of Abhinav Bharat as of now. Thing applies to Indian Mujahideen too. What are they? Who is running them? Let the government come clear. You can ban an outfit only after identifying it; no use floating balloons. Sometimes the Congress floats the balloon of Abhinav Bharat and the other time of Indian Mujahideen, but refrains from coming clean on the issue.

S: Gujarat elections are near. What in your view is your greatest challenge?

M: We are the greatest challenge to us. For, we have raised our level so high that people measure us against that. Modi works 16 hours…why doesn't he work 18, people ask. People's expectations from Modi are great. We have to break our own records.

Revolt against Modi

S: Today there is a revolt in your party. There is a challenge against you?

M: I have left this to the public. Let them decide. I have won every election in the last ten years. I hope we shall win this too.

S: Would you like to give some message to the Muslims?

M: I am a small man, brother. I don't have a right to give message to anyone. I am a servant…shall keep on doing service. I would like to say to my Muslim brothers that they should not become a vote-bank for someone to exploit. Muslims have been turned into mere votes in contemporary Indian politics. Muslims should dream. Let their dreams and those of their children be fulfilled. They should use their vote with an open mind. But, firstly, they should be looked upon as citizens of India and human beings. Their travails should be understood. If I am thought to be of some help to them, I surely will. But they too shall have to keep an open mind…think over.